· LE CORDON BLEU ·

complete cook

HOME COLLECTION

MURDOCH
BOOKS

Contents

History of Le Cordon Bleu School

The name Le Cordon Bleu (meaning the blue ribbon) is rich in history and heritage. The title originated with the 16th century French order of knights, L'Ordre du Saint Esprit (the order of the Holy Spirit). The members, royalty included, were called Cordon-Bleus after the broad ribbons on which they wore the cross of the Holy Spirit. The sumptuous banquets that accompanied their award ceremonies became legendary and the term Cordon Bleu was from then on associated with culinary excellence.

The school was founded in 1895 by journalist Marthe Distel, who wrote a weekly journal called 'La Cuisinière Cordon Bleu'. She invited some of the greatest chefs in Paris to teach and gave her first demonstration in January 1896 in the Paris Palais Royal, where guests were given a glimpse of the latest culinary technology—the electric stove.

Le Cordon Bleu grew, changed and flourished in the following decades. Originally a purely Parisian institution, the school quickly gained international acclaim and an enviable reputation, attracting students from around the world. By 1905 students were coming from as far away as Japan to learn about classical French cuisine. The Daily Mail wrote in 1927: "It is not unusual to find up to eight different nationalities in a classroom".

One of France's most famous chefs, author of 'L'Art Culinaire Moderne' (translated into five languages) and 'La Cuisine Familiale Pratique', Henri Paul Pellaprat, disciple and friend of Auguste Escoffier, taught at the school for over 40 years.

In 1933, one of Chef Pellaprat's students, Rosemary Hume, established 'L' Ecole du Petit Cordon Bleu' in London. In 1942, during the war, Dione Lucas, a London Cordon Bleu teacher, opened a School and a Restaurant in New York. The success of the London school was confirmed in 1951 by its participation in catering for the Coronation of Queen Elizabeth II. The famous recipe for Coronation Chicken was created for this event.

After the Second World War, Le Cordon Bleu, Paris continued to prosper and grow under the direction of Madame Elizabeth Brassart. She welcomed two generations of cooks to Le Cordon Bleu, revised the curriculum and saw the school gain official recognition.

An American woman named Julia Child began studying at Le Cordon Bleu, Paris in 1948 and was awarded the Grand Diplôme du Cordon Bleu. She proceeded to facilitate the teaching of French cuisine in the United States, and went on to become a well-known celebrity chef and food writer.

By the 1950s, Le Cordon Bleu represented not only the highest level of culinary training but had become a symbol of Paris itself. The famous film 'Sabrina' was set in Paris, with a young Audrey Hepburn taking a class at the Paris School where she was taught to make a classic French omelette.

For over a century Le Cordon Bleu has grown to become a leading authority on culinary techniques, training and development. In 1984 André J. Cointreau, a descendant of the founders of the Rémy Martin and Cointreau liqueur companies, became President of Le Cordon Bleu. He strengthened the curriculum, recruited the finest chefs of France and relocated the Paris school. The London school became fully part of the Le Cordon Bleu group in 1990.

Expansion continues around the globe, not only with respect to the number of colleges (20 in 10 countries) but also in the scope of programmes offered. Bachelor of Business degrees in Restaurant and International Hotel and Resort Management; Master of Arts in Gastronomy; and various Master of Business Administration degrees now complement Le Cordon Bleu Cuisine and Patisserie programmes.

Consulting partnerships in the culinary and hospitality industries have been established, as well as an extensive culinary product line and a wide range of publications for culinary professionals and enthusiasts. Le Cordon Bleu International is dedicated to promoting the advancement of education, training and the appreciation of gastronomy worldwide. Because of this mission the name evokes images of quality, tradition and a commitment to excellence at every level.

Foreword

Murdoch Books and Le Cordon Bleu are proud to present the Le Cordon Bleu Complete Cook. This very special book contains a selection of over 500 of the best recipes from our 26-book series 'Home Collection' (which has sold over five million copies worldwide in less than four years).

Founded in Paris in 1895, Le Cordon Bleu has over 100 years' experience in culinary education training with schools situated in France, Great Britain, Japan, Korea, Australia, Canada, USA, Brazil, Peru and Mexico. A corporate office in New York ensures that Le Cordon Bleu and its 20 schools are at the heart of many different markets.

Le Cordon Bleu has a global team of over 80 Master Chefs who come from Michelin-starred restaurants and prestigious hotels. They share their knowledge of classic French techniques—the fundamentals of world cuisine and pâtisserie—with students from over 50 countries, inspiring them to appreciate and develop their skills, potential and creativity. Le Cordon Bleu maintains close links with the evolving culinary industry by attending over 30 international events each year.

Throughout the world, Le Cordon Bleu also serves as a technical consultant to several companies in the gourmet and hospitality industries. This includes our newly formed partnership with Radisson Seven Seas Cruises. Le Cordon Bleu Master Chefs direct Signatures, the first gourmet restaurant at sea, as well as providing passengers with the option to create dishes at the Le Cordon Bleu Classe Culinaire de Croisières, the first-ever culinary workshop on board a cruise ship.

Enjoy our compilation of the best recipes from the Home Collection Series in one large volume, to inspire you with delicious and mouth-watering recipes to impress your friends and family.

How to use this book

BEFORE YOU START

The golden rule of cooking is to always read a recipe from start to finish before you begin preparing, or even shopping, in case there is work that needs to be done ahead of time. For example, puff pastry takes about a day to make, pulses sometimes have to be soaked overnight and ice-cream machine discs need to be fully frozen in advance. There may also be fruit and vegetable preparation such as peeling capsicums or tomatoes, or salting eggplants, which should usually be done before the recipe is started. And you should always check that you have the required equipment, such as a food processor or electric beaters and the correct size containers for baking. Organising and preparing a recipe, weighing out ingredients beforehand and getting all the equipment ready on the work surface will ensure that once you start to cook there should be no unpleasant surprises. Remember also to check that your oven or grill is preheated at the appropriate moment if necessary. Preparation is known as *mise-en-place*.

CHEF'S TECHNIQUES

Reading through the recipe before you start will also allow you to look up any techniques and ingredients that might be cross-referenced in Chef's techniques. These pages are at the back of the recipe section (pages 518–57) and give very detailed instructions, with step-by-step photographs, for commonly used techniques, such as making stock or mayonnaise, peeling capsicums and prawns, deep-frying or kneading bread dough. Following these should give you all the instruction that you need for any more tricky techniques, in more detail and with fuller illustrations than if we were to put them in the recipe method. This section also includes basic recipes for different types of pastry with step-by-step photographs. You will find that within the recipe itself the ingredient list will simply state '1 quantity puff pastry, see page 542'. It is up to you whether you make your own, following the recipe, or use the same weight of bought pastry. Similarly, the recipe method might state 'prepare the crab following the method in the Chef's techniques on page 523' so you can follow the step photography and in-depth method.

EQUIPMENT PAGES

For those setting up a kitchen or buying new cookery equipment, the following pages give advice as to the most useful, hard-wearing and appropriate equipment to choose with explanations as to their use and whether there is an alternative available. These are set out by common group, e.g. bakeware, knives.

MENU PLANNERS

We have compiled a selection of menu planners, themed by event, such as Cocktail Party or Summer Lunch, to give you an idea of how to compile a selection of dishes for a special occasion meal. The number of people each menu serves is stated and the quantities of each dish adjusted accordingly. Even if you don't follow the exact list of dishes, the quantities should give you an idea of how to feed larger numbers of people. In the introduction to this section we also give advice about how to choose recipes for feeding larger numbers of guests, how to present dishes and quantities to serve.

GLOSSARY

A glossary of ingredients, technical and kitchen terms (pages 558–64) allows you to look up any unknown or unfamiliar ingredients or techniques. Some French and Italian terms are also included along with examples of 'kitchen French'. This glossary is also useful for reading menus.

Equipment

KNIVES AND CUTTING IMPLEMENTS

KITCHEN KNIVES

Buy the best you can afford. Make sure they are comfortable to hold and that the handle and blade are well balanced. You will need a large knife for chopping, a medium knife and a small serrated knife for fruit with tough skins and tomatoes—the serrations easily pierce the skins, thus helping keep the flesh intact. For slicing bread loaves, a serrated bread knife is best, otherwise the loaf is squashed rather than cut. Store knives in a wooden block to keep them sharp—if they clash against things in a drawer they will quickly become blunt. A cleaver is useful for cutting through bones. Use a hand-held steel to keep knife edges keen, and sharpen before every use. For baking, buy a palette knife with a long flexible blade for spreading.

SPECIALIST KNIVES

These are required if you plan to be more adventurous with your cooking. For opening oysters, you will need an oyster knife—it has a short, flat blade with two cutting edges that slides easily between shells. A disc of metal on the handle protects your hand. For basic meat preparation, a boning knife with a very strong, thin blade will help. The width of the blade means you can make narrow cuts, even when the whole length of the blade is pushed into the meat. A fish knife with a long, flexible blade makes boning and filleting fish less of a challenge. Small paring knives with curved blades make preparing vegetables easier. A ham knife with a long, narrow, fluted blade makes slicing cold meats and smoked salmon more simple.

SPECIALIST CUTTING TOOLS

A mezzaluna is a double-handled knife with one or two curved blades, which are rocked from side to side to chop herbs. Some come with a special board with a dip for holding the ingredient. Citrus zesters and canelle knives easily peel zest off citrus fruit in thin or thick shreds using a row of small holes or a deeper V-shaped cutting edge. Kitchen scissors should have tough blades, preferably with a serrated edge. The lower handle should be large enough to grip with three fingers. Poultry shears have a cutting point near the pivot for gripping bones as you cut them. A mandolin will help you cut wafer thin slices of anything. Buy one with a moveable blade to vary the thickness. The rippled blade can be used for crinkle cutting or matchsticks.

GRATERS, PEELERS AND GRINDERS

Graters vary in shape, but the important part is the cutting edge, which should be very sharp. A box grater does not slip easily and is good for grating large quantities. A Microplane® grater has very sharp blades and works well for smaller quantities as it can be held over a bowl or a dish of food. Good vegetable peelers shave off only a thin skin. Grinding and crushing can be done in a bowl (mortar) with a slightly rough surface, using a crushing stick (pestle) that fits the curve of the bowl and provides the second grinding surface. Pepper mills with a steel grinding mechanism are best for efficiency and an adjustable grind. Salt should only be ground in a salt mill with a non-corrosive nylon grinder.

LE CORDON BLEU ❀ COMPLETE COOK

Equipment

SAUCEPANS, FRYING PANS AND CASSEROLES

SAUCEPANS

Buy saucepans that are a good quality and the most expensive you can afford. There is a huge range, but stainless steel pans with a sandwiched base containing a metal such as copper, which conducts heat well, are a good choice for even heat distribution. Copper with stainless steel lining are excellent but expensive. Stainless steel is non-reactive so it will not be affected by the use of an acid. Choose saucepans with comfortable handles, bearing in mind that you don't want the handle to heat up as the pan does. Lids must have a tight seal. You will need one large pan and a couple of smaller ones for everyday use. Buying a set of saucepans will often give you a good range of sizes. A non-stick pan is essential if you often make scrambled eggs.

FRYING PANS

Like saucepans, frying pans should be of good quality. Cast iron ones are heavy but last a very long time. Test their weight before you buy to make sure they are right for you. Non-stick frying pans have to be used with wooden or plastic implements but are easy to clean. Buy good-quality ones and treat them carefully. A frying pan with an ovenproof handle is useful for making anything that needs to be finished in the oven or under a grill, such as a frittata or tarte Tatin. An omelette pan is a useful size for both omelettes and pancakes and non-stick versions are most useful. Tiny cast iron or non-stick pans are available for making blinis and also for perfectly shaped fried eggs. A ridged or flat griddle pan is good for cooking over a high heat.

CASSEROLES AND OVENPROOF DISHES

These should be of good quality and be flameproof so they can transfer from oven to stovetop. Casseroles should be heavy enough to absorb and retain heat and need tight-fitting lids so moisture cannot escape. Cast iron or enamelled dishes are generally the best as they conduct heat well. You will need several sizes as it is important that the recipe fits the casserole—a small amount of stew will dry out in a large casserole. Baking and gratin dishes should be fully ovenproof and able to withstand high heat. For these, enamel, cast-iron and stoneware are good options as they are attractive for serving. Soufflé dishes and ramekins are made from ceramic, porcelain or glass (all are interchangeable) and are presentable for the table.

SPECIALIST PANS

These are pans that you may not use every day but which are useful to have. A pasta boiler with a fitted drainer is useful, not only for cooking pasta, but also potatoes and other vegetables. A sauté pan is useful both for frying and for making risotto. It has sloping sides and is slightly deeper than a frying pan. If you heat up a lot of milk or soups, you may want a milk pan, which has a pouring lip. If you plan on making stock you will need a stock pot: this is a deep saucepan that will hold several litres of liquid. A stainless steel one will last well. For making jam, you need a jam pan with sloping sides and a pouring lip on one side. Steamer sets have one or two steaming trays, which fit neatly onto a saucepan.

Equipment

BAKEWARE

ROASTING TINS AND BAKING TRAYS

Roasting tins should be made from stainless steel or anodised aluminium so that they can be used over direct heat without buckling. You will need several sizes if you do a lot of roasting. One tin needs to be big enough for a turkey or large joint of meat. Racks that sit in the tin for holding poultry or meat are useful for keeping the food above the fat and also collecting the fat and juices underneath. Baking trays should be heavy-duty with a lip at one end. The open sides mean that you can easily slide things on and off without having to lift and risk damaging them. They need to be heavy-duty and preferably steel, so that they conduct heat well and don't buckle in a very hot oven.

CAKE TINS

Cake tins are designed to respond to all-round heat. They act as both container and mould for their contents. Black, non-stick surfaces will brown baked goods faster than shiny, metal ones which reflect heat, so for dark tins you may need to reduce the oven by 10°C. You will need a size appropriate to your recipe. Loose-based versions are easy to unmould but make sure that the bases fit tightly or they will leak. A springform tin can be used for cheesecakes, cakes and gateaux. The spring clip means the side can be gently eased away from delicate textures. Swiss roll tins are shallow trays. Muffin or bun trays are available in different sizes and non-stick versions work well. Fluted madeleine moulds are available as a sheet or tray.

TART TINS, TART RINGS AND PIE DISHES

For quiches and tarts, buy a metal, fluted tart tin with a loose base so you can easily remove the tart. Recipes call for all sorts of sizes, but a 20 cm/8 inch (serves 6) or 25 cm/10 inch (serves 8) tin should fit most recipes. Tart rings can also be used: these are placed on a baking sheet and the ring lifted off when the tart is cooked. Individual tartlet tins are good for attractive presentation if you enjoy entertaining. These come in many different sizes from single serves to petits-fours. A pie dish should have a good lip so you can stick the pastry down well, otherwise the pastry will slide down into the pie as it cooks. Oval (for savoury fillings) or round dishes (for sweet fillings) are available in ceramic, glass or porcelain.

SPECIALIST TINS AND MOULDS

For loaves of bread, pound cakes or terrines, you will need a loaf tin. Buy one with welded, non-leaking seams. Most recipes for breads and cakes will fit in an average 17 x 11 x 8 cm or 19 x 12 x 9 cm tin, despite the measurements given in the recipe. Fancy-shaped tins like brioche (a deep, fluted tin with sloping sides), angel cake (a round, deep tin with sloping sides and a funnel down the centre) and kugelhopf moulds (fluted tins with a rounded base and a funnel down the centre) are also available. Use these as specified in the recipe. Charlotte tins have sloping sides and small, flat handles at the top. Smaller moulds such as dariole moulds and tiny metal pudding moulds are used for both baking and cold desserts.

Equipment

KITCHEN UTENSILS

SPOONS AND SPATULAS

Spoons are useful for stirring, mixing and beating. Wooden spoons are good because they don't conduct heat, don't scratch and are non-reactive. Some spoons have a flat edge and corner to help you get into the side of a saucepan. Metal spoons are used for folding ingredients as their sharp edges cut easily through the mixture without squashing out air. A perforated spoon is useful for draining. Ladles are made for serving liquids. Rubber spatulas scrape a bowl completely clean and are particularly useful for removing food from food processors and blenders. Wooden spatulas are useful for non-stick frying pans. Fish slices need to have enough flexibility to slide under things and a large enough surface area to pick things up.

SIEVES AND COLANDERS

Sieves come in a range of sizes. Larger colanders are best for draining. Make sure they have a pattern of holes which will drain easily. Round-based stainless steel sieves have a coarse mesh suitable for sifting and puréeing (they don't react with the acid in fruit). The mesh comes in different grades of fineness. Nylon mesh sieves are for fine sifting and puréeing fruit and are also non reactive. A chinoise is a conical colander or sieve which is useful for puréeing. The cone shape directs the liquid out in a narrow flow. Mouli-legumes are rotary sieves that purée fruit and vegetables by forcing them through a flat metal sieve, removing any lumps or hard bits that can then be discarded. They have a range of plates to purée to fine, medium or coarse.

CHOPPING BOARDS

A good chopping board is an essential piece of equipment. There is endless debate as to whether wooden or polyethylene boards are more hygienic and views change on a daily basis. Whichever you choose, your board should be kept spotlessly clean. All boards should be large enough to cope with large amounts of chopping. A small indent around the edge is useful for catching juices if you are using the board for carving. A set of coloured polyethylene boards is useful if you want to keep separate boards for meat, fish, garlic etc. A piece of marble, though not good for cutting as it will blunt knives, is an excellent cool surface for making pastry.

WHISKS AND BEATERS

Whisks beat air into mixtures or beat lumps out. Balloon whisks consist of loops of stainless steel joined by a handle. They range from large for egg white, through to small for sauces and dressings. Buy flexible whisks that are not too stiff or they will not whip well. Rotary whisks must be good quality to work efficiently and they give slightly less volume than balloon whisks. Flat whisks, which consist of a wire coiled around a loop, are useful for using in saucepans or containers with flat bottoms or on flat plates. A set of electric beaters is invaluable for cake-making and for beating large amounts of egg white. Some come with stands, others are single large whisk attachments for free-standing appliances.

Equipment

KITCHEN UTENSILS

BOWLS

You can never have too many bowls in a kitchen. Glass, heatproof bowls or stainless steel bowls are useful both for whisking egg whites and melting chocolate, as well as all other mixing. A very large mixing bowl is invaluable for large quantities, especially for bread-making. Plastic bowls are a good non-breakable option. However, they are not good for whisking egg white as they hold grease and prevent the whites aerating. A set of small, stacking bowls is useful for holding ingredients that are measured out prior to starting a recipe (mise-en-place). As the ingredients are used, the bowls can be stacked out of the way. A deep, rounded bowl is good with an electric mixer as the ingredients are contained and don't fly out.

PASTRY-MAKING EQUIPMENT

Pastry brushes are made with either nylon or natural bristles and can be flat or round. Be careful when using nylon bristles with hot liquids as they may melt. Cooling racks are raised wire racks used for cooling cakes and pastries so the air can circulate under them easily. Choose a large wire rack that can comfortably hold a large item or several small ones. Rolling pins should be long enough to roll out a full sheet of pastry in one go as this will ensure a smooth surface. They can be of any thickness, but thinner ones are often easier to handle. Blowtorches are used to caramelise sugar on the top of brulées and small ones can be found in cookware shops or hardware stores.

MASHERS AND MINCERS, PROCESSORS AND BLENDERS

Potato mashers work on all cooked vegetables. Old-style mashers with a cut grid often work better than those made with a wire coil. They may be made of strong plastic or stainless steel. Ricers are used for mashing and puréeing. They look like giant garlic presses and will hold a couple of potatoes at a time. Mincers need to be heavy-duty. They are clamped to a table edge to hold them in place while meat is forced through the hopper and onto the grinding plate. They are very useful for making good-quality mince from steaks etc. Food processors and blenders are good for chopping ingredients together. Blenders make a smoother purée but need more liquid to work efficiently. Baby whizzes (mini processors) are good for small amounts.

JUICE EXTRACTORS AND SQUEEZERS

Citrus fruit squeezers are available in glass, ceramic, plastic, stainless steel and wood. The squeezers with a strainer around the edge, which collects the pips, and a container underneath for collecting the juice are the most useful. Juicers should have a large enough reamer to fit snugly into the fruit without splitting it. If you make lots of fresh orange juice then find one which fits oranges well or buy a citrus press with a squeezing mechanism and keep it solely for that. For squeezing out just a few drops of citrus juice, there is a spouted reamer which plugs into the fruit. Electric juicers are useful for large quantities and for juicing fruit and vegetables such as apples and carrots. Buy a good-quality one that will last well and is easy to clean.

Equipment

KITCHEN UTENSILS

MEASURING EQUIPMENT

You only need one set of scales. A balance scale holds the weights on one side and the ingredients on the other. It can weigh very small amounts. An electronic scale has a digital display but is often less accurate for small weights under 30 g (1 oz). Spring weight scales have a scale pan on top of a calibrated scale and they have an adjustable tension screw. Measuring jugs should be plastic or glass so you can read them easily. Choose one with the calibrations visible on both the inside and outside. Measuring cups and spoons are used for dry and liquid measures. They are available in metal or plastic and in fractions and multiples of cup and spoon measures. Dry measurements should be levelled off with a knife for accuracy.

THERMOMETERS

Thermometers are essential for accurate and safe measurements in the kitchen. A kitchen thermometer is used for measuring oil temperatures when deep-frying, and for measuring sugar temperatures when making sugar syrup or jam. Before using glass thermometers, warm them in water as they can crack if added to a hot liquid when they are very cold. An oven thermometer is used to ensure that the thermostat is registering accurately in your oven. They hang from the oven shelf. A meat thermometer is pushed into a joint of meat to tell how done it is, or into whole poultry to check that the internal temperature is hot enough for the bird to be cooked through. Poultry should be at least 82–85°C inside to kill any bacteria.

CUTTERS AND SLICERS

Cutters for biscuits and pastry come in different shapes and sizes. They can be bought in graded sets, both plain and fluted. Store in their tins and dry thoroughly to stop them rusting. Tiny, decorative cutters and decorative pastry cutters can be used for all manner of sweet and savoury decorations. They work on doughs and icings and are good for cutting vegetable shapes from slices of carrot etc. A cheese slicer cuts thin slices much more effectively than a knife and it works well on harder cheeses. A cheese wire is essential if you buy large pieces of hard cheese as the wire cuts through easily in a straight line without making crumbs. An egg slicer is used to cut a whole, peeled egg into neat slices with a frame of wires.

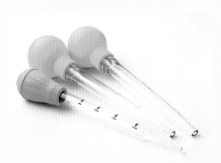

MISCELLANEOUS KITCHEN EQUIPMENT

It is worth buying good-quality pieces of kitchen equipment whether they are used every day or less often. There is nothing more irritating than something which does not work properly. It is worth buying a good-quality tin opener that grips properly and cuts efficiently. A cherry stoner/olive pitter is useful if you want to make cherry jam. It should have a decent spring action so you don't crush the cherries. Bulb basters are useful both for basting and for removing the fat from the surface of liquids. Buy a plastic one as the glass ones break easily. Larding and trussing needles are useful standbys that you may need occasionally. Buy them as you need them. Storage boxes are also useful. Buy ones you can use in both the fridge and freezer.

How to plan a menu and present food

When planning a menu, whatever the occasion, it is best to follow a few simple rules. First decide on a food theme. This can be as simple as choosing comfort food in winter and salads or light dishes in summer, or it might be based around a seasonal ingredient such as spring lamb or the Christmas turkey. You could even base your theme around a particular cuisine, perhaps French, Italian or American.

Don't forget to plan your menu around food that is in season and so at its best. If you have planned to serve asparagus with hollandaise sauce and then discover asparagus is not in season, prepare something else instead. If you are in any doubt, ask your greengrocer, fishmonger and butcher what is best.

Next, do a little research into your guests to find out if any of them have food allergies or are vegetarians. If so, you will have to plan your meal around these demands or provide an alternative dish or two. Most people find the easiest way to do this is to serve a vegetarian starter for everyone: that way you only need to make one separate main course.

Whether you are having two or three courses, you need to think about whether the dishes follow each other well, without being repetitive or clashing in style and flavours. For example, if you serve a seafood or fish starter then you will probably not want fish as a main course. Likewise, you should not serve more than one course containing pastry. You probably wouldn't want to serve a creamy pasta dish to start, followed by a rich buttery main course. For balance, try to alternate heavy and light dishes across the range of starter, main and dessert.

QUANTITIES

One of the aspects of entertaining that people often find the most difficult is judging the quantities of food needed for a large group of people. There are a few simple things to bear in mind.

For sit-down meals involving fewer people you can serve food which is already portioned, eg whole fish, steaks or chicken breasts. Allow one each.

For large groups of people, offer a choice of easily portioned dishes such as a whole ham or boeuf bourguignon. The more choices of dish that you offer, the smaller a portion each person will need. And the larger the number of people eating, the smaller the amount of food they will consume per head.

So, for forty people you would not need to make ten quantities of a recipe that serves four. Eight or nine quantities would probably be ample.

It is always a good idea to serve bread and butter. This takes the edge off appetites and makes sure the more hungry people have something to fill up with. There is a vast array of breads available today, so choose something to suit your theme.

PRESENTING A BUFFET

Buffets should offer a wide range of dishes for people to choose from, with main courses that should ideally feature both meat and seafood alternatives.

Unlike a sit-down meal, where the dishes appear one-by-one and are rarely seen all assembled on the table together, a buffet, laid out en masse, should look eye-catching and delicious.

Choose plain coloured, simply styled plates to show off your food to its best advantage. Keep your decorations and garnishes simple, especially if you have a lot of dishes on the table. Choose a theme for a garnish, such as small bundles of herbs, and use it for everything appropriate. Large dishes often benefit from a small garnish but smaller dishes may look fussy. Be careful about decorations that look unattractive once half the dish has disappeared, such as rings of tomato or lemon slices around the edge of a large platter. Keep colours simple and use appropriately coloured garnishes.

Keep the dish piled high in the centre; this shows off the food better than when it lies flat. But do not put too much on a plate or it will be hard to serve and quickly look messy.

Meat can be sliced in advance but make sure the serving platter has been warmed or the meat will grow cold quickly. Warm plates in the oven, by leaving in hot water, or by heating in the microwave for 30 seconds in a stack with a small amount of water between each plate. Take care beforehand to work out how you will keep food hot or cold.

Arrange petits-fours and canapés in contrasting rows. Diagonal rows look better than horizontal or vertical ones.

Most importantly, make sure that everything is absolutely fresh—there is nothing as unappetising as wilted or tired-looking food.

Menu Planner

SUNDAY BUFFET BRUNCH
for 12 people

Croissants

Stewed rhubarb with ginger · 424 ♦♦

Salmon kedgeree · 142 ♦♦

Eggs Benedict · 101 ♦♦

Frittata · 102 ♦♦

Blueberry muffins · 488 ♦♦

Bagels · 470   or
Croissants · 429

Danish pastries · 485

SPRING LUNCH
for 4 people

Ratatouille

FIRST COURSE
Smoked trout pâté · 3o

MAIN COURSE
Rack of lamb with
herb crust · 255

Ratatouille · 338

Sautéed potatoes · 323

DESSERT
Crêpes Suzette · 379

AFTERNOON TEA
for 6 people

Viennese fingers

Cheese and herb muffins · 113

Leek tartlets · 43

Crumpets · 481 or
English muffins · 480

Viennese fingers · 493

Gingernuts · 494

Black Forest gateau · 501

Dundee cake · 502

♦◀ Multiply the recipe by 1½   ♦♦ Double the recipe   ♦♦♦ Triple the recipe

Menu Planner

WEDDING BREAKFAST
for 24 people

Creamed Roquefort (top) and Crostini

FIRST COURSE
Creamed Roquefort and walnuts · 47

*Crostini of roasted capsicum
and basil · 47 ♦♦*

MAIN COURSE
*Whole baked salmon with
watercress mayonnaise · 163 ♦♦*

Mustard seed potato salad · 122 ♦♦♦

*Artichoke, spinach and
pine nut salad · 130 ♦♦♦*

Tabbouleh · 125 ♦♦♦

DESSERT
Iced raspberry soufflé · 405 ♦♦♦

Cherry brandy snap baskets · 406 ♦♦♦

CHRISTMAS LUNCH
for 8 people

Roast turkey

FIRST COURSE
Celeriac and Stilton soup · 75 ♦♦

MAIN COURSE
*Roast turkey with bread sauce
and gravy · 207*

Roast potatoes · 316 ♦♦

*Roasted parsnips with honey
and ginger · 336*

Green beans with bacon · 321

DESSERT
Traditional Christmas pudding · 399

Whisky sauce · 371

Brandy butter · 371

Mince pies · 511

NEW YEAR'S EVE DINNER
for 6 people

Chocolate rum truffles

APPETISER
Mini blinis with caviar · 24

FIRST COURSE
Lobster bisque · 71 ♦♦

MAIN COURSE
*Breast of duck with
winter vegetables · 208 ♦♦*

Gratin dauphinois · 339 ♦♦

DESSERT
Orange flower crème caramel · 420

Langues-de-chat · 514

Chocolate rum truffles · 457

♦↤ Multiply the recipe by 1¹/2   ♦♦ Double the recipe   ♦♦♦ Triple the recipe

Menu Planner

SUMMER BUFFET
for 30 people

Sherry trifle

Bruschetta with Parma ham, Gorgonzola
and sun-dried tomatoes · 26 ◆◆◆

Spiced prawn balls · 38

Minted pea and coriander triangles · 54

Colcannon and smoked
chicken canapés · 59

Leek and brie flamiche · 110 ◆◆

Chèvre and watercress quiche · 112 ◆◆

Coulibiac · 180 ◆◆

Coronation chicken · 192 ◆◆◆

Grilled marinated vegetables · 331 ◆◆◆

Fattoush · 128 ◆◆◆

Caprese · 126 ◆◆◆

Waldorf salad · 119 ◆◆◆

DESSERT
Millefeuille · 441 ◆◆◆

Sherry trifle · 400 ◆◆◆

Chocolate and chestnut terrine · 418 ◆◆

ITALIAN WINTER LUNCH
for 4 people

Garlic prawns

FIRST COURSE
Garlic prawns · 154

MAIN COURSE
Osso buco · 251

Green beans with bacon · 321

DESSERT
Zabaglione with sponge fingers · 410

SUNDAY ROAST
for 6 people

Roast potatoes

FIRST COURSE
Cream of cauliflower soup · 68 ◆◆

MAIN COURSE
Roast beef and Yorkshire
puddings · 239

Roast potatoes · 316 ◆◆

Braised witlof · 337

Vichy carrots · 326

Broccoli purée with blue cheese · 328

Thickened roast gravy · 346

DESSERT
Treacle tart · 512

Crème anglaise · 365

◆◀ Multiply the recipe by 1½   ◆◆ Double the recipe   ◆◆◆ Triple the recipe

Menu Planner

COCKTAIL PARTY
for 30 people

Salsa oysters

Roquefort in witlof leaves · 25

Onion tartlets · 27

Crab fritters with a lime and yoghurt
mayonnaise · 44

Spinach and feta parcels · 36

Smoked salmon
pancake rolls · 37

Mini brochettes · 49

Beef and horseradish canapés · 35

Blue cheese and tomato canapés · 35

Creamy oysters and
salsa oysters · 148

Chocolate dipped fruit · 454 ◆◆◆

LIGHT SUPPER
for 8 people

Summer prawn and cucumber soup

FIRST COURSE
Summer prawn and cucumber soup · 97

MAIN COURSE
Goat's cheese with a watercress
and lamb's lettuce salad · 127 ◆◆

DESSERT
Fruit terrine · 414

CELEBRATION SUPPER
for 25 people

Honey-glazed spiced ham

FIRST COURSE
Gravlax · 143 ◆◆

Spinach and crab roulade · 145 ◆◆

Quiche Lorraine · 107 ◆◆

Caesar salad · 120 ◆◆◆

MAIN COURSE

Honey-glazed spiced ham · 272

Boeuf bourguignon · 236 ◆◆◆

Chicken casserole with mushrooms
and onions · 216 ◆◆◆

Sautéed potatoes · 323 ◆◆◆

Mixed glazed vegetables · 315 ◆◆◆

Green beans with bacon · 321 ◆◆◆

DESSERT
Pecan pie · 448 ◆◆

Baked apple and
fruit charlotte · 394 ◆◆

Chocolate profiteroles · 408 ◆◆◆

◆◀ Multiply the recipe by 1½   ◆◆ Double the recipe   ◆◆◆ Triple the recipe

Menu Planner

SUMMER DINNER
for 6 people

Veal with lemon and capers

FIRST COURSE
*Smoked salmon soup with
lime Chantilly cream · 94*

MAIN COURSE
Veal with lemon and capers · 253 ◆◀

Grilled marinated vegetables · 331

Sautéed potatoes · 323 ◆◀

DESSERT
Pavlovas with fragrant fruit · 402

AUTUMN DINNER
for 4 people

Mixed glazed vegetables

APPETISER
Gougères · 115

FIRST COURSE
Chicken liver terrine · 188

MAIN COURSE
Sole meunière · 173

Mixed glazed vegetables · 315

DESSERT
Lemon tart · 444

VEGETARIAN DINNER
for 4 people

Gratin of summer berries

FIRST COURSE
*Warm fennel and cherry
tomato salad · 138*

MAIN COURSE
*Herb tagliatelle with mushrooms
and olive oil · 297*

Country sourdough · 465

DESSERT
Gratin of summer berries · 381

◆◀ Multiply the recipe by 1¹/₂   ◆◆ Double the recipe   ◆◆◆ Triple the recipe

hors d'oeuvres

Mini blinis with caviar

*Brightly coloured and extremely appetising, these small
pancakes topped with sour cream and caviar
or roe are bound to disappear very quickly.*

*Preparation time 45 minutes
+ 30 minutes resting
Total cooking time 35 minutes
Makes 40–45*

10 g (¼ oz) fresh yeast or
5 g (⅛ oz) dried yeast
155 ml (5 fl oz) lukewarm milk
2 teaspoons sugar
70 g (2¼ oz) plain flour
50 g (1¾ oz) buckwheat flour
2 eggs, separated
40 g (1¼ oz) butter, melted
but cooled
sour cream, to garnish
caviar or lumpfish roe, to garnish
sprigs of fresh dill or chervil,
to garnish

One Dissolve the yeast in the lukewarm
milk, then mix in the sugar, flours, egg
yolks and a large pinch of salt. Cover
and set aside to rest for 30 minutes in a
warm place. After resting, the batter
should be foamy and thick. Mix in the
melted butter.

Two Beat the egg whites with a pinch of
salt until soft peaks form. Gently fold
into the batter.

Three Over medium heat, melt a little
butter in a non-stick frying pan. Using a
small spoon, place dollops of the batter
in the pan, trying to make them as
uniform as possible and being careful
not to overcrowd them. Once the batter
begins to set around the edges and the
surface is bubbly, carefully flip the blinis
over. Cook for another 2–3 minutes, or
until brown. Transfer to a wire rack to
cool (you can overlap them, but do not
stack). Repeat until all the batter has
been used.

Four If necessary, use a small round
cutter to trim the blinis to the same size.
Arrange on a serving platter, place a
spoonful of sour cream in the centre of
each and top with caviar or roe. Finish
with a sprig of dill or chervil.

CHEF'S TIP *If you have any fresh
yeast left over, it can be stored in
the refrigerator, lightly wrapped in
greaseproof paper, for up to 2 weeks.*

*Other types of caviar appropriate for
this recipe include salmon or red caviar.*

LE CORDON BLEU · COMPLETE COOK

Roquefort in witlof leaves

The butter used in this recipe helps to soften both the texture and the distinctive salty taste of the Roquefort, a blue-vein cheese from southern France.

Preparation time 20 minutes
Total cooking time Nil
Makes 40–45

260 g (8¼ oz) Roquefort or other strong blue cheese
140 g (4½ oz) unsalted butter, at room temperature
1 tablespoon port
4 witlof (chicory)
2 tablespoons chopped walnuts
sprigs of fresh parsley, to garnish

One Place the cheese, butter and port in a food processor and process until smooth. Season to taste with freshly ground black pepper and more port if desired. Transfer to a bowl and set aside.

Two Remove any damaged outer leaves from the witlof and discard. Cut about 5 mm (¼ inch) from the bottom and carefully remove all the loose leaves. Repeat until all the leaves are loose.

Three Put the cheese mixture into a piping bag fitted with a medium star nozzle and pipe a small rosette of cheese at the bottom of each witlof leaf. Sprinkle each with some chopped walnuts, then arrange the leaves on a round platter with the tips pointing outwards like the petals of a flower. Form the parsley into a small bouquet and place it in the centre. Serve the leaves immediately.

CHEF'S TIP *The cheese filling can be prepared ahead of time and stored, covered with plastic wrap, in the refrigerator, but once the witlof is cut it tends to discolour, so prepare the leaves just before serving.*

Bruschetta with Parma ham and Gorgonzola

*Italians are great bread-eaters. Bruschetta are
thin slices of bread, grilled and rubbed with a clove
of cut garlic—the original garlic bread.*

Preparation time 10 minutes
Total cooking time 5 minutes
Makes 8

1 loaf Italian country bread
2 cloves garlic, halved
60 ml (2 fl oz) extra virgin olive oil
8 pieces sun-dried tomato in olive oil
200 g (6½ oz) Gorgonzola cheese
4 slices Parma ham, cut in half

One To prepare the bruschetta, cut the bread into thin slices and grill or toast to golden brown. Rub one side of each slice of bruschetta with the cut surface of the garlic. Drizzle with the olive oil and sprinkle with salt and freshly ground black pepper.

Two Drain the sun-dried tomato, scrape off any seeds and cut into thin strips. Press or spread the cheese onto the bruschetta, lay the Parma ham on top and garnish with strips of tomato. Season with freshly ground black pepper and serve.

CHEF'S TIPS *If Gorgonzola is too strong for your taste, use a creamier, milder cheese like Dolcelatte instead.*

As a variation, marinate diced fresh tomatoes, garlic and chopped fresh basil leaves in enough balsamic vinegar to moisten well. Drain away the excess juice and place a spoonful on the warm slice of bruschetta.

LE CORDON BLEU ❖ COMPLETE COOK

Onion tartlets

These delectable golden onion tartlets must be served warm. The onion filling can be replaced with a mushroom filling, as described in the chef's tip below. If short of time, you could use ready-made shortcrust pastry.

Preparation time 45 minutes
+ 35 minutes chilling
Total cooking time 45 minutes
Makes 24

PASTRY
200 g (6¹/2 oz) plain flour
¹/4 teaspoon salt
40 g (1¹/4 oz) unsalted butter,
cut into cubes and chilled
2 egg yolks
4 tablespoons water

ONION FILLING
30 g (1 oz) unsalted butter
2 onions, finely chopped
1 small bay leaf
2 sprigs of fresh thyme

160 ml (5¹/4 fl oz) thick
(double) cream
4 eggs
4 egg yolks
pinch of ground nutmeg

One Butter two 12-hole shallow patty pans or tart trays.

Two To make the pastry, sieve together the flour and salt into a large bowl. Using your fingertips, rub the butter into the flour until the mixture resembles fine breadcrumbs. Make a well in the centre and add the egg yolks and water. Work the mixture together with a palette knife to form a rough ball. Turn out onto a lightly floured work surface, form into a ball and cover with plastic wrap. Chill in the refrigerator for 20 minutes.

Three To make the onion filling, melt the butter in a pan over medium heat. Add the onion, bay leaf and thyme with a pinch of salt. Cover and cook slowly for

15 minutes, then remove the lid and cook for about 15 minutes, or until the onion is dark golden. Remove the bay leaf and thyme and set aside to cool.

Four Roll out the dough to a thickness of 2 mm (¹/8 inch), then refrigerate it for 5 minutes. Preheat the oven to moderate 180°C (350°F/Gas 4). Using a round cutter, slightly larger than the holes in the patty pans, cut out 24 rounds. Place the rounds in the pans, pressing down on the bottom so that the dough extends slightly over the tops of the holes. Put in the refrigerator to chill for 10 minutes.

Five Whisk together the cream, eggs, egg yolks, nutmeg and salt and pepper.

Six Divide the onion filling among the tartlet shells, then cover with the egg mixture. Bake for 12–15 minutes, or until the tops of the tartlets are lightly browned. Remove them from the pans while they are still warm and serve them immediately.

CHEF'S TIP *To replace the onion with a mushroom filling, melt 30 g (1 oz) butter in a saucepan over medium heat, add 3 finely chopped French shallots and cook for about 3 minutes. Toss 200 g (6¹/2 oz) finely chopped mushrooms in 1 tablespoon lemon juice, add to the shallots and cook for 10 minutes more, or until dry. Set the filling aside to cool, then use to fill the tartlets, as above.*

Chicken liver pâté

This simply made pâté dip (pictured top right) has lots of flavour. If you want a stronger taste, try making it with duck liver.

Preparation time 15 minutes
+ 15 minutes cooling
Total cooking time 10 minutes
Serves 4 as an appetiser

115 g (3¾ oz) unsalted butter,
at room temperature
2 French shallots, finely chopped
2 cloves garlic, finely chopped
225 g (7¼ oz) chicken livers, trimmed
sprig of fresh thyme
1 bay leaf
large pinch each of ground nutmeg,
clove and cinnamon
1 tablespoon brandy or port
2 tablespoons cream or crème fraîche

One Place 30 g (1 oz) of the butter in a frying pan and add the shallots and garlic. Cook over gentle heat until they soften and turn transparent.

Two Over medium heat, add the liver, thyme, bay leaf, spices and some salt and pepper to the shallot mixture. Fry for 3 minutes. The liver should be cooked through but still pink in the centre. Set aside to cool.

Three Remove the thyme and bay leaf and process the mixture in a food processor until smooth. Push the mixture through a sieve if you prefer an even smoother texture. Beat in the remaining butter with a wooden spoon, then add the brandy or port. Carefully fold in the cream or crème fraîche and season to taste with salt and freshly ground black pepper. Spoon into a serving bowl and serve with Melba toast or toasted bread fingers.

CHEF'S TIP *You can prepare the pâté in advance and refrigerate for up to 3 days. You might find it too firm to be eaten straight from the refrigerator—the flavour and texture is better if it is allowed to soften for about 30 minutes at room temperature before serving.*

Salmon rillettes

This modern version of the classic French meat rillettes—similar to pâté—uses both fresh and smoked salmon (pictured bottom right).

Preparation time 10 minutes
+ 1 hour chilling
Total cooking time 10 minutes
Serves 4 as an appetiser

125 g (4 oz) salmon fillet, skinned
and boned
60 g (2 oz) smoked salmon slices,
finely chopped
80 g (2¾ oz) unsalted butter,
at room temperature
60 ml (2 fl oz) Greek-style yoghurt
1 teaspoon lemon juice
2 tablespoons chopped fresh chives

One Steam the salmon for 8–10 minutes, or until it is cooked through and starting to flake. Cool on a clean tea towel or several pieces of paper towel.

Two Using a whisk or fork, mix the smoked salmon slices with the butter until as smooth as possible. Add the yoghurt, lemon juice and chives. Mix until the ingredients are well combined, season to taste and set aside.

Three Gently crush the fresh salmon to make large flakes and add to the smoked salmon mixture. Mix until completely incorporated. Transfer to a small serving bowl or terrine and place in the refrigerator for 1 hour, or until set. Serve with Melba toast or French bread.

CHEF'S TIP *You can also make a mackerel rillette by replacing the fresh salmon with three or four skinned and boned fresh mackerel fillets, about 125 g (4 oz). Replace the smoked salmon with the same quantity of smoked mackerel and substitute lime juice for the lemon juice.*

Smoked trout pâté

*A stylish but easy-to-make pâté, with a combination
of fresh and smoked trout. For a variation, you could also
use smoked and fresh salmon or mackerel.*

*Preparation time 30 minutes + cooling
+ 1 hour refrigeration
Total cooking time 5 minutes
Serves 6*

1 tablespoon white wine vinegar
1 bay leaf
4 white peppercorns
115 g (3¾ oz) fresh trout fillet,
skin on
315 g (10 oz) smoked trout fillet,
skinned
200 g (6½ oz) cream cheese
100 g (3¼ oz) unsalted butter,
softened
3 teaspoons lemon juice
sprigs of fresh parsley, chervil or dill,
to garnish

One Put the vinegar, bay leaf, peppercorns and 100 ml (3¼ fl oz) water in a
shallow pan and bring slowly to
simmering point. Place the fresh trout
skin side down in this poaching liquid,
cover and gently cook for 3–4 minutes,
or until the fish is cooked through.
Allow to cool in the liquid. Using a fish
slice or spatula, lift the trout onto a plate
and remove and discard the skin and
any bones.

Two Place the fresh trout and smoked
trout fillets in a food processor and
process until they form a smooth purée.
Add the cream cheese, butter, lemon
juice and some salt and black pepper
and process until all the ingredients are
thoroughly combined. Divide the trout
pâté among six 250 ml (8 fl oz)
ramekins, about 8 cm (3 inches) in
diameter, and place in the refrigerator
for 1 hour. To serve, garnish with a sprig
of parsley, chervil or dill and accompany
with Melba toast.

CHEF'S TIP *This makes an excellent
cocktail dip if it is served soft at cool
room temperature. Alternatively, put the
mixture into a piping bag and pipe it
onto small rounds of toast as a canapé.
Garnish with a sprig of dill or chervil.*

Crudités

A colourful selection of crunchy fresh vegetables served with a choice of dipping sauces is an ideal summer lunch or light appetiser.

*Preparation time 35 minutes
+ 1 hour chilling
Total cooking time Nil
Serves 8–10*

SOUR CREAM DIP
*250 ml (8 fl oz) sour cream
2 tablespoons mayonnaise
25 g (³/4 oz) Parmesan, grated
1 teaspoon lime or lemon juice
¹/2 teaspoon Worcestershire sauce
1 teaspoon horseradish sauce
¹/2 teaspoon Dijon mustard
¹/4 teaspoon celery salt*

*1 telegraph cucumber
2 sticks celery
1 red capsicum (pepper)
1 yellow capsicum (pepper)
1 head broccoli
12 fresh baby corn
75 g (2¹/2 oz) snow peas (mangetout)
12 baby carrots
20 cherry tomatoes*

HERB DIP
*2 tablespoons Dijon mustard
4 tablespoons red wine vinegar
250 ml (8 fl oz) olive oil
¹/2 tablespoon each of chopped fresh
chives, basil, parsley and tarragon*

One To prepare the sour cream dip, mix all the ingredients in a bowl. Chill for at least 1 hour before serving.

Two With a fork, zester or a canelle knife, scrape down the length of the cucumber to create a ridged pattern, then cut into 5 mm (1/4 inch) slices. Cut the celery and capsicums into 5–8 cm (2–3 inch) long sticks. Blanch the broccoli, corn, snow peas and carrots in boiling water for 1 minute. Drain,

refresh in cold water and drain again. Remove the broccoli stem and discard. Cut the bushy green part of the broccoli into bite-sized pieces. Arrange all the vegetables on a serving platter. Cover with damp paper towels, then wrap in plastic wrap and refrigerate.

Three To prepare the herb dip, place the mustard in a bowl and whisk in the red wine vinegar. Gradually whisk in the oil before adding the chopped herbs. Season to taste with salt and pepper, then serve the vegetables with the dips on the side.

Eggplant caviar

The name of this dish comes from the rather grainy appearance of the eggplant. Delicious served with crisp Melba toast or warmed pitta bread.

*Preparation time 10 minutes
+ 1 hour refrigeration
Total cooking time 30 minutes
Serves 6*

800 g (1 lb 10 oz) eggplant
(aubergines)
50 g (1¾ oz) pitted black olives,
chopped
1 clove garlic, crushed
4 tablespoons finely chopped
fresh chives
155 ml (5 fl oz) olive oil
½ teaspoon paprika

One Preheat the oven to moderate 180°C (350°F/Gas 4). Cut the eggplant in half lengthways. Brush the cut sides with a little olive oil and sprinkle with salt and pepper. Bake for 25–30 minutes, or until the flesh is very soft.

Two Drain the eggplant to remove any liquid. Scrape out the flesh with a spoon, chop the flesh and put in a bowl.

Three Add the black olives, garlic and half the chives. Mix everything together using a fork, squeezing the eggplant flesh against the side of the bowl to break it down. Add the olive oil very slowly, stirring it into the mixture with the fork. Add the paprika and season to taste with salt and pepper. Refrigerate for 1 hour.

Four Spoon into a chilled bowl, sprinkle the top with the reserved chives and serve with Melba toast.

CHEF'S TIP *For a special presentation, use two spoons to shape the mixture into quenelles, passing it back and forth from one spoon to the other to form ovals. Sprinkle with chopped chives.*

Prawn gougères

Traditionally, a gougère is a round or ring-shaped cheese choux pastry.
This variation uses plain choux pastry to make small puffs that
are filled with a cold prawn and mayonnaise mixture.

Preparation time 40 minutes
Total cooking time 25 minutes
Makes about 20

CHOUX PASTRY
60 g (2 oz) plain flour
125 ml (4 fl oz) water
50 g (1³/4 oz) unsalted butter, cubed
2 eggs, lightly beaten
pinch of ground nutmeg

1 beaten egg, for glazing
270 g (8³/4 oz) cooked peeled prawns
(see Chef's tip)
125 g (4 oz) mayonnaise
1 tablespoon finely chopped
fresh chives

One Preheat the oven to moderate 180°C (350°F/Gas 4) and lightly butter two baking trays.

Two Make the choux pastry, following the method in the Chef's techniques on page 545 and adding the pinch of nutmeg to the pan with the butter.

Three Spoon the choux pastry into a piping bag fitted with a small plain nozzle. Pipe out small balls of dough about the size of walnuts onto the prepared baking trays, leaving a space of 3 cm (1¼ inches) between each ball. Lightly brush the top of each ball with the beaten egg, being careful not to let any excess egg drip down onto the baking tray, as this may prevent the balls from rising evenly.

Four Bake the choux balls in the oven for 30 minutes, or until they are puffed up and golden brown. Remove from the oven and transfer the choux balls to a wire rack to cool.

Five Roughly chop the prawns, then mix with the mayonnaise and chives. Season to taste with salt and black pepper. Refrigerate until ready to use.

Six Once cooled, cut the choux balls in half and scoop out any soft dough from

inside. Fill each ball with a small spoonful of the prawn mixture. Replace the tops, arrange on a platter and serve.

CHEF'S TIP *If you are purchasing unpeeled prawns, you will need to buy about 640 g (1 lb 4¹/2 oz).*

LE CORDON BLEU ✤ COMPLETE COOK

Blue cheese and tomato canapés

Serve warm while the cheese is still melting and these canapés (pictured far left)
will disappear in an instant. Use day-old bread that will hold together better than fresh.

Preparation time 15 minutes
Total cooking time 20 minutes
Makes 60

15 thin slices white or
brown bread
2½ tablespoons tomato paste (purée)
200 g (6½ oz) firm blue cheese,
such as Stilton, crumbled
1½ tablespoons chopped fresh basil
or oregano

One Preheat the oven to moderately hot 190°C (375°F/Gas 5). Using a 4 cm (1½ inch) plain pastry cutter, cut out four circles from each slice of bread, discarding the trimmings. Place the rounds on two baking trays and bake for about 15 minutes, turning them halfway through cooking.

Two Spread the rounds with the tomato paste and put them back on the baking trays. Cover each one with blue cheese and sprinkle with half the basil or oregano. Return them to the oven for 2 minutes, or until the cheese just starts to melt, but is not so liquid that it runs off the canapés. Season with black pepper, sprinkle with the remaining herbs and serve immediately.

CHEF'S TIPS *For a variation, other blue cheeses such as Roquefort can be used, but will give a much stronger salty taste.*

To prepare ahead of time, cool the bread circles after baking. Just before serving, spread with the tomato paste and top with the cheese and herbs. Either cook in the oven or under a very hot grill to melt the cheese and heat them through.

Beef and horseradish canapés

A classic combination of roast beef and horseradish sauce
in bite-sized portions (pictured left).

Preparation time 15 minutes
Total cooking time 5 minutes
Makes 32

8 thin slices white or
brown bread
150 g (5 oz) rare roast beef,
finely chopped
30 g (1 oz) fresh horseradish,
finely grated
or 2 teaspoons horseradish cream
60 ml (2 fl oz) thick (double) cream,
lightly whipped, or sour cream
sprigs of fresh chervil sprigs,
to garnish

One Preheat the grill. Using a 4 cm (1½ inch) plain pastry cutter, cut out four circles from each slice of bread and discard the trimmings. Toast the circles on each side under the grill and cool on a rack.

Two Mix the chopped beef with the horseradish and cream. Season with salt and black pepper, bearing in mind the heat of the horseradish.

Three Using a teaspoon, mound the beef mixture neatly onto the rounds of bread. To serve, garnish with chervil.

CHEF'S TIP *For a variation, use the same ingredients, but do not chop the beef. Mix the horseradish, lightly whipped cream and salt and black pepper in a bowl. Pipe or spoon onto the toast, then place thinly sliced rounds of beef on top. Dust half the canapés with paprika and place thin slices of gherkin on the other half.*

Spinach and feta parcels

These delicious small parcels, resembling purses,
have a lovely crisp exterior and a soft creamy centre.

Preparation time 30 minutes
+ 15 minutes cooling
Total cooking time 20 minutes
Makes about 45

75 g (2½ oz) unsalted butter, melted
1 tablespoon olive oil
250 g (8 oz) English spinach, torn
120 g (4 oz) feta cheese, crumbled
with a fork
60 g (2 oz) ricotta or curd cheese
1 egg, beaten
1 tablespoon chopped fresh parsley
1 tablespoon chopped fresh basil
6 sheets filo pastry

One Brush two baking trays with the melted butter.

Two Heat the oil in a frying pan. Add the spinach and cook for 2 minutes, stirring continuously. Stir in the feta and ricotta until they become soft and coat the spinach. Season to taste with salt and freshly ground black pepper. Remove the pan from the heat, cool slightly, then stir in the egg, parsley and basil. Set aside for about 15 minutes to cool completely.

Three Preheat the oven to moderately hot 190°C (375°F/Gas 5). Following the method in the Chef's techniques on page 549, lay a sheet of filo pastry flat on a work surface and brush one side with melted butter. Lay a second sheet of filo pastry on top and brush with more melted butter. Repeat to produce three double sheets, each with two layers of filo. Cut each double sheet into 8 cm (3 inch) squares, discarding any leftover pastry. Put 1 teaspoon of spinach and cheese filling in the centre of each filo square, then gather up the corners over the filling. Gently pinch the filo, just above the filling, to seal without splitting the pastry.

Four Place the parcels on the baking trays, drizzle with some of the remaining melted butter, then bake for 15 minutes, or until crisp and golden brown.

Smoked salmon pancake rolls

*One of the attractive features of this recipe, which successfully combines
the flavours of smoked salmon and horseradish, is that the
pancakes can be prepared in advance and frozen.*

*Preparation time 1 hour + 15 minutes
resting + 1 hour refrigeration
Total cooking time 10 minutes
Makes 30–35*

MANDARIN PANCAKES
*125 g (4 oz) plain flour
2 teaspoons sesame oil*

*150 g (5 oz) cream cheese,
at room temperature
1 tablespoon horseradish cream
1/2 teaspoon lemon juice
200 g (6 1/2 oz) smoked salmon slices
chopped fresh chives or herbs,
to garnish*

One To make the pancake dough, bring 90 ml (3 fl oz) water to the boil, and then follow the method for preparing mandarin pancakes in the Chef's techniques on page 537.

Two Stack the pancakes on a plate and keep them wrapped in a slightly damp cloth to prevent them from drying out.

Three Soften the cream cheese in a small bowl and mix with the horseradish and lemon juice until smooth.

Four Place a pancake on a work surface and trim off the upper third of the circle. Spread with a thin layer of the cheese mixture, then cover with a layer of salmon. Roll up as tightly as possible. Wrap in plastic wrap to keep it from unrolling and set aside. Repeat with the remaining pancakes. Refrigerate for at least 1 hour.

Five Just before serving, trim the ends of each pancake roll, then slice into 1.5 cm (5/8 inch) pieces and pierce with a cocktail stick. Scatter a few chives or fresh herbs in the centre of each roll, arrange on a platter and serve.

CHEF'S TIP *The pancakes can be prepared in advance and frozen. Briefly steam to soften before using.*

Spiced prawn balls

The fried sesame seeds enclosing the tasty prawn mixture will give a strong, distinctive flavour and a lovely golden brown colour to these delicious savoury snacks.

Preparation time 15 minutes
+ 20 minutes chilling
Total cooking time 15 minutes
Makes 24

750 g (1½ lb) large raw prawns
1 tablespoon oil
2 cloves garlic, crushed
1 cm (½ inch) fresh ginger,
finely chopped
¼ teaspoon salt
2 teaspoons sugar
1 teaspoon chopped fresh coriander
1 teaspoon cornflour
½ egg white (see Chef's tip)
100 g (3¼ oz) sesame seeds
oil, for deep-frying

One Peel and devein the prawns, following the method in the Chef's techniques on page 522. Pat dry with paper towels.

Two Put the prawns in a food processor and process to a coarse purée. Transfer to a bowl and add the oil, garlic, ginger, salt, sugar, coriander and cornflour and mix well to combine.

Three Lightly whisk the egg white until it just stands in soft peaks, then add just enough of the egg white to the spiced prawn mixture to obtain a smooth, stiff mixture that will hold a shape.

Four Divide the mixture into 24 evenly sized balls. Roll them in the sesame seeds to coat, set them on a baking tray and chill in the refrigerator for 20 minutes.

Five Heat the oil in a deep-fat fryer or deep saucepan (see Chef's techniques, page 537). Cook the balls in three batches, for about 4–5 minutes, or until they are golden brown and crispy on the outside and cooked through. Drain on crumpled paper towels. Arrange them on a serving plate and serve hot.

CHEF'S TIP *It can be difficult to divide an egg white in half. The easiest way is to lightly beat it first to break it up a little and stop it clinging together.*

Satay beef sticks

*Widely cooked throughout South-East Asia, a satay consists
of marinated meat, fish or poultry, threaded onto bamboo
or wooden skewers, grilled and served with a sauce.*

*Preparation time 35 minutes
+ 2–3 hours marinating
Total cooking time 15 minutes
Makes 20*

1/4 teaspoon ground aniseed
1/4 teaspoon ground cumin
1 teaspoon ground turmeric
1 teaspoon ground coriander
1 French shallot, chopped
1 clove garlic, finely chopped
1.5 cm (5/8 inch) fresh ginger,
finely chopped
1 stalk lemon grass, white part only,
finely chopped
1 tablespoon brown sugar
35 ml (1 1/4 fl oz) peanut (groundnut)
oil
1 teaspoon soy sauce
200 g (6 1/2 oz) beef fillet or sirloin,
cut into 20 thin strips

SATAY SAUCE
1 clove garlic
80 g (2 3/4 oz) smooth peanut butter
40 ml (1 1/4 fl oz) coconut milk
a few drops of Tabasco,
or to taste
2 teaspoons honey
2 teaspoons lemon juice
2 teaspoons light soy sauce

One Soak 20 short wooden skewers in water for 1 hour to prevent them burning under the grill. To make the marinade, add the ground aniseed, cumin, turmeric and coriander to the shallot, garlic, ginger, lemon grass and brown sugar in a medium bowl. Mix well and add the oil and soy sauce.

Two Thread a strip of beef onto each wooden skewer, weaving the skewers through the meat, and place in a shallow dish. Thoroughly coat in the marinade and refrigerate for 2–3 hours.

Three To make the satay sauce, put the garlic in a small pan and cover with cold water. Bring to the boil and simmer for 3 minutes, refresh under cold water, then drain and finely chop. Combine the garlic with the peanut butter, coconut milk and 60 ml (2 fl oz) water in a medium saucepan. Stir over medium heat for 1–2 minutes, or until smooth and thick, then add the Tabasco, honey, lemon juice and soy sauce. Stir until the sauce is warm and thoroughly blended. If the mixture starts to separate, stir in 1–2 teaspoons water. Cover with plastic wrap and place in the refrigerator until ready to use.

Four Preheat a grill or barbecue until hot. Cook the satay sticks for 1–2 minutes on each side, turning three or four times during cooking. Once they are cooked, arrange on a plate and serve with the satay sauce.

Red mullet and tapenade on toast

*Tapenade, a simple spread from Provence in France,
is made by puréeing black olives, anchovies, capers,
olive oil and lemon juice (pictured bottom right).*

Preparation time 10 minutes
+ 15 minutes marinating
Total cooking time 10 minutes
Makes 16

2 fillets red mullet,
about 170 g (5½ oz), skinned
and boned
1 clove garlic
2 tablespoons olive oil
4 slices sandwich bread,
crusts removed
75 g (2¼ oz) tapenade
16 pink peppercorns
16 sprigs of fresh dill
small wedges of lemon, to garnish

One Preheat the oven to hot 220°C (425°F/Gas 7). Cut each fish fillet into eight pieces. Place the garlic clove in the olive oil, add the fish, toss well and leave to marinate for 15 minutes.

Two Toast the bread and spread with a thin layer of tapenade. Cut each slice diagonally into four triangles and arrange on a baking tray. Place the marinated fish on the prepared toasts and, just before serving, place in the oven for 2–3 minutes, or until the fish is just cooked (it will flake when lightly pressed with a fork).

Three Remove from the oven and transfer to a serving tray. Place a small dot of the tapenade on the top, then a pink peppercorn in the centre. Decorate with a sprig of dill and a lemon wedge.

CHEF'S TIP *Tapenade is available ready-made from gourmet delicatessens or you can use the quick and simple version in the recipe on page 52.*

Parma ham and melon fingers

*An extremely refreshing all-time favourite
that is best made with paper-thin slices of
Parma ham or prosciutto (pictured top right).*

Preparation time 10 minutes
Total cooking time Nil
Makes 32

1 small melon
11 slices Parma ham or prosciutto

One Cut the melon in half lengthways and, using a spoon, remove the seeds and gently scrape clean. Slice each half into eight wedges.

Two With a sharp knife, starting at one end of a melon wedge, slice between the flesh and the thick skin of the melon. Cut each piece of peeled melon in half.

Three Cut each slice of Parma ham or prosciutto into three long strips.

Four Wrap a strip of Parma ham or prosciutto around each wedge of melon and secure with a cocktail stick.

Prawn bouchées

Bouchées are small round cases of puff pastry with a tasty filling.
These were fashionable at the French court of Louis XV and
his wife, renowned for her hearty appetite.

Preparation time 15 minutes
+ 35 minutes chilling
Total cooking time 20 minutes
Makes 8

½ quantity puff pastry (see page 542)
1 egg, beaten

FILLING
30 g (1 oz) unsalted butter
30 g (1 oz) plain flour
250 ml (8 fl oz) fish or shellfish stock,
or milk
250 g (8 oz) cooked peeled prawns
2 tablespoons chopped
mixed fresh herbs

One Brush a large baking tray with butter, and refrigerate until needed. Roll out the pastry on a lightly floured surface to a thickness of 5 mm (¼ inch). Brush off any excess flour and cut out eight circles with a 7 cm (2¾ inch) fluted round cutter. Sprinkle the tray with a little cold water, turn the circles over and put on the tray. Brush with the egg, chill for 5 minutes, then brush again. Using a floured 5 cm (2 inch) plain round cutter, press into the pastry three-quarters of the way through to mark an inner circle. Refrigerate for 30 minutes.

Two Preheat the oven to hot 220°C (425°F/Gas 7). Brush the top of each pastry circle again with beaten egg. Bake on the middle shelf of the oven for 10–12 minutes, or until the pastry circles are well risen, crisp and golden. Remove from the oven and cut around the centre circle to remove the lid while still warm. Scrape out the excess soft pastry from inside the little cases. If you wish, return to the oven for 30 seconds to dry. (You can turn off the oven and use the residual heat to do this.)

Three To make the filling, melt the butter in a pan, add the flour and cook over low heat for 1 minute. Remove from the heat and pour in the stock or milk, blend thoroughly with a wooden spoon and return to the stove. Stir continuously over low heat until the sauce is free of lumps. Increase the heat and stir until the mixture boils, then simmer for 2–3 minutes. Just before serving, stir in the prawns to warm through. Finally add the herbs and season to taste with salt and pepper.

Four Spoon the filling into the pastry cases while both are still warm. If you wish, garnish with chopped herbs or extra prawns. You may replace the lid or not.

CHEF'S TIPS *If using frozen cooked prawns, they must be well thawed and drained before using them. Do not wash them, or thaw in cold water, as they will lose a lot of flavour.*

After cutting out the pastry circles, they are turned over on the tray to help them to rise with straight sides.

If the cooked cases are left to cool, reheat in a moderate 180°C (350°F/Gas 4) oven for 5 minutes and fill with the hot filling.

Leek tartlets

*These small tartlets filled with leek and cumin are ideal
served warm with drinks. Alternatively, they could be
made as larger tarts and served as a first course.*

*Preparation time 45 minutes
+ 15 minutes chilling
Total cooking time 40 minutes
Makes 30*

FILLING
*40 g (1¼ oz) unsalted butter
1 large leek, white part only,
thinly sliced
1 bay leaf
pinch of dried thyme
pinch of salt
¼ teaspoon ground cumin
160 ml (5¼ fl oz) thick
(double) cream
1 egg
1 egg yolk*

*1 quantity shortcrust pastry
(see page 544)*

One To make the filling, melt the butter in a saucepan over low heat. Add the leek, bay leaf, thyme and salt. Cover and cook slowly for 5 minutes, then uncover and continue cooking for 5–10 minutes, or until the mixture is dry. Remove the bay leaf. Add the cumin, mix well and set aside to cool.

Two Grease three 12-hole (30 ml/1 fl oz) mini muffin tins or patty pans. Roll out the shortcrust pastry on a lightly floured surface to a thickness of 3 mm (⅛ inch), and refrigerate for 5 minutes. Preheat the oven to warm 170°C (325°F/Gas 3).

Three Using a 7 cm (2¾ inch) plain round cutter, cut out 30 rounds from the pastry. Press the rounds into the muffin tins or patty pans, pressing well along

the bottoms so the dough extends slightly above the edge of the tins. Refrigerate the lined tins for 10 minutes.

Four Whisk together the cream, egg and egg yolk, and season with salt and pepper. Fill each tartlet shell with ½ teaspoon of the leek mixture, then carefully pour in the cream mixture. Bake for 10–15 minutes, or until the filling is set. Remove the tartlets from the tins while still warm. If they stick, loosen them carefully with the tip of a small knife.

Crab fritters with a lime and yoghurt mayonnaise

Warm crab and herb fritters are served here with a light
tangy dipping sauce. The yoghurt and lime in the sauce provide
a refreshing contrast to the richness of the mayonnaise.

Preparation time 20 minutes
Total cooking time 15 minutes
Makes about 30

LIME AND YOGHURT MAYONNAISE
2 teaspoons grated lime rind
125 g (4 oz) Greek-style yoghurt
125 g (4 oz) mayonnaise
lime juice, to taste

CRAB FRITTERS
250 g (8 oz) white fish fillets, such as
whiting, sole or haddock, skinned
1 egg white
60 ml (2 fl oz) thick (double) cream
250 g (8 oz) cooked white crab meat
2 tablespoons chopped mixed fresh
herbs, such as dill, chives,
parsley and tarragon
250 g (8 oz) fresh breadcrumbs

oil, for deep-frying

One To make the lime and yoghurt mayonnaise, stir the lime rind into the yoghurt. Mix in the mayonnaise and lime juice to taste, then season with salt and pepper. Cover with plastic wrap and set aside in the refrigerator.

Two To make the crab fritters, purée the fish in a food processor. Add the egg white, season well and process again until well blended. Using the pulse button on the processor, carefully add the cream. Do not overwork or the cream will separate. Transfer the mixture to a large bowl and set inside a larger bowl of ice. Using a large metal spoon or plastic spatula, fold in the crab meat and mixed herbs. Using two teaspoons, shape the mixture into small ovals, or roll by hand into balls, about 3 cm (1¼ inches) in diameter. Sprinkle the breadcrumbs onto a sheet of paper and roll the balls in them to coat, using the paper to help so that you don't handle the soft mixture too much.

Three Following the method in the Chef's techniques on page 537, deep-fry the fritters for 4–6 minutes. Season with salt and serve warm with the lime and yoghurt mayonnaise on the side.

CHEF'S TIP *Once shaped and coated, the crab fritters can be covered with plastic wrap and refrigerated for up to 24 hours before frying.*

Cranberry chicken cups

*These delicate, creamy little mouthfuls are quick to prepare
and guaranteed to impress.*

*Preparation time 20 minutes
Total cooking time 10 minutes
Makes 26*

*6 sheets filo pastry
150 g (5 oz) unsalted butter, melted
3 cooked skinless chicken breast fillets,
cut into 1 cm (½ inch) cubes
1 tablespoon cranberry sauce
3 tablespoons crème fraîche
2 spring onions, finely chopped
½ teaspoon finely grated lemon rind
fresh coriander leaves,
to garnish
thin strips of lemon rind,
to garnish*

One Preheat the oven to moderately hot 200°C (400°F/Gas 6). Following the method for layering filo pastry in the Chef's techniques on page 549, lay a sheet of filo out on a work surface and lightly brush it with the melted butter. Place a second sheet on top and brush with butter, then repeat this to make three layers. Do the same with the remaining filo.

Two Using a round 7 cm (2¾ inch) cutter, cut 26 discs from the filo pastry and, buttered side down, press gently into individual fluted tartlet tins, 5 cm (2 inches) across and 2 cm (¾ inch) deep, or patty pans.

Three Place small circles of greaseproof paper into the pastry cases and fill with baking beads or rice. Bake the pastry cases for 10 minutes, or until golden. Remove the beads and paper and cool the pastry in the tins.

Four Mix together the chicken, cranberry sauce, crème fraîche, spring onion, lemon rind and some salt and pepper. Spoon into the tartlet cases and garnish each with a coriander leaf and a little lemon rind.

CHEF'S TIP *The chicken can be replaced with cooked turkey, duck or flaked smoked trout.*

Creamed Roquefort and walnuts

These delicious easy-to-make toasts (pictured top left)
are best served within 30 minutes of being made,
so that they keep their crisp texture.

Preparation time 15 minutes
Total cooking time 10 minutes
Makes 40

25 g (3/4 oz) walnuts, roughly chopped
10 slices wholegrain bread,
about 5 mm (1/4 inch) thick
60 g (2 oz) Roquefort or
other strong blue cheese
60 g (2 oz) cream cheese
chopped fresh parsley,
to garnish

One Spread the walnuts on a baking tray and toast them under a preheated grill for 3–5 minutes, shaking the tray frequently to ensure that they are evenly browned and do not burn. Alternatively, toast the nuts for 7–10 minutes in a moderate oven at 180°C (350°F/Gas 4). Set aside to cool.

Two Cut the bread slices into 4 cm (1½ inch) circles with a plain round cutter. Toast lightly on both sides under the grill, then set aside.

Three Break up the Roquefort with a fork, then add the cream cheese and mix well. Stir in half the walnuts, then spread over the rounds of toast. To finish, sprinkle with the remaining chopped walnuts and a little parsley.

Crostini of roasted capsicum and basil

The name crostini comes from the Italian word 'crosta', meaning 'crust'.
Crostini are small rounds of toasted bread with toppings such as pâté,
cheese or, as in this case, roasted vegetables (pictured bottom left).

Preparation time 25 minutes
Total cooking time 10 minutes
Makes 12

1/2 small red capsicum (pepper),
cut in half
1/2 small green capsicum (pepper),
cut in half
2 tablespoons shredded fresh basil
70 ml (2¼ fl oz) olive oil
1/2 baguette
1 clove garlic
shavings of Parmesan cheese,
to garnish

One Preheat the oven to moderately hot 200°C (400°F/Gas 6). To grill the capsicum, follow the method in the Chef's techniques on page 535.

Two Cut the capsicum into thin strips and put them into a bowl with the basil and 1 tablespoon of the olive oil, or just enough to bind the mixture. Season with salt and freshly ground black pepper.

Three Cut the baguette into 1.5 cm (5/8 inch) thick slices. Toast the slices on both sides under a preheated grill or in a toaster, then brush them with the remaining oil. Rub the garlic clove over the crostini and spoon some of the roasted capsicum mixture onto each one. Serve immediately, topped with the Parmesan shavings.

Melting morsels

As the name suggests, these rich cheese biscuits melt in the mouth.
They can be prepared up to a week in advance as they keep well
if stored in an airtight container in a cool place.

Preparation time 35 minutes
+ 50 minutes chilling
Total cooking time 10 minutes per tray
Makes 64

90 g (3 oz) plain flour
pinch of celery salt
90 g (3 oz) unsalted butter,
cut into cubes and chilled
75 g (2½ oz) Cheddar cheese, grated
15 g (½ oz) Parmesan cheese, grated
1 egg yolk
1 egg, beaten
10 g (¼ oz) Parmesan cheese, finely
grated, for the topping

One Preheat the oven to moderately hot 190°C (375°F/Gas 5). Brush two baking trays with melted butter and refrigerate.

Two Sift the flour, celery salt and a pinch of salt and freshly ground black pepper together into a medium bowl. Add the butter cubes and, using two round-bladed knives, cut the mixture from the centre to the edges of the bowl with a quick action.

Three When the flour has almost disappeared into the butter, add the Cheddar and Parmesan and continue cutting for a few moments more until the mixture is blended and coming together in rough lumps. Make a well in the centre and cut in the egg yolk until combined. Gather together by hand to form a ball.

Four Wrap the dough loosely in plastic wrap and flatten slightly. Chill for about 20 minutes until firm.

Five Place the dough on a lightly floured work surface. Cut in half and roll out each half to a 20 cm (8 inch) square, 4 mm (¼ inch) thick. Cut each square into 16 small squares, then cut each square in half to form triangles. Using a palette knife, carefully place on enough triangles to comfortably fill the two baking trays, and chill for 30 minutes.

Six Brush each biscuit with beaten egg and sprinkle with a pinch of the extra Parmesan. Bake for 10 minutes, or until golden brown. Place on a wire rack to cool. Repeat with the remaining mixture, preparing the trays as instructed in step 1.

CHEF'S TIP *Try varying the topping by sprinkling with finely chopped nuts and rock salt, poppy seeds or Parmesan mixed with a pinch of cayenne.*

LE CORDON BLEU ✠ COMPLETE COOK

Mini brochettes

*It is important to marinate the ingredients as this
will bring more flavour to the brochettes and make
sure that the meat is deliciously tender.*

*Preparation time 25 minutes
+ 1 hour marinating
Total cooking time 15 minutes
Makes 20*

*180 ml (5¾ fl oz) veal or
chicken stock (see pages 518–9)
2 cloves garlic, crushed
2 teaspoons chopped fresh ginger
2 tablespoons dark soy sauce
2 teaspoons sesame oil
1 skinless chicken breast fillet, cut
into 1 cm (½ inch) cubes
½ red capsicum (pepper), cut
into 1 cm (½ inch) cubes
½ yellow capsicum (pepper), cut
into 1 cm (½ inch) cubes
2 spring onions, sliced diagonally
1 teaspoon cornflour*

One Put the stock in a pan and simmer
until is syrupy and reduced by a third.

Two Mix the reduced stock with the
garlic, ginger, soy and sesame oil to
make the marinade. Leave to cool.

Three Thread the chicken, capsicum and
spring onion onto the skewers, then
place the brochettes in a flat dish and
season well. Pour half the marinade over
the brochettes. Cover with plastic wrap
and refrigerate for at least 1 hour.

Four To make the dipping sauce, heat the
remaining marinade in a small pan, then
mix the cornflour with a little water and
stir in until the sauce boils and thickens.
Set aside and keep warm.

Five Drain the brochettes and cook under
a preheated grill for 3 minutes, turning,
until the meat is cooked through. Serve
with the dipping sauce.

Spring rolls with pork stuffing

*These rolls are deep-fried—if you do not have a deep-fat fryer,
it is possible to use a heavy-based pan. The results will be just
as good, but extreme care should be taken with the hot oil.*

Preparation time 40 minutes
+ 30 minutes chilling
Total cooking time 40 minutes
Makes about 40

2 tablespoons oil
250 g (8 oz) minced pork
1/2 Chinese cabbage, shredded finely
2 spring onions, sliced
1 teaspoon grated fresh ginger
30 g (1 oz) bamboo shoots,
finely chopped
3 button mushrooms, thinly sliced
1/2 teaspoon dried sage
1 teaspoon soy sauce
2 teaspoons cornflour
20 spring roll wrappers,
about 20 cm (8 inches) square
soy sauce, to serve

One Heat the oil in a large pan over high
heat, add the pork and cook, stirring,
for about 3 minutes. Transfer to a bowl
to cool. When cool, add the Chinese
cabbage, spring onion, ginger, bamboo
shoots, mushrooms, dried sage, soy
sauce and 1 teaspoon of the cornflour.
Stir well, then season to taste.

Two Add a little water to the remaining
teaspoon of cornflour to make a paste.
Prepare the spring rolls by following the
method in the Chef's techniques on page
537. Place in the refrigerator to chill for
at least 30 minutes before cooking.

Three Heat the oil in a deep-fat fryer or
saucepan (see Chef's techniques, page
537). Fry the rolls in batches of four or
five for 3–5 minutes, or until cooked and
golden brown. The spring rolls will float
to the surface of the oil when cooked.
Drain on crumpled paper towels and
serve hot with the soy sauce.

CHEF'S TIP *These could also be made
using filo pastry. Brush sheets of filo
with melted butter, wrap the filo around
the filling, then bake them in a
moderately hot 200°C (400°F/Gas 6)
oven for 10 minutes, or until crisp.*

Smoked salmon and trout roulade on pumpernickel

Pumpernickel, a coarse, dark bread made using a high proportion of rye flour, has a slightly sour taste, which complements the rich creaminess of the smoked fish topping.

Preparation time 25 minutes
+ 30 minutes chilling
Total cooking time Nil
Makes 20

100 g (3¼ oz) smoked trout fillet
100 g (3¼ oz) cream cheese
1 tablespoon lemon juice
200 g (6½ oz) smoked salmon slices
200 g (6½ oz) pumpernickel, sliced
sprigs of fresh chervil or parsley,
to garnish

One Remove any skin or bones from the trout and place in a food processor with 85 g (2¾ oz) of the cream cheese. Process until blended and smooth, then season with salt and pepper. Add the lemon juice and process to combine.

Two Lay the smoked salmon slices on a piece of plastic wrap in a 15 x 20 cm (6 x 8 inch) rectangular shape, with the edges of the slices overlapping. Spread an even layer of the smoked trout mixture over the salmon, then roll the slices up from the widest side, using the plastic wrap to help lift as you roll. Wrap the salmon and trout roulade in

plastic wrap and place it in the freezer for 30 minutes, or until set and firm enough to slice.

Three Using a 4.5 cm (1¾ inch) cutter, cut 20 rounds from the pumpernickel. Spread the remaining cream cheese on the pumpernickel circles. Remove the salmon roulade from the freezer, discard the plastic wrap and cut across the roulade, using a very sharp knife, to make about 20 slices. Top each piece of pumpernickel with a roulade slice and decorate with a sprig of chervil or parsley. Cover with plastic wrap and keep chilled until ready to serve.

Prosciutto, smoked ham and mustard roulade

Simple to prepare, yet full of flavour, these are ideal for serving with cocktails or pre-dinner drinks (pictured bottom right).

Preparation time 15 minutes
+ 10 minutes chilling
Total cooking time 5 minutes
Makes about 35

100 g (3¼ oz) smoked ham, chopped
60 g (2 oz) mayonnaise
1 tablespoon Dijon mustard
100 g (3¼ oz) prosciutto slices
3 petits pains (small French rolls)
sprigs of fresh chervil, to garnish

One To make the filling, purée the ham in a food processor, add the mayonnaise and mustard and process to bind. Season to taste with salt and freshly ground black pepper.

Two Lay the slices of prosciutto, slightly overlapping, on a sheet of plastic wrap and spread the filling mixture over the prosciutto with the back of a spoon. Roll up the prosciutto lengthways and put in the freezer for 10 minutes to firm.

Three Thinly slice the petits pains and toast until golden brown. Cut the prosciutto roll into thin slices and place a slice on each piece of toasted bread. Garnish with the fresh chervil.

Crostini with tapenade

Crostini are Italian croûtes, ideal with soups or as an accompaniment to vegetable dishes and salads. Here they are served with a tapenade (pictured top right), which is very intense in flavour and should be spread thinly.

Preparation time 15 minutes
Total cooking time 25 minutes
Makes about 60

1 French baguette
olive oil, for cooking
60 g (2 oz) black olives, pitted
1 small clove garlic
8 anchovy fillets

One Preheat the oven to moderate 180°C (350°F/Gas 4). Cut the bread into very thin slices. Pour enough of the oil into a large frying pan to lightly coat the base and heat gently. Lightly fry the bread, in batches, on both sides, then transfer to a baking tray. Bake in the oven until both sides are golden. Remove and cool to room temperature.

Two To make the tapenade, place the olives, garlic and anchovy fillets in a food processor and work into a paste with a spreadable consistency, adding a little olive oil if it is too dry. Season with freshly ground black pepper, but avoid salt—the saltiness of the anchovies will be enough. Spread the tapenade sparingly over the crostini.

Minted pea and coriander triangles

Despite being a little time-consuming to prepare, the advantage of these tasty savouries is that they can be made in advance and baked in the oven as required, making them ideal party fare, especially for vegetarians.

*Preparation time 55 minutes
+ 20 minutes cooling
Total cooking time 30 minutes
Makes 30*

*sprig of fresh mint
175 g (5³/4 oz) peas
1 tablespoon vegetable oil
1 onion, cut into cubes the same size
as the peas
2 potatoes, about 150 g (5 oz),
cooked and mashed
2 teaspoons ground coriander
1 tablespoon chopped
fresh coriander
1 tablespoon finely chopped fresh mint
1 tablespoon lemon juice,
to taste
6 sheets filo pastry
60 g (2 oz) unsalted butter,
melted*

One Place the sprig of mint in a pan of salted water and bring to the boil. When boiling, add the peas and cook for 2 minutes. Pour into a colander to drain, then remove and discard the mint.

Two Heat the oil in a frying pan over low heat, add the onion and cook for 7 minutes, or until the onion is soft and translucent. Increase the heat to medium, add the peas and potato and stir to combine. Transfer the vegetables to a small bowl and set aside for about 20 minutes to cool.

Three When cool, stir in the ground and fresh coriander, the chopped mint and lemon juice, then season to taste with salt and black pepper. Preheat the oven to moderately hot 190°C (375°F/Gas 5). Brush two baking trays with some melted butter.

Four Lay the filo out on a work surface Brush each with melted butter following the Chef's techniques on page 549. Cut across each sheet to form five strips, each about 8 cm (3 inches) wide. Place 2 teaspoons of filling on the corner of one end of each strip. Fold the pastry over diagonally to form a triangle at the end. Then keep on folding diagonally until you reach the other end of the strip.

Five Place the triangles on the prepared baking trays, brush the tops with a little melted butter and bake for 15 minutes, or until the filo pastry is crisp and golden brown.

CHEF'S TIP *These triangles can be prepared a day in advance and refrigerated before baking. Serve them straight from the oven.*

Cheese palmiers

*These small savouries are delicious served with a cocktail or to accompany a soup.
They can either be made as palmiers or as cheese straws. If you don't have time
to make your own puff pastry, use 375 g (12 oz) block puff pastry.*

Preparation time 30 minutes
+ 45 minutes refrigeration
Total cooking time 10 minutes
Makes 40

2 egg yolks
1 egg
1/4 teaspoon caster sugar
80 g (2 3/4 oz) Parmesan cheese, grated
1/2 teaspoon paprika
1 quantity puff pastry (see page 542)

One Beat together the egg yolks, egg, sugar and about 1/4 teaspoon salt and strain into a clean bowl.

Two Brush two baking trays with melted butter and put them in the refrigerator. In a bowl, combine the Parmesan, paprika, 1/2 teaspoon salt and some black pepper.

Three Divide the pastry in two and on a lightly floured surface, roll each piece into a 30 x 15 cm (12 x 6 inch) rectangle, about 3 mm (1/8 inch) thick. Brush lightly with the egg and sprinkle with the Parmesan mixture. Roll over the Parmesan with a rolling pin to press it into the pastry, then carefully slide the pastry sheets onto two trays and refrigerate for 15 minutes.

Four Transfer the pastry sheets to a lightly floured surface and trim back to 30 x 15 cm (12 x 6 inch) rectangles. With the back of a knife, lightly mark six 5 cm (2 inch) strips on each sheet, parallel with the shortest side. Sprinkle with a little water.

Five Fold the two outer strips of each pastry sheet inwards. Their non-cheese undersides will now be on the top. Brush with a little water and fold over onto the next marked strips, brush with water again and fold onto each other. Transfer to a tray and chill for 15 minutes.

Six Cut into 5 mm (1/4 inch) slices and place the palmiers, cut side down and well apart, on the prepared baking trays. Press down to lightly flatten, turn over and put in the refrigerator to chill for 15 minutes.

Seven Meanwhile, preheat the oven to moderately hot 200°C (400°F/Gas 6). Bake the palmiers for 8 minutes, or until golden and crisp. Remove to a wire rack to cool.

CHEF'S TIPS *As a variation, you could add some dried mixed herbs, finely chopped sun-dried tomato or anchovy to the cheese.*

To make cheese straws, use the same ingredients and follow the method for steps 1–3. Cut 1 cm (1/2 inch) wide strips from the pastry and twist each several times to form a long, loose ringlet. Place on the baking trays and press both ends down firmly. Chill for about 15 minutes, then bake for 12–15 minutes, or until golden and crisp. Cut each straw into 10 cm (4 inch) lengths and cool on a wire rack.

Cornish pasties

In the eighteenth and nineteenth centuries, Cornish pasties were eaten by miners as a complete meal. There was meat at one end and apple or jam at the other, with scrolled initials in the pastry to indicate the difference. This recipe is for smaller savoury pasties that can be served as finger food.

Preparation time 35 minutes
+ 30 minutes chilling
Total cooking time 30 minutes
Makes 48

PASTRY
500 g (1 lb) plain flour
pinch of salt
200 g (6¹/₂ oz) unsalted butter,
cut into cubes and chilled
50 g (1³/₄ oz) lard,
cut into cubes and chilled
6–8 tablespoons water

FILLING
1 potato, about 80 g (2³/₄ oz),
roughly chopped
¹/₄ swede, about 100 g (3¹/₄ oz),
roughly chopped
15 g (¹/₂ oz) unsalted butter
¹/₂ onion, finely chopped
125 g (4 oz) lean minced beef
50 g (1³/₄ oz) kidneys, finely chopped,
optional

milk, for brushing

One To make the pastry, sift the flour and salt into a large bowl and add the butter and lard. Using a fast, light, flicking action of thumb across fingertips, rub the butter and lard into the flour until the mixture resembles fine breadcrumbs. Make a well, add 1 tablespoon of the water and mix with a round-bladed knife until small lumps form. Continue to add the tablespoons of water, making a different well for each one and only using the last tablespoon if necessary. When the mixture is in large lumps, pick up and lightly pull together. Knead the pastry on a lightly floured surface until just smooth. Wrap in plastic wrap and chill in the refrigerator for 20 minutes. Brush two baking trays with melted butter and set aside.

Two To make the filling, put the potato and swede in a food processor and, using the pulse button, finely chop but do not purée. Melt the butter in a frying pan, add the onion and cook gently for 4 minutes. Add the potato and swede, increase the heat to medium and cook for 2 minutes, stirring occasionally, until just tender. Add the beef and kidney, increase the heat to high and fry, stirring continuously, for 5 minutes. Drain off the excess fat, season well with salt and pepper and leave to cool.

Three On a lightly floured surface, cut the pastry in half and roll out each half to 2 mm (¹/₈ inch) thick. With a 6 cm (2¹/₂ inch) round cutter cut out 24 circles from each half of pastry, and place a teaspoon of the filling on one side, 5 mm (¹/₄ inch) from the edge. Moisten the edge of the pastry with water and fold the unfilled side over to form a semicircle, pressing the edges together well to seal. Using a fork, press down on the edge of the pastry to form a decorative pattern. Make a hole in the top of each pasty with the point of a knife to make a small steam vent. Lay the pasties on the prepared baking trays. Place them in the refrigerator to chill for 10 minutes.

Four Preheat the oven to moderately hot 200°C (400°F/Gas 6). Brush the top of the pasties with a little milk and bake in the oven for 15 minutes, or until the pasties are golden brown.

Corn and chicken fritters

*Golden kernels of juicy sweet corn with the distinctive flavour
of coriander and soy sauce make these fritters irresistible.*

*Preparation time 20 minutes
+ refrigeration
Total cooking time 45 minutes
Makes about 65*

*2 eggs, lightly beaten
2 x 420 g (13¼ oz) cans sweet corn,
well drained
30 g (1 oz) cornflour
400 g (12¾ oz) skinless chicken
breast fillet, finely chopped
2 tablespoons chopped
fresh coriander
1 tablespoon caster sugar
1 tablespoon soy sauce
oil, for frying*

One In a large bowl, combine the eggs, sweet corn, cornflour, chicken, coriander, sugar and soy sauce and mix well. Cover the mixture and leave to chill in the refrigerator for at least 1 hour, or overnight if possible.

Two In a large frying pan, heat 3 mm (⅛ inch) of oil. Using a tablespoon, drop in enough corn mixture to make 3 cm (1¼ inch) circles, taking care not to overcrowd the pan. Fry for 3 minutes, or until golden, then turn over to brown the second side. Lift out and drain on crumpled paper towels.

Three Repeat with the remaining mixture, adding more oil to the pan when necessary. Serve the fritters warm.

CHEF'S TIPS *Make the first fritter a small one, taste to check the seasoning and, if necessary, add salt and pepper to the mixture before cooking the rest.*

These fritters are delicious topped with some Greek-style yoghurt and a drizzle of sweet chilli sauce.

Colcannon and smoked chicken canapés

These delicious appetisers of smoky chicken and cranberry chutney have an Irish twist, with a filling of buttery potato and cabbage.

Preparation time 35 minutes
+ 30 minutes refrigeration
Total cooking time 45 minutes
Makes 24

PASTRY
200 g (6½ oz) plain flour
¼ teaspoon salt
40 g (1¼ oz) unsalted butter,
cut into cubes and chilled
2 egg yolks
3 tablespoons water

COLCANNON
120 g (4 oz) floury potatoes
55 g (1¾ oz) cabbage
1 tablespoon oil
½ small onion, finely chopped
60 g (2 oz) smoked chicken,
finely chopped

CRANBERRY CHUTNEY
55 g (1¾ oz) cranberries,
fresh or frozen
2 teaspoons soft brown sugar
2 teaspoons white wine vinegar

One Brush two 12-hole shallow patty pans or tart trays or 24 individual tartlet tins, 3 cm (1¼ inches) across and 1.5 cm (⅝ inch) deep, with some melted butter.

Two To make the pastry, sieve together the flour and salt into a large bowl. Using your fingertips, rub the butter into the flour until the mixture resembles fine breadcrumbs. Make a well in the centre and add the egg yolks and water. Work the mixture together with a palette knife until it forms a rough ball. Turn out onto a lightly floured work surface, form into a ball and cover with plastic wrap. Place in the refrigerator to chill for 20 minutes.

Three Preheat the oven to warm 170°C (325°F/Gas 3). Roll out the dough between two sheets of greaseproof paper to a thickness of 2 mm (⅛ inch). Using a round cutter slightly larger than the holes in the patty pans, cut out 24 rounds. Place the rounds in each pan, pressing down on the bottom so that the dough extends slightly above the edge of the holes. Place in the refrigerator to chill for 10 minutes. Lightly prick the base of the pastry and bake for about 12–15 minutes, or until lightly browned, then cool completely before use.

Four To make the colcannon, place the potatoes in a pan of salted, cold water, cover and bring to the boil. Reduce the heat and simmer for 15–20 minutes, or until the potatoes are tender to the point of a sharp knife. Drain, return to the pan and shake over low heat for 1–2 minutes to remove excess moisture. Mash or push through a fine sieve into a bowl and season with salt and black pepper.

Five Place the cabbage in a pan of salted, cold water and bring to the boil. Blanch for 1 minute, then remove and finely chop. Heat the oil in a frying pan, add the onion and cook for 1 minute over high heat, stirring occasionally. Add the potato and cabbage and stir to combine with the onion. Continue cooking over medium heat for 10 minutes, or until the mixture has a mottled brown appearance, then add the chicken, season with salt and black pepper and keep warm.

Six To make the cranberry chutney, place the cranberries, sugar, vinegar and 1 tablespoon water in a small pan. Bring slowly to the boil, stirring to dissolve the sugar, then raise the heat to medium and simmer for 5–10 minutes, or until the mixture is almost dry and is thick and reduced. Remove the pan from the heat and set aside.

Seven Fill the cooled tartlets with a teaspoon of the colcannon and top with a small amount of the chutney. Arrange on a platter and serve warm or cold.

Puff pastry with asparagus and mushrooms

Ideal for serving with drinks or as a brunch dish, these crisp pastries are filled with subtle flavours that come together harmoniously in a creamy sauce. If you don't have time to make your own puff pastry, use 375 g (12 oz) block puff pastry.

Preparation time 30 minutes
+ 20 minutes chilling
Total cooking time 25 minutes
Makes 6

15 asparagus spears, trimmed
1 quantity puff pastry (see page 542)
1 egg, beaten
45 g (1½ oz) unsalted butter
30 g (1 oz) plain flour
250 ml (8 fl oz) milk
60 ml (2 fl oz) crème fraîche or cream
250 g (8 oz) button or oyster mushrooms, thickly sliced
melted butter, for brushing

One Bring a saucepan of salted water to the boil. Tie the asparagus into a bundle and cook for 4 minutes, or until tender, following the method in the Chef's techniques on page 535. Refresh, drain well and set aside.

Two On a lightly floured surface, roll out the pastry to a rectangle approximately 20 x 30 cm (8 x 12 inches) and 5 mm (¼ inch) thick. With a large sharp knife, trim to straighten the two long sides and cut into two long strips. Cut each strip into three diamonds or squares. Place slightly apart on a damp baking tray and chill for 20 minutes.

Three Meanwhile, preheat the oven to moderately hot 200°C (400°F/Gas 6). Brush the top surface of the pastry with the beaten egg. Do not brush the edges of the pastry as the egg will set and prevent the pastry from rising. Lightly score the tops of the pastry cases in a crisscross pattern with a thin knife. Bake for about 10 minutes, or until well risen, crisp and golden. Split in two horizontally with a sharp knife. Scrape out and discard any soft dough.

Four Melt 30 g (1 oz) of the butter in a saucepan, add the flour and cook for 1 minute over low heat. Remove from the heat, pour in the milk and blend thoroughly with a wooden spoon or whisk. Return the saucepan to low–medium heat, stir briskly until boiling and simmer for 2 minutes, stirring continuously. Add the crème fraîche or cream and stir over the heat for another minute. Remove from the heat and cover with foil. In a wide pan, melt the remaining butter and toss the mushrooms over medium heat for 2 minutes, or until cooked. Trim the asparagus tips to 6 cm (2½ inch) lengths. Cut the remainder of the tender stalks into 2 cm (¾ inch) lengths. Add the mushrooms and small pieces of asparagus to the sauce and mix briefly.

Five To assemble the pastry cases, spoon the warm sauce onto the six pastry bases and place the asparagus tips on top. Brush them with a little melted butter and replace the pastry lids. Warm through in the oven at warm 160°C (315°F/Gas 2–3) for about 5 minutes before serving.

CHEF'S TIPS *The pastry can be baked, split and scraped out the day before. Reheat in a warm oven before filling.*

Note that you may have a little of the mushroom mixture left over after filling the pastry cases, depending on the size of asparagus you use. This is delicious eaten on toast as a snack.

Potato and smoked fish croquettes

These deliciously crisp, golden brown potato croquettes are flavoured with smoked fish and garlic. They can be served with tomato sauce, garlic mayonnaise or salsa.

Preparation time 30 minutes
+ 15 minutes chilling
Total cooking time 45 minutes
Makes 40

500 g (1 lb) floury potatoes, such as
King Edward
20 g (³/4 oz) unsalted butter
1 egg yolk
pinch of ground nutmeg
1 tablespoon olive oil
2 cloves garlic, crushed
100 ml (3¹/4 fl oz) thick
(double) cream
150 g (5 oz) smoked haddock, trout or
salmon, flaked or thinly sliced
60 g (2 oz) plain flour
3 eggs, beaten
1 tablespoon peanut (groundnut) oil
150 g (5 oz) fresh breadcrumbs
oil, for deep-frying

One Cut the peeled potatoes into equal-sized pieces for even cooking. Place them in a medium saucepan, cover with cold water and add a large pinch of salt. Bring to the boil, lower the heat and simmer for at least 20 minutes, or until they are quite tender.

Two Drain the potatoes and dry them by shaking them in their pan over low heat. Push them through a sieve to purée or finely mash and add the butter, egg yolk, nutmeg and some salt and pepper. Transfer the mixture to a large bowl to cool.

Three Heat the olive oil in a saucepan, add the garlic and cook for 1 minute to soften. Stir in the cream and reduce by half. Add the fish to the potato mixture with the reduced cream. Season with salt and pepper and mix to combine well.

Four Season the flour with salt and pepper and place in a shallow tray. Place the beaten egg and peanut oil in a shallow bowl and the breadcrumbs on a large piece of greaseproof paper. Shape the potato mixture into ovals about 2 x 4 cm (³/4 x 1¹/2 inches) in size and roll each one carefully in the flour, patting off the excess. Dip them in the egg, then drain off the excess and then roll them in the breadcrumbs, lifting the edges of the paper to help the breadcrumbs to fully coat the croquettes. Sometimes it is necessary to coat the croquettes twice in the egg and breadcrumbs, especially if your mixture is a little too soft to hold its shape well. Put in the refrigerator for 15 minutes.

Five Heat the oil in a deep-fat fryer or deep saucepan (see Chef's techniques, page 537). Deep-fry, in batches, for 3–4 minutes, or until golden brown. Lift out, draining off any excess oil, and drain on crumpled paper towels. Serve with a sauce and lime wedges.

CHEF'S TIP *The potato must not be too wet or the moisture will cause the croquettes to split and absorb the oil. Using breadcrumbs on a large piece of paper enables you to coat the croquettes without too much mess. Always shake off or press on excess breadcrumbs or they will fall into the oil when frying, burn and then cling to the croquettes as unsightly specks.*

LE CORDON BLEU 🛡 COMPLETE COOK

Blue cheese puffs

Any type of blue cheese, such as Stilton or the creamy Italian Dolcelatte,
can be used to make these puffs. However, if you use the strong salty
Roquefort cheese, omit the salt in the recipe.

Preparation time 10 minutes
Total cooking time 25 minutes
Makes about 55

CHOUX PASTRY
100 g (3¼ oz) unsalted butter
100 g (3¼ oz) strong or plain flour
2 eggs, beaten

100 g (3¼ oz) blue cheese, finely
chopped
pinch of dry mustard, optional
oil, for deep-frying
finely chopped fresh chives, to garnish

One To make the choux pastry, melt the butter and 200 ml (6½ fl oz) water in a large pan over low heat, then follow the method in the Chef's techniques on page 545. Stir in the cheese and season to taste with salt, pepper and the mustard if desired.

Two Heat the oil in a deep-fat fryer or deep saucepan (see Chef's techniques, page 537). Using two lightly oiled teaspoons, scoop out a small amount of the mixture with one spoon and push off with the other to carefully lower into the hot oil.

Three Cook the mixture in batches until puffed, golden brown and crisp, turning with a long-handled metal spoon to ensure even colouring. Drain well on crumpled paper towels.

Four Sprinkle the warm puffs lightly with the chives and serve immediately.

CHEF'S TIP *The puff mixture can be prepared in advance, covered with plastic wrap and refrigerated for a few hours before deep-frying.*

soups

Vichyssoise

This rich, creamy leek and potato soup was created in
New York in the 1920s by a French chef. Although Vichyssoise
is typically served chilled, it can also be drunk hot.

Preparation time 25 minutes
+ 2 hours chilling
Total cooking time 40 minutes
Serves 4

30 g (1 oz) unsalted butter
3 large leeks, white part only,
finely sliced
1 celery stick, finely sliced
150 g (5 oz) potatoes, cubed
1 litre chicken stock (see page 519)
100 ml (3¼ fl oz) double
(thick) cream
50 ml (1¾ fl oz) cream, for whipping
1 tablespoon chopped fresh chives

One Place the butter in a large pan and melt over low heat. Add the leek and celery and cover them with buttered greaseproof paper. Cook the vegetables, without allowing to colour and stirring occasionally, for 15 minutes, or until they are soft.

Two Add the potatoes and stock and season to taste with salt and freshly ground black pepper.

Three Bring the soup to the boil, then reduce the heat and simmer for about 15 minutes, or until the potatoes become

very soft. Purée the soup in batches in a food processor or blender, pour into a bowl, stir in the cream and season to taste with salt and pepper. Cover with plastic wrap and allow to cool before placing in the refrigerator to chill for at least 2 hours.

Four Serve the soup in chilled bowls. Spoon some lightly whipped cream onto the centre of the soup and sprinkle with chives to garnish.

French onion soup

*Known in France as Soupe à l'oignon gratinée,
this onion soup has always been a very popular
first course on cold winter evenings in Paris.*

Preparation time 20 minutes
Total cooking time 1 hour 5 minutes
Serves 6

45 g (1½ oz) unsalted butter
1 small red onion,
finely sliced
400 g (12¾ oz) white onions,
finely sliced
1 clove garlic, finely chopped
25 g (¾ oz) plain flour
200 ml (6½ fl oz) white wine
1.5 litres brown stock (see page 518)
or water
1 bouquet garni (see page 520)
1 tablespoon sherry

CROUTES
12 slices French baguette
200 g (6½ oz) Gruyère cheese,
finely grated

One Melt the butter in a large heavy-based pan over medium heat. Add the onions and cook for 20 minutes, stirring often, until caramelised and dark golden-brown. This step is very important as the colour of the onions at this stage will determine the final colour of the soup. Stir in the garlic and the flour and cook, stirring continuously, for 1–2 minutes.

Two Add the white wine and stir the mixture until the flour has blended in smoothly. Bring to the boil slowly, stirring continuously. Whisk or briskly stir in the stock or water, add the bouquet garni and season with salt and freshly ground black pepper. Simmer gently for about 30 minutes, then skim the surface of excess fat if necessary. Add the sherry to the soup and adjust the seasoning to taste.

Three To make the croûtes, toast the bread slices until they are dry and golden on both sides.

Four Ladle the soup into warm bowls and float a few croûtes on top of each one. Sprinkle with Gruyère cheese and place under a preheated grill until the cheese melts and becomes lightly golden brown. Serve immediately.

CHEF'S TIP *The flour can be omitted from this recipe if you prefer soup with a lighter texture.*

Cream of cauliflower soup

*In France, this soup is known as Potage à la du Barry. It is named
after a mistress of Louis XV of France, Comtesse du Barry, whose
name is mysteriously given to a number of dishes that contain cauliflower.*

Preparation time 25 minutes
Total cooking time 35 minutes
Serves 4

300 g (10 oz) cauliflower, chopped
15 g (½ oz) unsalted butter
1 small onion, finely chopped
1 small leek, white part only,
finely sliced
15 g (½ oz) plain flour
750 ml (24 fl oz) milk

GARNISH
90 g (3 oz) small cauliflower florets
100 g (3¼ oz) clarified butter (see
page 520) or 100 ml (3¼ fl oz) oil
4 slices bread, cut into cubes
50 ml (1¾ fl oz) cream,
for whipping
chopped fresh chervil,
to garnish

One Place the cauliflower in a large pan
with 100 ml (3¼ fl oz) water. If the
cauliflower is not completely covered by
the water, add some milk to cover. Bring
to the boil, turn down the heat and
simmer for 7 minutes, or until soft.
Purée the cauliflower and cooking liquid
together in a blender or food processor
until smooth.

Two In a medium pan, melt the butter
over low heat. Add the onion and leek,
press on a buttered piece of greaseproof
paper and a lid and cook for 5 minutes,
or until soft but not coloured. Add the
flour and cook for at least 1 minute,
stirring continuously, until pale blonde
in colour. Remove from the heat, stir in
the milk until the mixture is smooth,
then return to the heat and bring to the
boil, stirring continuously. Add the
purée of cauliflower to the pan and

season to taste. Remove from the heat,
cover and keep to one side.

Three To make the garnish, bring a small
saucepan of salted water to the boil and
cook the cauliflower florets for about
2 minutes, then refresh them in cold
water. Drain well in a colander or sieve
and set aside.

Four Heat a frying pan with the clarified
butter or oil over high heat. Add the
bread cubes and fry, stirring gently, until

golden brown. Remove, drain on
crumpled paper towels and salt while
warm to keep them crisp.

Five Reheat the soup, season with salt
and freshly ground black pepper and
pour into bowls. Use the cream to thin
the soup if it is too thick. Alternatively,
lightly whip the cream and then stir into
the soup so that the swirls show as
streaks through it. Just before serving,
sprinkle with the cauliflower florets,
chervil and croutons.

Cream of tomato soup

This soup is best made with fresh tomatoes that are in season and very ripe. The result is a soup with a beautifully sweet tomato flavour.

Preparation time 15 minutes
Total cooking time 35 minutes
Serves 6

1¹⁄₂ tablespoons olive oil
1 onion, sliced
2 cloves garlic, chopped
3 large stalks of fresh basil
1 sprig of fresh thyme
1 bay leaf
2 tablespoons tomato paste (purée)
1 kg (2 lb) very ripe tomatoes,
quartered
pinch of sugar
250 ml (8 fl oz) chicken stock
(see page 519)
100 ml (3¹⁄4 fl oz) cream
fresh basil leaves, shredded, to garnish

One Heat the oil in a pan and gently cook the onion for 3 minutes, or until it is soft without being coloured.

Two Add the garlic, basil stalks, thyme, bay leaf, tomato paste and the fresh tomatoes. Season with the sugar, salt and black pepper. Pour in the chicken stock and bring to the boil, reduce the heat, cover and simmer for about 15 minutes. Discard the bay leaf.

Three Purée the soup in a blender or food processor and strain through a fine sieve. Return to the pan, stir in the cream and reheat. Check the seasoning. Serve garnished with the fresh basil.

CHEF'S TIP *If tomatoes are not in season and lack flavour, the same quantity of canned tomatoes could be used.*

Mussel soup

This is a delicious and delicate mussel velouté soup, lightly flavoured with saffron and cooked in a sauce of white wine and fish stock.

Preparation time 35 minutes
+ 10 minutes soaking
Total cooking time 30 minutes
Serves 4

1.25 kg (2 lb 8 oz) mussels
50 g (1¾ oz) unsalted butter
1 celery stick, finely chopped
4 French shallots, thinly sliced
30 g (1 oz) fresh parsley, chopped
300 ml (10 fl oz) dry white wine
300 ml (10 fl oz) fish stock
(see page 519)
350 ml (11¼ fl oz) cream
2 large pinches of saffron threads
20 g (¾ oz) plain flour
40 g (1¼ oz) unsalted butter, cut into
cubes and chilled
2 egg yolks
fresh chervil leaves,
to garnish

One Scrub the mussels well. Using a blunt knife, scrape off any barnacles and trim away the hairy beard on the straight side. Discard any mussels that remain open when tapped gently on a work surface (see page 523).

Two Melt 30 g (1 oz) of butter in a large saucepan and gently cook the celery and shallots until soft but not brown. Add the mussels, parsley and wine. Cover and simmer for 4 minutes, or until the mussels have opened. Take the mussels out of the pan and reserve the cooking liquid. Throw away any that have not opened and remove the mussels from the shells of those that have opened.

Three Strain the reserved liquid and simmer to reduce by half. Add the fish stock and 300 ml (10 fl oz) of the cream and simmer. Add the saffron and black pepper, to taste. Combine the remaining 20 g (¾ oz) of butter and the flour together in a bowl and whisk into the soup. Simmer the soup to cook the flour and then add the chilled butter, shaking the pan until it has blended in.

Four Mix the egg yolks and the rest of the cream together in a bowl, pour in a little hot soup and then add to the pan. Do not allow it to boil, simply warm the soup or the yolks will cook to small scrambled pieces.

Five Add the mussels to the soup to heat them through. Serve garnished with some fresh chervil leaves.

CHEF'S TIP *The mussels must be alive when cooked as they deteriorate quickly. If they remain open and do not close when tapped on a work surface, they are dead and should not be used. Any mussels which remain closed after cooking are also dead.*

Lobster bisque

Smooth, creamy bisques are thought to have Spanish origins. In the province of Biscay they were originally made with pigeons or quail before shellfish took over as the main ingredient in the seventeenth century.

Preparation time 30 minutes
Total cooking time 30 minutes
Serves 4

1 large or 2 small uncooked lobsters,
about 700–800 g
(1 lb 7 oz–1 lb 10 oz) in total
2 tablespoons olive oil
1/2 carrot, cut into cubes
1/2 onion, cut into cubes
1/2 small celery stick, cut into cubes
2 1/2 tablespoons brandy
150 ml (5 fl oz) dry white wine
4 large tomatoes, peeled, seeded and
quartered (see page 534) or 50 g
(1 3/4 oz) tomato passata
1 bouquet garni (see page 520)
1.5 litres fish stock (see page 519)
85 g (2 3/4 oz) rice flour
2 egg yolks
1 tablespoon thick (double) cream
1 teaspoon finely chopped
fresh tarragon

One If you have bought live lobsters, kill them by the method in the Chef's techniques on page 524. If you prefer not to do this, ask your fishmonger to do it.

Two Prepare the lobster following the method in the Chef's techniques on page 525. Heat the oil in a large pan, add the lobster pieces in their shell and stir for 2 minutes over high heat. Add the carrot, onion and celery, reduce the heat and cook for 2 minutes.

Three Add the brandy and immediately ignite at arm's length, then allow the flames to subside or cover with a lid. Pour in the wine and stir to blend in any sticky juices from the pan base. Add the tomato or passata, bouquet garni and stock and bring to the boil.

Four Using a slotted spoon, remove the lobster pieces from the stock, roughly break into small pieces with a knife and return to the pan with the rice flour. Stir to combine, bring to the boil and simmer for 10 minutes.

Five Pass the soup through a fine sieve, pressing the solids with the back of a spoon to extract the juices, then discard the contents of the sieve, pour the liquid into a clean pan and season to taste with salt and black pepper. The bisque should just coat the back of a spoon. If not, bring to the boil and simmer to reduce.

Six Mix the egg yolks and cream together in a bowl, stir in about 125 ml (4 fl oz) of the hot bisque, then pour back into the pan. Check the seasoning and reheat for 5 minutes, stirring continuously, without boiling. Sprinkle with the tarragon and serve in warm bowls or a soup tureen.

Scotch broth

*This warming Scottish soup is sometimes served as two courses,
the unstrained broth followed by the tender meat. Traditionally made
with mutton, it is now more often made with lamb.*

*Preparation time 30 minutes
+ 1–2 hours soaking
Total cooking time 1 hour 30 minutes
Serves 4*

*30 g (1 oz) pear barley
400 g (12¾ oz) lamb neck or mutton,
boned (ask your butcher to do this)
30 g (1 oz) unsalted butter
1 small carrot, finely diced
½ small turnip, finely diced
1 small leek, finely diced
½ small onion, finely diced
60 g (2 oz) frozen peas
30 g (1 oz) fresh parsley, chopped*

One Place the barley in a bowl, cover well with cold water and allow to soak for 1–2 hours. Drain the barley and rinse under cold running water. Bring a pan of water to the boil, add the barley and cook for 15 minutes, or until tender. Drain the barley and set aside.

Two Trim any excess fat from the meat then cut the meat into small cubes. Half fill a medium pan with salted water and bring to the boil. Add the lamb and cook for 2 minutes, then drain and plunge the lamb into a bowl of cold water. This process will give clarity to the soup and further remove traces of fat. Rinse the pan, half fill with salted water once more and bring to the boil. Add the meat, reduce the heat and simmer for

30–40 minutes, or until the meat is tender. Strain, reserving the meat, and measure the cooking liquid to 1 litre, adding extra water if necessary.

Three Place the butter in a large saucepan and melt over medium heat. Add the diced vegetables to the pan and cook, stirring frequently, until tender but not coloured. Drain the vegetables and wipe out the pan with paper towels. Replace the vegetables then mix in the lamb, barley and peas. Add the stock and bring to the boil. Reduce the heat and simmer for 30 minutes, while frequently skimming the surface to remove excess fat and impurities. Season to taste and serve the soup with a sprinkling of parsley to garnish.

Chicken consommé

*A consommé is a classic clear soup made from meat, chicken or fish stock.
The name comes from the French word 'consommer', meaning to finish or use up
and is so called because all the goodness of the meat goes into the soup.*

Preparation time 45 minutes
Total cooking time 3 hours 15 minutes
Serves 4

1.25 kg (2 lb 8 oz) chicken legs
250 g (8 oz) lean minced beef
1 teaspoon oil
1 small carrot, roughly chopped
1 small leek, roughly chopped
1 small celery stick, roughly chopped
1 small onion, halved
2 cloves, stuck into the onion
1 bouquet garni (see page 520)
1 teaspoon salt
6 peppercorns
2 egg whites

TO SERVE
10 g (¼ oz) butter
½ small leek, white part only, cut into
julienne strips (see Chef's tips)
½ small carrot, cut into
julienne strips
½ celery stick, cut into
julienne strips

One Preheat the oven to moderately hot 200°C (400°F/Gas 6). Remove the skin from the chicken legs and discard. Scrape the meat from the bones, following the method in the Chef's techniques on page 530, place in a food processor and process until finely minced. Place the minced chicken and the beef in a bowl in the refrigerator. Coarsely chop the bones, place in a roasting tin and bake for 30–40 minutes, or until well browned.

Two Heat the oil in a heavy-based pan, add the carrot, leek and celery and cook until lightly coloured. Set aside. Heat a cast-iron or stainless steel pan and add the onion, cut side down. Cook over medium heat until the onion has blackened.

Three Place the bones, carrot, leek, celery, onion, bouquet garni, salt and peppercorns in a large stockpot and cover with 2 litres cold water. Add the egg whites to the minced meat and mix with a wooden spoon, then add 500 ml (16 fl oz) water and mix well. Add to the stockpot and mix well. Put the stockpot over medium heat and bring slowly to the boil, stirring every 2 minutes. Reduce the heat and leave to gently simmer for 2 hours.

Four Line a fine sieve with a clean tea towel and place over a clean pan. Gently ladle the consommé into the sieve and strain into the pan.

Five To serve, melt the butter in a small frying pan. Add the julienned vegetables and a pinch of salt and cook, covered, over low heat for 10–15 minutes, or until the vegetables are cooked but still firm. Strain and pat dry to remove the excess butter, then place in four bowls and pour in the hot consommé.

CHEF'S TIPS *Julienne strips are even-sized strips of vegetables the size and shape of matchsticks. They cook quickly and are very decorative.*

To remove the maximum amount of fat, the consommé is best made a day in advance and refrigerated overnight, or until the excess fat solidifies on the surface. Skim off the fat before reheating the consommé over a pan of gently simmering water.

Borscht

This vegetarian version is based on a recipe from Ukraine,
where borscht is the national soup. It is characterised by its thickness and
the deep red colour of its main ingredient—beetroot.

Preparation time 40 minutes
Total cooking time 45 minutes
Serves 6

1 tablespoon tomato paste (purée)
500 g (1 lb) fresh beetroot, cut into
   julienne strips (see Chef's tip)
1 carrot, cut into julienne strips
125 g (4 oz) parsnips, cut into
   julienne strips
4 celery sticks, cut into
   julienne strips
1 onion, finely chopped
2 cloves garlic
350 g (11¼ oz) cabbage,
   coarsely shredded
6 ripe tomatoes, peeled, seeded and
   roughly chopped (see page 534)
30 g (1 oz) fresh parsley,
   finely chopped
60 g (2 oz) plain flour
125 ml (4 fl oz) sour cream

One Bring 3 litres of water to the boil in
a large saucepan and season well. Add
the tomato paste, beetroot, carrot,
parsnip and celery, stir well and simmer
for 15 minutes. Add the onion, garlic
and cabbage and simmer for 15 minutes.

Two Check the soup for seasoning and
add the tomato. Simmer for 5 minutes
and stir in the parsley. Thicken the soup
by mixing the flour into the sour cream,
then stirring it into the soup over low
heat until well combined.

Three Borscht should be slightly piquant,
but not sweet—add salt and sugar if
necessary. This is best made a day in
advance and reheated just before serving.

CHEF'S TIP *Julienne strips are vegetables*
cut the size and shape of matchsticks.

Celeriac and Stilton soup

*Celeriac tastes like a sweeter and more nutty version of celery,
and is partnered here by Stilton, the king of English cheeses.*

Preparation time 5 minutes
Total cooking time 40 minutes
Serves 4

1¹/₂ tablespoons oil or 30 g (1 oz)
unsalted butter
1 onion, sliced
200 g (6¹/₂ oz) celeriac, peeled and
thinly sliced
100 g (3¹/₄ oz) Stilton cheese,
crumbled
fresh watercress, to garnish

One In a large pan, heat the oil or butter and add the onion. Cover the pan and cook over low heat until the onion is soft and translucent. Add the celeriac and 1 litre water, cover and bring to the boil. Reduce the heat and simmer for 30 minutes, or until the celeriac is very soft.

Two Add 75 g (2¹/₂ oz) of the Stilton and purée the mixture in a blender or food processor. Return the soup to a clean pan and reheat gently. Season with salt and pepper to taste, bearing in mind that Stilton can be very salty.

Three Serve with the remaining cheese crumbled over the surface. Garnish with a watercress and black pepper.

CHEF'S TIP *Celeriac discolours when it is peeled so, if preparing in advance, place it in a bowl, cover with water and add a tablespoon of lemon juice.*

Bouillabaisse

Fishermen in Marseilles made this fragrant soup using fish that were difficult to sell. These were tossed into a simmering pot, hence the name Bouillabaisse, from 'bouillir' (to boil) and 'abaisser' (to reduce). You can use any combination of the fish below in the soup, increasing the amount of one if another is not available.

Preparation time 3 hours
Total cooking time 1 hour 10 minutes
Serves 4–6

1 John Dory, filleted and bones
reserved (see page 526)
2 sole, filleted and bones reserved
500 g (1 lb) monkfish or ling,
filleted and bones reserved
1 small sea bream, filleted and
bones reserved
500 g (1 lb) conger eel, cut into pieces
90 ml (3 fl oz) olive oil
2 cloves garlic, finely chopped
pinch of saffron threads
1 carrot, fennel bulb and leek, white
part only, cut into julienne strips
(see Chef's tip)
24 thin slices French baguette,
for croûtes
3 cloves garlic, cut in half, for croûtes
chopped fresh basil, to garnish

SOUP
1 small leek, onion and fennel bulb,
sliced thinly
1 celery stick, sliced thinly
2 cloves garlic
2 tablespoons tomato paste (purée)
500 ml (16 fl oz) white wine
pinch of saffron threads
2 sprigs of fresh thyme
1 bay leaf
4 sprigs of fresh parsley

ROUILLE SAUCE
1 egg yolk
1 tablespoon tomato paste (purée)
3 cloves garlic, crushed into a paste
pinch of saffron threads
250 ml (8 fl oz) olive oil
1 baked potato, about 200 g (6½ oz)

One Season the fish and eel with salt and pepper and toss with half the oil, the garlic, saffron, carrot, fennel and leek. Cover and refrigerate.

Two To make the soup, heat the remaining oil in a stockpot over high heat, add the reserved bones and cook for 3 minutes. Stir in the leek, onion, fennel, celery and garlic and cook for 2 minutes, then mix in the tomato paste and cook for 2 minutes. Pour in the wine and simmer for 5 minutes. Finally, add 1 litre water, the saffron and herbs and simmer for 20 minutes.

Three Strain the mixture through a sieve, pressing down to extract as much juice as possible, then discard the solids. Place the soup in a saucepan and simmer for 15 minutes until slightly thickened, skimming to remove any foam that floats to the surface.

Four To make the rouille, whisk the egg yolk in a small bowl with the tomato paste, garlic, saffron and some salt and black pepper. Continue to whisk while slowly pouring the oil into the mixture. Press the flesh of the potato through a sieve and whisk into the sauce.

Five Lightly toast the French baguette under a preheated grill, cool, then rub both sides with the cut sides of the half cloves of garlic to make garlic croûtes. Set aside.

Six Cut each fish fillet into six and add to a large pot with the eel and julienne vegetables. Pour the hot soup over and simmer for 7 minutes, or until the fish is cooked. Remove the fish and vegetables and place in a large earthenware or metal dish.

Seven Whisk three tablespoons of the rouille into the soup to thicken it a bit, then pour the soup over the fish and sprinkle with the basil. Serve with the garlic croûtes and the remaining rouille.

CHEF'S TIP *Julienne strips are vegetables cut to the size and shape of matchsticks.*

about saffron...

Threads of saffron, the world's most expensive spice, are the red stigmas of a type of crocus. The use of saffron is traditional in bouillabaisse—it adds both colour and an earthy fragrance to the broth. The best quality saffron comes from either Spain, Iran or Kashmir. It is always expensive and is usually packaged in small boxes or jars.

Cream of asparagus soup

*Asparagus is one of the most delicious of the spring vegetables.
In this simple soup, which can be served hot or cold,
the flavour of the asparagus comes to the fore.*

Preparation time 15 minutes
Total cooking time 20 minutes
Serves 4

800 g (1 lb 10 oz) green or white
asparagus
500 ml (16 fl oz) chicken stock
(see page 519)
265 ml (8½ fl oz) cream or thick
(double) cream
pinch of sugar
1 tablespoon cornflour or potato flour
1–2 tablespoons water or milk
2 tablespoons chopped fresh chervil,
to garnish

One Peel and discard the tough skin from the base of the asparagus and trim the thick ends. Wash and drain. Cut off the tips 3 cm (1¼ inches) down the asparagus and set aside. Slice the stalks into thin rounds. Bring a pan of salted water to the boil, add the asparagus tips and simmer briefly for about 2 minutes. Drain and place in a bowl of iced water to stop them from cooking further.

Two Add the chicken stock and 250 ml (8 fl oz) of cream to a large pan with the sugar and some salt and pepper and bring to the boil. Add the sliced asparagus and cook gently for 10 minutes.

Three Purée in a food processor or blender, then pass through a fine sieve. Return the mixture to a clean pan and heat again. In a small bowl, mix the cornflour or potato flour with the water or milk to form a smooth paste. Pour a little hot asparagus mixture into the paste. Blend, return to the pan, and bring to the boil, stirring continuously. (This ensures a lump-free result when using a dry, starchy powder to thicken a hot liquid.) Season to taste with salt and freshly ground black pepper.

Four Pour the soup into a dish or bowls. Swirl the remaining 15 ml (½ fl oz) of cream in the centre, arrange some asparagus tips on top and sprinkle with the chopped chervil.

Cream of vegetable soup

You can use different vegetables for this soup, depending on the season. This is a thick, winter version, but a spring vegetable soup is also delicious.

Preparation time 15 minutes
Total cooking time 1 hour
Serves 6

100 g (3¼ oz) unsalted butter
300 g (10 oz) potatoes, cut into cubes
1 carrot, cut into cubes
½ onion, cut into cubes
2 small leeks, white part only,
thinly sliced
1 celery stick, thinly sliced
1 bouquet garni (see page 520)
200 ml (6½ fl oz) cream
chopped fresh chervil or parsley,
to garnish

One Heat the butter in a saucepan, add the vegetables, cover, and cook over a low heat until soft. Add the bouquet garni. Pour on 1.5 litres water, bring to the boil, reduce the heat and simmer for 30 minutes. Lift out and discard the bouquet garni.

Two Purée the soup, in batches, in a blender or food processor, then sieve into a clean pan and cook over low heat for 10 minutes.

Three Add the cream and season with salt and pepper. Serve very hot, sprinkled with the chervil or parsley.

New England clam chowder

*Clams are very popular on the east coast of the United States,
where they are caught in the coastal waters and eaten raw or cooked the
same day. Make sure the clams you use for this chowder are very fresh.*

*Preparation time 40 minutes
+ 30 minutes soaking
Total cooking time 1 hour 15 minutes
Serves 4*

1 kg (2 lb) clams
20 g (¾ oz) unsalted butter
20 g (¾ oz) plain flour
500 ml (16 fl oz) white wine
1 bay leaf
2 sprigs of fresh thyme
1 tablespoon oil
90 g (3 oz) smoked bacon,
cut into cubes
1 onion, chopped
2 celery sticks, sliced
120 g (4 oz) potatoes, cut into
small cubes
185 ml (6 fl oz) thick (double) cream
1 teaspoon shredded fresh
parsley

One Rinse the clams under running water two or three times to remove as much grit as possible. Drain.

Two Melt the butter in a large saucepan over low heat. Add the flour and mix with a whisk or a wooden spoon and cook for 3 minutes. Set aside and allow to cool.

Three Add the wine, bay leaf and thyme to a large stockpot, bring to the boil and cook for 5 minutes over medium heat. Add the clams, cover and simmer for 5–7 minutes, or until the clams have opened. Strain the clams and the cooking liquid over a bowl, keeping the liquid for later, and discard any clams that did not open. Set the remaining clams aside to cool. Once cooled, remove the clam meat from the shells, chop up the flesh and set aside.

Four Strain the cooking liquid again through a fine sieve into the pan with the butter and flour mixture. Whisk together, place over medium heat and simmer for about 10 minutes, skimming the top twice, and then set aside.

Five In a large stockpot, heat the oil over medium heat and cook the bacon for 5 minutes, or until nicely coloured. Reduce the heat, add the onion, cover and cook, without allowing the onion to colour, for about 3 minutes. Add the celery and cook, covered, for 6 minutes, then add the potato and cook, covered, for 3 minutes. Pour in the thickened clam liquid, cover and simmer for 15–20 minutes, or until the potatoes are just done. Add the chopped clams and the cream and simmer for 5 minutes. Serve the soup sprinkled with the shredded parsley.

CHEF'S TIP *Shellfish can contain lots of sand and grit. Always rinse several times, using lots of running water.*

Prawn bisque

*The first seafood bisques were a sort of crayfish purée, thickened with bread.
Today, all kinds of shellfish are used and the soup is usually finished
with fresh cream. The result is a rich and elegant soup.*

Preparation time 35 minutes
Total cooking time 1 hour
Serves 6

600 g (1¼ lb) small cooked prawns,
unpeeled
30 g (1 oz) unsalted butter
1 small carrot, chopped
½ small onion, chopped
1 celery stick, chopped
½ leek, chopped
1 tablespoon brandy
1 tablespoon tomato paste (purée)
2 ripe tomatoes, cut into quarters
3 sprigs of fresh tarragon
1 bouquet garni (see page 520)
150 ml (5 fl oz) white wine
350 ml (11¼ fl oz) fish stock
(see page 519)
300 ml (10 fl oz) cream
small pinch of cayenne pepper
40 g (1¼ oz) unsalted butter, cut into
cubes and chilled
1 teaspoon rice flour (optional)
fresh chopped dill, to garnish

One Set aside 18 whole prawns for decoration. Roughly chop the remainder with their shells.

Two Heat the butter in a large saucepan and add the carrot, onion, celery and leek. Cover and cook over low heat until the vegetables are soft, but not coloured. Add the chopped prawns and their shells and cook gently for about 5 minutes. Add the brandy and boil, scraping the base of the pan to pick up any sticky juices, then allow the liquid to evaporate. Add the tomato paste, tomato and tarragon sprigs and cook for about 30 seconds, stirring continuously, then add the bouquet garni. Pour in the white wine and allow it to evaporate to a syrup before adding the fish stock and the cream. Bring to the boil, reduce the heat, cover and simmer gently for about 15–18 minutes.

Three Mix vigorously and then strain the liquid through a fine sieve. Check the seasoning, adding salt and cayenne pepper if necessary. Mix in the chilled butter, shaking the pan until it has blended in. The soup will thicken as the liquid takes in the butter to form an emulsion.

Four If the bisque is not thick enough, mix the rice flour with a little water and then gradually whisk into the hot bisque until it reaches the right consistency. If it is too thick, dilute with a little fish stock.

Five Divide the whole prawns among six bowls. Pour the soup over them and garnish with chopped dill.

Minestrone

*Although there are many variations of this hearty soup, according
to the region of origin and the season, it will always consist of
vegetables and broth with the addition of pasta or rice.*

*Preparation time 45 minutes
+ overnight soaking
Total cooking time 2 hours 20 minutes
Serves 6–8*

250 g (8 oz) dried beans, such as
kidney beans or navy beans
150 g (5 oz) diced salt pork or
belly bacon
2 tablespoons olive oil
1 large onion, chopped
2 carrots, diced
2 potatoes, diced
1 celery stick, diced
2 cloves garlic, chopped
1 tablespoon tomato paste (purée)
3 litres brown stock (see page 518)
or water
1 bouquet garni (see page 520)
1/4 cabbage, finely sliced
150 g (5 oz) dried macaroni or
any small pasta
grated Parmesan cheese,
to serve

One Cover the beans with cold water and leave to soak for 8 hours or overnight. Drain, place them in a large pan with 2 litres water and simmer for 1½ hours, or until tender.

Two Meanwhile, place the salt pork or bacon in another pan and cover with cold water. Bring to the boil, strain and refresh in cold water. Spread on paper towels to dry.

Three In a large heavy-based pan, heat the olive oil and lightly brown the salt pork or bacon over medium heat for 3 minutes. Add the onion, carrot, potato, celery and garlic, then reduce the heat and cook for 5 minutes without allowing to colour.

Four Add the tomato paste and cook for 3 minutes. Add the stock and simmer for 10 minutes, skimming any fat from the surface. Add the bouquet garni and cabbage and simmer for 5 minutes. Remove from the heat and set aside. Drain the beans and add to the soup.

Five Return the soup to the heat and simmer for 10 minutes. Add the pasta and cook for another 15 minutes, or until the pasta is soft. Check the seasoning and remove the bouquet garni. Just before serving, sprinkle the grated Parmesan over the top.

Minted green pea soup with croutons

Mint and green peas are a classic culinary partnership, here puréed together into a deliciously fragrant soup with a fairly light consistency.

Preparation time *25 minutes*
Total cooking time *40 minutes*
Serves 4

1 small butter or round lettuce, sliced
12 spring onions or 1 small onion, sliced
450 g (14 oz) frozen baby peas, thawed
1–2 sprigs of fresh mint
1.2 litres chicken stock (see page 519)
4 slices bread
oil, for cooking
30 g (1 oz) unsalted butter
30 g (1 oz) plain flour
150 ml (5 fl oz) cream

One Put the lettuce, spring onion or onion, peas, mint and stock in a large saucepan. Bring to the boil, then reduce the heat and simmer for 25 minutes. Purée in batches in a blender or food processor, then pass through a fine sieve.

Two Remove the crusts from the bread and cut into small cubes. Heat the oil and fry the cubes until lightly browned, stirring to colour evenly. Drain on crumpled paper towels and salt lightly while hot to keep them crisp.

Three Melt the butter in a large pan over medium heat, stir in the flour and cook for 1 minute without browning. Remove from the heat, add the puréed soup and mix well. Return to low to medium heat and bring slowly to the boil, stirring continuously. Add the cream and season. To serve, put the croutons in bowls and pour the soup over the top.

CHEF'S TIP *To vary the garnish, cook an extra 30 g (1 oz) of baby peas and use them to replace the croutons.*

Pumpkin soup

Pumpkins are winter squashes, native to America. Their golden colour and firm texture makes them perfect in soups, and the lemon grass gives a tangy taste to cut their sweet flavour.

Preparation time 30 minutes
Total cooking time 45 minutes
Serves 6

750 g–1 kg (1¹/₂ lb–2 lb) pumpkin
3 large potatoes, chopped
3 large tomatoes, halved and seeded
1 stalk lemon grass, white part only, bruised with the side of a large knife
1.2 litres chicken stock (see page 519), vegetable stock or water
1¹/₂ tablespoons long-grain rice
pinch of nutmeg
15 g (¹/₂ oz) unsalted butter, optional
3 tablespoons thick (double) cream

One Cut a wide circle around the pumpkin stem with a small, sharp, pointed knife and remove the top. Using a large metal spoon, scrape the seeds from the pumpkin and discard, then either scrape as much flesh as possible from the pumpkin with the spoon or cut the pumpkin into wedges. Slice just inside the skin to release the flesh and chop it roughly.

Two Place the pumpkin, potato, tomato and lemon grass in a large saucepan with the stock or water. Season with salt and ground black pepper to taste. Bring to the boil, then reduce the heat and simmer for 25–30 minutes, or until the potatoes are soft. Remove the lemon grass stalk and discard.

Three While the soup is simmering, add the rice to a pan of boiling salted water and stir to the boil. Cook for 12 minutes, or until tender. Drain the rice in a sieve and rinse under water. Set aside and leave to drain well.

Four Transfer the soup to a blender or food processor and purée until smooth. Return to a clean pan, add the nutmeg and adjust the seasoning. The soup should be thick, but still drinkable from a spoon. If the consistency seems too thick, add a little milk. Stir in the rice, butter and cream, then heat through and serve garnished with black pepper.

Garlic and zucchini soup

Two whole bulbs of garlic may seem a powerfully large amount, but you will find it takes on a mellow creaminess when cooked.

Preparation time 35 minutes
Total cooking time 1 hour 15 minutes
Serves 4–6

olive oil, for cooking
1 onion, finely chopped
2 bulbs garlic, peeled and thinly sliced
2 potatoes, peeled and thinly sliced
2 litres chicken stock (see page 519)
or water
2 zucchini (courgettes)
1 tablespoon finely chopped fresh basil

One Heat about 4 tablespoons of olive oil in a large heavy-based pan, add the onion and garlic and cook over medium heat for 5–10 minutes, or until golden brown. Add the potato and cook for 2 minutes, stirring continuously. Add the stock, season to taste and simmer for 30 minutes. Allow to cool a little.

Two Trim the ends from the zucchini. Cut into quarters lengthways, then cut into short pieces. Set aside.

Three Purée the soup in a blender or food processor until smooth. Return to the pan and bring to the boil. Skim any foam from the top if necessary, then add the zucchini and cook for 20–25 minutes, or until the zucchini is tender. Just before serving, stir in the basil and adjust the seasoning. Serve garnished with a few extra basil leaves.

Creamy garlic soup with black olive crostini

*This unusual recipe has its roots in the garlic-based soups of
the Mediterranean. The black olive crostini would also go beautifully
with many of the other cream soups in this book.*

Preparation time 20 minutes
Total cooking time 45 minutes
Serves 4

90 g (3 oz) unsalted butter
2 heads of garlic, peeled into
individual cloves
2 onions, finely chopped
300 g (10 oz) floury potatoes,
cut into cubes
500 ml (16 fl oz) milk
500 ml (16 fl oz) chicken stock
(see page 519) or water

BLACK OLIVE CROSTINI
4 slices stale French baguette
100 g (3¼ oz) black olives, pitted
and finely chopped
50 ml (1¾ fl oz) olive oil

One Melt 30 g (1 oz) of the butter in a medium saucepan over medium heat. Add the garlic cloves and cook for about 5–7 minutes, or until the garlic is golden. Add the onion, cook for 2–3 minutes, then add the potato and the remaining 60 g (2 oz) of butter and continue to cook for 7–10 minutes, or until the onion begins to soften. Stir frequently as the starchy potatoes will want to stick to the pan. Pour in the milk and stock or water, then cook gently for 15 minutes, or until the potatoes are very soft.

Two Purée the soup in batches in a food processor or blender. Return to the rinsed pan and season to taste with salt and freshly ground black pepper. Cover to keep warm and set aside.

Three To make the black olive crostini, toast the four round slices of French baguette under the grill until golden brown on both sides. Place the finely chopped olives in a small bowl and moisten with the oil to lightly bind. Season to taste with salt and freshly ground black pepper and spread onto the crostini.

Four Ladle the soup into bowls and serve with the crostini.

Cream of chicken soup

This soup is quick and easy to prepare. It is based on a simple stock made from chicken wings, which can be ready in just 30 minutes. You could also use the more traditional stock from the Chef's techniques (see page 519).

Preparation time 10 minutes
Total cooking time 50 minutes
Serves 6

1 leek, roughly chopped
1 small carrot, roughly chopped
1 small onion, roughly chopped
1 celery stick, roughly chopped
400 g (12³/4 oz) chicken wings
2 sprigs of fresh tarragon
1 bouquet garni (see page 520)
6 black peppercorns
1 clove
35 g (1¹/4 oz) unsalted butter
35 g (1¹/4 oz) plain flour
250 ml (8 fl oz) cream
1 skinless chicken breast fillet
sprigs of fresh tarragon, to garnish
2 egg yolks

One Put the leek, carrot, onion, celery, chicken wings, tarragon, bouquet garni, peppercorns and clove in a large pan. Pour in 1.5 litres water to cover and bring to the boil. Reduce the heat and simmer for about 30–35 minutes. Skim the surface of the soup frequently for a clear finish.

Two Pour the stock through a colander and measure about 1 litre of the liquid, reserving the rest. In a medium pan, melt the butter, add the flour and cook gently, stirring continuously, for 1 minute, or until a smooth paste is formed and the flour is cooked. Remove from the heat. Pour the 1 litre of hot stock into the cooled butter and flour mixture a little at a time and stir well between each addition. Return the pan to the heat and continue to stir until the mixture boils and thickens. Add 200 ml (6¹/2 fl oz) of the cream and return to the boil. Season to taste with salt and pepper.

Three Cook the chicken breast for 8 minutes in enough of the stock to just cover it. Drain and cut into small cubes. Remove the leaves from the remaining tarragon stems and place in boiling salted water. Cook for 30 seconds, then drain. Mix the egg yolks with the rest of the cream. Bring the soup back to the boil, remove from the heat and add the egg mixture. Stir well. Do not boil the soup any further. Add the chicken cubes and sprinkle with the tarragon to serve.

Seafood and lemon soup

Choose from a selection of local fresh or frozen shellfish to make this very elegant and refined dish. Savour the richness of the seafood, refreshed by the citrus tang of lemon.

Preparation time 25 minutes
Total cooking time 20 minutes
Serves 6–8

400 g (12¾ oz) cockles
500 g (1 lb) small mussels
400 g (12¾ oz) clams or pipis
100 ml (3¼ fl oz) dry white wine
3 French shallots, finely chopped
6 scallops (ask your fishmonger to open the shells, remove the scallops and trim them)
2 small squid (ask your fishmonger to skin the squid and prepare them for cooking)
300 ml (10 fl oz) fish stock (see page 519)
100 ml (3¼ fl oz) cream
20 g (¾ oz) unsalted butter, cut into cubes and chilled
1 small carrot, cut into julienne strips (see Chef's tip)
1 celery stick, cut into julienne strips
½ leek, cut into julienne strips
100 g (3¼ oz) small cooked prawns, peeled (see page 522)
finely grated rind of 1 lemon
chopped fresh chervil or parsley, to garnish

One Wash the cockles, mussels and clams in lots of water and repeat twice. Be especially thorough when washing the cockles or clams as they can be very sandy. Place the shellfish in a large pot with the wine and shallots, bring the mixture slowly to the boil and cook for 2–3 minutes, or until the shells open. Discard any that do not open. Lift the shellfish out of the cooking liquid and remove the flesh from the shells.

Two Add the scallops to the cooking liquid and poach for 1–3 minutes, then remove and cut into small cubes. Cut the squid into small cubes and fry in a pan with a little hot oil, drain on crumpled paper towels and set aside.

Three Pour the cooking liquid from the shellfish through a muslin-lined sieve into a clean pan and add the fish stock and cream. Place over high heat and boil for 3–5 minutes, or until a very light sauce is obtained. Strain, then mix in the butter, shaking the pan until it has blended in.

Four Cook the carrot, celery and leek in salted boiling water for 3–4 minutes. Drain, pour on cold water to stop the cooking, then drain again and add all the vegetables and seafood, including the prawns, to the sauce. Stir gently and allow all the ingredients to heat through. Mix in some of the lemon rind and check the seasoning, adding more rind to taste.

Five Serve the soup, sprinkled with chervil or parsley.

CHEF'S TIP *Julienne strips are vegetables cut to the size and shape of matchsticks.*

about shellfish...

Shellfish such as cockles, clams and mussels need to be bought from a reputable source. They should always be bought alive and need considerable care and attention in both storage and cooking. Buy shellfish on the day you intend to cook them and throw any dead ones away (tap them on the work bench—if they do not close they are dead).

Cream of mushroom soup

This soup combines wild and cultivated mushrooms to create a rich, complex flavour. Try using some of the new varieties becoming more widely available to create different flavours.

Preparation time 20 minutes
Total cooking time 30 minutes
Serves 6

200 g (6½ oz) wild mushrooms, such
as chanterelles or cèpes
300 g (10 oz) button mushrooms
30 g (1 oz) unsalted butter
4 French shallots, finely chopped
500 ml (16 fl oz) chicken stock
(see page 519)
300 ml (10 fl oz) cream
5–6 sprigs of fresh chervil
30 g (1 oz) unsalted butter,
cut into cubes and chilled
60 ml (2 fl oz) cream, for whipping

One Put the wild mushrooms in a sieve and shake off some of the sand and dirt. Thoroughly clean them by tossing in a large bowl of water—don't leave them in the water or they'll absorb too much liquid. Finely slice. Wipe the button mushrooms with paper towels.

Two Melt the butter in a medium saucepan. Add the shallots and cook over low heat, covered, for 1–2 minutes. Add the mushrooms, cover and cook for 2–3 minutes. Pour the chicken stock and the cream into the saucepan and season with salt and pepper. Add three or four chervil sprigs and simmer for about 12–15 minutes.

Three Pour the soup into a blender or food processor and purée. Sieve the purée into a clean saucepan, heat gently and toss in the chilled butter, shaking the saucepan until it has blended in. Season to taste with salt and pepper.

Four Whip the cream until soft peaks form and season with salt and pepper.

Five Pour the soup into bowls. Use two dessertspoons to form neat, oval quenelle shapes from the whipped cream by passing a little cream from spoon to spoon. Float a cream quenelle on top of each bowl of soup and decorate with the remaining chervil.

CHEF'S TIP *Cèpes are also known as porcini. If the wild mushrooms are only available dried, use half the weight specified and soak overnight in just enough cold water to cover. The soaking liquid has a strong flavour and can be used instead of some of the stock.*

Chicken, bacon and lentil soup

Lentils are excellent for thickening winter soups and are here partnered with chicken and the traditional bacon. Brown and green lentils have the best texture for soups, but yellow and red lentils can also be used.

Preparation time 40 minutes
+ overnight soaking
Total cooking time 1 hour 40 minutes
Serves 4

300 g (10 oz) brown or green lentils
1 chicken, weighing 1.8 kg (3lb 10 oz)
50 g (1¾ oz) unsalted butter
100 g (3¼ oz) bacon, cut into cubes
1 carrot, sliced
1 small onion, sliced
1 celery stick, sliced
1 bouquet garni (see page 520)
sprigs of fresh parsley,
to garnish

One Soak the lentils in cold water overnight. Rinse and drain well.

Two Remove the skin from the chicken. Then remove the breast meat and set aside. Chop up the legs, wings and the carcass. In a large stockpot, melt the butter and add the bacon and chicken legs, wings and carcass and brown over medium heat for 7–10 minutes. When nicely coloured, add the vegetables, bouquet garni, 3 litres cold water and the lentils. Place back on the heat and allow to simmer for 1 hour, occasionally skimming the foam off the top.

Three Meanwhile, season the chicken breasts with salt and pepper and pan-fry over medium heat for 5 minutes on each side, or until cooked to a golden-brown. Set aside to cool.

Four Take the chicken pieces out of the stockpot with tongs and remove the meat, discarding the bones. Place the chicken meat back in the stockpot and simmer for about 15 minutes. Remove the bouquet garni, then purée the soup in a blender or food processor. Return to a clean pan over low heat and season with salt and freshly ground black pepper to taste.

Five Cut the cooled chicken breasts into small cubes and add to the soup to heat through. Serve garnished with a few sprigs of parsley.

CHEF'S TIP *If you want to enrich the flavour of this soup, a few spoons of cream and butter can be mixed in just before serving.*

Fish soup

French cuisine has a number of wonderful traditional fish soups,
making good use of fresh fish simmered with herbs and wine.
This is a light soup, but with a surprising depth of flavour

Preparation time 30 minutes
Total cooking time 1 hour
Serves 6

1 John Dory, about 400 g (12¾ oz),
    filleted (see Chef's tips)
4 red mullet, about 600 g (1¼ lb),
    filleted
2 red gurnard or coral trout, about
    400 g (12¾ oz), filleted
500 g (1 lb) conger eel, skinned
    and cleaned
50 ml (1¾ fl oz) olive oil
1 small carrot, finely chopped
½ small onion, finely chopped
½ leek, cut into 2 cm (¾ inch) cubes
3 cloves garlic, chopped
2 sprigs of fresh thyme
1 bay leaf
1 tablespoon tomato paste (purée)
80 g (2¾ oz) fresh parsley, chopped
4 tomatoes, quartered and seeded
200 ml (6½ fl oz) white wine
3 tablespoons brandy
200 ml (6½ fl oz) cream
2 large pinches of cayenne pepper
2 large pinches of saffron threads

One Wash the fish fillets and conger eel thoroughly. Pat dry with paper towels and cut into 3–5 cm (1¼–2 inch) cubes. Cover and refrigerate until ready to use.

Two Heat the olive oil in a pan, add the carrot, onion, leek and garlic and cook over low heat for 5 minutes. Add the thyme sprigs, bay leaf and the tomato purée. Mix well for 5 minutes. Stir in the pieces of fish and cook for another 5 minutes. Add 2 litres water, the chopped parsley and tomato and simmer for about 30 minutes. Pour in the white wine and brandy and stir over low heat for about 2 minutes.

Three Pour the mixture through a fine sieve and press very hard to extract all the liquid. Discard the solids. Pour the liquid into a clean pan and heat gently. Add the cream, cayenne pepper, saffron threads and season to taste. Cook gently over low heat for 5 minutes. Serve the soup sprinkled with black pepper.

CHEF'S TIPS *Ask your fishmonger to scale, gut, head and fillet the fish and to skin and clean the eel.*

If one kind of fish is not available, you can increase the amount of one of the others to make up the quantities. The eel can be replaced by a high-fat fish such as mackerel or herring.

Vegetable and saffron consommé

*This beautifully light consommé is very low in fat
and would make an elegant first course for
those who are watching their weight.*

Preparation time 30 minutes
Total cooking time 1 hour 5 minutes
Serves 6

VEGETABLE STOCK
1 onion, roughly chopped
1 carrot, roughly chopped
1 celery stick, roughly chopped
1/2 fennel bulb, roughly chopped
1 leek, roughly chopped
*80 g (2¾ oz) button mushrooms,
chopped*
*2 ripe tomatoes, quartered, seeded
and chopped*
2 cloves garlic, halved
6 white peppercorns
small pinch of ground nutmeg
*1 tablespoon finely grated
orange rind*
1 bouquet garni (see page 520)
2 large pinches of saffron threads

*1/2 small leek, cut into julienne strips
(see Chef's tip)*
1/2 small carrot, cut into julienne strips
1/2 stick celery, cut into julienne strips
*1 ripe tomato, peeled and diced (see
page 534)*
6 quail eggs
*chopped fresh chives and chervil,
to garnish*

One To make the vegetable stock, put the vegetables in a large saucepan and pour in 1.5 litres water. Mix in the garlic, peppercorns, nutmeg, rind, bouquet garni and a large pinch of salt. Bring to the boil, cover and reduce the heat to low until the liquid reaches a simmer. Simmer gently for 45 minutes.

Two Strain the stock through a fine sieve and discard the vegetables. Measure out 1 litre of the stock, adding water if

necessary, and pour into a large, clean pan. Add the saffron and set aside.

Three Add the leek, carrot and celery to a saucepan of boiling salted water. Cook for 5 minutes, or until tender, and drain. Add these to the measured stock with the tomato and season to taste, then reheat without boiling.

Four Bring a small pan of salted water to the boil. Gently lower in the quail eggs and simmer for 3–4 minutes. Remove the shells and place in a soup dish. Pour over the hot consommé and sprinkle with the chopped chives and chervil.

CHEF'S TIP *Julienne strips are vegetables cut to the size and shape of matchsticks.*

Smoked salmon soup with lime Chantilly cream

*If you order a smoked salmon as a whole side for Christmas
or another special occasion, don't throw away the trimmings.
Keep them in the freezer to make this elegant soup.*

Preparation time 30 minutes
Total cooking time 1 hour
Serves 8

30 g (1 oz) unsalted butter
1 onion, finely chopped
3 French shallots, finely chopped
½ fennel bulb, finely chopped
1 celery stick, finely chopped
1 leek, finely chopped
1 carrot, finely chopped
750 g (1½ lb) smoked salmon
trimmings
375 ml (12 fl oz) white wine
1 bouquet garni (see page 520)
10 white peppercorns
1 star anise
1 tablespoon mixed chopped fresh
herbs, such as parsley and chervil
1.8 litres fish stock (see page 519)
or water
150 ml (5 fl oz) thick (double) cream
50 g (1¾ oz) smoked salmon,
to garnish
chopped fresh chives, to garnish

LIME CHANTILLY CREAM
150 ml (5 fl oz) cream, for whipping
finely grated rind of 1 lime

One Melt the butter in a large frying pan over medium heat and add the onion, shallots, fennel, celery, leek and carrot. Cook, stirring, for 10 minutes, or until the vegetables are soft but not coloured. Remove half the vegetables from the pan and set aside.

Two Add the salmon trimmings to the vegetables in the pan and cook gently for 2 minutes, without colouring. Add the wine, bouquet garni, peppercorns, star anise and mixed herbs and season with salt and freshly ground black pepper.

Bring to the boil and cook until the liquid has reduced by half. Add the fish stock. Reduce the heat and simmer for 25 minutes, skimming the surface frequently. Strain through a sieve and discard the salmon trimmings, vegetables and seasonings.

Three Transfer the liquid to a clean saucepan, add the reserved vegetables and cook for 10 minutes over medium heat. Strain once more, discarding the vegetables, return the soup to the saucepan and stir in the cream. Season to taste with salt and pepper, then set aside and keep warm.

Four To make the lime Chantilly cream, lightly whisk the cream until it just holds its shape. Gently fold in the lime rind.

Five Serve the soup hot or cold with a spoonful of lime Chantilly cream in the centre. Top with a small roll of thinly sliced salmon and a sprinkling of chopped chives.

Apple and parsnip soup

Don't save your fruit for dessert—a fruit and vegetable soup makes a wonderful beginning to a meal. Granny Smiths are just right for this recipe as they are not too sweet.

***Preparation time** 30 minutes*
***Total cooking time** 40 minutes*
Serves 6

30 g (1 oz) unsalted butter
1 onion, chopped
2 celery sticks, chopped
5 parsnips, chopped
3 Granny Smith apples,
or similar variety,
peeled and chopped
1 bouquet garni (see page 520)
1.5 litres chicken stock (see page 519)
sprigs of fresh thyme, to garnish
chopped walnuts, to garnish

One Heat the butter in a medium saucepan, add the onion, cover with buttered greaseproof paper and a lid and cook over low heat until the onion is transparent, but not coloured. Add the celery, parsnip and apple and season with salt and pepper. Cook for a few minutes, then add the bouquet garni and cover with the chicken stock.

Two Bring the soup to the boil, then reduce the heat and simmer gently for 25 minutes, or until the vegetables are soft. Skim the surface, remove the bouquet garni, transfer the soup to a food processor or blender and process until smooth. Return the soup to a clean saucepan, season again to taste and reheat gently.

Three Divide the soup into bowls. Arrange a little thyme and some chopped walnuts in the centre of each soup to serve.

CHEF'S TIP *For a different garnish, stir 1 tablespoon of Calvados into 100 ml (3¼ fl oz) thick (double) cream. Gently swirl the flavoured cream into the soup just before serving.*

Gazpacho

Of Arabic origin, the name of this soup means 'soaked bread'.
Gazpacho originates from Seville in the south of Spain, but many
Spanish regions have their own versions of the soup.

Preparation time 35 minutes
+ 2 hours refrigeration
Total cooking time Nil
Serves 6–8

GAZPACHO
75 g (2½ oz) fresh white bread,
crusts removed
30 ml (1 fl oz) red wine vinegar
2 cloves garlic
¾ telegraph cucumber, unpeeled
and roughly chopped
1 onion, chopped
½ green capsicum (pepper),
roughly chopped
1.75 kg (3½ lb) ripe tomatoes,
quartered and seeded
125 ml (4 fl oz) olive oil

TO GARNISH
¼ telegraph cucumber, unpeeled
½ green capsicum (pepper)
4 slices of bread, crusts removed
and toasted

One In a food processor or blender, process the bread into fine breadcrumbs and add the vinegar, garlic, cucumber, onion, capsicum, tomato and a teaspoon of salt. Purée and then push the liquid through a sieve.

Two Return the mixture to the food processor or blender and slowly pour in the olive oil in a thin steady stream. Alternatively, pour the mixture into a large bowl and briskly stir or whisk in the oil.

Three Check the flavouring, season with salt and freshly ground black pepper and add a little more vinegar if required for a refreshing tang. Check the consistency—the soup should be thinnish, so you may

need to add a little more water to dilute it. Cover the bowl with two layers of plastic wrap and chill in the refrigerator for at least 2 hours.

Four To prepare the garnish, cut the remaining cucumber in half lengthways and use the point of a teaspoon to scoop out the seeds. Cut the cucumber, capsicum and bread into small cubes.

Five Pour the soup into well-chilled bowls and pass round the cucumber,

capsicum and croutons in separate dishes for each person to sprinkle onto their own soup.

CHEF'S TIPS *To serve, you could add two or three ice cubes to chill the soup, or for more colour, chop a red capsicum along with the green.*

This soup can be made a day in advance for a mature, well-rounded flavour, but cover it well—it has a strong smell that can affect other foods close to it in the refrigerator.

Summer prawn and cucumber soup

This unusual and refreshing soup has its origins in the Middle East. Very easy to make, it should be served chilled, accompanied by flat bread, for a perfect al fresco lunch.

Preparation time 20 minutes
+ 30 minutes standing
+ 2–3 hours refrigeration
Total cooking time 10 minutes
Serves 6–8

250 g (8 oz) cucumber
1 egg, optional
375 ml (12 fl oz) chicken stock
(see page 519)
155 ml (5 fl oz) tomato juice
2 x 450 g (14¼ oz) cartons
Greek-style yoghurt
125 ml (4 fl oz) cream
60 g (2 oz) cooked peeled prawns,
roughly chopped
12 cooked prawns, unpeeled
1 clove garlic, crushed
1 teaspoon chopped fresh mint
1 teaspoon chopped fresh chives

One Peel and cut the cucumber into 1 cm (½ inch) cubes, salt them lightly and leave on a plate for about 30 minutes. Rinse under cold water, drain and dry on crumpled paper towels.

Two Bring a small saucepan of salted water to the boil, lower in the egg and simmer for 7 minutes. Lift the egg out into a bowl of iced water to stop the cooking process and tap to just crack the shell. Leave in the water until just cool enough to remove the shell, then return the egg to the cold water. When fully cooled, chop roughly.

Three In a large bowl, mix together the chicken stock, tomato juice and yoghurt. When quite smooth, add the cucumber, cream and chopped prawns to the soup. Season to taste with salt and freshly ground black pepper. Cover and put in the refrigerator for 2–3 hours.

Four Meanwhile, peel and devein the whole prawns, following the method in the Chef's techniques on page 522, leaving the tails intact. Cover and store in the refrigerator.

Five Rub the inside of each soup bowl with the crushed garlic. Pour in the soup and sprinkle with the egg, chopped mint and chopped chives. Hang two of the whole prawns on the side of each bowl and serve the soup immediately with fresh bread.

CHEF'S TIP *To keep a hard-boiled egg from overcooking, it must be cooled immediately in iced water. The quick cooling also prevents an unsightly greeny grey ring from forming around the yolk.*

eggs and cheese

Scrambled eggs with smoked salmon

Scrambled eggs are delicious served with toast, as a filling for croissants or, alternatively, in puff pastry cases. The key to making really creamy scrambled eggs is not to overcook them.

Preparation time 10 minutes
Total cooking time 5 minutes
Serves 4–6

125 g (4 oz) smoked salmon
10 eggs
80 ml (2¾ oz) double (thick) cream
20 g (¾ oz) unsalted butter
sprigs of fresh parsley,
to garnish

One Set aside a few whole pieces of smoked salmon for decoration. Finely chop the rest and set aside.

Two In a bowl, whisk the eggs with the cream and season with salt and pepper.

Three Melt the butter in a frying pan. Add the eggs and cook over medium heat, stirring constantly, for about 3–5 minutes, or until the eggs are thick and creamy but still have a flowing consistency. Stir in the chopped salmon and serve immediately, garnished with the whole pieces of salmon and some parsley. Serve with fingers of toast.

CHEF'S TIPS *Scrambled eggs will continue cooking even when the frying pan is removed from the stove, so it is important that everything is ready to serve as soon as the eggs are done.*

If you prefer, you can leave the salmon in whole pieces and serve it beside the eggs.

This combination of eggs and smoked salmon also makes a delicious filling for warm fresh croissants.

LE CORDON BLEU COMPLETE COOK

Eggs Benedict

Toasted English muffins, topped with grilled bacon and lightly poached eggs, are smothered in rich buttery hollandaise sauce. This American speciality is a truly memorable breakfast or brunch treat.

Preparation time 25 minutes
Total cooking time 10 minutes
Serves 4

HOLLANDAISE SAUCE
2 egg yolks
2 tablespoons water
90 g (3 oz) clarified butter
(see page 520), melted
½ teaspoon lemon juice

8 rashers bacon, rind removed
4 English muffins
3 tablespoons vinegar
8 eggs
4 pitted black olives, cut in half,
or 8 slices of truffle

One Make the hollandaise sauce by following the method in the Chef's techniques on page 521. Cover the surface of the finished sauce with a disc of baking paper and keep warm over the hot water, off the heat.

Two Grill the bacon until crisp and toast the muffins. Put the bacon on the muffins and keep them warm.

Three To poach the eggs, fill a large shallow pan with water and bring to the boil. Reduce the temperature to low and add the vinegar. The water should be barely simmering. Crack the eggs one at a time into a small bowl and carefully slide them into the water two or three at a time. Cook for 2–3 minutes, or until the egg white is firm but not hard. Remove the eggs with a slotted spoon, and drain well.

Four Top each muffin and bacon with an egg. Cover with the hollandaise sauce, decorate with the olive halves and serve.

Eggs en cocotte with smoked trout and leek

Eggs that are 'en cocotte' are baked in the oven in ramekins placed in a bain-marie. These eggs, served with trout or leek, make a wonderful first course or brunch dish (pictured top right).

Preparation time 15 minutes
Total cooking time 35 minutes
Serves 4

30 g (1 oz) unsalted butter
1 small leek, halved and
finely sliced
185 g (6 oz) smoked trout,
finely flaked
120 ml (4 fl oz) cream
4 eggs
3 teaspoons snipped fresh chives

One Melt the butter in a saucepan. Add the leek, cover and cook gently for 8 minutes, or until soft but not brown. Meanwhile, brush four 150 ml (5 fl oz) ovenproof ramekins or soufflé dishes with a little melted butter.

Two Remove the leek from the heat and stir in the trout and a third of the cream. Season, spoon into the dishes and leave to cool. The cocottes can be prepared up to this stage the night before, covered and refrigerated.

Three Preheat the oven to warm 170°C (325°F/Gas 3). With the back of a teaspoon, make a slight indent in the centre of the mixture in each of the dishes. Break an egg into each cocotte, spoon a tablespoon of cream on each and sprinkle with salt and pepper and 2 teaspoons of the chives. Place the ramekins in a roasting tin and pour enough boiling water into the tin to come halfway up the sides of the ramekins and make a bain-marie.

Four Bake for 20–25 minutes, or until the whites are set and the yolks cooked but still tremble when lightly shaken. Set each cocotte on a cold plate, sprinkle with the remaining chives and serve immediately with fingers of freshly made buttered toast.

Frittata

Unlike the French omelette, an Italian frittata usually requires all ingredients to be mixed with the eggs before being cooked to a fairly firm texture (pictured bottom right).

Preparation time 20 minutes
Total cooking time 30 minutes
Serves 4–6

120 g (4 oz) skinless chicken
breast fillet
60 g (2 oz) unsalted butter
120 g (4 oz) mushrooms, sliced
2 cloves garlic, chopped
1 red capsicum (pepper), sliced
into short strips
10 eggs, beaten and seasoned with
salt and pepper
120 g (4 oz) Gruyère or
Cheddar cheese, grated

One Preheat the oven to hot 220°C (425°F/Gas 7).

Two Cut the chicken breast into small 1 cm (½ inch) cubes and season with salt and pepper. Melt the butter in an ovenproof frying pan over medium heat. Once melted, cook the chicken for 2–3 minutes, or until lightly browned.

Three Add the mushrooms and cook for 5–7 minutes, or until any liquid has evaporated. Add the garlic and red capsicum. Season with salt and freshly ground black pepper and cover. Lower the heat and cook for 5–8 minutes, or until the capsicum is tender.

Four Add the beaten eggs and stir to distribute evenly. Continue stirring for about 2–3 minutes, or until the eggs begin to set.

Five Sprinkle the cheese over the eggs and transfer the frying pan to the oven. Cook for 5–8 minutes, or until the cheese has melted and the eggs are cooked through. Remove from the oven and slide the frittata onto a plate. Cut into wedges to serve.

LE CORDON BLEU ✻ COMPLETE COOK

Twice-baked individual cheese soufflés

*A soufflé with a difference—you can relax. Prepare these
'individual' soufflés the day before and watch them
rise again ready to thrill your brunch guests.*

*Preparation time 35 minutes
+ cooling time
Total cooking time 45 minutes
Serves 8*

*315 ml (10 fl oz) milk
tiny pinch of grated nutmeg
1 small bay leaf
1 small French shallot, halved
4 whole peppercorns
30 g (1 oz) unsalted butter
30 g (1 oz) potato flour or
15 g (1/2 oz) flour mixed with
15 g (1/2 oz) cornflour
15 g (1/2 oz) unsalted butter,
cut into very small cubes
3 eggs, separated
90 g (3 oz) Cheddar cheese
1/4 teaspoon dry mustard powder
1 egg white
155 ml (5 fl oz) cream
2 tablespoons grated Parmesan
or Gruyère cheese*

One In a small saucepan, warm the milk with the nutmeg, bay leaf, shallot and peppercorns. When bubbles form around the edge of the pan, remove from the heat.

Two Melt the butter in a large saucepan, remove from the heat and stir in the potato flour. Strain the milk and pour into the pan, blend well and return to the heat. Whisk briskly until the mixture comes to the boil. Remove from the stove and scatter the butter cubes over the surface. Cover the pan with a lid and leave to cool slightly. Meanwhile, preheat the oven to moderate 180°C (350°F/Gas 4) and lightly butter eight 150 ml (5 fl oz) ramekins.

Three Uncover the sauce and stir in the melted layer of butter, followed by the egg yolks, Cheddar, mustard, and salt and pepper, to taste. In a large bowl, whisk the four egg whites until stiff. Using a large metal spoon or a spatula, stir 1 tablespoon of the egg white into the cheese mixture to loosen it, then add the remainder in one go, carefully folding until just combined.

Four Divide the mixture among the ramekins, pouring it in gently to avoid losing any volume. Place the ramekins in a roasting tin and pour in enough boiling water to come three-quarters of the way up the sides of the ramekins to make a bain-marie. Bake for 25 minutes, or until the soufflés have lightly risen and are firm to the touch. Remove the ramekins from the water and leave them to cool. (Cover and keep overnight in the refrigerator if you wish to prepare the soufflés the night before.)

Five Just before serving, preheat the oven to moderately hot 200°C (400°F/Gas 6). Return the ramekins to their roasting tin, pour some cream into each, dividing it equally, and season each one lightly. Sprinkle with Parmesan and pour boiling water into the roasting tin, as before. Bake for 10–15 minutes, or until risen and golden brown. Lift out carefully and place each dish on a plate. Serve immediately.

about soufflés...

The secret to making soufflés is to cook the mixture at the right temperature. This allows the air to puff up the soufflé before the mixture around it cooks and sets the structure in shape. If the soufflé is then cooled and reheated, as the air expands again it will push the structure back up.

Eggs Florentine

This classic dish is made from a layer of spinach and lightly poached eggs topped with a creamy cheese sauce. For perfect poached eggs, use the freshest eggs possible.

Preparation time 25 minutes
Total cooking time 30 minutes
Serves 4

MORNAY SAUCE
15 g (½ oz) unsalted butter
2 tablespoons plain flour
250 ml (8 fl oz) milk
pinch of ground nutmeg
40 g (1¼ oz) Gruyère cheese, grated
2 egg yolks

60 g (2 oz) unsalted butter
500 g (1 lb) English spinach leaves, cleaned
3 tablespoons vinegar
8 eggs

One To make the mornay sauce, melt the butter in a heavy-based pan over low–medium heat. Sprinkle with the flour and cook for 1–2 minutes without colouring, stirring constantly with a wooden spoon. Remove from the heat and slowly add the milk, whisking or beating vigorously to avoid lumps. Return to medium heat and bring to the boil, stirring. Simmer for 3–4 minutes, or until the sauce coats the back of a spoon. Stir in the nutmeg, then remove from the heat, cover and keep warm.

Two In a large shallow pan, melt the butter over low heat and add the spinach. Cook for about 5–8 minutes, or until dry. Set aside and keep warm.

Three Whisk the cheese into the mornay sauce, then whisk in the egg yolks. Season, to taste. Place over low heat and mix until the cheese is melted, then heat until very hot but not boiling. Set aside, cover the surface with a piece of baking paper and keep warm.

Four To poach the eggs, fill a large shallow pan with water and bring to the boil. Reduce the temperature to low and add the vinegar. The water should be barely simmering. Crack the eggs one at a time into a small bowl and carefully slide them into the water two or three at a time. Cook for 2–3 minutes, or until the white is firm but not hard. Remove with a slotted spoon and drain well.

Five Divide the cooked spinach evenly among four warmed plates. Place two poached eggs in the centre of the spinach and cover with the hot mornay sauce. Serve immediately.

LE CORDON BLEU COMPLETE COOK

Quiche Lorraine

This open tart originated in the Lorraine region around the sixteenth century. The name quiche comes from the German word 'Küchen', meaning cake. A quiche can contain many fillings, but a quiche Lorraine is traditionally made with cream, eggs and smoked bacon, and is considered a classic of French cuisine.

Preparation time 30 minutes
Total cooking time 1 hour 5 minutes
Serves 4–6

1/2 quantity shortcrust pastry
(see page 544)
1 egg, beaten

FILLING
oil, for cooking
180 g (5³/4 oz) smoked bacon,
rind removed and cut
into thin strips
3 eggs
ground nutmeg, to taste
250 ml (8 fl oz) cream
80 g (2³/4 oz) Gruyère cheese, grated

One Lightly grease a 22 cm (9 inch) round loose-bottomed flan tin. Roll out the dough on a lightly floured surface to a thickness of 3 mm (1/8 inch) and line the tin (see Chef's techniques, page 547). Preheat the oven to moderate 180°C (350°F/Gas 4). Bake blind for about 25 minutes, or until firm (see Chef's techniques, page 547). Remove the beads and paper and brush the bottom of the pastry with the beaten egg. Bake for another 7 minutes

Two To make the filling, heat a little oil in a frying pan. Sauté the bacon, drain on paper towels and set aside. Whisk the eggs and season to taste with salt and pepper and nutmeg. Mix in the cream and strain through a sieve.

Three Sprinkle the bottom of the pastry with the bacon and cheese. Gently pour in the egg mixture until the pastry is three-quarters full. Bake for about 20–30 minutes, or until the filling is well coloured and is set. Serve hot.

LE CORDON BLEU ✣ COMPLETE COOK

Caramelised onion, spinach and blue cheese quiche

*The delicious combination of vegetables
with blue cheese and a hint of nutmeg makes
a perfect filling for this vegetarian quiche.*

*Preparation time 30 minutes
+ 50 minutes refrigeration
Total cooking time 1 hour 45 minutes
Serves 8–10*

*1 quantity shortcrust pastry
(see page 544)*

FILLING
*2 tablespoons vegetable oil
500 g (1 lb) onions, thinly sliced
1 teaspoon caster sugar
100 ml (3¼ fl oz) red wine
50 g (1¾ oz) unsalted butter
250 g (8 oz) frozen English spinach,
thawed and squeezed dry
pinch of ground nutmeg
200 ml (6½ fl oz) thick (double)
cream
200 g (6½ oz) strong blue cheese,
such as Roquefort or Stilton
4 eggs, beaten*

One Brush a 24 x 3.5 cm (9½ x 1¼ inch) loose-bottomed flan tin with melted butter and line with the pastry, following the method in the Chef's techniques on page 547.

Two Preheat the oven to moderate 180°C (350°F/Gas 4) and blind bake the pastry for 10 minutes, or until firm, following the method in the Chef's techniques on page 547. Remove the beads and paper and bake the pastry for 5–10 minutes, or until it is dry. Remove and cool. Raise the oven temperature to moderately hot 190°C (375°F/Gas 5).

Three To make the filling, heat the oil in a large saucepan. Add the onion and cook gently for 8 minutes, or until translucent. Raise the heat, add the sugar and cook for 5–10 minutes, or until the onion begins to caramelise. Next, pour in the wine and cook until the liquid has evaporated and the onion

is soft. Season with salt and pepper. Remove from the pan and set aside.

Four In the pan, melt the butter, add the spinach and fry over high heat, stirring constantly, until the spinach is dry when pressed with the back of a spoon. (Wet spinach will make the quiche soggy.) Season with salt, pepper and the nutmeg, turn out on to a chopping board and chop finely.

Five In a saucepan, warm the cream and cheese gently, stirring, until the cheese melts, but does not boil. Season and cool before adding the egg. Fill the pastry case with the onion, then the spinach. Smooth the surface a little but do not pack down. Pour in the cream mixture and bake for 30 minutes, then lower the temperature to warm 160°C (315°F /Gas 2–3) and bake for 20 minutes to cook the centre of the quiche. Cover with foil if it is getting too brown. Serve warm.

about blue cheese...

Blue cheese is often used for cooking because its strong taste is robust enough to compete with other flavours. Creamy soft-rind blues, such as bleu de bresse, would be lost in a recipe such as this. Blue cheeses are ripened internally by blue moulds which add a particular strong taste. True Roquefort is produced from ewe's milk and left to ripen for 3 months in the limestone caves of Les Causses in south-central France. It has all-over marbling that is more green than blue in colour.

Leek and Brie flamiche

The flamiche derives its name from the Flemish word for cake, as originally it was a type of cake made from bread dough and served with butter. Nowadays, however, the name usually refers to a pie filled with vegetables or cheese, or both, as in this particular recipe.

Preparation time 1 hour 5 minutes
+ 30 minutes chilling
Total cooking time 55 minutes
Serves 4–6

PASTRY
250 g (8 oz) plain flour
1 teaspoon salt
60 g (2 oz) unsalted butter
1 egg
1 egg yolk

1 egg, beaten

FILLING
60 g (2 oz) unsalted butter, cubed
400 g (12¾ oz) leeks, white part
only, thinly sliced
150 g (5 oz) Brie cheese
1 egg
1 egg yolk
50 ml (1¾ fl oz) thick (double) cream

One To make the pastry, sift the flour and salt together into a bowl. Using your fingertips, rub in the butter until the mixture resembles fine breadcrumbs. Make a well in the centre and add the egg, egg yolk and 2½ tablespoons water. Mix well, form into a ball and refrigerate for 20 minutes, wrapped in plastic wrap.

Two To make the filling, melt the butter in a deep frying pan and slowly cook the leek, covered, for 5 minutes. Cook for a further 5 minutes, uncovered, or until all the liquid has evaporated, being careful not to allow the leek to brown. Transfer the leek to a colander and set aside to cool.

Three Preheat the oven to warm 170°C (325°F/Gas 3). Grease a 20.5 x 2.5 cm (8¼ x 1 inch) loose-bottomed flan tin. Divide the pastry in half and roll out one half on a lightly floured surface to a thickness of 3 mm (⅛ inch) and line the prepared tin (see Chef's techniques, page 547), leaving a 1 cm (½ inch) overhang.

Roll out the second piece of dough on a lightly floured surface to a 22.5 cm (8¾ inch) circle, and then refrigerate until needed.

Four Remove the rind of the cheese and cut the cheese into small cubes. Spread the leek over the bottom of the pastry, and sprinkle with the cheese. Whisk together the egg, egg yolk and cream. Pour over the leek and cheese. Brush the edge of the pastry with the beaten egg and place the second piece of pastry on top. Trim the top pastry sheet so that it is even with the lower sheet. Pinch the dough well to seal the two pieces together, and trim the edges by pressing down with the thumb against the edge of the tin. Brush the top with the egg and refrigerate for 10 minutes.

Five Brush again with the beaten egg and cut a hole in the centre with a small round cutter. Bake for 40–45 minutes, or until golden. Set on a wire rack to cool slightly before removing from the tin. Leave for 5 minutes before cutting.

about leeks...

The secret to cooking leeks is to sauté them very slowly until their crunchiness turns to a sweet softness. Always wash leeks well as they often contain dirt right through their structure of layers—slice them lengthways before cutting off the root so you can wash them under running water without them coming apart.

Chèvre and watercress quiche

The rather peppery flavour of the watercress complements the creamy goat's cheese filling in this recipe. This quiche could also be made as individual tartlets and served either warm or cold.

Preparation time 30 minutes
Total cooking time 1 hour 15 minutes
Serves 4–6

FILLING
250 g (8 oz) watercress
3 eggs
100 ml (3¼ fl oz) thick (double) cream
ground nutmeg, to taste
150 g (5 oz) chèvre (goat's cheese), cut into 1.5 cm (⅝ inch) slices

½ quantity shortcrust pastry (see page 544)
1 egg, beaten

One To make the filling, remove the large stems from the watercress, rinse and pat dry with paper towels. Bring 2 litres water to the boil, add some salt and cook the watercress for 10 seconds. Drain, then refresh in iced water for 3 minutes, and then drain again. Squeeze out any excess water, then roughly chop the watercress. Season well.

Two Preheat the oven to moderate 180°C (350°F/Gas 4). Grease a 20.5 x 2.5 cm (8¼ x 1 inch) loose-bottomed flan tin. Roll out the dough on a lightly floured surface to a thickness of 3 mm (⅛ inch) and line the prepared tin (see Chef's techniques, page 547). Bake blind for about 25 minutes, or until firm (see Chef's techniques, page 547). Remove the beads and paper, and brush the bottom of the pastry with the beaten egg. Bake for another 7 minutes

Three Whisk the eggs with the cream, and season with nutmeg, salt and pepper. Sprinkle the bottom of the tart with the watercress, and arrange the slices of chèvre on top. Add the egg mixture and bake for 30–40 minutes, or until set and a knife inserted into the centre comes out clean. Set on a wire rack to cool slightly before removing from the tin. Leave the quiche for 5 minutes before cutting.

Cheese and herb muffins

*Cheese and herb muffins are an excellent accompaniment
to soups and stews. Or, of course, you can eat them
on their own, spread thickly with butter.*

Preparation time 25 minutes
Total cooking time 20 minutes
Makes 12 muffins

225 g (7¼ oz) self-raising flour
155 g (5 oz) wholemeal self-raising
flour
pinch of cayenne pepper
pinch of salt
2 tablespoons finely chopped
fresh parsley
2 tablespoons finely chopped
fresh chives
2 tablespoons fresh thyme leaves
125 g (4 oz) Cheddar cheese, grated
2 eggs
250 ml (8 fl oz) milk
125 g (4 oz) unsalted butter, melted

One Preheat the oven to hot 210°C
(415°F/Gas 6–7). Brush a 12-hole
(125 ml/4 fl oz) muffin tin with melted
butter or oil. Sift the flours, cayenne
pepper and salt into a large bowl, and
return the husks to the bowl. Stir in the
herbs and Cheddar cheese and make a
well in the centre.

Two Whisk the eggs and milk together in
a jug, and pour into the well in the dry
ingredients along with the butter. Stir
with a metal spoon until the ingredients
are just combined. Do not overmix—the
mixture should be lumpy.

Three Spoon the mixture into the muffin
tin, filling each hole about three-quarters
full. Bake for 20 minutes, or until a
skewer comes out clean when inserted
into the centre of a muffin. Leave the
muffins in the tin for 5 minutes before
lifting out onto a wire rack to cool.
Serve spread with butter while the
muffins are still warm.

Brie parcels with pears and almonds

This sophisticated brunch dish can be served with grilled tomatoes, some watercress or a green salad. It would also make an elegant first course for a lunch or dinner party.

*Preparation time 25 minutes
+ 30 minutes chilling
Total cooking time 15 minutes
Serves 4*

120 g (4 oz) whole blanched almonds
1 large or 2 small ripe pears, peeled
and thinly sliced
30 ml (1 fl oz) balsamic or
tarragon vinegar
250 g (8 oz) ripe Brie cheese
12 sheets filo pastry
150 g (5 oz) unsalted butter,
melted

One Preheat the grill to high. Place the almonds into a food processor and blend for 30 seconds, or until they resemble fine breadcrumbs. Turn out onto a baking tray and place under the grill to toast. Do not walk away while this is happening as the almonds will burn very quickly. Season the toasted almonds with a little salt and pepper.

Two Place the pear slices in a bowl and sprinkle with the vinegar, toss to coat well and set aside. Cut the Brie in half through the middle to make two large flat pieces with a rind on one side of each. Lay one piece on a work surface, rind downwards, and place the pear slices on top of the cheese in a neat layer to completely cover the top of the cheese. You may need to do several layers in order to use up all the pear. Sprinkle with any remaining vinegar, season with salt and pepper and place the second piece of Brie on top, so that the rind is uppermost and the edges are even all the way round. Wrap the cheese tightly in plastic wrap, place on a plate and chill for a minimum of 30 minutes. When chilled, cut into eight even-sized

pieces and toss them in the almonds, taking care to keep the wedges whole.

Three Preheat the oven to hot 220°C (425°F/Gas 7). Brush one sheet of filo with the melted butter, cover with another sheet, brush again, then add a third sheet. Cut into two 20 cm (8 inch) squares. Discard the trimmings. Place one wedge of the Brie in the centre of each square and gather up the edges to form a purse, squeezing the pastry together to make a 'drawstring' effect. Brush gently with a little more butter.

Repeat with the remaining pastry and Brie, making sure the Brie remains chilled or it will melt too quickly. When ready to cook, put the parcels on a greased baking tray and bake for 10 minutes, or until golden. Serve immediately.

CHEF'S TIP *A few ripe, peeled and sliced apricots or peeled seedless grapes can be used instead of the pears, or if time is limited, omit both the fruit and the vinegar and spread the opened-out cheese with 2 tablespoons of a fruit chutney instead.*

Gougères

In Burgundy these cheese-flavoured choux pastry puffs are traditionally served cold with wine during tastings in the local cellars.

Preparation time 25 minutes
Total cooking time 25 minutes
Makes 25–30

1 quantity choux pastry (see page 545)
40 g (1¼ oz) Gruyère or Cheddar
cheese, finely grated
1 egg, beaten

One Preheat the oven to warm 170°C (325°F/Gas 3). Lightly grease two baking trays. Mix half the cheese into the thick and glossy choux pastry.

Two Spoon the pastry into a piping bag fitted with a small plain nozzle. Pipe out 2.5 cm (1 inch) balls of dough onto the prepared trays, leaving a space of 3 cm (1¼ inches) between each ball. Using a fork dipped in the beaten egg, slightly flatten the top of each ball. Sprinkle with the remaining grated cheese. Bake for 20–25 minutes, or until the balls have puffed up and are golden brown. Serve hot.

CHEF'S TIP *This is a very simple and light finger food to serve with pre-dinner drinks. Gougères are sometimes served in restaurants with drinks and referred to as 'amuse-gueule', the French term for appetiser.*

salads

Salade niçoise

Niçoise indicates that a dish usually contains tomatoes and black olives—staples from the region of southern France around Nice. Originally this salad did not include cooked vegetables, but, as the salad gained popularity, local chefs made their own adaptations, including the addition of potatoes.

Preparation time *40 minutes*
+ 20 minutes cooling
Total cooking time *1 hour 20 minutes*
Serves 4

200 ml (6¹/₂ fl oz) olive oil
1 bay leaf
4 sprigs of fresh thyme
400 g (12³/₄ oz) piece of fresh tuna, skin removed
300 g (10 oz) waxy or salad potatoes
240 g (7¹/₂ oz) green beans
50 ml (1³/₄ fl oz) white wine vinegar
1 green capsicum (pepper), cut into julienne strips (see Chef's tip)
1 red capsicum (pepper), cut into julienne strips
2 red onions, thinly sliced
1 bibb or butter lettuce
4 tomatoes, cut into quarters
4 hard-boiled eggs, shelled and quartered
50 g (1³/₄ oz) can anchovies, drained
30 black olives

One Preheat the oven to slow 150°C (300°F/Gas 2). Put the oil, bay leaf, thyme and tuna in a small pan. Warm over low heat for 5 minutes, then put in the oven for 30 minutes, or until the tuna feels firm to the touch. Cool for 20 minutes in the oil, remove and drain on a rack. Strain the oil and set aside.

Two Put the unpeeled potatoes in cold, salted water. Bring to the boil and cook for 30–35 minutes, or until the tip of a knife easily pierces them. Remove from the water and leave to cool. Peel, then slice into thick rounds.

Three Trim the beans and cook in boiling salted water for 8 minutes, or until tender. Refresh in cold water and drain.

Four To make the vinaigrette, whisk the vinegar and some salt together, then gradually whisk in the reserved oil.

Five Toss the potatoes, green beans, capsicum and onion with a little vinaigrette and season to taste. Break the tuna into bite-sized pieces and mix with some of the vinaigrette. Arrange a few leaves of lettuce on each plate. In the centre, place a mound of the potatoes. Top with the green beans, capsicum and onion and finish with the tuna. Arrange the tomato and egg around the edge and finish with the anchovies and olives. Serve the remaining vinaigrette on the side or drizzle over the salad to serve.

CHEF'S TIP *Julienne strips are vegetables cut to the size and shape of matchsticks.*

Waldorf salad

Traditionally made with apple, celery, walnuts and mayonnaise, this salad was created in New York's Waldorf Astoria Hotel in the 1890s. This version is based around the same key ingredients with the addition of Parma ham.

Preparation time *30 minutes*
Total cooking time *5 minutes*
Serves 6–8

2 celery hearts
60 g (2 oz) walnut halves
½ lemon
4 apples
1 French shallot, very finely chopped
1 clove garlic, very finely chopped
1 tablespoon vegetable oil
6 slices Parma ham or prosciutto
1 cos or romaine lettuce

DRESSING
2 teaspoons Dijon mustard
4 tablespoons olive oil
4 tablespoons thick (double) cream

One Using a large sharp knife, cut the celery hearts into thin slices, wash well and set aside to drain thoroughly.

Two Preheat the grill to medium. Spread the walnuts out on the baking tray and grill for 1–2 minutes, or until brown, taking care that they don't burn.

Three Grate the rind of the lemon finely into a large bowl and squeeze in all but a tablespoon of the juice. One at a time, peel, quarter and slice the apples and toss them gently into the lemon in the bowl to stop them going brown. Add the shallot and garlic with the walnuts, drained celery and a little salt and black pepper.

Four To make the dressing, place the remaining tablespoon of lemon juice in a small bowl and mix with the mustard. Using a small balloon whisk, beat in the olive oil a few drops at a time until the dressing is smooth and emulsified, then beat in the cream for a few seconds until combined. Taste the dressing and season with salt and black pepper.

Five Heat the vegetable oil in a heavy-based, non-stick frying pan and fry the Parma ham for 30 seconds, or until shrivelled slightly. Drain on paper towels, then cut into small strips with scissors or a sharp knife and leave until cool and crispy.

Six Slice the lettuce leaves very thinly and use to line a serving bowl. Drizzle the dressing over the apple and celery, stir gently to mix and toss together with the lettuce. Sprinkle the strips of Parma ham over the salad just before serving.

Caesar salad

This salad is often thought of as an American dish, but was actually created by Caesar Cardini in Tijuana, Mexico in the 1920s.

Preparation time 20 minutes
Total cooking time 15 minutes
Serves 4

DRESSING
2 egg yolks
1 tablespoon lemon juice, or to taste
160 ml (5¼ fl oz) olive oil
4 anchovy fillets, finely chopped
2 cloves garlic, finely chopped

2 eggs
1 cos lettuce
4 slices of white bread, crusts removed
80 ml (2¾ fl oz) olive oil
35 g (1¼ oz) Parmesan cheese, grated
2 tablespoons finely chopped
fresh parsley

One To make the dressing, beat the egg yolks and lemon juice with a whisk or blender. Add the oil in a thin steady stream and beat until thick and smooth. Stir through the anchovies and garlic and season to taste with salt, pepper and extra lemon juice. Set aside.

Two To hard-boil the eggs, place them in a small saucepan and cover with cold water. Bring to a gentle boil and cook for 10 minutes. Drain and cool in cold water, then peel and chop finely.

Three Tear the lettuce into bite-size pieces and set aside in the refrigerator. To make the croutons, cut the bread into even cubes. Heat the oil in a frying pan

and brown the bread until golden. Remove the croutons and drain on crumpled paper towels.

Four In a large serving bowl, toss the lettuce in the dressing. Sprinkle with the remaining ingredients to serve.

CHEF'S TIP *To make the salad into a more substantial meal, add smoked duck breast, chicken or salmon.*

Kaleidoscope salad

This attractive salad has a bold dressing of fresh ginger, olive oil and coriander and makes an ideal accompaniment to outdoor or grilled food. It can be made up to 12 hours in advance to develop the flavours.

Preparation time 20 minutes
Total cooking time 25 minutes
Serves 4–6

2 corn cobs
13 cm (5 inch) length of cucumber
1 small fennel bulb
1/2 red capsicum (pepper)
6 spring onions, finely sliced
4 large ripe tomatoes
105 g (3 1/2 oz) shelled fresh peas
2 tablespoons chopped fresh parsley
1 tablespoon chopped fresh coriander
1 tablespoon chopped fresh basil

DRESSING
2.5 cm (1 inch) piece fresh ginger
1 clove garlic, crushed
125 ml (4 fl oz) olive oil
45 ml (1 1/2 fl oz) rice vinegar
1 teaspoon Tabasco
1 teaspoon ground coriander

One Preheat a grill to hot. Remove the papery husk and fibres from the outside of the corn cobs and place under the grill for about 25 minutes, turning several times, until the corn is mottled brown and tender. Remove from the grill and, when the cobs are cool enough to handle, place on a board standing upright and cut off the kernels using a downward action with a sharp knife. Place the kernels in a large bowl.

Two Cut the cucumber in half lengthways, remove the seeds with a teaspoon and cut the flesh into dice. Add to the corn. Discard any tough, outer layers of fennel. Remove the seeds, stalk and membrane from the pepper, then cut this and the fennel into dice. Add to the bowl with the spring onions.

Three Halve two of the tomatoes and remove the seeds with a teaspoon. Cut the flesh into dice and add to the bowl with the peas, parsley, coriander and basil. Gently combine everything with a large spoon, taking care not to break up the tomato.

Four To make the dressing, finely grate the ginger and place in a bowl with the garlic. Using the back of a teaspoon, mash to a paste with 1/4 teaspoon salt. Add the olive oil, rice vinegar, Tabasco, ground coriander and season with 1/2 teaspoon salt and 3/4 teaspoon black pepper. Whisk the dressing, pour over the vegetables and toss gently. Slice the remaining tomatoes and arrange around the plates. Spoon the salad into the centre to serve.

Mustard seed potato salad

A flavoursome potato salad made with whole small potatoes and a mustard mayonnaise.

Preparation time 10 minutes
Total cooking time 35 minutes
Serves 4

2 kg (4 lb) small salad or new potatoes, scrubbed

MAYONNAISE
2 egg yolks
275 ml (9 fl oz) lightly flavoured vegetable oil
1 tablespoon white wine vinegar
2 heaped tablespoons wholegrain mustard

One Bring a pan of salted water to the boil. Add the potatoes and boil for 30–35 minutes, or until tender to the point of a knife. Drain well and place in a bowl.

Two To make the mayonnaise, bring all the ingredients to room temperature and set a large bowl on a damp tea towel to prevent it from moving. Add the egg yolks and a pinch of salt to the bowl and mix together with a balloon whisk or electric beaters.

Three Put the oil in a jug that is easy to pour from. While whisking constantly by hand or with electric beaters, pour a steady thin stream of oil into the mixture. Begin with a small amount of oil and stop pouring periodically to allow each addition to emulsify to a thick creamy mixture. Continue until 100 ml (3¼ fl oz) of the oil has been added and the mayonnaise has begun to thicken.

Four Add the vinegar to make the texture slightly thinner. Continue gradually adding the oil, then stir in the wholegrain mustard. Adjust the flavour by adding more vinegar, salt and pepper if necessary. Add 1–2 tablespoons of boiling water if it curdles or separates. Add the mayonnaise to the potatoes and stir until evenly coated. Serve warm.

Celeriac remoulade

This French classic makes a delicious first course or light lunch.
A mustardy mayonnaise enhances the crunchy celeriac's
flavour, along with some gherkins, capers and anchovies.

Preparation time 35 minutes
+ 1 hour standing
Total cooking time Nil
Serves 4–6

1.25 kg (2½ lb) celeriac
juice of 1 lemon
2 tablespoons capers
8 gherkins, finely chopped
2 ripe tomatoes, peeled, seeded and
diced (see page 534)
30 g (1 oz) fresh herbs, such as chervil,
basil and dill
105 g (3½ oz) small salad leaves
8 anchovy fillets, to garnish

REMOULADE SAUCE
2 egg yolks
2 heaped tablespoons Dijon mustard
or 1 heaped teaspoon dried mustard
powder
pinch of cayenne pepper
275 ml (9 fl oz) lightly flavoured
vegetable oil

One Cut the celeriac in half and peel away the skin, cutting 3 mm (1/8 inch) deep into the flesh to remove all of the fibrous skin. Roughly grate the celeriac into a bowl, season and toss in the lemon juice. Cover with plastic wrap and set aside for 30–60 minutes.

Two To make the remoulade sauce, bring all the ingredients to room temperature and set a large bowl on a damp tea towel to prevent it from moving. Add the egg yolks, mustard, cayenne pepper and a pinch of salt to the bowl and mix with a balloon whisk or electric beaters.

Three Put the oil in a jug that is easy to pour from. While whisking constantly by hand or with electric beaters, pour a steady thin stream of oil into the mixture. Begin with a small amount and stop pouring periodically to allow each addition to emulsify to a thick creamy mixture. Continue until the sauce resembles whipped cream. If it curdles or separates, add 1–2 tablespoons of boiling water.

Four Squeeze out the excess liquid from the celeriac and mix with the remoulade sauce. Rinse the capers, dry and chop them if they are large, then stir these and the gherkins into the celeriac. Serve decorated with the tomato, herbs and salad leaves, then top with the anchovy fillets.

Tabouleh

*This grain salad (shown top right) originated in the Lebanon
and is made with generous amounts of fresh
mint, parsley and bulgar wheat.*

*Preparation time 20 minutes
+ 30 minutes soaking
Total cooking time Nil
Serves 4*

*250 g (8 oz) bulgar wheat
1 telegraph cucumber
30 g (1 oz) fresh mint, finely chopped
40 g (1¼ oz) fresh flat-leaf parsley,
finely chopped
6 spring onions, finely chopped
90 ml (3 fl oz) olive oil
100 ml (3¼ fl oz) lemon juice
cos or romaine lettuce leaves, to serve*

One Place the bulgar wheat in a bowl and pour in enough hot water to just cover the wheat. Leave to soak for 20–30 minutes. Peel the cucumber and cut in half lengthways. Using a teaspoon, remove the seeds from the centre, then finely dice the flesh. Place the cucumber, mint, parsley and spring onion in a medium bowl with the olive oil and lemon juice.

Two Tip the bulgar wheat into a sieve to drain off any excess water. Fluff up the grains with a fork, add to the bowl with the herbs and season generously with salt and black pepper.

Three Serve with a pile of lettuce leaves. To eat, place some tabouleh in the centre of each lettuce leaf and fold the lettuce into a parcel.

Rustic Greek salad

*A hearty salad with the Greek flavours of feta,
oregano, black olives and ripe tomatoes (shown bottom right).*

*Preparation time 15 minutes
Total cooking time Nil
Serves 4*

*1 romaine or cos lettuce
3 ripe tomatoes
125 g (4 oz) Kalamata olives
1 French shallot, finely chopped
250 g (8 oz) feta cheese
1 tablespoon fresh oregano leaves,
chopped
60 ml (2 fl oz) olive oil
60 ml (2 fl oz) lemon juice*

One Shred the romaine or cos lettuce finely and arrange on plates. Cut the tomatoes into slim wedges and arrange them over the lettuce with the olives and chopped shallot.

Two Cut the feta cheese into 2 cm (¾ inch) cubes and scatter these over the salad with the oregano. Season with salt and black pepper.

Three Whisk together the oil and lemon juice and pour it over the salads.

CHEF'S TIP *Greek salads are always made with wonderfully fresh ingredients and often include plenty of chopped herbs for flavour. The ingredients, including the herbs, can be varied according to seasonal availability and individual preference.*

Insalata caprese

This lovely combination of tomato, mozzarella and basil is an Italian classic. Balsamic vinegar and good olive oil make up the dressing.

Preparation time 15 minutes
Total cooking time Nil
Serves 4 as an accompaniment

4–6 large ripe tomatoes
300 g (10 oz) fresh mozzarella cheese or bocconcini
1 tablespoon olive oil
2 tablespoons balsamic vinegar
10 g (¼ oz) fresh basil leaves

One Cut the tomatoes horizontally into thin slices and slice the mozzarella to a similar thickness. Sprinkle the base of a serving plate with salt and black pepper, then arrange the sliced tomato and mozzarella in slightly overlapping circles on the plate.

Two Drizzle with the olive oil and balsamic vinegar and sprinkle over the basil leaves, tearing any large leaves with your fingers. Season with salt and black pepper. The salad can be served immediately or covered and set aside at room temperature for several hours, which will allow the flavours to infuse. If you wish to do this, drizzle only half the olive oil and balsamic vinegar over the top, then drizzle over the remainder just before serving.

CHEF'S TIP *Choose tomatoes of any type, just as long as they have some flavour—vine-ripened tomatoes are best. If tomatoes are not at their peak, choose to make another salad instead.*

LE CORDON BLEU ✠ COMPLETE COOK

Goat's cheese with a watercress and lamb's lettuce salad

*The bitter watercress, tangy goat's cheese and home-made herb
olive oil marry beautifully to make a simple salad that
is ideal to serve as a light meal with fresh bread.*

*Preparation time 25 minutes
+ 3–4 days marinating
Total cooking time 2 minutes
Serves 4*

*300 g (10 oz) goat's cheese
(see Chef's tips)
3 sprigs of fresh thyme
1 large sprig of fresh rosemary
15 fresh basil leaves
6 whole black peppercorns,
lightly crushed
4 juniper berries, lightly crushed
400 ml (12¾ fl oz) olive oil
50 g (1¾ oz) pine nuts
100 g (3¼ oz) watercress
100 g (3¼ oz) lamb's lettuce*

One Place the goat's cheese on a board and cut off the skin with a sharp knife. Cut into roughly 1 cm (½ inch) cubes and place loosely in a 1-litre preserving jar with an airtight lid, tucking the thyme, rosemary and basil leaves in between the cheese cubes as you go. Drop the crushed peppercorns and juniper berries into the jar and pour in the olive oil. The oil must cover the cheese completely, so add a little more if the shape of your jar requires it. Place in the refrigerator for 3–4 days for the flavours of the herbs to infuse the cheese.

Two Preheat a grill to medium and place the pine nuts on a tray. Grill them for 2 minutes, turning several times and taking care not to let the nuts burn. Leave to cool.

Three Separate the watercress out into sprigs. Just before you are ready to serve, place in a bowl with the lamb's lettuce and sprinkle over the pine nuts

and the marinated goat's cheese, drizzling about a quarter of the oil over the leaves. Season with salt and plenty of black pepper and serve immediately.

CHEF'S TIPS *Choose a firm goat's cheese like chèvre for this recipe—soft goat's cheese will break down too much in the oil.*

If there is any cheese left over in the jar, it will keep for up to a month in the fridge if it is covered completely in oil. However, if you are storing it for this long, remove the basil beforehand.

Fattoush

*This Middle Eastern salad, flavoured with fresh mint
and parsley, is traditionally garnished
with toasted Arab or Lebanese bread.*

Preparation time 40 minutes
Total cooking time 5 minutes
Serves 4

4 ripe tomatoes, peeled, seeded and
diced (see page 534)
1 small cos or romaine lettuce
1 small cucumber
1 green capsicum (pepper)
2 French shallots, finely chopped
4 spring onions, finely sliced
4 tablespoons finely chopped fresh
mint
4 tablespoons finely chopped fresh
flat-leaf parsley
2 pitta breads or other flat breads

DRESSING
1 clove garlic
1 teaspoon salt
60 ml (2 fl oz) lemon juice
125 ml (4 fl oz) olive oil
few drops of Tabasco

One Put the tomato in a bowl. Shred the
lettuce and add to the tomato. Peel the
cucumber, slice it into quarters lengthways and remove the seeds with a
teaspoon. Cut the flesh into cubes and
add to the bowl. Cut the capsicum into
similar-sized cubes. Add to the bowl
with the shallots, spring onion, mint and
parsley. Stir gently to combine.

Two To make the dressing, crush the
garlic and mix with the salt to form a
paste. Use a fork to whisk the lemon
juice, olive oil and Tabasco into the
garlic, then season with black pepper.

Three Toast the pitta bread on both sides
until crisp. Cut into 1 cm (½ inch)
squares and add to the salad. Pour in the
dressing and toss gently before serving.

Coleslaw

If you have never before made coleslaw, you will be amazed at how different real home-made slaw tastes from that sold in plastic tubs by supermarkets.

Preparation time *30 minutes*
Total cooking time *Nil*
Serves 6–8

MAYONNAISE
2 egg yolks
1 heaped tablespoon Dijon mustard
or 1 heaped teaspoon dried mustard powder
275 ml (9 fl oz) lightly flavoured vegetable oil
1 tablespoon white wine vinegar

¹/₂ white cabbage
1 onion
2 carrots

One To make the mayonnaise, bring all the ingredients to room temperature and set a large bowl on a damp tea towel to prevent it from moving. Add the egg yolks, mustard, some ground white pepper and a pinch of salt, and mix well with a balloon whisk or electric beaters.

Two Put the oil in a jug that is easy to pour from. While whisking constantly by hand or with electric beaters, pour a steady thin stream of oil into the mixture. Begin with a small amount of oil and stop pouring periodically to allow each addition to fully emulsify to a thick, creamy mixture. Continue until 100 ml (3¹/₄ fl oz) of the oil has been added and the mayonnaise has begun to thicken.

Three Add the wine vinegar to make the texture slightly thinner. Continue gradually adding the oil and adjust the flavour by adding more vinegar, salt and white pepper if necessary. If it curdles or separates, add 1–2 tablespoons of boiling water

Four Finely slice the cabbage and onion and coarsely grate the carrot. Place these in a large bowl and mix together gently with your hands. Using your hands or a large metal spoon (the former is a little messy, but gentler and more effective) mix in enough mayonnaise to coat the vegetables. Season to taste and serve.

CHEF'S TIPS *Up to half the light vegetable oil can be replaced with olive oil, but the flavour of olive oil is too strong to use alone.*

Any unused mayonnaise can be covered tightly and stored in a clean preserving or jam jar in the refrigerator for up to three days.

Artichoke, spinach and pine nut salad

*This fresh-tasting salad could be served either
as a first course, or with crusty bread as
a light lunch on a hot summer day.*

Preparation time 40 minutes
Total cooking time 30 minutes
Serves 4

4 large fresh artichokes
juice of 2 lemons
*150 g (5 oz) baby English spinach
leaves*
80 g (2³/4 oz) pine nuts, toasted
2 tablespoons olive oil
40 g (1¹/4 oz) grated Parmesan cheese
16 black olives, halved and pitted

One Prepare the fresh artichoke hearts, following the method in the Chef's techniques on page 534. When you place the artichokes in the pan of boiling water, use the juice from one of the lemons in the water. Once you have cooked and prepared the artichoke hearts, cut them into bite-sized wedges, cover and set aside.

Two Toss the spinach leaves with the pine nuts in a large bowl. Whisk the olive oil with 1 tablespoon lemon juice and freshly ground black pepper, to taste, and use to dress the spinach. Divide the artichoke pieces among four bowls and pile the spinach up in the centre. Top the salad with the Parmesan and black olives.

Smoked chicken salad with macadamia nut dressing

*This delicious salad contains all the ingredients for a wonderful
lunch or light supper—smoked chicken and asparagus
with peppery rocket and slices of French baguette.*

Preparation time 20 minutes
Total cooking time 15 minutes
Serves 4

185 g (6 oz) asparagus
12 thin slices French baguette
150 g (5 oz) rocket leaves
2 smoked chicken breasts, about
180 g (5¾ oz) each
sprigs of fresh chervil, to garnish

DRESSING
60 g (2 oz) macadamia nuts
3 tablespoons white wine vinegar
2 tablespoons olive oil
3 tablespoons macadamia or
hazelnut oil

One Bring a large pan of salted water to the boil. Use a vegetable peeler to remove the outer layer from the lower two-thirds of each asparagus spear, then snap the woody ends off at their natural breaking point and discard. Cut the spears into 2.5 cm (1 inch) lengths and add to the water. Reduce the heat and simmer until the tips are tender. Remove and run under cold water, then drain on paper towels.

Two To make the dressing, preheat the grill to medium. Grill the macadamia nuts on a baking tray for 5 minutes, taking care not to let them burn. Cool slightly and then chop.

Three Put the baguette slices on a tray in a single layer and grill for 5 minutes on each side until crisp and golden.

Four Whisk together the vinegar, olive oil and macadamia oil in a bowl with a small balloon whisk, then stir in the macadamia nuts and season to taste with salt and black pepper.

Five Place the rocket in a large bowl. Give the dressing a stir to distribute the nuts and then drizzle a little over the leaves, tossing to thoroughly coat them. Arrange the baguette slices and the rocket on four plates.

Six Cut the smoked chicken into bite-sized pieces. Place the chicken and asparagus in a small bowl, stir the dressing and pour over a little to coat. Place the chicken and asparagus on the rocket and top with the chervil.

Salmon salade niçoise

This typical Provençal salad from Nice is traditionally made with tuna, but here it is served with a fillet of salmon. Perfect for a light summer supper.

Preparation time 20 minutes
Total cooking time 1 hour
Serves 4

310 g (10 oz) small salad potatoes
250 g (8 oz) green beans
8 quail eggs
1 green capsicum (pepper), cut into julienne strips (see Chef's tip)
1 red capsicum (pepper), cut into julienne strips
2 French shallots, finely sliced
4 ripe tomatoes, cut into wedges
4 x 155 g (5 oz) salmon fillets, skinned
1 small round lettuce
100 g (3¼ oz) rocket
20 black olives

VINAIGRETTE
2 tablespoons balsamic vinegar
100 ml (3¼ fl oz) olive oil

One Bring a large pan of salted water to the boil and add the unpeeled potatoes. Return to the boil and then simmer for 30–35 minutes, or until they are tender to the point of a knife. Drain, then plunge the potatoes into a bowl of iced water for 5 minutes to stop the cooking process. Drain again and cut in quarters.

Two Bring a large pan of fresh salted water to the boil and trim the ends off the beans. Put in the pan and boil for 8 minutes, or until tender, then place into iced water as above to stop the cooking process and retain the colour of the beans. Drain well.

Three Bring a small pan of salted water to the boil and boil the quail eggs for about 4 minutes, or until hard-boiled. When cooked, run the eggs under cold water, set aside to cool, then shell the eggs and cut them in half.

Four To make the vinaigrette, place the balsamic vinegar into a small bowl and whisk in the olive oil and some salt and black pepper with a small balloon whisk.

Five Place the potato quarters, green beans, capsicum, shallots and tomato in a large bowl and toss very gently with half the vinaigrette.

Six Heat a lightly oiled chargrill pan or frying pan over high heat and, when hot, cook the salmon fillets for 10 minutes, or until cooked through, turning once. Remove from the pan and keep warm. Place the lettuce and rocket on four plates and arrange the potato mixture, quail eggs and olives on top. Place a piece of salmon on each salad and drizzle with the remaining vinaigrette.

CHEF'S TIP *Julienne strips are vegetables cut to the size and shape of matchsticks.*

Seared scallop and mango salsa salad

A very pretty starter for a special occasion. The scallops and salsa can be prepared ahead, leaving just the brief cooking of the scallops to the last minute.

Preparation time 30 minutes
Total cooking time 5 minutes
Serves 4

16 large scallops
1 tablespoon olive oil
15 g (¹/2 oz) unsalted butter
baby salad leaves, to serve
sprigs of fresh coriander, to garnish

MANGO SALSA
2 ripe mangoes
6 ripe tomatoes, peeled, seeded and diced (see page 534)
15 g (¹/2 oz) fresh coriander leaves, finely chopped
2 large French shallots, finely chopped
2 green chillies, finely chopped
juice of 2 limes

One If the scallops are in their shells, remove them by sliding a knife underneath the white muscle and orange roe. Wash the scallops to remove any grit or sand, then pull away the small tough shiny muscle and the black vein, leaving the orange roe intact (see Chef's techniques, page 524). Dry the scallops on paper towels, cover and chill.

Two To make the salsa, dice the mangoes into small cubes and mix with the tomato, coriander leaves, shallots, chilli and lime juice. Season with salt and black pepper. Cover and chill until ready to serve.

Three Heat the olive oil in a non-stick frying pan, add the butter and, when it has melted and starts foaming, place the scallops in the pan. Cook for about 3–4 minutes, or until lightly golden on both sides and just tender to the touch. Arrange a bed of baby salad leaves on four plates and spoon over the mango salsa. Top with the warm scallops, any juices and the coriander sprigs and serve the salad immediately.

Duck salad with plum dressing

*This easy and unusual salad has a wonderful flavour
and is glamorous enough to serve as a dinner party starter.*

Preparation time 20 minutes
Total cooking time 10 minutes
Serves 4

DRESSING
*1 x 250 g (8 oz) tinned plums
in syrup, stoned*
1 tablespoon honey
*1 teaspoon Worcestershire
sauce*
1 tablespoon dark soy sauce
1/2 teaspoon Tabasco

4 x 220 g (7 oz) duck breasts
4 slices white bread
60 g (2 oz) unsalted butter
1 tablespoon olive oil
2 cloves garlic, crushed
4 spring onions
185 g (6 oz) curly endive (frisée)

One To make the dressing, place the plums and their syrup, the honey, Worcestershire, soy sauce and Tabasco in a small pan. Bring to the boil over medium heat and simmer for 5 minutes, then remove from the heat and allow to cool. Once cooled, place the plum mixture with all the liquid into a blender or food processor and process until completely smooth. Check the seasoning, adding salt and black pepper only if necessary, and transfer to a small bowl. Cover and chill.

Two Prick the duck breasts all over with a fork and place, skin side down, in a hot frying pan. Cook for 5 minutes, or until the skin is browned and the fat melted out. Turn over and cook the other side for 2 minutes, or until cooked through.

Three Remove the crusts from the bread and cut the bread into 2 cm (3/4 inch) cubes. In a large heavy-based frying pan, heat the butter, oil and garlic over medium heat until the butter has melted, raise the heat a little, then add the cubes of bread and cook for 2–3 minutes, stirring frequently to ensure that they cook to an even golden colour but taking care that they do not burn. Remove the frying pan from the heat, drain the croutons on crumpled paper towels and sprinkle them with a little salt and black pepper.

Four Remove the skin from the duck breasts if you prefer and slice across into 5 mm (1/4 inch) thick slices. Slice the spring onions diagonally and tear the curly endive into bite-sized pieces. Toss the spring onion, endive and half the croutons in about 1 tablespoon of the plum dressing just to coat and pile into a dish. Arrange the duck slices on top and scatter over the remaining croutons. Serve immediately with the remaining plum sauce offered separately.

Chicken liver salad with bacon and croutons

*Chicken liver has a delicate flavour and soft moist texture
when cooked. When pan-fried it is best served slightly pink in
the centre. Here, the sherry vinegar dressing cuts its richness.*

Preparation time 15 minutes
Total cooking time 15 minutes
Serves 4

345 g (11 oz) mixed salad leaves
200 g (6¹/2 oz) smoked bacon, rind
removed, cut into thin strips
100 ml (3¹/4 fl oz) oil
2 slices bread, crusts removed,
cut into small cubes
440 g (14 oz) chicken livers
30 g (1 oz) unsalted butter
3 French shallots, finely chopped
2 tablespoons vinegar

VINAIGRETTE DRESSING
1¹/2 tablespoons Dijon mustard
3 tablespoons sherry vinegar
100 ml (3¹/4 fl oz) oil

One Wash and dry the salad leaves and
then refrigerate, covered with a tea
towel, to prevent wilting.

Two Fry the bacon in a dry pan over
medium heat. Lift out and drain on
crumpled paper towels. Set aside.

Three Heat the oil in a shallow pan, add
the bread cubes and fry, stirring, until
golden brown. Lift out and drain on
crumpled paper towels. Sprinkle lightly
with salt and keep warm.

Four Clean the chicken livers, removing
the small green area that can be bitter,
and cut into small pieces. Heat the
butter in a shallow pan and toss the liver
over high heat for 2 minutes. Add the
shallots and fry for a further 2 minutes,
then season with salt and pepper and
transfer to a plate. The liver should be
barely pink and juicy inside. Add the
vinegar to the pan and heat to dissolve

any sticky juices. Pour over the liver and
keep warm.

Five To make the vinaigrette dressing,
put the mustard, sherry vinegar and salt
and pepper to taste in a bowl and add
the oil in a slow, steady stream, mixing
continuously with a fork or small whisk
until fully blended.

Six Put the salad leaves in a bowl, pour
over the dressing and carefully toss to
coat thoroughly without bruising the
leaves. Serve topped with the bacon,
croutons and liver with its juices.

LE CORDON BLEU ❦ COMPLETE COOK

Warm lentil salad with mustard seed vinaigrette

This traditional French salad, high in protein, can be served with crustaceans such as prawns. Normally, the small French puy lentils are used as they hold their shape well. However, other green or brown lentils could be used. Red lentils are not suitable as they soften to a purée.

Preparation time 15 minutes
+ overnight soaking
Total cooking time 40 minutes
Serves 6

250 g (8 oz) lentils
50 g (1¾ oz) unsalted butter
100 g (3¼ oz) carrots, diced
½ onion, diced
100 g (3¼ oz) smoked bacon, diced
300 ml (10 fl oz) chicken stock
(see page 519)
1 lettuce

VINAIGRETTE
30 g (1 oz) wholegrain mustard
2 teaspoons white wine vinegar
100 ml (3¼ fl oz) olive or peanut
(groundnut) oil
3 tablespoons chopped fresh parsley

One Soak the lentils in cold water overnight, then drain. Melt the butter in a large saucepan, add the vegetables and bacon and cook gently until the vegetables are soft, but not brown. Add the lentils and stock. Cover and simmer very gently for 30–35 minutes, or until the lentils are tender. Season with salt and pepper.

Two Pour the mixture into a sieve and allow the liquid to drain off. Transfer the lentils, vegetables and the bacon to a large bowl.

Three To make the vinaigrette, whisk together the mustard and white wine vinegar. Season well and very slowly add the olive oil, whisking constantly. Finally, add the parsley. Toss through the warm lentils, vegetables and bacon. Arrange a bed of lettuce leaves on a plate and pile the salad in the centre.

Warm fennel and cherry tomato salad

The dressing for this salad is an aromatic herb oil, made a week in advance to allow the flavours to infuse. If making extra, the oil keeps well and is perfect for drizzling over grilled meat and fish.

Preparation time 10 minutes
+ 1 week infusing
Total cooking time 30 minutes
Serves 4

AROMATIC OIL
50 ml (1³/4 fl oz) sesame oil
250 ml (8 fl oz) olive oil
100 ml (3¹/4 fl oz) hazelnut oil
1 bay leaf
1 sprig of fresh thyme
1 sprig of fresh rosemary

3 large or 4 small fennel bulbs with green fronds
1 sprig of fresh thyme
375 g (12 oz) ripe cherry or baby plum tomatoes
45 g (1¹/2 oz) Pecorino or Parmesan cheese, shaved

One Begin by making the aromatic oil at least one week in advance. Place the oils, bay leaf, thyme and rosemary in a pan and heat gently for 5 minutes, without boiling. Season well. Cool, then transfer to a sterilised screwtop bottle or jar and store the oil in the refrigerator for a week, turning the bottle occasionally. After a week, decant the oil into a clean bottle, discarding the herbs.

Two To make the salad, trim the fronds from the tops of the fennel bulbs and reserve for garnish, then cut the fennel into eighths, leaving a little of the base on each section to hold it together. Brush generously with about 75 ml (2¹/2 fl oz) of the aromatic oil.

Three Heat a chargrill pan until it is very hot and brush with a little of the oil. Alternatively, the vegetables can be placed under a preheated grill, but then they will not have the attractive charred lines. Place the fennel on the pan and cook for about 10 minutes each side, or until tender, caramelised and lightly charred. When the fennel is cooked, set aside and keep warm.

Four Heat the remaining oil in a large shallow pan until very hot. Carefully place the thyme and tomatoes in the hot oil and fry for 2–3 minutes, or until the skins are just splitting. Remove with a slotted spoon, discarding the thyme and reserving the oil, and pile up on a plate with the fennel and any juices. Top with the Pecorino or Parmesan and reserved fennel fronds. Season with some salt and black pepper and drizzle with some of the oil from cooking the tomatoes. Serve immediately with fresh bread.

Warm chicken and mushroom salad

*The warmth of the chicken and mushroom brings
out the tangy flavour of the Dijon dressing.*

Preparation time 20 minutes
Total cooking time 15 minutes
Serves 4

2 skinless chicken breast fillets
oil, for cooking
40 g (1¼ oz) unsalted butter
200 g (6½ oz) mixed wild mushrooms,
trimmed
1 French shallot, finely chopped
240 g (7½ oz) mixed salad leaves
2 teaspoons Dijon mustard
2 teaspoons red wine vinegar
100 ml (3¼ fl oz) olive oil
sprigs of fresh chervil, to garnish

One Season the chicken breast fillets, then heat a little oil in a frying pan and fry for 4 minutes on each side, or until tender. Remove from the pan, cover with foil and set aside.

Two Heat a little more oil in the pan, then add the butter and fry the mushrooms for 3–5 minutes, or until they are tender and lightly coloured. Add the shallot and cook for 1 minute. Season to taste and remove with a slotted spoon.

Three Wash and dry the salad leaves and tear them into bite-sized pieces. Set aside in a large bowl.

Four Remove the foil from the chicken and slice at an angle lengthways.

Five Whisk together the mustard and vinegar. Continue whisking and slowly add the oil. Pour half the dressing over the salad leaves and toss well; place a mound in the centre of each plate. Toss the mushrooms in half the remaining dressing and sprinkle over the salad. Arrange the chicken on top. Drizzle with the remaining dressing and garnish with sprigs of fresh chervil.

fish and seafood

Salmon kedgeree

*An old favourite with a twist: salmon and dill
replace the traditional smoked haddock.
Prepare the ingredients the day before.*

Preparation time 20 minutes
Total cooking time 16 minutes
Serves 4

2 eggs, at room temperature
50 g (1¾ oz) unsalted butter
*375 g (12 oz) salmon fillet, cooked
and flaked*
*250 g (8 oz) long-grain rice, cooked
and well drained*
1 egg, beaten
3 tablespoons cream
*1–2 teaspoons chopped fresh dill or
snipped fresh chives*

One Bring a small pan of water to the boil, gently put in the two eggs, return to the boil and simmer for 7 minutes. Remove the eggs with a spoon and place in a bowl of iced water to cool. Tap the shells with the back of a spoon to craze them, then peel. Roughly chop the eggs on a plate. The yolks should still be a little moist.

Two Melt the butter in a frying pan, add the salmon and heat for 30 seconds. Add the rice and the chopped egg and, using a fish slice, toss the ingredients over high heat for 2 minutes, or until hot. Keep your movements light and the mixture loose as you do not want to compact the rice.

Three Add the beaten egg with the cream. Continue to toss for 3–5 minutes, scraping the base of the pan, until the egg has set. Season, to taste. Pile onto a warm serving dish and scatter with the fresh dill or chives to serve.

CHEF'S TIPS *For the best result, the rice needs to be dry, so cook it the day before, drain well, cover and refrigerate.*

Don't worry that the boiled eggs initially seem underdone as they will continue to cook in the kedgeree.

Gravlax

*This method of curing salmon in salt, sugar and dill is Scandanavian in origin.
The salmon is left to marinate for 1¹/2 days and is then
served with a traditional sweet dill and mustard dressing.*

Preparation time 1 hour
+ 36 hours refrigeration
Total cooking time Nil
Serves 10

1.8 kg (3 lb 10 oz) salmon fillet,
skin on but scales removed
115 g (3³/4 oz) rock or sea salt
85 g (2³/4 oz) caster sugar
4 tablespoons chopped fresh dill
1¹/2 tablespoons black peppercorns,
crushed
2 teaspoons coriander seeds,
crushed
1 teaspoon ground mixed spice
6 tablespoons roughly chopped
fresh dill

DILL AND MUSTARD DRESSING
2 teaspoons sweet German mustard or
2 teaspoons grain mustard mixed
with 2 teaspoons honey
2 teaspoons chopped fresh dill
2 teaspoons white wine vinegar or
cider vinegar
220 ml (7 fl oz) vegetable oil

One Wash the salmon, dry it with paper towels and lay on a tray or plate, skin side down. Mix together the salt, sugar, dill, peppercorns, coriander seeds and mixed spice and spoon it over the fish. Cover with plastic wrap, place a baking tray on top and roughly 500 g (1 lb) of weight to lightly press the salmon (this could be cans spaced out along the fish). Refrigerate for 24 hours.

Two Remove the weights and covering, discard the solids from the marinade, then rinse off the remaining marinade with cold water and pat the salmon dry with paper towels. Place on a clean tray or plate, skin side down.

Three Press the dill leaves onto the salmon, then cover with plastic wrap and press well with your fingers to make the dill stick. Refrigerate for 12 hours.

Four To make the dill and mustard dressing, mix all the ingredients except the oil together in a bowl with some salt and black pepper, then slowly drizzle the oil into the bowl, whisking to emulsify with the other ingredients.

Five Uncover the salmon, remove any excess dill, then lift onto a board. With a long, thin-bladed knife held at an angle of 45 degrees and 6–8 cm (2¹/2–3 inches) from the tail, cut a slice towards the tail and continue slicing to produce short thin slices. Serve with the dressing.

CHEF'S TIP *For a variation, try this beetroot and mustard mixture. Follow the recipe to the end of Step 2, then combine 50 g (1³/4 oz) mustard seeds (soaked in cold water for 30 minutes, then drained) and 250 g (8 oz) very finely chopped cooked beetroot. Press onto the salmon and continue as above.*

Spinach and crab roulade

*Thick slices of this light spinach roulade with
a creamy crab filling are perfect for brunch,
a light lunch or served as a first course.*

Preparation time 45 minutes
Total cooking time 40 minutes
Serves 6

FILLING
20 g (³/4 oz) unsalted butter
1 tablespoon plain flour
200 ml (6¹/2 fl oz) milk
225 g (7¹/4 oz) white crab meat,
fresh, frozen or tinned
pinch of cayenne pepper

ROULADE
450 g (14¹/4 oz) English spinach, large
stalks removed, or 185 g (6 oz)
frozen spinach
15 g (¹/2 oz) unsalted butter, melted
4 eggs, separated
pinch of ground nutmeg

One To make the filling, melt the butter in a heavy-based pan over low-medium heat. Sprinkle the flour over the butter and cook for 1 minute without allowing it to colour, stirring constantly with a wooden spoon. Remove the pan from the heat and slowly add the milk, whisking or beating vigorously to avoid lumps. Return to low heat and briskly stir with a wooden spoon or whisk until the mixture is smooth and begins to thicken, then turn up the heat and stir briskly until boiling. Simmer for about 3–4 minutes, or until the sauce coats the back of a spoon. Cover with a piece of buttered greaseproof paper pressed onto the surface and set aside.

Two To make the roulade, first line a 30 x 25 cm (12 x 10 inch) swiss roll or baking tin with non-stick baking paper. If using fresh spinach, half-fill a large pan with water and bring to the boil, then add a generous pinch of salt and the spinach. Return to the boil and cook for 1–2 minutes, then drain the spinach, run under cold water and squeeze dry. Chop finely, using a large sharp knife. If using frozen spinach, thaw it, drain well, squeeze out the excess water and chop finely. Put the fresh or frozen spinach in a large bowl and add the butter.

Three Preheat the oven to moderately hot 200°C (400°F/Gas 6). Stir the egg yolks and nutmeg into the spinach and season

well. In a large bowl, whisk the egg whites until stiff and standing in peaks, then stir a large tablespoon of egg white into the spinach mixture to loosen it. Add the remaining egg white in one addition and, using a large metal spoon, carefully cut and fold into the spinach. Pour into the prepared tin, lightly smoothing it to the edges with a palette knife. Bake for about 10 minutes, or until the mixture is just set and springs back to the light touch of a finger. Meanwhile, spread a tea towel onto the work surface and cover it with non-stick baking paper.

Four Reheat the filling mixture, then stir in the crab, cayenne pepper and salt and pepper, to taste, and heat right through.

Five Turn the spinach roulade over onto the paper and tea towel and remove the tin and the paper lining. Quickly spread with the crab filling then, with the shortest edge towards you, pick up the cloth and the paper and push the roulade away from you, holding it quite low, so that the roulade rolls up like a swiss roll. Stop when the last of the roulade is underneath, then lift it onto a dish. Cut the roulade into thick slices and serve immediately.

CHEF'S TIP *This is perfect to serve alone, but can also be served with a sauce such as hollandaise or Béarnaise.*

Ceviche

Ceviche originated in South America and is the perfect way to show off the freshest fish. The acidity of the lime dressing magically 'cooks' the raw fish until it is opaque, just as if heat had been used.

Preparation time 55 minutes
+ 4 hours refrigeration
Total cooking time 1 minute
Serves 6

600 g (1¼ lb) bream, snapper or
seabass fillets, skinned
(see Chef's tips)
juice of 6 limes
1 small onion, finely chopped
1 green capsicum (pepper), halved,
seeded and finely chopped
½ fresh red chilli, seeded and
finely chopped
½ cucumber, cut into 5 mm
(¼ inch) cubes
1 small avocado, peeled and cut into
5 mm (¼ inch) cubes
4 tomatoes, peeled, seeded
and diced (see page 534)
sprigs of fresh parsley or chervil,
to garnish

WATERCRESS VINAIGRETTE
100 g (3¼ oz) watercress, tough
stems removed
1¼ tablespoons white
wine vinegar
100 ml (3¼ fl oz) olive oil

One Cut the fish into 5 mm (¼ inch) wide slices. Put in a non-metallic dish, pour the lime juice over the top, cover and refrigerate for about 2 hours.

Two Drain the fish, then add some salt and black pepper, the onion, pepper, chilli, cucumber and avocado and mix gently to combine. Cover with plastic wrap and refrigerate for 1–2 hours. Chill six serving plates.

Three To make the watercress vinaigrette, add the watercress to a pan of boiling salted water and cook for about 1 minute, then drain and run the watercress under cold water. Pat dry with paper towels to remove any excess water, then purée in a blender or food processor with the white wine vinegar and olive oil. Season with some salt and black pepper.

Four To serve, place an 8 cm (3 inch) pastry cutter in the centre of a chilled plate and spoon the ceviche into it until full, packing down lightly with the back of a spoon. Remove the cutter and repeat on the other plates. Decorate the plates with the watercress vinaigrette and garnish with the diced tomato and parsley or chervil. Serve with some crusty bread.

CHEF'S TIPS *If you can only buy a whole bream, snapper or seabass, buy an 800 g (1 lb 10 oz) fish and fillet it yourself (see Chef's techniques, page 526).*

For a creamy variation to this dish, add 250 ml (8 fl oz) coconut milk with the vegetables.

Smoked salmon and leek terrine with sauce verte

*Beautifully light but with a good depth of flavour, this dish makes
a perfect appetiser or lunch. Cooking the leeks in fish stock helps
them to press together and makes it easier to slice the terrine.*

Preparation time 1 hour
+ 4 hours refrigeration
Total cooking time 20 minutes
Serves 10

1.5 litres fish stock
(see page 519)
30 very small whole leeks, trimmed of
tough green leaves and roots
10–15 large English spinach leaves,
stalks removed
560 g (1 lb 2 oz) long slices of
smoked salmon
rocket leaves, to garnish

SAUCE VERTE
105 g (3½ oz) watercress, tough
stems removed
45 g (1½ oz) fresh chervil, chopped
45 g (1½ oz) fresh dill,
chopped
45 g (1½ oz) fresh parsley
few drops of lemon juice
350 ml (11 fl oz) crème fraîche or
sour cream

One In a large pan, bring the fish stock to the boil. Place the leeks in the stock, reduce the temperature and gently simmer for 20 minutes, or until tender. Drain well, then set the leeks aside and allow to cool.

Two Blanch the spinach in boiling water for 30 seconds. Drain, then plunge into iced water. Carefully lift the leaves out individually and place on paper towels or a cloth and pat dry.

Three Using plastic wrap, line a 1-litre, 21 x 10 cm (8½ x 4 inch) terrine mould, then line the base and sides with some of the smoked salmon, allowing a long overhang at one end. Add a layer of spinach, allowing for an overlap over one side of the terrine.

Four Tightly pack two layers of leeks lengthways into the bottom of the lined terrine and season well, then add a layer of half the remaining salmon, followed by one layer of leeks and seasoning. Cover with the remaining salmon and top this with two layers of leeks and seasoning. Fold over the salmon and spinach overhangs to enclose the filling and cover with plastic wrap. Cut a piece of cardboard to fit inside the terrine, cover it twice with foil and place a 1 kg

(2 lb) weight on top (this can be cans). Refrigerate for 4 hours.

Five To prepare the sauce verte, place the watercress, herbs and a little water into a blender and blend to a fine purée. Push through a coarse sieve, add the lemon juice and salt and black pepper and fold in the crème fraîche. Cover with plastic wrap and place in the refrigerator until ready to serve.

Six To serve, slice the terrine and arrange on plates with a spoonful of the sauce verte and some rocket leaves to garnish.

Creamy and salsa oysters

Two versions of classic oyster dishes. The creamy version is made with white wine, bacon and cream and is flashed under the grill to give a golden topping. If you prefer less heat, just omit the chilli. The salsa oysters are not cooked and come with a fiery tomato, red onion and lime dressing.

Preparation time 50 minutes
Total cooking time 15 minutes
(Creamy oysters)
Serves 4

24 oysters

CREAMY
2 teaspoons Tabasco
120 g (4 oz) bacon rashers,
rind removed
4 egg yolks
100 ml (3¼ fl oz) white wine
80 ml (2¾ fl oz) thick (double) cream,
lightly whipped
½ fresh red chilli, seeded and
finely chopped
1 tablespoon olive oil
1 small red capsicum (pepper),
cut into julienne strips (see
Chef's tip)

OR

SALSA
410 g (13 oz) ripe tomatoes, peeled,
seeded and diced (see page 534)
1 red onion, finely chopped
juice of 2 limes
1 teaspoon Tabasco
1 teaspoon roughly chopped
fresh coriander
3 teaspoons roughly chopped fresh
parsley
fresh coriander leaves, to garnish

One Shuck the oysters following the method in the Chef's techniques on page 522. Add the oysters to their liquid in the bowl and refrigerate. Clean the deeper halves of the shells and set them aside. Discard the flat halves.

Two To make the creamy oysters, add half the Tabasco to the oysters before refrigerating them. Place the bacon in a small pan, cover with cold water, bring to the boil and simmer for 4 minutes. Drain, then run the bacon under cold water to remove excess salt. Tip the bacon onto paper towels to drain, then cut into matchsticks.

Three Place the egg yolks, wine and remaining Tabasco in a heatproof bowl over a pan of simmering water, ensuring the bowl is not touching the water. Whisk vigorously until the mixture has increased to three or four times the original volume and leaves a trail across the surface when lifted on the whisk. Remove the bowl from the pan, whisk until it cools to room temperature, then fold in the cream and chilli and set aside.

Four Preheat the grill. Heat the oil in a saucepan and fry the bacon until golden. Add the capsicum and cook for 1 minute until soft but not coloured. Heat the oysters and their juices in another pan over low heat for 1 minute. Take care not to overheat or the oysters will toughen. Put the warm oysters back in their shells and place in an ovenproof dish (a layer of rock salt will help them balance). Pour over the juices and place the bacon and capsicum mixture on top. Spoon the egg mixture over and place the oysters under the grill for 2 minutes, or until golden. Serve immediately.

Five To make the salsa oysters, mix together all the ingredients except the whole coriander leaves. Season, cover with plastic and leave for 20 minutes at room temperature. Place an oyster in each shell and spoon over some juices and a little salsa, then garnish with a coriander leaf. Arrange on a bed of salad leaves or crushed ice.

CHEF'S TIP *Julienne strips are vegetables cut to the size and shape of matchsticks.*

about oysters...

Oysters need to be bought from a reliable source as they have a reputation for harbouring toxins. There are several different varieties available including Pacific, Portuguese, American and 'natives'. Like any other fresh produce, oysters that are in season will be at their best. Ask your fishmonger if you need advice.

Dressed crab

In Britain, the most traditional way to enjoy fresh crab is to 'dress' it.
This enduring favourite is well worth the effort and evokes
the feeling of an old-fashioned English seaside holiday.

Preparation time 40 minutes
Total cooking time 10 minutes
Serves 1–2

2 eggs, at room temperature
1 cooked crab, about 750 g–1 kg
(1½–2 lb) (see Chef's tip)
1–2 tablespoons mayonnaise, to taste
60–100 g (2–3¼ oz) fresh
breadcrumbs
Worcestershire sauce or Tabasco,
to taste
3 tablespoons chopped fresh parsley
2–3 anchovy fillets, to garnish
2–3 teaspoons drained capers,
to garnish
15 g (½ oz) stuffed green olives,
sliced, to garnish
2–4 slices brown bread
20 g (¾ oz) unsalted butter,
at room temperature
1 lime or lemon, cut into wedges

One To hard-boil the eggs, place them in a small saucepan and cover with cold water. Bring to a gentle boil and cook for 10 minutes. Drain and cool in cold water. Peel the eggs and push the whites and yolks separately through a fine sieve.

Two Prepare the crab, following the method in the Chef's techniques on page 523. Scrape all the creamy brown meat from the shell and sieve it into a bowl. Stir in the mayonnaise and breadcrumbs to bind, adding more of each if the flavour of the dark meat is too strong. Season with salt, freshly ground pepper and Worcestershire sauce or Tabasco.

Three Crack open the claws and remove all the white meat, checking that there are no shell splinters left (see Chef's tip). Season to taste.

Four Place the white meat from the claws and body of the crab towards the two outer sides of the cleaned and dried shell. Spoon the brown meat into the centre, then arrange the chopped parsley on the seams in between. Cover half of the white meat with the egg white; spoon the egg yolk on the dark meat. Garnish with anchovies, capers and sliced olives. Butter the bread thinly, and serve the dressed crab with the bread and butter, and lime or lemon wedges to the side.

CHEF'S TIP *When choosing a crab, select one that feels heavier than it looks. If possible, buy a fresh crab, as frozen crabs lose a lot of flavour and liquid as they defrost. Male crabs have larger claws than females.*

Coquilles Saint-Jacques mornay

*Coquilles Saint Jacques is the French term for scallops, meaning
Saint James's shells. Here they are baked in the half shell and classically
coated with piped potato and a Gruyère cheese sauce.*

Preparation time 25 minutes
Total cooking time 45 minutes
Serves 4

8 large fresh scallops in their shells
55 g (1³/4 oz) Gruyère cheese,
finely grated

DUCHESSE POTATOES
1 kg (2 lb) floury potatoes, peeled
and cut into pieces
25 g (³/4 oz) unsalted butter
2 egg yolks
pinch of grated nutmeg

MORNAY SAUCE
15 g (¹/2 oz) unsalted butter
15 g (¹/2 oz) plain flour
250 ml (8 fl oz) milk
1 egg yolk
55 g (1³/4 oz) Gruyère cheese, grated

One To prepare the scallops, follow the method in the Chef's techniques on page 524. Place the scallops flat on a board and slice each one into three circles, leaving the orange roe whole. Cover and refrigerate until needed.

Two Scrub the scallop shells and place in a pan of cold water. Bring to the boil and simmer for 5 minutes. Drain and leave the shells to cool and dry.

Three To make the duchesse potatoes, place the potatoes in a large pan of salted, cold water. Cover and bring to the boil, then reduce the heat and simmer for 15–20 minutes, or until the potatoes are tender to the point of a sharp knife. Drain, return to the pan and shake over low heat for 1–2 minutes to remove excess moisture. Purée the potatoes, following the method in the

Chef's techniques on page 536, then stir in the butter and egg yolks and season with nutmeg, salt and pepper. Spoon the mixture into a piping bag with a 1.5 cm (⁵/8 inch) star nozzle. Preheat the oven to moderately hot 200°C (400°F/Gas 6).

Four To make the mornay sauce, melt the butter in a heavy-based pan over low–medium heat. Sprinkle with the flour and cook for 1 minute without allowing the sauce to colour, stirring continuously with a wooden spoon. Remove from the heat and slowly add the milk, blending thoroughly. Return to the heat and bring slowly to the boil, stirring constantly. Lower the heat and

cook for 3–4 minutes, or until the sauce coats the back of a spoon. Remove from the stove, stir in the egg yolk and cheese, then season with salt and black pepper.

Five Pipe shell shapes or small overlapping circles of duchesse potato to form a border around the edge of each shell. Place on a baking tray with a rim so that the round edge of each shell rests on the rim to stop the filling running out. Place a sliced scallop and whole roe in each rounded shell, season with salt and black pepper and spoon over the mornay sauce. Sprinkle the cheese over the sauce and bake for 12–15 minutes, or until golden brown.

Asparagus, artichoke and lobster salad

*This is an elegant salad for a special occasion. The walnut oil adds
a delicious nutty flavour to the dressing, but don't be tempted
to increase the quantity as it has a strong flavour.*

Preparation time 1 hour + chilling
Total cooking time 35 minutes
Serves 4

COURT BOUILLON
1 large carrot, finely sliced
2 onions, finely sliced
2 celery sticks, finely sliced
1 leek, white part only, finely sliced
3 sprigs of fresh thyme
1 bay leaf
10 black peppercorns
500 ml (16 fl oz) white wine
3 tablespoons salt

3 uncooked lobster tails
24 stalks asparagus

DRESSING
60 ml (2 fl oz) sherry vinegar
1 French shallot, finely chopped
60 ml (2 fl oz) walnut oil
120 ml (4 fl oz) vegetable oil
1 tablespoon chopped fresh chervil
or chives

4 large artichoke hearts,
from a jar or can
sprigs of fresh chervil, to garnish

One To make the court bouillon, place all the vegetables with the thyme sprigs, bay leaf, peppercorns and wine in a large pot and bring to the boil. Cook for 5 minutes over high heat. Add the salt and 4 litres water and return to the boil. Add the lobster tails, bring to the boil and cook for 12 minutes. Remove the pot from the heat and allow the lobster to cool slightly.

Two When the lobster is cool enough to handle, remove it from the bouillon. Discard the bouillon. Remove the tail flesh in a single piece, following the method in the Chef's techniques on page 524. Slice the meat into medallions. Cover and refrigerate.

Three Wash the asparagus under cold, running water. Using a small knife, remove the spurs from the asparagus stems, starting from the top and working down, then remove the outer layer from the lower two thirds of the stem using a vegetable peeler. Snap off the woody ends at their natural breaking point and discard. Lining up the tips, tie the stalks in bundles of six to eight and cook in

4 litres of salted water, following the method in the Chef's techniques on page 535. When cooked, place in a bowl, cover and refrigerate.

Four To make the dressing, whisk together the vinegar and shallot. Gradually whisk in the oils, then the chervil or chives. Season and set aside. Rinse the artichokes well, pat dry, toss them in a little dressing and season to taste. Repeat with the asparagus, being careful not to break the tips. Refrigerate the vegetables until ready to use. To serve, arrange the artichokes, asparagus and lobster medallions on serving plates. Drizzle the remaining dressing around the artichoke, then garnish with chervil.

CHEF'S TIP *The cooked lobster tail shells can be frozen and used another time when preparing a seafood bisque or broth.*

about lobsters...

True lobsters have large front pincers but as this recipe just calls for the tails you can use rock lobster or crayfish instead. Buy live lobsters so you know they are fresh and then kill them humanely by putting them in the freezer for a couple of hours beforehand, following the instructions in the Chef's techniques on page 524.

Garlic prawns

*Ideal as an appetiser or light summer lunch,
serve this Spanish-inspired dish with lots of crusty
bread to soak up the lemony garlic butter.*

Preparation time *20 minutes*
Total cooking time *10 minutes*
Serves 4

120 g (4 oz) curly endive (frisée)
*1 red chilli, seeded and very
thinly sliced*
1 tablespoon fresh chervil
24 raw tiger prawns, unpeeled
*2 teaspoons vegetable or
olive oil*
4 cloves garlic, crushed
*125 g (4 oz) unsalted butter,
cut into cubes*
*finely grated rind and juice of
1 lemon*
*1 tablespoon finely chopped
fresh parsley*

One Mix together the endive, chilli and chervil and pile onto four plates.

Two Peel and devein the prawns, leaving the tails intact, following the method in the Chef's techniques on page 522.

Three Heat the oil in a large, heavy-based frying pan. Add the prawns and, over medium–high heat, fry for 1 minute on each side, or until cooked through. Remove and keep warm.

Four Add the garlic to the pan and cook for 1 minute. Add the butter and cook for 4 minutes, or until it is nut brown. Remove from the heat and add the lemon rind and juice and chopped parsley to the garlic butter.

Five Quickly shake the pan once or twice to combine the juices, then add the prawns and toss briefly to warm through. Arrange around the salad and drizzle with any pan juices.

Crab cakes

These crispy crab cakes make a perfect light lunch with salad, or you can make lots of small ones to serve as appetisers at a barbecue or as part of a summer picnic.

Preparation time 55 minutes
+ 20 minutes cooling + 30 minutes refrigeration
Total cooking time 20 minutes
Serves 4–6

2 tablespoons vegetable oil
1 onion, finely chopped
2 cloves garlic, crushed
1½ tablespoons grated fresh ginger
1 small red capsicum (pepper), halved, seeded and cut into cubes
8 spring onions, finely chopped
480 g (15 oz) white crab meat, drained well if frozen
2 teaspoons Tabasco
2 tablespoons chopped fresh parsley
3 tablespoons fresh breadcrumbs
½ teaspoon Dijon mustard
1 egg, beaten
200 g (6½ oz) plain flour, seasoned
100 g (3¼ oz) fresh breadcrumbs
60 g (2 oz) Parmesan cheese, grated
2 eggs, beaten, for coating
oil, for deep-frying
lemon wedges, to serve

One Heat the oil in a frying pan and cook the onion, garlic and ginger for 1 minute. Add the capsicum and spring onion and cook for 2 minutes until soft. Put on a plate and leave for 20 minutes to cool completely. Then stir in the crab meat, Tabasco, parsley, breadcrumbs, mustard and some salt and black pepper. Add the egg and bind together.

Two Divide the mixture into four, six or 12, depending on what size cakes you want. Using lightly floured hands and a lightly floured surface, shape into patties. Place on a tray, cover and refrigerate for 30 minutes, or until firm.

Three Place the flour on one plate, the breadcrumbs and Parmesan on another and the beaten egg in a bowl. Toss the crab cakes in the flour, then pat off any excess. Place in the egg and use a brush to help coat. Remove with a fish slice and toss in the breadcrumbs and Parmesan. Reshape the cakes, pressing the crumbs firmly onto them with your fingers, then place on a tray.

Four Heat 1 cm (½ inch) oil in a non-stick frying pan and cook the cakes, in small batches, over medium heat for 1–2 minutes each side, or until golden. Drain on crumpled paper towels and serve with lemon wedges.

CHEF'S TIP *To keep the crab cakes warm and crisp while you're cooking the rest, place on a rack in a warm oven.*

Fritto misto with a garlic dip

*There are a number of ways to prepare Italy's well-known mixed fry.
Here the fish is simply dipped in flour, egg and then breadcrumbs
before being fried to a crispy golden brown.*

Preparation time 1 hour
Total cooking time 20 minutes
Serves 6 as a starter
or 2 as a main course

2 French shallots, finely chopped
150 ml (5 fl oz) dry white wine
1 bay leaf
1 sprig of fresh thyme
300 g (10 oz) mussels, scrubbed and
beards removed (see page 523)
150 g (5 oz) squid
oil, for deep-frying
4 eggs, lightly beaten, for coating
90 g (3 oz) plain flour, seasoned
200 g (6½ oz) fresh breadcrumbs
150 g (5 oz) barramundi, plaice, sole
or flounder fillet, cut into strips
150 g (5 oz) blue-eye cod, ling or cod
fillet, cut into large, bite-sized cubes
185 g (6 oz) mayonnaise
1 tablespoon Greek-style yoghurt
2 cloves garlic, finely chopped
fresh parsley and lemon wedges,
to garnish

One Put the shallot, wine, bay leaf and thyme in a large saucepan, cover and bring to the boil. Add the mussels, discarding any that are already open, cover and reduce to medium heat. Cook for 2 minutes, shaking the saucepan occasionally, until the mussels open (discard any that do not open). Drain and remove from the shells.

Two To prepare the squid, remove the wings from the tube, peel off the skin and remove the head. Remove the clear cartilage quill from the opening of the tube, cut off the tentacles and rinse the tube under running water. Drain, pat dry with paper towels and then slice the squid into rings.

Three One-third fill a large heavy-based pan with oil and heat to 190°C (375°F) (see page 537). Put the egg, flour and breadcrumbs into separate dishes. Toss the fish, mussels and squid in the flour, shake off the excess, then dip into the egg and finally coat with the breadcrumbs, shaking off the excess. Deep-fry the crumbed seafood in batches until golden brown, drain on crumpled paper towels and sprinkle lightly with salt. If keeping warm for a few minutes, do so on a wire rack in a warm oven, uncovered to keep them crisp.

Four To make the garlic dip, stir together the mayonnaise, yoghurt and garlic and serve in a bowl to accompany the seafood. Garnish with the parsley and lemon wedges.

Sardines with walnut and parsley topping

*The crisp walnut topping gives these grilled fresh sardines a lovely texture.
They can be served as a main course or appetiser with warm olive oil,
lemon wedges, rocket leaves and plenty of fresh bread.*

Preparation time 40 minutes
Total cooking time 20 minutes
Serves 4

WALNUT AND PARSLEY TOPPING
150 g (5 oz) unsalted butter
4 French shallots, finely chopped
2 cloves garlic, crushed
4 tablespoons fresh white breadcrumbs
110 g (3³/4 oz) walnuts, finely chopped
2 teaspoons chopped fresh parsley

*16 x 50 g (1³/4 oz) fresh sardines,
scaled and gutted*
2 tablespoons plain flour, seasoned
50 ml (1³/4 fl oz) olive oil
2 tablespoons olive oil, warm, to serve
lemon wedges, to serve

One To make the walnut and parsley topping, melt the butter in a pan over moderate heat, add the shallots and garlic, cover and cook for 3 minutes, or until the shallots are soft and translucent. Remove from the heat, season, then add the breadcrumbs, walnuts and parsley and mix thoroughly.

Two Preheat the grill to high. Wash the sardines, then dry well on paper towels. Place the flour and oil on separate plates. One at a time, roll the sardines in the flour to coat, shaking off the excess. Dip into the oil, coating on both sides, then transfer half to the grill pan. Grill for 3 minutes on each side and keep warm while you cook the second batch.

Three Sprinkle the walnut and parsley topping over the sardines and press firmly onto the skin. Grill again, in two batches, until the topping is golden brown. Drizzle with the warm olive oil and serve with lemon wedges.

Trout flans with chive and lemon sauce

These delicately flavoured and fine textured flans, served with
a smooth lemon butter sauce, make an elegant first course
to impress your friends and dinner guests.

Preparation time 30 minutes
Total cooking time 30 minutes
Serves 4

TROUT FLANS
fresh flat-leaf parsley leaves
300 g (10 oz) trout, skinned, trimmed
and boned
1/4 teaspoon salt
pinch of cayenne pepper
1 egg
150 ml (5 fl oz) thick (double) cream
200 ml (6 1/2 fl oz) milk

CHIVE AND LEMON SAUCE
1 French shallot, finely chopped
juice of 1 lemon
150 g (5 oz) unsalted butter, cut into
small cubes and chilled
1 tablespoon very finely chopped
fresh chives

One Preheat the oven to warm 160°C (315°F/Gas 2–3). Prepare four 8 x 4 cm (3 x 1 1/2 inch) ramekins by cutting four rounds of baking paper to the same diameter. Grease them, then line with the rounds of baking paper, brushing the lining with softened butter and pressing out any air holes. Press one or two parsley leaves onto the baking paper, then refrigerate.

Two To make the flan mixture, cut the trout into 1 cm (1/2 inch) cubes and put in a food processor with the salt, cayenne pepper and the egg. Blend until smooth. Scrape down with a spatula and process again. With the machine still running, add the cream and milk, stopping the moment the liquid is incorporated—the trout mixture should resemble a cake batter. Pass the mixture through a sieve into a jug.

Three Pour the mixture into the ramekins and tap them on a work surface to remove any air bubbles. Smooth the tops and transfer the ramekins to a small roasting tin lined with one or two sheets of paper towel to stop the ramekins slipping. Pour enough boiling water into the tin to come halfway up the sides of the ramekins. Bake for 15–20 minutes. Insert a small knife in the centre of a ramekin for 3 seconds. If the blade comes out hot, the flans are cooked. Remove from the roasting tin and set aside to rest.

Four To make the chive and lemon sauce, put the shallot and lemon juice in a small pan. Add 2 tablespoons water, bring to the boil and cook for 5–7 minutes, or until almost dry. Reduce the heat to low, then whisk in the butter, a few pieces at a time, without letting the sauce boil. Strain into a clean pan and season to taste with salt and white pepper. Just before serving, whisk in the chives.

Five Loosen the flans from the inside of the ramekins with a knife. Turn the flans out onto individual serving plates. Carefully remove the paper, drizzle the sauce around and serve immediately.

CHEF'S TIP *When making a lightly coloured sauce, use ground white pepper rather than black pepper.*

Tiger prawns with sautéed capsicum

This colourful dish is perfect as a starter or a light main course.
It derives its superb flavour from the sweetness of the
capsicum, spiked with lemon oil and fresh ginger.

Preparation time 30 minutes
+ 1 hour infusion
Total cooking time 5 minutes
Serves 4

LEMON OIL
60 ml (2 fl oz) oil
finely grated rind of ¼ lemon

1.25 kg (2 lb 8 oz) raw large tiger
or king prawns
1 red capsicum (pepper)
1 yellow capsicum (pepper)
1 tablespoon grated fresh ginger
1 tablespoon crushed garlic
60 ml (2 fl oz) dry sherry
2 tablespoons lemon juice
2 teaspoons light soy sauce

One To make the lemon oil, warm the oil in a small saucepan over low heat until lukewarm. Add the lemon rind, then leave the oil to cool and infuse for 1 hour. Strain before using.

Two Leaving the heads attached, peel and devein the prawns following the instructions in the Chef's techniques on page 522. Remove the eyes. Pat the prawns dry on paper towels.

Three Cut both the capsicums in half and remove the stems and seeds. Dice into 5 mm (¼ inch) cubes and set aside.

Four Heat the lemon oil in a wok over high heat until it begins to smoke. Add the ginger, garlic and capsicum and stir-fry for 1 minute, then add the prawns and stir-fry for 1 minute more. Stir in the sherry, lemon juice and soy sauce and stir-fry for about 3 minutes, or until the prawns are just tender. Serve hot, with fresh crusty bread and a green salad.

LE CORDON BLEU ❖ COMPLETE COOK

Moules marinière

*This is a classic French way to prepare mussels, cooked simply
in white wine and onions and enriched with cream.*

Preparation time 15 minutes
Total cooking time 10 minutes
Serves 4

60 g (2 oz) unsalted butter
2 onions, chopped
2 kg (4 lb) mussels, scrubbed and
beards removed (see page 523)
400 ml (12¾ fl oz) dry white wine
1 bay leaf
1 large sprig of fresh thyme
200 ml (6½ fl oz) thick
(double) cream
60 g (2 oz) fresh parsley, finely
chopped

One In a deep pan, melt the butter, add
the onion and cook over medium heat
until transparent and soft, stirring
continuously to prevent the onion from
colouring. Stir in the mussels, wine, bay
leaf and thyme and place a tight-fitting
lid on the pan. Turn the heat to high and
cook rapidly for 2–3 minutes, shaking
the pan periodically, until all the mussels
have opened. Discard any mussels that
do not open.

Two Remove the mussels from the liquid
and set them aside. Strain the liquid
through a fine sieve into a clean pan and
reheat. Stir in the cream and season to
taste with salt and freshly ground black
pepper. Divide the mussels among four
bowls and pour the liquid over them.
Just before serving, sprinkle with the
chopped parsley.

Three Provide a finger bowl and a spare
bowl for the shells. Serve with hot crusty
bread to soak up the juices.

CHEF'S TIP *Mussels can be kept alive
overnight by placing them in a bowl in
the fridge covered with a damp cloth to
keep them closed and moist.*

Seared tuna with chickpea salad

*These tuna steaks are infused with Oriental flavours and are seared
quickly to great effect. The chickpea salad is very versatile,
and is also lovely with grilled vegetables or chicken.*

Preparation time 10 minutes + overnight
soaking + 3–4 hours marinating
Total cooking time 1 hour 5 minutes
Serves 4

125 g (4 oz) dried chickpeas
(see Chef's tip)
4 tuna steaks
1 bay leaf
1 French shallot, chopped
1 small clove garlic, crushed
1 red chilli, seeded and chopped
1 red capsicum (pepper), chopped
1 avocado
2 tablespoons chopped fresh coriander
leaves
4 lime wedges, to serve

MARINADE
100 ml (3¼ fl oz) olive oil
finely grated rind and juice of
1½ limes
6 stalks of fresh coriander,
roughly chopped or slightly bruised

One Soak the chickpeas overnight in
plenty of cold water.

Two Combine the marinade ingredients
and mix well. Place the tuna steaks in a
shallow glass or ceramic dish and pour
on a third of the marinade, turning to
coat both sides. Cover with plastic wrap
and refrigerate for 3–4 hours, turning
the tuna occasionally.

Three Drain the chickpeas and place in a
large pan with enough water to cover.
Add the bay leaf, bring to the boil, then
reduce the heat and simmer for 1 hour,
or until tender. Drain and set aside.

Four To make the chickpea salad, place
the chickpeas, shallot, garlic, chilli and

capsicum in a bowl and toss well. Peel
and dice the avocado and fold into the
salad with the coriander. Strain the
remaining marinade into the salad and
season to taste.

Five Preheat the grill to high. When the
grill is hot, cook the tuna for about

2 minutes on each side, or chargrill for
1 minute on each side. Serve on warmed
plates with a wedge of lime, and the
chickpea salad on the side.

CHEF'S TIP *To save time, you can use
250 g (8 oz) canned chickpeas. Drain
well and add to the salad in step 4.*

LE CORDON BLEU COMPLETE COOK

Whole baked salmon with watercress mayonnaise

*Baked in foil to retain the salmon's flavour and moist texture,
this impressive centrepiece is the perfect dish for a large al fresco
gathering. Serve with new potatoes and summer vegetables.*

Preparation time 1 hour 10 minutes
+ 1 hour refrigeration
Total cooking time 40 minutes
Serves 10–12

1.5–1.75 kg (3–3½ lb) whole salmon,
cleaned and scaled
(ask your fishmonger to gut the
fish and remove the scales)
1 small onion, thinly sliced
1 small bay leaf
1 sprig fresh thyme
5 fresh parsley stalks
90 ml (3 fl oz) dry white wine
sprigs of watercress,
to garnish
lemon wedges, to garnish

WATERCRESS MAYONNAISE
120 g (4 oz) watercress, tough
stems removed
315 g (10 oz) mayonnaise
few drops of lemon juice

One Lift up the gill flap behind the cheek of the salmon head and, using kitchen scissors, remove the dark, frilly gills. Repeat on the other side of the fish. If any scales remain, hold the tail and, using the back of a knife, scrape the skin at a slight angle, working towards the head. Trim the fins. Cut across the tail to shorten it by half, then cut a V shape into the tail. Wash the salmon under cold water and open it on the belly side where the fishmonger has slit it. Remove the blood vessel lying along the backbone with a spoon. Rinse and wipe inside and out with paper towels.

Two Preheat the oven to moderate 180°C (350°F/Gas 4). Butter a piece of foil large enough to wrap around the fish and place on a large baking tray. Lay the salmon just off centre and place the onion and herbs inside the belly. Season with salt and black pepper, then pour over the wine. Fold over the foil and seal the edges tightly.

Three Bake for 30–40 minutes, or until the fish feels springy and firm to the touch. Open the foil and leave to cool. Remove the flavourings and lift the salmon onto greaseproof paper, draining off any liquid. Prepare the salmon for serving following the Chef's techniques on page 527, then cover with plastic wrap and put in the refrigerator for 1 hour, or until needed.

Four To make the watercress mayonnaise, add the watercress to a pan of boiling salted water and cook for 1 minute, then drain and run under cold water. Pat dry with paper towels to remove any excess water, then purée the watercress in a blender or food processor. Beat the purée gradually into the mayonnaise. If it is too dry, add a few drops of lemon juice. Season to taste with salt and freshly ground black pepper.

Five To serve, decorate the fish with some watercress mayonnaise and serve the remainder separately. Garnish with the watercress sprigs and lemon wedges.

Grilled lobster with a buttery Pernod sauce

Seafood gains a wonderful new dimension when served with a buttery sauce brightened with a dash of Pernod. The aniseed flavour of the sauce is enhanced by the infusion of star anise.

Preparation time 15 minutes
Total cooking time 30 minutes
Serves 4

PERNOD SAUCE
1 star anise
2 tablespoons Pernod
200 g (6¹/2 oz) unsalted butter, cubed

4 raw lobster tails
40 g (1¹/4 oz) unsalted butter, melted

One To make the Pernod sauce, place 125 ml (4 fl oz) water in a small saucepan with the star anise and bring to the boil. Reduce the heat to low and simmer for 10 minutes, or until reduced to about 2 tablespoons. Stir in half the Pernod. Whisking constantly, gradually add the butter, a few pieces at a time. Season to taste with salt and ground white pepper, then place the pan in a bowl or pan of hot water to keep warm.

(The sauce will separate if placed back over direct heat.)

Two Add the lobster tails to a large pot of boiling water and cook for 2 minutes, or until the shells turn bright orange. Drain and refresh in cold water.

Three Place the lobster tails on a cutting board with the soft undershells facing down. Using a large knife, but without cutting all the way through, split the tails in half lengthways down the back, then open them up.

Four Preheat the grill to high. Brush the lobster flesh with the melted butter, season lightly, then grill, cut side down, for 5 minutes. Turn and grill the other side for 5–10 minutes, or until the flesh is firm.

Five Transfer to serving plates. Stir the remaining Pernod into the sauce, then spoon a little sauce over the tail and serve the remainder on the side.

CHEF'S TIP *You could also use cooked whole lobsters in this recipe. First remove the claws by twisting where they meet the body, then crack them with a nutcracker or meat mallet and set aside to serve later with the grilled lobsters.*

Place the lobsters face down on a cutting board. Using a large knife, but without cutting all the way through, split the lobsters in half lengthways down the back, then open them up. Remove the vein along the tail, the small sac just behind the mouth, and any coral or grey-green liver (tomalley). Brush the flesh with melted butter, season lightly and grill under a hot grill until heated through, turning during cooking.

Roasted salmon with a basil and capsicum sauce

*The smoky sweetness of roasted capsicum marries with peppery basil
in this inspirational sauce which makes salmon fillets, simply cooked,
so sumptuous. Enjoy in the garden with a glass of chilled wine.*

Preparation time 15 minutes
Total cooking time 8–12 minutes
Serves 4

2 red capsicums (peppers)
100 ml (3¼ fl oz) olive oil
*4 salmon fillets, scaled but
not skinned*
30 ml (1 fl oz) vegetable oil
30 g (1 oz) unsalted butter
2 tablespoons shredded fresh basil

One Preheat the oven to hot 220°C (425°F/Gas 7). Lightly brush the whole capsicums with some olive oil, then place them on a baking tray and roast for 15–20 minutes, or until the skin is blackened and blistered and the capsicums are soft. Cover them with plastic wrap, or place in a plastic bag. (This will cause the capsicums to sweat, making the skins peel off more easily.) Allow them to cool. Peel away the skin, then halve and seed the capsicums.

Two To make the sauce, place the capsicums in a blender or food processor, add the remaining olive oil and work to a smooth purée. Season to taste with salt and freshly ground black pepper, and transfer to a small pan.

Three Season the salmon fillets with salt and freshly ground pepper. Heat the vegetable oil and butter in a flameproof dish over high heat. Place the salmon in the dish, skin side up, then transfer to the oven and bake for 2 minutes. Turn and bake for 6 minutes, or until the salmon is cooked through and the skin is lightly coloured.

Four Gently heat the sauce, then add the basil. Transfer the salmon to warm plates and pour the sauce around. Serve at once with a mixed green salad.

Smoked haddock gougères

A cheese-flavoured crown of choux pastry here holds a filling of smoked haddock, leek, tomato and dill. For a variation, you could try a mixture of fish such as salmon, trout or monkfish, or perhaps some shellfish.

Preparation time 35 minutes
Total cooking time 45 minutes
Serves 6

CHOUX PASTRY
150 g (5 oz) plain flour
100 g (3¼ oz) unsalted butter,
cut into cubes
pinch of salt
4 eggs, lightly beaten
100 g (3¼ oz) Cheddar cheese,
roughly grated
1 teaspoon Dijon mustard

FILLING
310 g (10 oz) smoked haddock fillet
15 g (½ oz) unsalted butter
1 small leek or 4 spring onions,
white part only, sliced
15 g (½ oz) plain flour
180 ml (5¾ fl oz) milk
1 large tomato, peeled, seeded (see page 534) and cut into 1 cm (½ inch) strips
1 teaspoon chopped fresh dill

1 egg, beaten
1 tablespoon grated Parmesan cheese
1 tablespoon lightly toasted fresh breadcrumbs
20 g (¾ oz) unsalted butter, melted
fresh dill, to garnish

One Lightly brush six 14.5 x 3 cm (5¾ x 1¼ inch) round gratin dishes with melted butter and refrigerate to set.

Two Make the choux pastry following the method in the Chef's techniques on page 545) and using 250 ml (8 fl oz) of water. When the pastry is smooth, thick and glossy, beat in the cheese and mustard and season well with salt and black pepper. Cover and set aside.

Three To make the filling, place the smoked haddock flat in a shallow pan and pour in enough cold water to cover. Slowly bring to the boil, covered, then turn off the heat and leave for 7 minutes.

Four Melt the butter in a deep pan, add the leek and cook over low heat for 3 minutes to soften. Sprinkle with the flour, stir in with a wooden spoon and cook for 1 minute. Remove from the heat, mix in the milk, then return to the heat and bring to the boil, stirring continuously. Simmer for 1 minute, or until the mixture thickens.

Five Preheat the oven to moderately hot 200°C (400°F/ Gas 6). Lift the fish from its cooking liquid, pat dry with paper towels, then use a fork to lightly take the fish off its skin in flakes. Gently stir the flakes into the filling with the tomato, dill and some salt and black pepper.

Six Put the choux pastry in a piping bag with a 1–1.25 cm (½–⅝ inch) nozzle. Pipe a circle around the outside of the base of each prepared dishes, then a second circle on top to cover the side of the dish. Spoon the filling into the middle of the choux circles and brush the top of the pastry lightly with the beaten egg. Combine the Parmesan and breadcrumbs, sprinkle over the filling, then drizzle with the melted butter. Place on a baking tray and bake for about 15–20 minutes, or until the pastry is risen and crisp. Sprinkle with the chopped dill to garnish.

CHEF'S TIPS *You can also spoon in the pastry to cover the sides of the dish and give a more peaked surface.*

To make one large gougère, use a deep 20 cm (8 inch) round ovenproof dish and bake for 30–35 minutes.

Snapper with fennel en papillote

Cooked in a parcel of greaseproof paper or foil to retain all the juices and flavours, the white wine, basil leaves and gentle anise flavour of fennel infuse the sweet snapper or mullet.

Preparation time 40 minutes
Total cooking time 35 minutes
Serves 4

2 x 400 g (12¾ oz) snapper or red mullet, filleted (see page 526)
2 large fennel bulbs with fronds
60 g (2 oz) unsalted butter
16 fresh basil leaves
80 ml (2¾ fl oz) white wine
4 teaspoons Pastis or Ricard (optional)

One Wash the fish, dry on paper towels and keep in the refrigerator until needed. With a small sharp knife, trim off the fronds at the top of the fennel bulbs, keeping the leaves and discarding the thick stalks. With a large sharp knife, cut the bulb in half from the top down through the root and then cut away and discard the root. Cut the fennel into 5 mm (¼ inch) thick slices.

Two Heat the butter in a pan, add the fennel, cover and cook over low heat for 25 minutes, or until soft to the point of a sharp knife. Remove from the heat and season with salt and black pepper. Preheat the oven to hot 220°C (425°F/ Gas 7).

Three Fold a piece of greaseproof paper or foil in two, then cut out a large half tear-drop shape, 5 cm (2 inches) bigger than the fish. Open the paper or foil out and you should have a heart shape. Repeat to make four in total, then lay the shapes flat and brush with melted butter. Spoon the fennel onto one side of each heart and spread to the size of the fish. Place a fish fillet on top and lightly season with salt and black pepper. Arrange four basil leaves on each piece of fish, then sprinkle each one with a tablespoon of white wine and a teaspoon of Pastis or Ricard. Top with the reserved sprigs of fennel leaf.

Four Fold the empty side of paper or foil over the fish and seal the edges by twisting and folding tightly. Put on a baking tray or in a shallow ovenproof dish and bake for 5–8 minutes.

Five Place the fish parcels on each plate and allow your guests to open them and release the aromas.

CHEF'S TIP *Other fish can be cooked by this method, such as perch, salmon or cod. The cooking times will vary according to the thickness and shape of the fish.*

Fish and chips

Tradition at its best: firm white fish that flakes at the touch of a fork, cooked in a crisp batter and served with home-made chips. For the best results, make sure that the fish is really fresh and eat piping hot.

*Preparation time 20 minutes
+ 30 minutes standing
Total cooking time 20 minutes
Serves 4*

*600 g (1¼ lb) floury potatoes, peeled
oil, for deep-frying
4 x 150–180 g (5–5¾ oz) pieces firm
white fish fillet, skinned
2–3 tablespoons seasoned flour
lemon wedges, to garnish*

BATTER
*160 g (5¼ oz) cornflour
160 g (5¼ oz) plain flour
3 teaspoons baking powder
315–500 ml (10–16 fl oz) beer*

One Cut the potatoes into 6–8 cm (2½–3 inch) long thin batons. Place in a bowl and cover with cold water.

Two To make the batter, sift the cornflour, plain flour, baking powder and some salt and black pepper into a bowl and make a well in the centre. Gradually pour in the beer, using a wooden spoon to beat it into the flour, until the mixture becomes a smooth batter the consistency of cream (the amount of liquid you need will depend on the flour you use). Cover and leave for 30 minutes at room temperature.

Three Meanwhile, fill a deep-fat fryer or heavy-based saucepan one third full of oil, following the method in the Chef's techniques on page 537, and heat to 160–170°C (315–325°F) (when a cube of bread is dropped into the oil, it will brown in 30 seconds). Drain and pat the chips dry, then fry until the bubbles subside and the chips have formed a thin, light-golden skin. Lift out the chips, allowing any excess oil to drip back into the deep-fat fryer, and transfer the chips onto crumpled paper towels.

Four Increase the temperature of the oil to 180°C (350°F) (a cube of bread dropped into the oil will brown in 15 seconds). Wash the fish and dry thoroughly on paper towels. Place the seasoned flour on a plate and coat the fish, shaking off the excess. Dip the fish into the batter until it is evenly coated, then lift out using fingers or forks to allow any excess mixture to drip off. Lower the fish carefully into the fryer or pan and fry, in batches if necessary, for 5 minutes, or until golden and crisp. Do not overcrowd the pan or the temperature will be lowered. Remove and drain on crumpled paper towels. Season with salt, place on a wire rack and keep warm.

Five Place the chips in the oil again and fry until golden and crisp. Remove and drain, season with salt and serve with the fish, lemon wedges and tartare or tomato sauce.

'Lasagne' of salmon with tomato and spinach

*There is no pasta in this special dish, but the effect is like a lasagne,
with layers of pink salmon, dark-green spinach leaves, white and
tomato sauces making for a stunning dinner-party recipe.*

Preparation time 1 hour
Total cooking time 1 hour 15 minutes
Serves 4

*4 x 150 g (5 oz) thick centre cuts of
fresh salmon fillet, skinned and cut
into 3 slices horizontally (ask your
fishmonger to do this)*
90 ml (3 fl oz) olive oil
2 onions, finely chopped
*1 kg (2 lb) ripe tomatoes, peeled,
seeded and diced (see page 534)*
2 cloves garlic, crushed
1 bouquet garni (see page 520)
45 g (1½ oz) unsalted butter
*750 g (1½ lb) English spinach
small pinch of ground nutmeg*
*12 small black olives, halved and
pitted, to garnish*
sprigs of fresh chervil, to garnish

BEURRE BLANC
3 French shallots, finely chopped
315 ml (10 fl oz) white wine
3 tablespoons cider vinegar
*1 tablespoon thick (double) cream
or crème fraîche*
*180 g (5¾ oz) unsalted butter,
cut into cubes and chilled*
*2 tablespoons finely chopped
fresh chives*

WHITE SAUCE
15 g (½ oz) unsalted butter
15 g (½ oz) plain flour
250 ml (8 fl oz) milk

One Separate the slices of salmon, brush with olive oil, cover and place in the refrigerator. Heat the oil in a pan, add the onion, cover and cook for 4 minutes, or until soft and translucent. Stir in the tomato, garlic, bouquet garni and season with some salt and black pepper. Cook for about 40 minutes, stirring occasionally, until the mixture is thick. Discard the bouquet garni, season and keep warm.

Two To make the beurre blanc, place the shallots, wine and vinegar in a pan, bring to the boil and cook to reduce by a quarter. Add the cream and remove from the heat, then whisk in the butter a piece at a time until you have a creamy, flowing sauce that coats the back of a spoon. Strain into a bowl, stir in the chives, cover with plastic wrap and sit over a pan of warm water.

Three To make the white sauce, melt the butter in a heavy-based pan over low–medium heat. Sprinkle the flour over the butter and cook for 1–2 minutes without allowing it to colour, stirring continuously with a wooden spoon. Remove the pan from the heat and slowly add the milk, whisking to avoid lumps. Return to medium heat and bring to the boil, stirring constantly. Cook for 3–4 minutes, or until the sauce coats the back of a spoon. Cover and keep warm. Preheat the grill.

Four Melt the butter in a large frying pan or wok, add the spinach and toss over high heat for 2 minutes, or until wilted. Add the nutmeg, salt and black pepper and place in a sieve over a bowl to allow the moisture to drain through. Season the fish and grill for 1 minute each side.

Five To serve, take four plates and place a salmon slice on each. Using half the spinach, spread a layer on each slice, then add half the white sauce, followed by half the tomato sauce. Cover with another slice of fish, the remaining spinach, white and tomato sauce, and finish with the remaining salmon. Spoon the beurre blanc around the base of the plate and garnish with the olive halves and chervil leaves.

about tomatoes...

Tomatoes have become remarkably popular since their arrival in Europe in the sixteenth century. The best flavoured are those that have been left to ripen on the vine. For immediate use they should be firm and bright coloured with no wrinkles or cracks. Pale red tomatoes can be left to ripen naturally in the light, but not in the sun. Uniformity of shape or colour bears no relation to the flavour.

Trout braised in Riesling

The Alsace region of France, which borders Germany, is well known for
its preparation of the freshwater fish caught in its rivers. In this recipe,
the fish is braised in Riesling, a typical Alsatian wine.

Preparation time *35 minutes*
Total cooking time *1 hour 10 minutes*
Serves 4

75 g (2½ oz) unsalted butter
3 onions, thinly sliced
150 g (5 oz) mushrooms, sliced
1 tablespoon chopped fresh parsley
2 large French shallots, chopped
230 ml (7¼ fl oz) Riesling wine
230 ml (7¼ fl oz) fish stock
(see page 519)
8 freshwater trout fillets, skinned and
all bones removed
230 ml (7¼ fl oz) thick
(double) cream
chopped fresh parsley, to garnish

One Preheat the oven to moderate 180°C (350°F/Gas 4).

Two In a heavy-based frying pan, melt 50 g (1¼ oz) of the butter over low heat. Add the onion with a pinch of salt and cook, covered, for 15 minutes without colouring, or until soft and translucent. Stir in the mushrooms and 230 ml (7¼ fl oz) water and cook, uncovered, until almost all the liquid has evaporated. Stir in the parsley, season and set aside to cool.

Three In a medium saucepan, melt the remaining butter over low heat and cook the shallots for 3 minutes without colouring. Add the wine and increase the heat to high. Bring to the boil and cook for 5 minutes. Pour in the stock, remove from the heat and set aside to cool.

Four Butter an ovenproof baking dish (which can be put over direct heat) large enough to hold the trout fillets in a single layer. Place a fillet, skinned side down, on a chopping board and sprinkle it with salt and pepper. Place 1–2 spoons of the onion and mushroom mixture onto the wide end of the fillet. Fold the tail end over and place in the buttered dish. Repeat with the remaining fillets, leaving a little space between each one.

Five Pour on the cooled wine and fish stock, place the baking dish on the stovetop and bring the liquid just to the boil. Cover and put in the oven for 5–8 minutes, or until the fish is opaque and feels firm to the touch. Carefully remove the fish on a plate, cover and keep warm while finishing the sauce.

Six Strain the cooking liquid through a fine sieve into a saucepan. Place over medium heat and simmer until reduced in volume by three quarters, to about 60 ml (2 fl oz). Add the cream, simmer for 5 minutes, then season. Arrange the trout fillets on a platter or individual plates, coat with the sauce and sprinkle with the parsley just before serving.

Sole meunière

A stylish classic: the sole is quickly pan-fried, then butter and lemon juice are poured over and the fish is eaten hot with parsley and lemon wedges. Dover sole is recommended for its firm texture and succulence, but any flat fish could be substituted.

Total preparation time 10 minutes
Total cooking time 10 minutes
Serves 4

4 sole fillets, skinned
100 g (3¼ oz) clarified butter or ghee
(see page 520)
100 g (3¼ oz) plain flour, seasoned
100 g (3¼ oz) unsalted butter, cut into
cubes and chilled
1 tablespoon lemon juice
2 teaspoons finely chopped fresh
parsley, to garnish
1 lemon, cut into wedges

One Wash the fish, then dry well on paper towels. In a large frying pan, heat the clarified butter.

Two Place the seasoned flour on a plate and roll the fillets in it to coat thoroughly, then pat off any excess. Place in the pan, skinned side up, and fry for about 2 minutes, turning once, or until lightly golden. Remove and place on hot plates.

Three Drain off the clarified butter used for frying and wipe out the pan with paper towels before returning to the heat. Add the butter to the pan and cook until golden and frothy. Remove from the heat, immediately add the lemon juice and, while still bubbling, spoon or pour over the fish.

Four Garnish with some parsley and serve with the lemon wedges.

Lobster Américaine

This is one of the most famous of all lobster dishes, with the flesh being cooked on the shell in a rich tomato and wine sauce. There is much dispute over the origins of the name—whether it should be 'Armoricaine', the ancient name for Brittany in France, or 'Américaine', after a French chef who had worked in America.

Preparation time 30 minutes
Total cooking time 50 minutes
Serves 4

4 x 500 g (1 lb) live lobsters or
2 x 1 kg (2 lb) live lobsters
100 ml (3¼ fl oz) vegetable oil
45 g (1½ oz) unsalted butter
1 onion, diced
1 carrot, diced
2 celery sticks, diced
150 ml (5 fl oz) dry white wine
2½ tablespoons brandy
500 ml (16 fl oz) fish stock (see page 519)
3 tablespoons tomato paste (purée)
500 g (1 lb) ripe tomatoes, halved and seeded
1 bouquet garni (see page 520)
fresh parsley, to garnish

One Kill the lobster, following to the method in the Chef's techniques on page 524. If you prefer not to do this, ask your fishmonger to do it.

Two Prepare the lobster, following the method in the Chef's techniques on page 525. To fry the lobster claws and tails, heat the oil in a large frying pan and add the claws and tails. Fry quickly, turning with long-handled tongs, until the lobsters change colour from blue to red and the tail flesh shrinks visibly from the shell. Lift onto a plate and continue to prepare the lobster according to the method on page 525.

Three Heat half the butter in the pan and fry the pieces of head shell quickly until the colour has changed, as before. Remove any flesh and set aside. Add the reserved shell from the tail with the onion, carrot and celery and cook for about 5 minutes, or until lightly brown. Add the wine and reduce by half before adding the brandy and stock.

Four Stir in the tomato paste and cook for 1 minute before adding the tomato halves. Cover the pan with a lid and, over gentle heat, cook for 20 minutes, or until the tomatoes are pulpy. While this is cooking, place the reserved coral and tomalley into a blender with the remaining butter and blend until smooth.

Five Remove the lid from the pan, add the bouquet garni and the reserved fried claws and cook for 10 minutes. Lift out the claws and cool before cracking to remove the flesh.

Six Strain the tomato mixture through a sieve into a clean pan, discarding the shell, tomato skins, bouquet garni and diced vegetables. Cook the tomato mixture, stirring occasionally, for about 4 minutes, or until lightly syrupy.

Seven Whisk the coral and tomalley flavoured butter into the sauce until smooth, then add the lobster tail flesh and simmer very gently for 1 minute (if overcooked, the lobster flesh will be tough). Remove the pan from the stove and leave the lobster tail to rest for 5 minutes in the sauce before removing and slicing into round slices. Gently warm the slices in the sauce with all the cracked claw and head meat. To serve, spoon onto hot plates and garnish with the parsley.

CHEF'S TIP *Lobsters generally have two large front claws. Although in some countries crayfish are also called lobsters, they do not have the large front claws.*

LE CORDON BLEU COMPLETE COOK

Sole Véronique with potato galettes

This classic French recipe uses white grapes in a white wine sauce to accompany poached lemon sole. Here the dish is served on crisp potato galettes.

Preparation time 1 hour
Total cooking time 1 hour 15 minutes
Serves 4

POTATO GALETTES
500 g (1 lb) floury potatoes, peeled and cut into even-sized pieces
4 egg whites
clarified butter (see page 520) or ghee, for frying

8 x 85 g (2¾ oz) lemon sole fillets
2 French shallots, finely chopped
100 ml (3¼ fl oz) dry white wine
200 ml (6½ fl oz) fish stock (see page 519)
200 g (6½ oz) seedless white grapes
300 ml (10 fl oz) cream

One To make the potato galettes, place the potatoes in a large pan of salted, cold water. Cover and bring to the boil, then reduce the heat and simmer for about 15–20 minutes, or until the potatoes are tender to the point of a sharp knife. Drain, return to the pan and shake over low heat for 1–2 minutes to remove excess moisture. Mash or push through a fine sieve, season with salt and black pepper and cool.

Two Meanwhile, wash the sole and dry well on paper towels. Fold the skinned side under at each end of the fillets to give eight fillets about 10 cm (4 inches) long. Butter a shallow 30 x 21 cm (12 x 8½ inch) ovenproof dish and sprinkle half the shallots over the base. Place the sole on the shallots, drizzle with one tablespoon each of the wine and stock and season lightly with some salt and black pepper. Cover with plastic wrap and set aside in the refrigerator.

Three Put the grapes in a pan of boiling water and cook for 15 seconds, then drain and plunge them into iced water to cool. Remove from the water, peel away their skins and reserve the grapes and skins separately.

Four Preheat the oven to moderate 180°C (350°F/Gas 4). In a bowl, whisk the egg whites until they hold in stiff peaks. Stir a quarter of the egg white into the potato then, using a spatula or large metal spoon, gently fold in the remaining egg white.

Five Place a 1 cm (½ inch) depth of clarified butter or ghee in a large heavy-based frying pan and place over moderate heat. Lightly oil the inside of an 8 cm (3 inch) round plain pastry cutter and put it in the pan. Place a 5 mm (¼ inch) layer of the potato inside the cutter. Gently loosen around the side with a palette knife and lift the cutter away. Repeat to fill the pan, leaving enough space between the galettes to turn them. Fry for 5 minutes each side, or until golden brown. Drain on crumpled paper towels, then remove to a wire rack in a low oven and keep warm.

Six Place the remaining shallots, wine and stock in a pan. Add the grape skins, bring to the boil, then simmer for about 20 minutes, or until the mixture is syrupy. Meanwhile, bake the sole for 10–12 minutes, or until opaque and cooked through. Stir the cream into the sauce and simmer for 5 minutes, or until syrupy, then strain into a clean pan, discarding the grape skins. Strain the cooking liquid from the fish into the sauce, reduce again to syrupy, then add the grapes and warm through.

Seven To serve, place a galette on each plate, arrange two sole fillets on top and coat with the sauce.

CHEF'S TIP *For a richer finish, mix together 3 tablespoons lightly whipped cream and 1 egg yolk. Coat the sauced fillets with the mixture, then grill to golden brown.*

Marmite dieppoise

A marmite is a covered metal or earthenware pot traditionally used for making soups and stews. This fish soup comes from Dieppe on the Normandy coast of France, which is renowned for its excellent fishing. Dieppoise dishes often include mussels, prawns and mushrooms.

Preparation time 1 hour
Total cooking time 25 minutes
Serves 4

1 large French shallot, chopped
400 ml (12¾ fl oz) white wine
2 sprigs of fresh thyme
1 bay leaf
500 g (1 lb) mussels, scrubbed and debearded (see page 523)
12 large prawns, peeled (see page 522)
12 scallops, cleaned (see page 524)
240 g (7½ oz) monkfish or salmon fillet, skinned and diced
240 g (7½ oz) mushrooms, sliced
300 ml (10 fl oz) thick (double) cream
20 g (¾ oz) fresh parsley, chopped

One Put the shallot, wine, thyme, bay leaf and mussels in a large flameproof pot with a lid. Bring to the boil over high heat. Reduce the heat and simmer, covered, for 2–3 minutes, tossing gently occasionally. Remove the mussels and set aside (discarding any that haven't opened), saving the liquid.

Two Bring the liquid to a simmer and stir in the prawns and scallops. Cover and simmer for 2–3 minutes, or until firm. Remove from the liquid and set aside. Add the fish to the liquid and poach for 5 minutes, or until cooked through. Remove the mussels from their shells.

Three Strain the liquid through muslin or a fine sieve. Place in a pan and bring to the boil. Add the mushrooms and cook until all the liquid has evaporated. Stir in the cream and boil for 5 minutes, or until thick enough to coat a spoon. Add the mussels, prawns, scallops and fish and simmer until hot. Season and gently stir through the parsley before serving.

LE CORDON BLEU ❖ COMPLETE COOK

Salmon, leek and potato gratin

*This wonderful recipe, combining fresh and smoked salmon, is perfect
for a special lunch or supper. A more economical version, also
delicious, could be made using a cheaper fresh fish, or even salt cod.*

Preparation time 20 minutes
Total cooking time 50 minutes
Serves 6

800 g (1 lb 10 oz) floury potatoes
220 g (7 oz) unsalted butter, softened
3 small leeks, thinly sliced
150 g (5 oz) salmon fillet, skinned
*200 g (6½ oz) smoked salmon,
diced*
300 ml (10 fl oz) cream
100 g (3¼ oz) grated Gruyère cheese
40 g (1¼ oz) unsalted butter, chopped
sprigs of fresh dill, to garnish

One Peel the potatoes and place them in a large pan of salted water. Bring to the boil, then reduce the heat and simmer for 20–25 minutes, or until the potatoes are tender to the point of a knife. Drain and finely mash the potatoes, or purée them, following the method in the Chef's techniques on page 536. Mix in half the softened butter, then set the potatoes aside and keep warm.

Two Melt the remaining softened butter in a frying pan over low heat. Gently cook the leeks for 2–3 minutes, without colouring them. Drain the excess butter and spread the leeks evenly in an oval gratin dish. Set aside.

Three Remove any fine bones from the salmon with a pair of tweezers (see page 527). Place the fillet in a steamer basket, then cover and steam for 5–10 minutes, or until the fish changes colour and begins to break apart when pressed with a fork. Break the fish into pieces and mix into the mashed potato with the smoked salmon.

Four Preheat the grill to hot. Bring the cream to the boil in a pan, then stir into the salmon and potato mixture. Mix well and season with salt and pepper to taste. Transfer to the gratin dish and sprinkle with the grated cheese. Dot with the butter and brown under the grill for 2–3 minutes, or until golden. Serve garnished with sprigs of dill.

CHEF'S TIP *To use salt cod in this recipe, rinse and soak it overnight, changing the water several times, then poach in milk with a few sprigs of fresh thyme, a bay leaf and a few garlic cloves until tender. Drain, break into small pieces, then add to the potato mixture.*

Coulibiac

This traditional Russian fish pie is packed with salmon, rice, hard-boiled eggs and mushrooms, then wrapped in puff pastry to form a pillow shape. A great dish for a party, especially when served with warm beurre blanc.

Preparation time 50 minutes
+ 15 minutes refrigeration
Total cooking time 1 hour 40 minutes
Serves 8

55 g (1¾ oz) long-grain rice
4 eggs
50 g (1¾ oz) unsalted butter
6 small spring onions, finely sliced
3 large French shallots, finely chopped
400 g (12¾ oz) mushrooms,
finely chopped
juice of ½ lemon
500 g (1 lb) salmon fillet, skin on
1 quantity puff pastry (see page 542)
2½ tablespoons finely chopped
fresh dill
1 egg yolk
100 g (3¼ oz) fromage frais
or Greek-style yoghurt

COURT BOUILLON
1 small carrot, roughly chopped
1 small onion, roughly chopped
1 bay leaf
4 fresh parsley stalks
1 sprig fresh thyme
6 black peppercorns
2 tablespoons white wine vinegar

One Cook the rice until tender, then drain well. Hard-boil 3 of the eggs for 10 minutes, place in a bowl of iced water to cool quickly, then coarsely grate or finely chop.

Two Melt half the butter in a pan and add the spring onion. Cover and cook for 4 minutes over low heat until soft and translucent. Season and set aside.

Three Melt the remaining butter, add the shallots and cook gently for 2 minutes. Add the mushrooms, lemon juice, salt and black pepper and cook until the mushrooms are dry.

Four To make the court bouillon, place all the ingredients except the vinegar in a pan with 1.5 litres water and a large pinch of salt. Bring to the boil, then simmer, covered, for 15 minutes. Add the vinegar and simmer for 5 minutes.

Five Add the salmon to the court bouillon and poach, covered, for 5 minutes. Remove from the heat, uncover and let the salmon cool in the liquid before transferring to a plate. Remove the flesh in large flakes from the skin and cover with plastic wrap. Discard any skin and bones.

Six Cut the pastry in half and, on a lightly floured surface, roll out one half to a 3 mm (⅛ inch) thick rectangle. Transfer to a baking tray without a lip and trim down to a rectangle big enough

to contain the salmon, about 23 x 35 cm (9 x 14 inches). Wrap and chill the trimmings, layering them flat. Leaving a 2.5 cm (1 inch) border on all sides, spread the rice in the centre of the pastry. Sprinkle with ½ tablespoon of dill, then the salmon, salt and pepper, mushroom mixture, egg and spring onion in separate layers.

Seven Lightly beat the remaining egg and brush over the pastry border. Roll the remaining pastry to about 45 x 30 cm (18 x 12 inches), then pick the pastry up on the rolling pin and place over the filling. Press the edges together to seal the top and bottom, then trim neatly and brush with egg. Roll out the reserved trimmings and cut strips to decorate the top of the pie. Lay them on as a lattice and put the pie in the refrigerator for 10–15 minutes.

Eight Preheat the oven to moderately hot 200°C (400°F/Gas 6). Beat the yolk and remaining egg together and brush over the pie. Wipe off any egg from the tray and make three small holes down the centre of the pie with a skewer. Bake for 30 minutes, until risen, crisp and golden.

Nine Stir the remaining dill into the fromage frais or yoghurt and serve with slices of the Coulibiac.

CHEF'S TIP *For a special dinner, the coulibiac could be served with a beurre blanc sauce (see page 352).*

Sole normande

This classic dish from Normandy was originally prepared by a Parisian chef in the early nineteenth century using cider rather than white wine and braising the fish in cream. Today, the dish usually includes mushrooms and seafood.

Preparation time 1 hour
Total cooking time 1 hour
Serves 4

8 sole fillets, skinned
500 ml (16 fl oz) dry white wine
2 French shallots, chopped
500 g (1 lb) mussels, scrubbed and
debearded (see page 523)
30 g (1 oz) unsalted butter
110 g (3¾ oz) mushrooms, sliced
1 lemon
250 ml (8 fl oz) thick (double)
cream
125 g (4 oz) small cooked prawns,
peeled (see page 522)
1 tablespoon chopped fresh parsley,
to garnish

One Place the sole fillets, skinned side up, on a chopping board. Lightly season with salt and pepper and carefully roll up, starting at the wide end. Secure with a toothpick. Cover with plastic wrap and chill until ready to use.

Two In a large pan, bring the wine and shallots to the boil and then simmer for 5 minutes. Add the mussels, cover and cook for 2–3 minutes. Discard any mussels that do not open. Strain and reserve the liquid. Remove the mussels from their shells, set aside to cool and discard the shells.

Three Preheat the oven to moderately hot 200°C (400°F/Gas 6). In a large pan, melt half the butter, add the mushrooms, a little lemon juice and 60 ml (2 fl oz) water and simmer for 5 minutes. Add the cooking liquid from the mussels and cook until reduced in volume by three quarters. Add the cream and simmer for another 5 minutes, or until the mixture

is thick enough to coat the back of a spoon. Season to taste with salt and white pepper.

Four Grease an ovenproof dish with the remaining butter and place the rolled sole fillets into it. Sprinkle the prawns and the mussels around and coat with the sauce. Cover with foil and bake for 7–10 minutes, then remove the toothpicks, sprinkle with the chopped parsley and serve.

LE CORDON BLEU ✠ COMPLETE COOK

Cioppino

*This superb Italian-sounding dish is said to have been created in
San Francisco by Italian immigrants. A combination of fish and seafood
with tomatoes and herbs, it is delicious served with crusty bread.*

Preparation time 45 minutes
Total cooking time 35 minutes
Serves 6–8

750 ml (24 fl oz) white wine
2 onions, finely chopped
2 bay leaves
4 sprigs of fresh thyme
*1 kg (2 lb) mussels, scrubbed and
debearded (see page 523)*
30 g (1 oz) fresh basil
80 ml (2³/4 fl oz) olive oil
1 green capsicum (pepper), chopped
1 stick celery, chopped
1 carrot, chopped
4 cloves garlic, chopped
*2 tablespoons tomato paste
(purée)*
*3 x 400 g (12³/4 fl oz) cans chopped
Italian tomatoes*
2 x 250 g (8 oz) lobster tails
500 g (1 lb) white fish fillets
500 g (1 lb) crab claws
1 kg (2 lb) large raw prawns
*500 g (1 lb) scallops, cleaned (see
page 524)*
4 cloves garlic, finely chopped
*2 tablespoons extra virgin
olive oil*

One Place the wine, half the onion, one
bay leaf, two sprigs of thyme and the
mussels in a large pan. Cover, bring to
the boil and cook for 5 minutes. Remove
the mussels from the pan with a slotted
spoon and discard any that have not
opened. Strain over a bowl, reserving the
cooking liquid.

Two Separate the leaves from the stems
of basil and set aside. Make a herb
bundle by tying the basil stems,
remaining thyme and bay leaf together
with string.

Three Heat the oil in a large pan and
cook the remaining onion, pepper,
celery, carrot and garlic for 3 minutes.
Add the tomato paste and cook for a
further 2 minutes, stirring regularly.
Add the tomatoes, herb bundle and
mussel liquid to the pan and bring to
the boil. Reduce the heat and simmer for
10 minutes.

Four Meanwhile, with a large sharp
knife, cut each lobster tail into three or
four pieces. Cut the fish into bite-sized
pieces and crack the crab claws with a
nutcracker or mallet. Remove the
mussels from their shells. Peel and
devein the prawns, keeping the tails
intact (see Chef's techniques, page 522).

Five Remove the herb bundle, then add
all the seafood except the mussels to the
pan. Simmer for 10 minutes, add the
mussels and heat through.

Six To make the basil sauce, finely chop
the reserved basil leaves and combine
with the garlic and olive oil. Season the
cioppino to taste, then stir in the basil
sauce and serve with thick slices of
crusty bread.

Seafood pie

A classic family dish, this seafood pie is made with white fish, mussels and prawns in a light wine sauce. It is topped with a purée of potato that is baked to lightly golden in the oven.

Preparation time 50 minutes
Total cooking time 1 hour 10 minutes
Serves 6

500 g (1 lb) mussels, scrubbed and debearded (see page 523)
150 g (5 oz) prawns
60 g (2 oz) unsalted butter
2 French shallots, finely chopped
1 leek, white part only, cut into julienne strips (see Chef's tips)
220 ml (7 fl oz) dry white wine
500 ml (16 fl oz) milk
1 onion, studded with 1 clove
1 bouquet garni (see page 520)
600 g (1 1/4 lb) mixed firm white fish fillets, such as lemon sole, plaice, cod and halibut, skinned and cut into 3 cm (1 1/4 inch) cubes
30 g (1 oz) plain flour
1 kg (2 lb) floury potatoes, peeled and cut into pieces
50 g (1 3/4 oz) unsalted butter, extra
1 egg yolk
4 tablespoons cream
small pinch of ground nutmeg

One Place the mussels in a cool place covered with a damp cloth. Peel and devein the prawns, following the method in the Chef's techniques on page 522.

Two In a pan, melt half the butter over low heat, then add the shallots, cover and cook for 2–3 minutes, or until soft. Add the leek and cook for 2 minutes, uncovered, then add a tablespoon of the wine and simmer until evaporated. Place the mixture in a shallow 28 x 20 cm (11 x 8 inch) ovenproof dish.

Three Place the mussels and remaining wine in a pan, bring slowly to the boil, covered, and cook for 2–3 minutes, or until all the mussels are open. Discard any unopened mussels. Drain, reserving the cooking liquid, then remove the mussels from their shells and scatter into the dish. Strain the liquid through a sieve lined with muslin or a damp piece of paper towel and set aside.

Four Add the milk, onion and bouquet garni to a pan, bring to barely simmering and cook for 5 minutes. Remove the onion and bouquet garni and add the fish, prawns and reserved mussel liquid. Heat to just simmering and poach the seafood for 2 minutes. Drain, reserving the liquid and keeping it hot, and add the seafood to the dish.

Five Melt the remaining butter in a pan over low heat, sprinkle on the flour and cook, stirring, for 1 minute without colouring. Remove from the heat and blend in the hot poaching liquid. Return to medium heat, bring to the boil, stirring constantly, and cook for about 3–4 minutes, or until it thickens and coats the back of a spoon. Season, then pour over the fish. Cover and refrigerate.

Six Preheat the oven to moderate 180°C (350°F/Gas 4). Place the potatoes in a pan of salted, cold water, cover and bring to the boil, then reduce the heat and simmer for 15–20 minutes, or until the potatoes are tender to a sharp knife. Drain, return to the pan and shake over low heat for 1–2 minutes to remove excess moisture.

Seven Purée the potatoes, following the method on page 536, then return to the pan. Beat in the extra butter, yolk and finally the cream. Season with nutmeg, salt and black pepper and spoon into a piping bag with a large star nozzle. Pipe a pattern over the surface of the fish, or spread the potato, then use a fork to peak it. Bake for 30 minutes, or until lightly golden.

CHEF'S TIPS *Julienne strips are vegetables cut to the size and shape of matchsticks.*

poultry

Chicken liver terrine

Chicken livers have a mild flavour and soft creaminess. Take care not to overcook a terrine—this one should be moist and juicy, with the bacon wrapping adding a contrast of flavour and texture.

*Preparation time 35 minutes
+ marinating + resting twice overnight
Total cooking time 1 hour 15 minutes
Serves 4–6*

20 g (³/4 oz) unsalted butter
1 small French shallot, finely chopped
185 g (6 oz) chicken livers, cut in half
315 g (10 oz) pork neck, cubed
1 teaspoon brandy
1 teaspoon port
¹/8 teaspoon five-spice powder
6 rashers bacon
3 tablespoons cream
1 small egg, beaten

One Heat the butter in a pan, add the shallot and heat through for 2 minutes. Remove from the heat, add the livers and pork and stir over very low heat for 3 minutes, or until the meat and liver are warm. Mix in the brandy, port and five-spice, season well and cover with plastic wrap. Cool slightly, then refrigerate overnight.

Two Preheat the oven to very hot 250°C (500°F/Gas 10). Line a 600 ml (20 fl oz) capacity deep terrine with some of the bacon and refrigerate until ready to use. Grind the marinated livers and meat through a meat grinder set with a fine grill or in a food processor. Mix in the cream and egg, spoon into the terrine and cover with the remaining bacon.

Three Bake for 30 minutes, or until the top has begun to brown, then turn the oven to its lowest temperature. Cook for a further 30–40 minutes, or until the tip of a small knife, inserted into the centre of the terrine for a few seconds, comes out hot. Remove from the oven and allow to cool for 20 minutes. Cut a piece of cardboard or wood to just smaller than the tin and cover with foil. Place this directly onto the terrine (inside the edge of the tin), weigh down with heavy cans and refrigerate for 8 hours or overnight.

Four To unmould, first loosen the edges with a knife and then place the terrine in hot water for 30 seconds. Turn over onto a serving dish and lift away the terrine. Slice and serve with small gherkins and salad.

Deep-fried chicken with cumin and sesame

*Sesame seeds give a crisp crunchy batter and
the tangy dipping sauce adds an eastern twist.*

Preparation time 20 minutes
Total cooking time 20 minutes
Serves 4

80 g (2³/4 oz) plain flour
60 g (2 oz) potato flour
1 teaspoon baking powder
2 teaspoons oil
90 g (3 oz) sesame seeds
¹/4 teaspoon ground cumin
3 small skinless chicken breast fillets
oil, for deep-frying

DIPPING SAUCE
¹/2 teaspoon grated fresh ginger
1 teaspoon finely chopped
spring onion
1 tablespoon vinegar
1 tablespoon soy sauce
2 tablespoons tomato ketchup
1 teaspoon sesame oil

One Sift together the flour, potato flour, baking powder and a good pinch of salt into a bowl. Add the oil and whisk while adding 150 ml (5 fl oz) water in a steady stream. Whisk until the batter is smooth, add the sesame seeds and cumin and cover with plastic wrap.

Two To make the dipping sauce, mix together all the ingredients and set aside.

Three Trim the chicken of excess fat and cut lengthways into thin strips. Season to taste, dip in the batter and deep-fry in moderately hot oil at 190°C (375°F) until golden, following the method in the Chef's techniques on page 537. Drain on paper towels and serve immediately with the dipping sauce.

LE CORDON BLEU COMPLETE COOK

Smoked chicken and sun-dried tomato terrine

Terrines are an impressive and elegant way to dress your dinner or buffet table, but a few slices served with a salad would also make an ideal first course or lunch.

Preparation time 1 hour 20 minutes
+ overnight refrigeration if possible
Total cooking time 1 hour 30 minutes
Serves 12

1 smoked chicken, weighing
about 1 kg (2 lb)
4 large chicken legs
2 egg whites
300 ml (10 fl oz) thick (double) cream
100 g (3¼ oz) sun-dried tomatoes,
shredded
100 g (3¼ oz) mixed fresh herbs,
chopped

**BLACK OLIVE AND
CAPER RELISH**
100 g (3¼ oz) pitted black olives,
sliced
100 g (3¼ oz) capers,
roughly chopped
1 clove garlic, chopped
30 g (1 oz) fresh chives, chopped
3 teaspoons olive oil

One With a sharp knife, cut down each side of the breastbone of the smoked chicken, remove the wings and set aside the two breast pieces. Remove the skin and cut away the leg meat from the chicken, discarding the bones. Mince or finely chop the leg meat in a food processor and set aside.

Two With a small sharp knife, scrape the flesh from the raw chicken legs, following the method in the Chef's techniques on page 530. Trim away the fine, shiny, white nerves and tendons—these will not break down during cooking and will spoil the smooth texture of the terrine. Work the raw meat to a fine purée in the food processor, then blend in the egg whites. Transfer to a bowl, cover and refrigerate for 15 minutes. Preheat the oven to warm 160°C (315°F/Gas 2–3).

Three Sit the bowl of puréed chicken over ice and slowly mix in the cream to just blend. Season with salt and pepper. Gently mix in the smoked leg meat, sun-dried tomatoes and herbs.

Four Line the length of the base of a 1.5 litre terrine with a strip of doubled greaseproof paper or foil, to overhang the sides and help you unmould the terrine after cooking. Half-fill the terrine with the chicken mixture, place the smoked chicken breasts on top and cover with the remaining chicken mixture. Cover the terrine with foil, firmly turning under to seal the edges.

Five Place the terrine in a roasting tin and pour enough boiling water into the tin to come halfway up the side of the terrine and make a bain-marie. Bake in the oven for 1½ hours, or until the juices run clear when tested with a skewer. Remove from the roasting tin and leave to cool in the mould. The terrine is best left in the refrigerator overnight to make slicing easier.

Six To make the relish, mix the olives with the capers, garlic and chives, then stir in the olive oil to bind. Loosen the edges of the terrine with a sharp knife, then turn out and cut into 12 slices. Serve with the relish.

CHEF'S TIP *In step 3, it is very important that the cream and meat purée be chilled. If not, there is a risk of the cream splitting. If the cream splits, the smooth light texture of the terrine is spoiled.*

about sun-dried tomatoes...

Sun-dried tomatoes are available completely dried or stored in oil. If you buy the ones stored in oil, rinse them in boiling water to remove any excess oil before you chop them. Semi-dried or sun-blushed tomatoes can also be used for this recipe.

Coronation chicken

Originally created by Rosemary Hume of The Cordon Bleu Cookery School, London,
for the foreign dignitaries at the coronation luncheon of Queen Elizabeth II, this dish now
appears on menus around the world. Here is an updated version of the traditional recipe.

Preparation time *30 minutes + cooling*
Total cooking time *1 hour*
Serves 4

1 chicken, weighing 1.5 kg (3 lb)
1 carrot, sliced
1 onion, halved
1 bouquet garni (see page 520)
6 peppercorns
oil, for cooking
2 French shallots, finely chopped
1 teaspoon curry powder
2 teaspoons tomato paste (purée)
60 ml (2 fl oz) red wine
pinch of sugar
1 slice lemon
few drops of lemon juice
1 tablespoon mango chutney
220 g (7 oz) mayonnaise
3–4 tablespoons lightly whipped cream
chopped spring onion, to garnish

One Place the chicken, carrot, onion, bouquet garni, peppercorns and a pinch of salt in a pan, add enough water to cover and bring to the boil. Reduce the heat and simmer for about 40 minutes, or until tender. Leave the chicken to cool in the liquid. When cold, remove the chicken and discard the skin and bones. Cut the chicken meat into bite-sized pieces and set aside.

Two Heat a little oil in a large saucepan, add the shallot and cook gently for 3–4 minutes. Add the curry powder and continue to cook for 1–2 minutes. Add the tomato paste, wine and 2 tablespoons water and bring to the boil. Add the sugar, salt and pepper, to taste, and the lemon and lemon juice. Reduce the heat and simmer for 5–10 minutes, or until reduced by half. Stir in the mango chutney, strain and cool.

Three Once the mixture has cooled, gradually add to the mayonnaise, to taste. Adjust the seasoning, adding a little more lemon juice if necessary. Stir in the whipped cream and chicken. Garnish with a little spring onion. Delicious served with rice salad.

CHEF'S TIP *For a rice salad to serve with Coronation chicken, mix together 185 g (6 oz) cooked rice with cubes of cooked carrot, strips of red capsicum, sliced celery cooked peas and peeled, seeded and quartered tomatoes. Moisten with a vinaigrette dressing.*

Chicken Kiev

*You can shallow-fry or deep-fry your Kiev to produce
a crisp coating for the chicken. The garlic butter bursts
with succulence and flavour as you cut into the chicken.*

Preparation time 40 minutes
Total cooking time 40 minutes
Serves 4

4 skinless chicken breasts fillets
120 g (4 oz) plain flour, seasoned
3 eggs, beaten
200 g (6½ oz) dried breadcrumbs,
sieved
oil, for cooking and deep-frying

GARLIC BUTTER
150 g (5 oz) unsalted butter
3 cloves garlic, crushed
50 g (1¾ oz) chopped fresh parsley

One Remove the thin fillets (tenderloins) from the underside of the chicken breasts and place on lightly oiled plastic wrap or greaseproof paper. Gently flatten them with a cutlet bat or small heavy pan and put in the refrigerator.

Two To make the garlic butter, soften the butter, then add the garlic, parsley, salt and pepper, and mix well. Spoon the butter along one end of a piece of oiled plastic wrap or damp greaseproof paper and roll it up into a sausage shape, twisting the ends. Refrigerate until firm.

Three Cut a short slit into the top of each chicken breast and make a pocket by cutting just under either side of the slit with the tip of a small sharp knife. Place a slice of garlic butter in each pocket. Place a flattened fillet over the top of each breast to cover the butter.

Four Put the seasoned flour, egg and breadcrumbs in separate dishes. Coat the chicken with the flour, then the egg and finally with the breadcrumbs. Coat again with the egg and breadcrumbs.

Five Preheat the oven to moderately hot 200°C (400°F/Gas 6). To shallow-fry, heat enough oil in a frying pan to come halfway up the sides of the chicken. Cook the Kievs over medium heat for 6 minutes each side, or until golden brown and cooked through. Transfer to a wire rack in the oven for a few minutes to allow the coating to crisp further.

Six To deep-fry, preheat the oil in the deep fryer to low 160°C (315°F) following the method in the Chef's technique on page 537. Fry the Kievs, two at a time, for 8–12 minutes, or until golden brown. Drain on crumpled paper towels. Keep warm in the oven on a wire rack while cooking the rest. Serve with a crisp salad and fresh bread.

Chicken en croûte

These succulent chicken breasts, married with mushrooms and bacon, are encased in crisp plaited pastry. This dish requires a little patience in the making, but the results are spectacular.

*Preparation time 1 hour
+ 40 minutes chilling
Total cooking time 1 hour 30 minutes
Serves 4*

*oil, for cooking
4 skinless chicken breast fillets
30 g (1 oz) unsalted butter
1 French shallot, finely chopped
1 clove garlic, finely chopped
250 g (8 oz) mushrooms, finely chopped
400 g (12¾ oz) puff pastry (see page 542)
4 thin rashers smoked back bacon or pancetta, rind removed
1 egg, lightly beaten*

SAUCE
*4 chicken wings, roughly chopped
1 onion, finely chopped
2 carrots, finely chopped
1 celery stick, finely chopped
1 mushroom, finely chopped
1 bay leaf
1 tablespoon sherry vinegar
100 ml (3¼ oz) dry Madeira or sherry
500 ml (16 fl oz) chicken stock
(see page 519)*

One Heat about 3 tablespoons oil in a frying pan and fry the chicken for 1 minute on each side to seal. Remove from the pan and set aside.

Two Heat the butter in a medium-sized saucepan, add the shallot and garlic, cover with greaseproof paper and a lid and cook gently until transparent and soft. Add the mushrooms and increase the heat. The mushrooms will produce juice, so cook uncovered until dry. Season, then transfer to a plate to cool.

Three Cut the pastry into quarters. Roll out each piece on a lightly floured surface to a 16 x 25 cm (6½ x 10 inch) rectangle. Transfer to a lightly floured baking tray and chill for 20 minutes. Slide off the tray onto a lightly floured work surface and make cuts at 2 cm (¾ inch) intervals down the two short sides of each rectangle. Make the cuts 8 cm (3 inches) long, towards the centre of the rectangle.

Four Place a chicken breast down the centre of each pastry rectangle. Put a quarter of the mushroom mixture on each chicken breast and lightly flatten, then cover with bacon or pancetta, folding round to hold the mushroom in place. Brush the pastry strips with egg. Take the top strip of pastry from one side and place over the chicken. Take the top strip from the other side and place on top, as if to plait. Continue down the chicken, overlapping slightly and leaving small gaps between the plaiting to let the steam escape and the pastry crisp. Trim the strips at the base of the chicken or tuck underneath. Place on a buttered baking tray and chill for 20 minutes. Preheat the oven to moderately hot 200°C (400°F/Gas 6).

Five To make the sauce, add about 3 tablespoons oil to a roasting tin and heat on top of the stove. Add the wings and bake for 30 minutes, or until golden brown. Transfer to the stove top, add the chopped vegetables, bay leaf and vinegar and simmer for 5 minutes, or until reduced by three-quarters and the pan juices are sticky. Add the Madeira or sherry and bring to the boil, add the stock, reduce the heat and simmer gently for 10 minutes, or until reduced by half. Skim frequently with a spoon. Strain into a clean pan and season to taste.

Six Brush the pastry parcels with egg, avoiding the cut edges or they will not rise. Bake for 25–30 minutes, or until golden and crisp. If the underside is not crisp, cover the top with foil and cook a little longer. Serve with the sauce and steamed asparagus spears.

Chicken brochettes with vegetable rice

Brochette is a French word for skewer or kebab and is also the term for this method of cooking. Marinating the chicken before grilling on the skewers makes the meat more tender and flavoursome.

Preparation time 30 minutes
+ refrigeration (1 hour or overnight)
Total cooking time 1 hour
Serves 4

4 skinless chicken breast fillets
1 large red capsicum (pepper),
halved and seeded
12 button mushrooms
1 onion
200 ml (6¹/2 fl oz) corn oil
100 ml (3¹/4 fl oz) soy sauce
juice of 1 lemon
1 onion, chopped
100 ml (3¹/4 fl oz) white wine vinegar
500 ml (16 fl oz) chicken stock
(see page 519)
2 tomatoes, peeled, seeded and diced
(see page 534)
1 teaspoon chopped fresh thyme
30 g (1 oz) capers, rinsed and chopped

VEGETABLE RICE
oil, for cooking
1 onion, finely sliced
200 g (6¹/2 oz) long-grain rice
¹/2 red capsicum (pepper), diced
¹/2 green capsicum (pepper), diced
60 g (2 oz) frozen baby peas, thawed

One Cut each chicken breast into six nuggets. Cut the capsicum into 12 rough squares. Remove the mushroom stalks and discard. Cut the onion in half and then into large pieces to match the capsicum. Thread the chicken, capsicum, mushroom and onion pieces alternately onto the skewers and place in a shallow dish. Mix together the corn oil, soy sauce and lemon juice, spoon over the brochettes and baste well. Cover and refrigerate for at least 1 hour but preferably overnight.

Two To make the vegetable rice, preheat the oven to moderately hot 200°C (400°F/Gas 6). In an ovenproof casserole, heat 2–3 tablespoons oil on the stove top, add the onion and cook gently until transparent but not coloured. With a wooden spoon, stir in the rice and cook for 1 minute. Add 400 ml (12³/4 fl oz) water and bring to the boil, stirring continuously. Season, cover the dish and put in the oven for 15 minutes, or until the rice is tender. Lightly mix in the red and green capsicum and the peas and season to taste. Turn the oven to very low, cover the rice and return to the oven to keep warm.

Three Lift the brochettes from the marinade, reserving the liquid, and grill for 4 minutes on each side, or until the chicken juices run clear when pierced with a skewer. Transfer to a tray, cover and keep warm in the oven.

Four Add the onion to the juices in the grill pan and place over low to medium heat on the stove top, stirring until lightly coloured. Pour on the vinegar and stir until reduced by half. Add the reserved marinade and cook for 2 minutes. Add the stock and cook for a further 10–15 minutes, or until reduced to a syrup. Stir in the tomato, thyme and capers and season to taste. Serve the rice and brochettes with the sauce spooned over the top.

Southern-fried chicken

Crumbed chicken, fried to crisp perfection, is one of the classic dishes from the Deep South of America. A great family favourite for eating with your fingers.

Preparation time 1 hour + marinating
Total cooking time 1 hour
Serves 4

1 chicken, weighing 1.6 kg
(3 lb 3½ oz)
1.2 litres buttermilk
2 tablespoons Tabasco
170 g (5½ oz) plain flour
1 teaspoon paprika
1 teaspoon dried oregano
1 teaspoon salt
½ teaspoon cayenne pepper
2 eggs
2 tablespoons oil
250 g (8 oz) fresh breadcrumbs
30 g (1 oz) unsalted butter
oil, for shallow-frying

One Cut the chicken into eight pieces, following the method in the Chef's techniques on page 528. In a large bowl, combine the buttermilk with the Tabasco and season to taste with salt. Marinate the chicken for at least 1 hour, or preferably overnight.

Two Drain the chicken and pat dry. Mix together the flour, paprika, oregano, salt and cayenne pepper in a dish and use to coat the chicken. Shake off the excess and set the chicken aside.

Three Beat the eggs with the oil and 2 tablespoons water. Dip the chicken pieces into the egg mixture, then roll in the breadcrumbs and press them on well. Place on a plate lined with paper towels. Preheat the oven to slow 150°C (300°F/Gas 2).

Four Heat the butter with about 2.5 cm (1 inch) oil in a large heavy-based frying pan over medium-high heat. Add the chicken pieces, skin side down, and reduce the heat to medium. Cook for about 10 minutes, or until nicely coloured. If necessary, cook in batches— do not overcrowd the pan, and leave enough space between the pieces to ensure even cooking. Turn the pieces over and cook until coloured. Transfer to a baking dish or roasting tin, cover loosely with foil and bake in the oven for 45 minutes. Drain on paper towels and serve immediately.

CHEF'S TIP *You could also make this recipe using 8 chicken drumsticks or thighs rather than a whole chicken.*

LE CORDON BLEU ✤ COMPLETE COOK

Lime-marinated chicken with Mediterranean bread

This refreshing dish combines the flavours of the Mediterranean and the tropics. Lime, yoghurt and coriander blend especially well together and are complemented by a light, crusty bread.

Preparation time 50 minutes
+ rising + marinating
Total cooking time 55 minutes
Serves 4

MEDITERRANEAN BREAD
(SEE CHEF'S TIPS)
440 ml (14 fl oz) lukewarm water
30 g (1 oz) fresh yeast
680 g (1 lb 6 oz) strong or plain flour
140 ml (4½ fl oz) extra virgin olive oil
3 teaspoons salt
100 g (3¼ oz) pitted black olives, roughly chopped
100 g (3¼ oz) sun-dried tomatoes, soaked, drained and roughly chopped (see Chef's tips)

410 g (13 oz) Greek-style yoghurt
2 fresh green chillies, seeded and chopped
2 cloves garlic, chopped
3 tablespoons roughly chopped fresh coriander
grated rind of 3 limes
juice of ½ lime
8 skinless chicken thigh fillets

One To make the Mediterranean bread, combine the warm water and yeast in a small bowl and stir together until smoothly blended. Sieve 440 g (14 oz) of the strong flour into a bowl and make a well in the centre. Pour the yeast and water into the well, followed by the olive oil. Using your hand with fingers slightly apart, gradually begin to draw the flour into the liquid in the well. Continue until all the flour has been incorporated and a loose batter is formed. Beat for 5 minutes in a slapping motion to develop its elasticity and free it from lumps. Clean the sides of the bowl with a scraper, cover with a damp cloth and leave at room temperature to rise for 1–1½ hours, or until doubled in volume.

Two Add the remaining flour, salt, olives and sun-dried tomatoes and mix well. Scrape down the side of the bowl, cover with a fresh damp cloth and leave until doubled in volume.

Three Preheat the oven to moderately hot 200°C (400°F/Gas 6). Lightly butter and flour two medium-sized baking trays. Divide the very soft dough in half (do not be alarmed by the very loose texture—this is quite normal). Be careful not to overhandle the dough or it will lose volume. Place on the trays and, with wet hands, gently pat and shape each piece to a rectangle about 2½ cm (1 inch) thick. Sprinkle with cold water and dust heavily with extra flour. Bake in the oven for 35–40 minutes, or until a skewer inserted into the centre of the bread comes out clean. Transfer to a cooling rack and leave for 20 minutes before serving.

Four For the marinated chicken, combine the yoghurt, chilli, garlic, coriander and lime rind and juice in a blender until smooth. Season with salt and pepper. Place half the mixture in a dish and lay the chicken on top. Cover with the remaining mixture and leave in a cool place for 30 minutes. Arrange the chicken on a baking tray or grill pan. Grill gently, turning frequently, for up to 15 minutes, or until cooked through. Serve with the Mediterranean bread.

CHEF'S TIPS *The Mediterranean bread is a perfect complement to the marinated chicken, but be sure to prepare it well in advance to give time for the dough to rise. The nature of this bread is for it to have an uneven, crusty texture. The olive oil gives the crustiness and not knocking back the dough during rising creates the holes in the loaf.*

If you are using sun-dried tomatoes in oil, there is no need to soak them before draining and chopping.

Roast chicken

Roast chicken is an all-time favourite with many families—the tantalising aroma, crisp golden skin and snowy-white flesh all add up to a traditional Sunday lunch. Use free-range for a wonderful rich flavour.

Preparation time 30 minutes
Total cooking time 1 hour 40 minutes
Serves 4

1 chicken, weighing 1.8 kg (3 lb 10 oz)
3 tablespoons oil
60 g (2 oz) unsalted butter
220 g (7 oz) chicken wings
1 French shallot, chopped
1 tablespoon chopped celery
1 tablespoon chopped carrot
1 tablespoon chopped onion
1 bouquet garni (see page 520)

One Preheat the oven to moderately hot 200°C (400°F/Gas 6). Truss the chicken for roasting by following the method in the Chef's techniques on page 529. Coat the bottom of a roasting tin with a tablespoon of oil. Season the chicken and rub with the remaining oil. Put the chicken on its side in the roasting tin and place the butter on top. Put in the oven and roast, basting every 5 minutes. After 15 minutes, turn the chicken onto its other side, continuing to baste every 5 minutes. After 15 minutes, turn the chicken onto its back and add the chicken wings. Roast, basting as before, for a further 20–30 minutes, or until the juices run clear.

Two Transfer the chicken and wings to an ovenproof plate, cover with foil, set aside and keep warm in a very low oven. Place the roasting tin on the stove top over low heat to clarify the fat. After 10 minutes, without stirring, the fat should be clear. Pour off the excess fat. Strain the chicken wings of excess fat and return to the roasting tin. Add the chopped vegetables and cook for 2 minutes, then add 500 ml (16 fl oz) water and the bouquet garni. Stir to loosen any bits stuck to the roasting tin, then pour into a saucepan. Bring to the boil, reduce the heat and simmer, skimming off the fat occasionally, for about 35 minutes, or until reduced in volume by three quarters. Strain and season with salt and pepper.

Three To serve, remove the string and place the chicken on a platter. Serve the roasting juices in a sauce boat.

CHEF'S TIP *To check that a chicken is cooked doesn't require any fancy gadgets or thermometers. Simply lift the chicken by inserting a carving fork into the cavity and allow the juices to drain. If the juices run clear, the chicken is cooked. If the juices have a pink tinge, give the bird another 5–10 minutes in the oven before testing it again.*

Cider apple chicken with mushroom sauce

The traditional French name for this recipe is Poulet Vallée d'Auge. The Auge Valley is in Normandy and this recipe makes good use of local ingredients: butter, Calvados, cider, cream and apples from the dairy farms and apple orchards.

Preparation time 25 minutes
Total cooking time 1 hour
Serves 4

1 chicken, weighing 1.8 kg (3 lb 10 oz)
60 g (2 oz) unsalted butter
oil, for cooking
60 ml (2 fl oz) Calvados
2 French shallots, finely chopped
500 ml (16 fl oz) cider
150 g (5 oz) button mushrooms, sliced
250 ml (8 fl oz) thick (double) cream
200 g (6½ oz) Golden Delicious apples
50 g (1¾ oz) clarified butter (see page 520)
4 tablespoons chopped fresh parsley

One Cut the chicken into four or eight pieces, following the method in the Chef's techniques on page 528, and season well. Heat half the butter and a little oil in a pan and sauté the chicken in batches, skin side down, until lightly browned. Pour off the excess fat, return all the chicken to the pan, add the Calvados and light with a match to flambé (keep a saucepan lid on one side in case of emergency). Add the shallots and cook gently until softened but not brown. Add the cider, cover and cook for 15 minutes, turning the chicken after 10 minutes.

Two Sauté the mushrooms in the remaining butter, covered, for 4 minutes. Add the mushrooms and cooking juices, and the cream to the chicken and cook for 5 minutes. Remove the chicken and keep warm.

Three Continue cooking the sauce for 10 minutes, or until it is reduced enough to coat the back of a spoon. Adjust the seasoning to taste. Return the chicken to the pan, bring to the boil, reduce the heat and simmer for 2 minutes to heat the chicken through.

Four Core the unpeeled apples and cut across into thin slices. Fry in clarified butter until golden brown on both sides. Garnish the chicken with the apples and the parsley.

Date-stuffed breast of chicken with Madeira sauce

This dish looks impressively complicated but is actually very quick and easy to prepare. The date and pistachio stuffing and rich Madeira sauce prevent the chicken breast from drying out.

Preparation time 45 minutes
Total cooking time 50 minutes
Serves 4

DATE STUFFING
30 g (1 oz) unsalted butter
60 g (2 oz) French shallots, finely chopped
85 g (2³/4 oz) pitted dates
75 g (2¹/2 oz) shelled pistachios, skinned and roughly chopped

4 chicken breasts with skin on (see Chef's tip)
30 g (1 oz) unsalted butter or 1¹/2 tablespoons oil
fresh chervil or parsley, to garnish

MADEIRA SAUCE
250 g (8 oz) French shallots, thinly sliced
200 ml (6¹/2 fl oz) Madeira wine
500 ml (16 fl oz) chicken stock (see page 519)
90 ml (3 fl oz) cream, optional
2 tablespoons chopped fresh chives

One To make the date stuffing, heat the butter in a small pan and cook the shallots over low heat for 4 minutes, or until soft but not coloured. Finely chop all but three of the dates. Remove the shallots from the heat and stir in the chopped dates and pistachios, then set aside to cool. Preheat the oven to moderate 180°C (350°F/Gas 4).

Two Remove the thin fillets (tenderloins) from the underside of the chicken breasts and place them between lightly oiled pieces of plastic wrap. Gently flatten them with a cutlet bat or small heavy-based pan. On the underside of each of the breasts, cut a central horizontal slit to half the depth of the flesh. Slide the knife flat inside the slit and to each side to form a pocket, then fill each pocket with the stuffing. Remove the plastic wrap from the small fillets. Place a fillet lengthways on each breast to cover the filling, bringing the edges of the pocket flesh over to seal, then secure with cocktail sticks by pushing them through across the top of the seal. Season to taste with salt and black pepper.

Three Heat the butter or oil in a large frying pan and place the chicken in the pan, skin side down. Cook over high heat for 4 minutes, or until just golden. Lift the chicken into a baking tray or shallow ovenproof dish and bake, skin side up, for 10–12 minutes, or until the juices from the thickest part of the flesh run clear when pierced with a skewer.

Four To make the Madeira sauce, use the pan and oil the chicken was fried in to cook the shallots over medium-high heat, turning frequently, for 15 minutes, or until golden brown. Tip off any excess fat and pour in three quarters of the Madeira. Bring to the boil, then reduce the heat and simmer for about 3–5 minutes, or until reduced to 2 tablespoons of light syrupy liquid. Add the stock and simmer until reduced by three quarters, then stir in the remaining Madeira and cream, if using. Reduce once again to a light coating consistency. Season with some salt and black pepper, then strain the sauce through a fine sieve into a jug. Stir in the chives, cover and keep warm.

Five Cut the reserved dates lengthways into quarters. Lift the chicken onto a chopping board, remove the cocktail sticks and cut on the diagonal into slices. Lift and fan out on four plates, pour the sauce around and garnish with the dates and a sprig of chervil or parsley. Serve with green vegetables and new potatoes.

CHEF'S TIP *If you can't find chicken breast fillets with skin on, then buy breasts on the bone and, using a small sharp knife, fillet the breast.*

Devilled spatchcock chickens

*The name spatchcock derives from medieval times,
when a traveller would arrive late at an inn and a bird
would be quickly 'despatched' and roasted.*

Preparation time 30 minutes
Total cooking time 1 hour
Serves 4

4 poussins, about 440 g
(14 oz) each
melted butter or oil, for cooking
60 g (2 oz) Dijon or English mustard
60 g (2 oz) fresh breadcrumbs
chopped fresh parsley, to garnish

One Remove the wishbones from the chickens, following the method in the Chef's techniques on page 529, and preheat the oven to moderate 180°C (350°F/Gas 4).

Two To open and flatten the chickens, rinse out the inside cavity, then with the breast side down, use kitchen scissors to cut along each side of the backbone and remove it. Turn the chickens breast side up and push down with the weight of two flat hands to break the breastbone. Tuck the pointed end wing joints under the breast. Run a metal skewer between the two bones of one of the middle wing joints, then through the breast and out through to the wing on the other side. Push another skewer through from one thigh to the other. Lay the chickens flat, breast side up, on an oiled baking tray.

Three Brush the chickens with the butter or oil and season lightly. Place under a low grill to lightly colour, then roast in the oven for 40–50 minutes, or until the juices run clear.

Four Spread the chicken skin evenly with the mustard, sprinkle with breadcrumbs, then drizzle with a little melted butter or oil. Place under a hot grill until golden brown and garnish with the chopped parsley to serve.

LE CORDON BLEU · COMPLETE COOK

Roasted poussins with herb butter

*This is a deliciously simple variation on a plain roast chicken.
Use whichever fresh herbs you have to hand and pick up
the same flavours in the buttery sauce.*

Preparation time 40 minutes
Total cooking time 1 hour 15 minutes
Serves 4

*2 poussins, weighing 440 g
(14 oz) each
90 g (3oz) unsalted butter, softened
3 tablespoons chopped mixed fresh
herbs (tarragon, chervil, parsley)
2 tablespoons oil
3–4 chicken wings
2 tablespoons chopped carrot
2 tablespoons chopped French shallot
2 tablespoons chopped onion
1 tablespoon chopped celery*

One Preheat the oven to moderately hot 200°C (400°F/ Gas 6). Prepare the poussins by gently sliding a finger under the skin at the neck end and loosening the skin from the flesh. Be careful not to tear the skin.

Two In a small bowl, mix together the butter and herbs and season to taste with salt and pepper. Using a piping bag with a small nozzle, pipe about 1½ tablespoons herb butter under the skin of each poussin, using your fingers to spread out the butter as much as possible. If you do not have a piping bag, simply use the handle of a fork or spoon to spread the herb butter under the skin. Truss the poussins for roasting, following the method in the Chef's techniques on page 529. Reserve the remaining herb butter for the sauce.

Three Heat a roasting tin on the stove top over medium-low heat. Add the oil and place the poussins on their side in the tin. Once the oil is hot, place the roasting tin in the oven and roast the poussins for about 10 minutes, basting with the pan juices every 5 minutes. Turn the poussins onto their other side and roast for 10 minutes, basting every 5 minutes. Turn the poussins onto their backs, add the chicken wings and roast for about 10 minutes, or until the poussin juices run clear, basting every 5 minutes.

Four Transfer the poussins and chicken wings to an ovenproof plate, cover with foil and keep warm in a very low oven. Place the roasting tin on the stove top over low heat to clarify the fat, if necessary. After 5–10 minutes, without stirring, the fat should be clear. Pour off the excess fat. Strain the chicken wings of excess fat and return to the roasting tin. Add the vegetables and cook for 2 minutes, then add 500 ml (16 fl oz) water. Stir to loosen the cooking juices from the roasting tin, then pour into a saucepan. Bring to the boil, then reduce the heat to simmer, skimming off the fat. Simmer for 35 minutes, or until reduced by three quarters. Strain into a smaller saucepan, discarding the chicken wings and vegetables. Whisk in the remaining herb butter, season with salt and pepper and pour into a sauce boat. Remove the string and cut the poussins in half. Serve with the sauce.

LE CORDON BLEU ✠ COMPLETE COOK

Roast turkey with bread sauce and gravy

The classic Christmas dinner: a golden turkey with bread sauce and gravy.
The turkey needs about 2 hours cooking time and can then sit for up to
45 minutes while the juices seep back into the meat to keep it moist.

Preparation time 35 minutes
Total cooking time 2 hours 50 minutes
+ 30 minutes standing
Serves 8

1 x 6 kg (12 lb) turkey, plus the neck
from the giblets if available
105 ml (3½ fl oz) vegetable oil
watercress, to garnish

GRAVY
1 small onion, roughly chopped
1 small carrot, roughly chopped
2 celery sticks, roughly chopped
30 g (1 oz) plain flour
500 ml (16 fl oz) chicken stock (see
page 519)

BREAD SAUCE
600 ml (20 fl oz) milk
½ onion, studded with 3–4 cloves
1 bouquet garni (see page 520)
2 cloves garlic, peeled and lightly
bruised
105 g (3½ oz) fresh white
breadcrumbs
grated fresh nutmeg
2½ tablespoons cream or 45 g (1½ oz)
unsalted butter, optional

One Clean the turkey inside and out, removing any feathers. With a sharp knife, cut off and reserve the end wing joints. Lift up the flap of skin at the neck and, using a small sharp knife, remove the wishbone following the method in the Chef's technique on page 529. Tie the legs together with string. Preheat the oven to moderate 180°C (350°F/Gas 4).

Two Place a large roasting tin over medium heat and heat the oil. Add the end wing joints and neck and cook until lightly browned, then arrange the turkey on top and bake for 1½–2 hours, basting with the juices and oil every 20 minutes. If the turkey begins to overbrown, cover with foil. The turkey is cooked if the juices run clear when you pierce a leg and thigh with a skewer. If pink, continue roasting until the juices are clear. Transfer the turkey to a large plate and leave in a warm place.

Three To make the gravy, tip off the excess fat from the pan, retaining about a tablespoon with all the juices. Add the onion, carrot and celery and cook over moderate heat, stirring occasionally, for 3–5 minutes, or until tender. Sprinkle on the flour, then stir in to mix evenly and cook for 1 minute. Add the stock gradually and stir over low heat to produce a smooth texture. Bring to the boil, then reduce the heat and simmer for 10 minutes. Strain, skim off the excess fat and season with some salt and black pepper.

Four To make the bread sauce, pour the milk into a small pan, add the onion, bouquet garni and garlic and bring slowly just to the boil. Remove from the heat and stand for 20–30 minutes. Strain and discard the flavourings, then return the milk to the pan and bring to the boil. Whisk in the breadcrumbs to produce a thick sauce and season with the nutmeg and some salt and black pepper. Stir in the cream or butter. Serve immediately, as the sauce will thicken on standing.

Five Carve the turkey (see the Chef's techniques on page 531). Serve with the bread sauce, gravy, stuffing and other traditional accompaniments.

about turkeys...

There are now several varieties of turkey on the market as well as the more common white-feathered variety found in most supermarkets and butchers. For a more flavoursome bird, try a Norfolk black or Cambridge bronze turkey, both of which can usually be ordered from good butchers.

Breast of duck with winter vegetables

This would be a great alternative to roast turkey for a small, grown-up Christmas lunch, especially if you don't want lots of leftovers. Delicious served with a home-made cranberry sauce.

Preparation time 40 minutes
Total cooking time 35 minutes
Serves 4

4 duck breasts, about 185 g (6 oz) each
100 g (3¼ oz) parsnips, cut into matchsticks
120 g (4 oz) small Brussels sprouts
155 g (5 oz) celeriac, cut into large cubes
100 g (3¼ oz) sweet potato, cut into large cubes
80 ml (2¾ fl oz) vegetable oil
155 g (5 oz) unsalted butter
120 g (4 oz) tinned chestnuts, halved
4 French shallots, chopped
220 ml (7 fl oz) balsamic vinegar
220 ml (7 fl oz) chicken stock
(see page 519)
sprigs of fresh rosemary, to garnish

One Remove any feathers or stubble from the duck breasts, keeping the skin intact. Using a small, sharp knife, trim away and discard any shiny white skin or sinew from the flesh side, then pat dry on paper towels. Lightly score a crisscross pattern in the skin to allow fat to run out during cooking, then season with salt and black pepper.

Two Bring a small pan of water to the boil and separately cook the parsnip for 1 minute, then the sprouts, celeriac and sweet potato for 2 minutes, or until just tender. Lift each out with a slotted spoon into a colander and run a few drops of cold water through each layer to stop the cooking. Drain well.

Three Heat half the oil in a large frying pan, add half the butter and, when melted and foaming, add the chestnuts and drained vegetables and fry for 7 minutes, or until golden. Season with salt and black pepper, remove from the pan and keep warm.

Four Heat the remaining oil and butter in the frying pan and add the duck breasts, skin side down. Cook over medium heat for 7 minutes, then turn over and cook for a further 2–3 minutes, or until the skin is crisp and the duck flesh succulent but still slightly pink in the centre.

Five Remove the duck from the pan and set aside in a warm place. Tip the excess fat from the pan, leaving about 1 teaspoon behind with any duck juices. Add the shallots and cook gently for 3 minutes, or until soft, then pour in the balsamic vinegar and boil for 1–2 minutes, or until reduced by one third. Add the stock and cook for 3–4 minutes, or until reduced again by one third. Season with some salt and black pepper and strain the sauce into a jug and keep warm.

Six To serve, slice the duck breasts diagonally into thin slices and serve with the vegetables and sauce. Garnish with small sprigs of rosemary and accompany with cranberry sauce or a chutney.

CHEF'S TIP *The duck breasts may also be served whole, especially if you need to keep them warm while eating a first course.*

Stuffed chicken breast with cucumber

The cucumber's origins date back to Roman times and with its cool and refreshing qualities it is included in many of today's recipes. This dish is beautifully light and brings a taste of summer all year round.

Preparation time 35 minutes
+ 20 minutes chilling
Total cooking time 40 minutes
Serves 6

1 chicken maryland (leg quarter),
skinned
1 egg white
185 ml (6 fl oz) thick (double) cream
30 g (1 oz) chopped mixed fresh herbs
6 skinless chicken breast fillets,
about 185 g (6 oz) each
1 telegraph cucumber
3 French shallots, finely chopped
100 ml (3¼ fl oz) dry white wine
500 ml (16 fl oz) chicken stock
(see page 519)
410 ml (13 fl oz) thick (double) cream,
extra

One Cut the flesh from the chicken maryland, scraping it from the bone (see page 530), and purée in a food processor. Lightly beat the egg white and add just over half of it to the chicken (discard the remainder). Season with salt and pepper, then use the pulse button to mix in the cream and herbs. Do not overprocess or the cream may split. Cover and chill for 15–20 minutes to firm up slightly.

Two Remove the thin fillets (tenderloins) from the underside of the chicken breasts and place on lightly oiled plastic wrap or greaseproof paper. Gently flatten them with a cutlet bat or small heavy-based pan and store in the refrigerator.

Three Make a short slit on the top of each chicken breast and make a pocket by cutting just under either side of the slit with the tip of a small sharp knife. Using a spoon or piping bag, fill each pocket with the prepared chicken purée; do not overfill or it will burst its shape in cooking. Place a flattened fillet over the top of each chicken breast to completely cover the chicken purée. Wrap each breast in buttered foil, twisting the ends tightly to seal. Poach in gently simmering water for 20–30 minutes. Remove from the heat and leave to rest in the hot poaching liquid.

Four Cut the unpeeled cucumber in half lengthways and, using the point of a teaspoon, scrape out the seeds. Cut three quarters of the cucumber into 5 cm (2 inch) lengths and cut into strips about the thickness of a little finger. Blanch in a small pan of boiling salted water for 2–3 minutes, rinse under cold water and drain. Roughly chop the remaining cucumber and set aside.

Five To make the sauce, place the shallots, wine and chicken stock in a wide pan and quickly bring to the boil. Boil for 5 minutes, or until it has reduced to a light syrupy consistency. Add the extra cream and boil until the mixture thickens slightly. Add the chopped cucumber and boil for a further 5 minutes. Transfer the sauce to a blender or food processor and purée well. Season with salt and pepper and strain through a sieve.

Six Serve the chicken breasts, either whole or sliced, with the cucumber strips and sauce.

Duck à l'orange

The rich, moist meat of a duck is perfectly complemented by the sharpness of oranges in this classic French recipe. You can prepare the orange sauce in advance, then put the dish together quickly just before serving.

Preparation time 30 minutes
Total cooking time 1 hour 45 minutes
Serves 4

4 oranges
1 lemon
30 g (1 oz) unsalted butter
180 g (5¾ oz) caster sugar
1 tablespoon Grand Marnier, optional
500 ml (16 fl oz) duck or
chicken stock (see page 519)
4 duck breasts, about 200 g
(6½ oz) each
1 teaspoon arrowroot
chopped fresh chervil, to garnish

One Using a peeler, thinly pare the coloured outer layer of rind from two of the oranges and the lemon. Then, with a small, sharp knife, cut away the white pith and discard it. Chop the orange and lemon flesh and set aside in a small bowl. Heat the butter in a pan, add the orange and lemon rind and toss gently for 2–3 minutes over low heat. Add 80 g (2¾ oz) of the caster sugar, increase the heat to medium and cook until the sugar has melted and just caramelised to a light golden brown. Stir in the chopped orange and lemon flesh and the Grand Marnier and cook gently until the juice from the flesh has evaporated and the pan is dry.

Two Pour in the duck or chicken stock and stir to combine. Bring to the boil, reduce the heat, cover and simmer for 1 hour. Strain through a fine sieve, discarding the rind and remnants of the fruit, then cover the sauce and set aside.

Three Thinly pare the rind from the remaining two oranges, without the white pith, into long strips. Put into a pan, cover with cold water and bring slowly to the boil. Drain the rind, refill the pan with cold water and repeat this procedure twice more to soften the rind and to remove any bitterness. With a small sharp knife, cut the rind into thin, needlelike shreds, about 1 mm (1/16 inch) thick, and set them aside. Put 100 ml (3¼ fl oz) water and the remaining sugar into a small pan and slowly bring

to the boil, stirring to dissolve the sugar. Add the shreds of peel and cook gently for 20 minutes to 'candy' the rind. Lift the rind from the syrup using a fork and place on an overturned sieve to drain, taking care to separate the strands.

Four Heat a wide, shallow pan over medium-high heat. Season the duck breasts with salt and freshly ground black pepper, then place them in the hot pan, skin side down, and cook until most of their fat has melted and run out, and the skin is crisp and brown. Turn the breasts over and cook briefly for 1–2 minutes on the second side. Remove from the pan, cover and allow to rest for 5–10 minutes before serving.

Five Reheat the sauce to boiling. In a small bowl, mix the arrowroot with 1 tablespoon water, stir in a little of the hot sauce, then pour back into the pan and stir the sauce to the boil. The milky appearance of the arrowroot mixture will become clear as it comes to the boil. Check the thickness of the sauce; it should coat the back of a spoon. Add a little more arrowroot and water if necessary, or pour in a few drops of water or stock if too thick. If too sweet, add a little lemon juice. Season to taste.

Six To serve, cut each breast into slices and fan out on a warm plate. Drizzle the sauce around the plate and garnish with a sprinkling of the candied citrus rind and some chervil.

Chicken cacciatore

*Literally meaning 'hunter-style' chicken in Italian, this ever popular
dish combines the flavours of mushrooms, capsicums
and onions with herbs in a rich tomato sauce.*

Preparation time 30 minutes
Total cooking time 1 hour
Serves 4

3 tablespoons olive oil
1 chicken, weighing 1.8 kg (3 lb 10 oz),
cut into 8 pieces (see page 528)
2 onions, thinly sliced into rings
1 clove garlic, finely chopped
100 g (3¼ oz) button mushrooms,
thinly sliced
1 small green capsicum (pepper),
thinly sliced
3 tablespoons tomato paste (purée)
185 ml (6 fl oz) dry white wine
400 g (12¾ oz) canned Italian
tomatoes
½ teaspoon dried rosemary
½ teaspoon dried oregano

One Heat the oil in a large frying pan.
Season the chicken, then fry, skin side
down, for 5 minutes. Turn and brown
on the other side. Remove and set aside.

Two Add the onion to the pan and cook
for 5 minutes, then add the garlic,
mushrooms and capsicum. Cook for a
further 3–4 minutes, or until the onions
are soft and golden. Mix in the tomato
paste and cook for 1–2 minutes, then
add the white wine. Bring to the boil,
stirring, then add the tomatoes, breaking
them down with a wooden spoon. Add
the rosemary, oregano and chicken.
Season to taste, cover and simmer for
20 minutes, stirring occasionally.

Three Check that the chicken is tender—
if not, cover and cook for 10 minutes
longer—then transfer to a serving plate.
If the sauce appears too liquid, boil,
uncovered, for 5 minutes. Season and
pour over the chicken before serving.

Stuffed chicken breast with celeriac purée

*A perfect combination of delicate and robust flavours
with a syrupy mango chutney sauce—the finished dish
is even greater than the sum of its delicious parts.*

Preparation time 40 minutes
Total cooking time 1 hour
Serves 4

STUFFING
2 chicken thighs
75 g (2½ oz) Greek-style yoghurt
2 tablespoons chopped celery

300 g (10 oz) celeriac, peeled and
chopped
few drops of lemon juice
3 tablespoons Greek-style yoghurt
4 skinless chicken breast fillets,
about 120 g (4 oz) each
1 tablespoon oil
1 tablespoon mango chutney
2 tablespoons sherry vinegar
500 ml (16 fl oz) chicken stock
(see page 519)
20 g (³/4 oz) unsalted butter
2 tablespoons each of diced carrot,
onion, celery and apple

One To make the stuffing, remove the skin from the thighs and scrape the meat from the bones, reserving the bones. Weigh 200 g (6½ oz) of the meat (discard any left over) and work until smooth in a food processor. Add the yoghurt, process until combined and transfer to a bowl. Add the celery and season. Mix and set aside.

Two Add the celeriac and lemon juice to a pan of boiling salted water and simmer for 20 minutes, or until the celeriac is tender. Drain, return to the pan and shake over the heat for 1 minute. Purée in a food processor with the yoghurt, season to taste and keep warm.

Three Preheat the oven to moderately hot 190°C (375°F/Gas 5). Cut a slit in the side of each chicken breast, about two thirds of the way through, and spoon in the stuffing, avoiding overfilling. Heat the oil in an ovenproof shallow pan and lightly brown the chicken breasts. Add the thigh bones to the pan and bake in the oven for 10 minutes. Remove the breasts, set aside and keep warm. Pour off the fat from the pan, then add the chutney and vinegar and cook on the stove top until syrupy. Add the stock and cook for 10 minutes, or until reduced by a third. Season to taste with salt and freshly ground black pepper, strain and set aside.

Four Melt the butter in a small pan, add the carrot, onion and celery and cook gently for 5 minutes, or until softened but not coloured. Add the apple and cook for 2 minutes. Spoon the vegetables onto serving plates and top with the chicken breasts and sauce. Serve with the celeriac purée.

LE CORDON BLEU COMPLETE COOK

Roast quail

This small game bird makes a lovely choice for a special dinner, with a whole quail for each guest. Here they are stuffed with a rice and bacon filling and served with a wine sauce.

Preparation time 1 hour
Total cooking time 1 hour
Serves 4

RICE AND BACON STUFFING
30 g (1 oz) unsalted butter
1 onion, finely chopped
85 g (2³/4 oz) basmati rice
55 g (1³/4 oz) speck or streaky bacon, diced
1 tablespoon chopped fresh parsley
2 teaspoons sultanas or raisins

4 quails
1 tablespoon peanut (groundnut) oil
45 g (1¹/2 oz) unsalted butter

WINE SAUCE
30 g (1 oz) unsalted butter
2 French shallots, finely chopped
100 ml (3¹/4 fl oz) sweet white wine, such as Sauternes
250 ml (8 fl oz) chicken or veal stock (see pages 518-9)

One To make the stuffing, melt the butter in a pan, add the onion and cook, covered, over low heat for 5 minutes, or until soft and translucent. Add the rice and 140 ml (4¹/2 fl oz) water. Bring to the boil, then reduce the heat and cook, covered, for 15–20 minutes, or until the rice has absorbed all the water. Remove from the heat and set aside. Heat a small heavy-based pan, add the speck or bacon and dry-fry until golden brown. Add to the rice with any fat that has run out. Stir in the parsley and sultanas, season with salt and black pepper, then set aside to cool.

Two Bone the quails following the method in the Chef's techniques on page 530. Preheat the oven to moderately hot 200°C (400°F/Gas 6). Lay the boned quails out flat, skin side down, season lightly with salt and black pepper, then spoon the stuffing into the centre of each bird. Draw the neck skin down over the stuffing and the sides in to cover. Hold the two cut edges of skin and zigzag a cocktail stick through their length to hold them together. Turn the quail over and, using the side of your little finger, gently plump the body cavity and make a division between it and the legs to give a good shape. Tuck the wing tips under at the neck end and pull the ends of the legs together by skewering through the thighs with a cocktail stick.

Three Heat the oil in a baking tray over medium heat, add the butter and, when melted and foamy, put in the quails, breast-side-down, and the reserved carcass bones. Turn to brown the quails and bones evenly on all sides, then bake for 15 minutes, basting every 5 minutes with the pan juices. Lift the quails and bones onto a plate and rest for 5 minutes.

Four To make the wine sauce, melt the butter in a pan, add the shallots and roasted quail bones and cook for about 1 minute, then add the wine and cook for 5 minutes, or until the liquid has reduced by about three quarters. Pour in the stock and continue to reduce by half. Skim off any excess fat from the pan, then strain the sauce and season with salt and freshly ground black pepper. Cover the surface with a piece of plastic wrap to stop the sauce from forming a skin and keep warm.

Five To serve, remove and discard the cocktail sticks, cut off the wing tip joints and place the birds on a serving platter or plates. Spoon the sauce around and serve with vegetables.

CHEF'S TIP *Quails vary in size, so if you have some stuffing left over, place it in a lightly buttered small ovenproof dish, cover with buttered foil and cook in the oven with the quails.*

Chicken casserole with mushrooms and onions

The lovely flavours of the onions, bacon and mushrooms combine perfectly
with the chicken to produce this popular casserole. The dish will
cook slowly in the oven, leaving you time to spend on other things.

Preparation time 25 minutes
Total cooking time 1 hour 20 minutes
Serves 4–6

12 pearl or pickling onions
60 g (2 oz) streaky bacon, rind
removed and cut into
1 cm (1/2 inch) strips
90 g (3 oz) clarified butter (see
page 520)
1.5 kg (3 lb) chicken, cut into 8 pieces
(see page 528)
100 g (31/4 oz) button mushrooms,
quartered or whole if very small
30 g (1 oz) plain flour
600 ml (20 fl oz) chicken stock
(see page 519)
1 bouquet garni (see page 520)
chopped fresh parsley, to garnish

One Preheat the oven to warm 170°C (325°F/Gas 3). Place the onions in a small pan with the bacon strips, cover with cold water and bring to the boil. Drain and rinse with cold water. Melt 60 g (2 oz) of the butter in a 2.5 litre deep flameproof casserole dish on the stove. Add the chicken pieces, in batches, skin side down, and fry for 10 minutes, or until well browned. Remove from the pan and pat dry with paper towels.

Two Tip off the excess fat from the casserole dish, leaving 2 tablespoons, then add the bacon, onions and mushrooms. Fry for 3 minutes, or until lightly browned, then remove. Melt the remaining butter in the casserole dish, add the flour and stir with a wooden spoon, scraping the base of the pan. Cook for 3 minutes, or until lightly

golden. Gradually add the chicken stock and mix continuously until smooth and heated through. Do not boil.

Three Return the chicken to the pan with the bouquet garni, season with salt and pepper and place the bacon, onions and mushrooms on top. Bring just to the boil, cover and bake for 45 minutes, or until the chicken is tender and, when pierced, the juices run clear, not pink.

Four Transfer the chicken to a serving dish, then with a slotted spoon, lift out the bacon and vegetables and sprinkle over the chicken. Cover to keep warm and, if necessary, reduce the sauce to a syrupy consistency. Season the sauce to taste and pour over the chicken. Sprinkle with the parsley and serve with rice, pasta, dumplings or boiled potatoes.

Tarragon and tomato chicken casserole

*This recipe comes from Lyon, France's third largest city
and its gastronomic capital, situated close
to the Burgundy vineyards.*

Preparation time 20 minutes
Total cooking time 45 minutes
Serves 4

1 chicken, weighing 1.2 kg (2 lb 6½ oz)
oil or butter, for cooking
200 ml (6½ fl oz) tarragon vinegar
(see Chef's tip)
15 g (½ oz) unsalted butter, softened
15 g (½ oz) plain flour
1 kg (2 lb) tomatoes, peeled, seeded
and cut into wedges (see page 534)
fresh tarragon, to garnish

One Cut the chicken into four or eight pieces, following the method in the Chef's techniques on page 528, and season well. Heat a little oil or butter in a frying pan and brown the chicken, in batches, on all sides, skin side down first. Remove the chicken and pour off any excess oil from the pan.

Two Return all the chicken to the pan and add half the tarragon vinegar. Cover and simmer for 10 minutes. Turn the chicken, cover and cook for 10 minutes, or until the juices run clear. Remove the chicken and keep the sauce warm.

Three Put the remaining vinegar in a pan and boil for 4 minutes. Mix the softened butter and flour, whisk into the reduced vinegar, then whisk this into the sauce. Return the chicken to the sauce, add the tomato and simmer for 10 minutes, or until the sauce just coats a spoon. Season and sprinkle with the chopped tarragon.

CHEF'S TIP *Make tarragon vinegar by putting a sprig in a bottle of red or white wine vinegar. After a week, strain out the tarragon. Other herbs do not usually have a strong enough flavour for this.*

Chicken fricassee with spring vegetables

*The word fricassee is French in origin and may have been
a marriage of two culinary terms: 'frire', which means to fry,
and 'casse', meaning ladle or dripping pan.*

Preparation time 25 minutes
Total cooking time 1 hour
Serves 4

1 chicken, weighing 1.8 kg (3 lb 10 oz)
30 g (1 oz) plain flour, seasoned
oil, for cooking
35 g (1¼ oz) unsalted butter
6 French shallots, thinly sliced
100 ml (3¼ fl oz) dry white wine
250 ml (8 fl oz) chicken stock
(see page 519)
1 bouquet garni (see page 520)
1 egg yolk
150 g (5 oz) sour cream or crème
fraîche
300 g (10 oz) baby carrots
300 g (10 oz) baby turnips
150 g (5 oz) large spring onions
1 teaspoon sugar
200 g (6½ oz) snow peas (mangetout),
topped and tailed
250 g (8 oz) asparagus
100 g (3¼ oz) button mushrooms

One Cut the chicken into eight pieces, following the method in the Chef's techniques on page 528. Coat the chicken pieces in the seasoned flour, shaking off and reserving the excess. Heat a little oil in a large frying pan over medium heat, add 15 g (½ oz) of the butter and cook the chicken quickly to seal without colouring; remove from the pan and set aside. Lower the heat, add the shallots to the pan and cook slowly, without colouring, until softened. Stir in the reserved flour, then pour in the wine, stirring until the mixture boils and thickens. Reduce the heat and simmer for 2 minutes, then stir in the stock and bouquet garni. Return the chicken to the pan, cover and simmer for 15 minutes. Remove the wings and breast meat, keeping them covered and warm, and cook for a further 5 minutes. Remove the chicken thighs and legs, leaving the cooking liquid in the pan.

Two Increase the heat and let the liquid boil for 5–10 minutes, or until reduced by half, skimming off the excess fat with a spoon. Mix the egg yolk with a tablespoon of sour cream in a bowl. Stir the remaining sour cream into the pan and bring to the boil, then simmer for 2 minutes. Remove from the heat, pour a little hot sauce onto the egg yolk mixture, blend and return to the pan, whisking or stirring until heated (do not allow to boil). Strain, season to taste and set aside.

Three Place the carrots, turnips and spring onions in separate small pans with just enough water to cover. Add a small pinch of salt, sugar and a third of the remaining butter to each pan, then press on buttered greaseproof paper to cover. Cook gently until the water has nearly evaporated and the vegetables are cooked and shiny, shaking the pan occasionally. Remove to a lightly buttered dish, arrange in separate piles and keep warm.

Four Cook the snow peas, asparagus and mushrooms in salted boiling water for 3–5 minutes, or until tender but still keeping a crisp bite. Drain well.

Five Arrange a piece of chicken breast and dark meat on each serving plate and coat with the sauce. Serve with the cooked vegetables.

Roasted duck with turnips

Roasting a duck on each side before turning it onto its back will ensure the breast fillets do not dry out. The salty bacon and sweetened turnips perfectly complement this succulent dish.

Preparation time 40 minutes
Total cooking time 1 hour 40 minutes
Serves 4

1.4 kg (2 lb 13 oz) duck, trussed
(ask your butcher to do this)
oil, for cooking
60 g (2 oz) unsalted butter,
softened
200 g (6¹/2 oz) duck trimmings
(wings or necks), chopped
1 kg (2 lb) turnips
300 g (10 oz) bacon, cut into 1 cm
(¹/2 inch) cubes
20 g (³/4 oz) unsalted butter
1 teaspoon sugar
1 French shallot, chopped
1 tablespoon chopped celery
1 tablespoon chopped carrot
1 tablespoon chopped onion
750 ml (24 fl oz) chicken stock
(see page 519)
1 bouquet garni (see page 520)

One Preheat the oven to moderately hot 200°C (400°F/Gas 6). Coat a roasting tin with 2 tablespoons of oil. Season the duck, rub it all over with oil and place it on its side in the pan. Dot with the softened butter, transfer to the oven and roast for 20 minutes, basting every 5 minutes. Turn the duck onto its other side and roast for 20 more minutes, basting as before. Turn the duck on its back, add the duck trimmings, then roast and baste for another 15 minutes.

Two Peel the turnips and use a melon-baller to scoop the flesh into little balls. Place the balls in cold water until ready to use.

Three In a frying pan, heat some oil and brown the bacon over medium heat.

Strain and set aside. Drain and dry the turnips; place in the pan with the butter, sugar and some salt. Cover with cold water and cook over high heat until evaporated. Roll the turnips until coated and shiny. Remove from the heat, add the bacon and set aside.

Four Remove the duck from the roasting pan; cover and keep warm. Remove and drain the trimmings. Drain the pan of all but 2 tablespoons of the oil and duck juices and place over low heat for 10 minutes, or until the juices are sticky and the fat is clear.

Five Add the trimmings and chopped vegetables and cook for 2 minutes. Add the stock and bouquet garni; stir well and pour into a pan. Bring to the boil, reduce the heat and simmer, skimming occasionally, for 20–30 minutes, or until the sauce is reduced by half. Strain, discarding the solids; season with salt and black pepper and keep warm.

Six Remove the string and place the duck on a platter. Reheat the bacon and turnips and arrange around the duck. Drizzle half the sauce over the bacon and turnips and serve the remaining sauce on the side.

CHEF'S TIP *For instructions on carving the duck, follow the Chef's techniques for carving turkey on page 531.*

LE CORDON BLEU COMPLETE COOK

Chicken chasseur

This classic French pan-fried chicken with a mushroom sauce is easy to prepare and will fully satisfy any guest. The recipe may be traditional but it's also versatile—try adding onions, wild mushrooms, tomatoes, button onions or smoked bacon to the sauce. Delicious with crusty bread or roast potatoes.

Preparation time 30 minutes
Total cooking time 1 hour 30 minutes
Serves 4

1 chicken, weighing 1.2 kg (2 lb 6½ oz), giblets optional
410 ml (13 fl oz) chicken stock (see page 519)
oil, for cooking
150 g (5 oz) button mushrooms, sliced
1 large French shallot, finely chopped
25 ml (¾ fl oz) brandy
25 ml (¾ fl oz) white wine
2–3 large sprigs fresh tarragon
2–3 sprigs fresh chervil

One Preheat the oven to moderately hot 200°C (400°F/Gas 6). Cut the chicken into four or eight pieces, following the method in the Chef's techniques on page 528, then roughly cut up the remaining carcass with a knife or kitchen scissors.

Two Put the carcass pieces and giblets, if using, into a roasting tin and roast for 25 minutes, or until browned. Remove from the oven and add the stock. Use a wooden spoon to loosen any bits stuck to the tin and simmer gently on the stove top for 30 minutes. Strain and reserve the liquid. Skim off any excess fat.

Three On the stovetop, heat a little oil in the roasting tin, add the chicken pieces, skin side down, and brown quickly and lightly on both sides. Transfer to the oven to finish cooking: the legs will need 20 minutes, the breast and wings 15 minutes. Check that the chicken is cooked by piercing with a fork or fine skewer—the juices should run clear. Remove the chicken from the tin and keep warm.

Four Pour the excess fat from the tin, leaving 1 tablespoon and any chicken juices. Reheat on top of the stove, then add the mushrooms and cook until lightly coloured. Add the shallot and cook without browning. Increase the heat if necessary and, when the tin is very hot, add the brandy. Bring to the boil and light with a match to flambé. Add the wine and reduce the heat to simmer for 1–2 minutes, or until reduced by half. Add the reserved chicken stock and reduce for 4–5 minutes. Season to taste. Finely chop the herbs and add to the sauce—do not allow to boil again. Spoon over the chicken to serve.

Coq au vin

The long list of ingredients is not as daunting as it appears. The chicken is marinated overnight in wine, vegetables and herbs to tenderise and flavour it, and the dish can quickly be put together the next day. This traditional recipe originated in the Burgundy region, famous for its fine red wines.

*Preparation time 50 minutes
+ overnight marinating
Total cooking time 2 hours
Serves 6–8*

MARINADE
*1 onion, chopped
1 carrot, chopped
5 juniper berries
10 peppercorns
1 clove
1 clove garlic
2 litres red wine
50 ml (1¾ fl oz) brandy
30 ml (1 fl oz) red wine vinegar
1 bouquet garni (see page 520)*

*3 kg (6 lb) chicken pieces
clarified butter or oil, for cooking
45 g (1½ oz) plain flour
800 ml (26 fl oz) chicken stock
(see page 519)
185 g (6 oz) smoked streaky bacon
200 g (6½ oz) pearl onions
20 g (¾ oz) caster sugar
20 g (¾ oz) unsalted butter
150 g (5 oz) button mushrooms*

CROUTONS
*4 slices bread, crusts removed
150 ml (5 fl oz) clarified butter (see
page 520) or oil
1 tablespoon chopped fresh parsley*

One To make the marinade, place all the ingredients into a large non-metallic bowl. Add the chicken pieces, cover and leave overnight in the refrigerator.

Two Remove the chicken pieces and dry with paper towels. Strain the marinade and reserve the vegetables and herbs separately from the liquid. Preheat the oven to moderately hot 200°C (400°F/Gas 6).

Three Heat a little clarified butter or oil in a deep flameproof casserole dish and sauté the chicken over high heat, skin side down first, until well browned on all sides. Add the reserved marinade, vegetables and herbs. Cook for 5 minutes, or until softened, stirring occasionally. Pour off any excess fat. Sprinkle the flour into the dish and mix well. Add the reserved marinade, hot stock and salt and pepper. Cover with greaseproof paper and a lid and cook in the oven for 45 minutes, or until the chicken is cooked through. Reduce the oven temperature to low. Remove the chicken to a clean casserole, strain the sauce and skim off the excess fat. Season if necessary. Pour over the chicken and return to the oven to heat through.

Four Meanwhile, put the bacon in a pan, cover with water and bring to the boil. Drain, rinse under cold water and trim away the rind. Cut into small pieces and fry in a little oil until golden; drain on paper towels. Put the onions, sugar and butter in a pan with just enough water to cover. Bring to the boil, then simmer until all the water has evaporated and the onions are tender (if necessary, add a little extra water and continue cooking). Glaze the onions by tossing in the butter and sugar in the pan until golden. Fry the mushrooms in hot oil and drain. Sprinkle the bacon, onions and mushrooms over the chicken, cover and keep warm.

Five To make croutons, cut each slice of bread into four triangles and fry in very hot clarified butter or oil until golden brown—be careful as the bread colours quickly. Dip the tips of the croutons in the parsley and arrange over the dish.

about cooking with wine...

Wine for cooking should be of a reasonable quality, one that you would be happy to drink. Cheaper wines will not add a good flavour to food and the flavour of expensive wines will be lost in the cooking process.

Breast of chicken with tarragon and mustard sauce

French tarragon (as opposed to its coarser cousin, Russian tarragon) has a subtle anise-like flavour, which perfectly complements other gently flavoured foods such as eggs, fish and chicken. The Latin name means 'little dragon', from the belief that the herb could cure the bites of venomous creatures.

Preparation time 15 minutes
Total cooking time 50 minutes
Serves 4

oil, for cooking
4 skinless chicken breasts
4 French shallots, finely sliced
100 ml (3¼ fl oz) dry white wine
500 ml (16 fl oz) chicken stock
(see page 519)
200 ml (6½ fl oz) thick (double)
cream or crème fraîche
80 g (2¾ oz) Dijon or tarragon
mustard
15 g (½ oz) fresh tarragon

One Preheat the oven to moderate 180°C (350°F/Gas 4). Heat about 1 tablespoon oil in a roasting tin on the stove top and fry the chicken breasts for 5 minutes on each side, or until golden brown. Transfer to the oven and cook for a further 5–10 minutes, or until the juices run clear when a skewer is inserted into the centre.

Two Remove the chicken from the tin and keep warm. Tip off the excess fat and transfer the roasting tin to the stove top. Add the shallots and fry until soft and lightly browned, then add the wine and reduce until almost dry. Add the stock and simmer for 5–10 minutes, or until syrupy.

Three Strain the sauce into a clean pan, add the cream and simmer for 5 minutes. Stir in the mustard and season to taste with salt and freshly ground black pepper. Chop the tarragon and sprinkle into the sauce at the last minute to prevent it discolouring. Serve the sauce over the chicken.

CHEF'S TIP *The shallots, which have a lovely flavour, could be left in the sauce. If you wish to do this, simply add the cream without straining the sauce first.*

LE CORDON BLEU COMPLETE COOK

Chicken Basque

The Basque country is located in the south-west of France and northern Spain. This traditional recipe uses local produce such as onions, peppers and tomatoes but we have substituted the more readily available Parma ham or prosciutto for the local cured ham from Bayonne, and olive oil instead of the traditional goose fat.

Preparation time 30 minutes
Total cooking time 1 hour 15 minutes
Serves 4

2 red capsicums (peppers)
2 green capsicums (peppers)
1 chicken, weighing 1.2 kg
(2 lb 6½ oz), cut into 8 pieces (see page 528)
oil, for cooking
1 large onion, finely sliced
3 cloves garlic, crushed
410 g (13 oz) tomatoes, peeled and quartered (see page 534)
100 ml (3¼ fl oz) white wine
90 g (3 oz) Parma ham or prosciutto, cut into strips
1 tablespoon chopped fresh parsley, to garnish

One Halve the capsicums, remove the seeds and membrane and slice the flesh into long strips.

Two Season the chicken with salt and pepper. Heat about 2 tablespoons oil in a large deep frying pan. Add the chicken pieces, skin side down first, and fry until lightly golden brown all over. Remove and drain on crumpled paper towels.

Three Tip off the excess oil, leaving just 1 tablespoon in the pan. Add the onion, garlic, capsicum and tomato and simmer for 10 minutes. Add the white wine, cover and leave to simmer for a further 30 minutes. Add the chicken, season lightly with salt and pepper, cover and simmer for 15–20 minutes. Check that the chicken is fully cooked by pricking it with a fork (the juices should run clear). Lift out the chicken pieces, cover with foil and keep warm. Season the sauce with salt and pepper, to taste.

Four Pan-fry the ham or prosciutto in a little oil, lifting directly from the pan with a slotted spoon, without draining on paper towels. Pour the sauce over the chicken, sprinkle with the ham or prosciutto and garnish with the parsley.

LE CORDON BLEU ❧ COMPLETE COOK

Chicken pie

Serve this delicious pie with simple boiled or mashed potatoes to mop up the chicken juices. Green beans or spinach would also be delicious accompaniments. Alternatively, for a crisper bite, serve with a mixed green side salad.

*Preparation time 45 minutes
+ 30 minutes resting
Total cooking time 1 hour 35 minutes
Serves 4–6*

*1 chicken, weighing 1.5 kg (3 lb)
8 slices pancetta, about 185 g (6 oz),
rind removed
60 g (2 oz) unsalted butter
1 hard-boiled egg, roughly chopped
100 g (3¼ oz) button mushrooms,
quartered
1 onion, finely chopped
60 ml (2 fl oz) white wine
250 ml (8 fl oz) chicken stock
(see page 519)
½ quantity puff pastry (see page 542)
1 egg, beaten
large pinch of chopped fresh herbs,
such as parsley, tarragon or chervil*

One Cut the chicken into eight pieces, following the method in the Chef's techniques on page 528, and remove the bones and skin. Season with salt and pepper, then wrap each piece of chicken in a slice of pancetta and secure with cocktail sticks or string.

Two Heat half the butter in a frying pan over medium heat and lightly brown the chicken in batches, turning regularly to seal them on all sides. Remove the chicken from the pan and drain on crumpled paper towels. Discard the cocktail sticks or string and place the chicken in a 1.5 litre pie dish with the hard-boiled egg. Pour off the excess fat from the pan, add the remaining butter and cook the mushrooms and onion over low heat for 5 minutes without letting them colour.

Three Add the white wine to the pan and simmer until only a little liquid is left. Pour over the chicken in the dish. Add sufficient stock to almost cover the chicken pieces.

Four Roll out the pastry so that it is a little bigger than the top of the dish. Brush the rim of the pie dish with beaten egg and line with 1 cm (½ inch) of spare pastry cut from around the pastry edge, pressing onto the dish firmly and brushing with beaten egg. Fold the pastry over a rolling pin and cover the pie dish. Be careful not to stretch the pastry or it will shrink out of shape while baking. Press the edges together to seal. With a small sharp knife, trim off the excess pastry. Do not angle the knife in towards the dish or it will encourage shrinkage later. With the back of the knife, notch the cut pastry edge. Brush the top surface with egg, but not the edges. Make a small hole for steam to escape, then decorate with pastry trimmings and brush them with egg.

Five Chill the pie for 30 minutes, to prevent the pastry shrinking during baking, and preheat the oven to moderately hot 190°C (375°F/Gas 5). Bake the pie for 20 minutes, or until the pastry is risen and golden. Reduce the oven to very slow 120°C (250°F/Gas ½) and cover the pie with foil to prevent over-browning while cooking the chicken through. Cook for 45 minutes. Break the crust in the centre, or loosen and lift off from the side, and add the chopped fresh herbs. Serve immediately.

CHEF'S TIP *This pie traditionally has a lot of thin gravy, delicious mopped up with potatoes. If you prefer a thicker sauce, chop up the mushrooms more finely, or roll the chicken pieces in seasoned flour after sealing and before putting in the pie dish.*

meat

Beef carpaccio with rocket and Parmesan

*Beef carpaccio is a classic Italian first course consisting
of very thin slices of raw beef served with a vinaigrette and
often topped with onions, or capers as in this recipe.*

*Preparation time 15 minutes
+ 30 minutes freezing
Total cooking time Nil
Serves 4*

350 g (11¼ oz) beef eye fillet or
tenderloin (see Chef's tips)
40 ml (1¼ fl oz) lemon juice
50 ml (1¾ fl oz) extra virgin olive oil
100 g (3¼ oz) piece of Parmesan
cheese, at room temperature
100 g (3¼ oz) rocket
3 tablespoons capers

One To prepare the carpaccio, trim the
beef of any fat and sinew. Wrap tightly
in plastic wrap and freeze for at least
30 minutes, or until very firm but not
rock-solid. Remove the plastic wrap
and, using a very sharp knife, slice the
meat as thinly as possible. Place each
beef slice between two layers of plastic
wrap and lightly pound the slices to
flatten them.

Two Divide the beef among four plates,
arranging the slices in a single layer,
overlapping them slightly. Cover with
plastic wrap and refrigerate until ready
to serve.

Three To make the dressing, whisk
together the lemon juice and olive oil.
Season to taste with salt and freshly
ground pepper and set aside.

Four Using a vegetable peeler, shave
cheese curls from the piece of Parmesan,
allowing six shavings per plate. Set aside
until ready to use.

Five Just before serving, toss the rocket
leaves in half the dressing and arrange
on the plates with the carpaccio.

Sprinkle with the Parmesan and capers.
Drizzle the carpaccio with the remaining
dressing and serve at once with freshly
ground black pepper.

CHEF'S TIPS *When making your own
carpaccio, it is very important to use a
good-quality cut of very fresh meat.
Alternatively, for the thinnest possible
slices of beef, your butcher may be able
to prepare the carpaccio for you. Order
the meat several days in advance for the
day you plan to serve it, and specify how
you would like it prepared. Ask your
butcher to lay out the slices on a sheet of
plastic wrap for easier handling.*

*This recipe can be adjusted to taste by
adding freshly chopped herbs such as
basil, as well as olives, anchovies or
roasted capsicums (peppers).*

LE CORDON BLEU COMPLETE COOK

Traditional corned beef with vegetables and dumplings

This corned beef is served with onions, carrots, turnips and light dumplings cooked in a well-flavoured beef stock. The marrow may be extracted from the bone with a teaspoon and is particularly good sprinkled with a little salt.

Preparation time 20 minutes
+ 3 hours soaking
Total cooking time 4 hours 30 minutes
Serves 6

1 kg (2 lb) piece of corned beef
(salt beef)
6 x 5 cm (2 inch) pieces
of marrowbone
1 bouquet garni (see page 520)
6 peppercorns
½ onion
6 onions, quartered
4 large carrots, quartered
2 turnips, quartered
2 teaspoons chopped fresh parsley

DUMPLINGS
225 g (7¼ oz) self-raising flour
pinch of salt
50 g (1¾ oz) suet, roughly grated
120 ml (4 fl oz) cold water

One Soak the beef in cold water for at least 3 hours, remove and rinse.

Two Place the marrowbones and beef in a large pan, cover with water and bring to the boil slowly, skimming off the foam as necessary.

Three Reduce the heat to a simmer. Add the bouquet garni, peppercorns and the ½ onion. Partially cover the pan and simmer for 3 hours. Check regularly and skim off any fat and scum. Remove and discard the bouquet garni, peppercorns and onion. Add the quartered onions, carrot and turnip and allow to simmer for 40 minutes.

Four Begin to prepare the dumplings 30 minutes before the beef is cooked. Sift the flour and salt into a bowl and stir in the suet. Make a well in the centre, add a little water and draw in the flour with a knife. Add enough water to make a soft, but not sticky dough, then knead gently until smooth. Shape, with floured hands, into about 20 dumplings. Add to the pan of beef and cook for about 20 minutes, or until the dumplings have puffed up and float. Remove with a slotted spoon.

Five Place the beef in a large dish surrounded by vegetables from the pot, dumplings and marrowbones. Cover and keep warm. Simmer the stock for about 30 minutes, skimming the surface as necessary, until it has thickened and reduced and has a good flavour. Ladle onto the meat and sprinkle with the chopped parsley.

CHEF'S TIP *These dumplings could be made to be served with other casseroles. To cook them separately, simply poach in 550 ml (18 fl oz) of simmering beef stock or well-salted water.*

LE CORDON BLEU COMPLETE COOK

Beef Wellington

*Beef Wellington is the name given to fillet of beef, lightly covered
with duxelles (shallots and mushrooms cooked in butter) and sometimes
liver pâté, then wrapped in puff pastry and cooked until golden.*

*Preparation time 1 hour
+ 15 minutes chilling
Total cooking time 1 hour 15 minutes
Serves 6*

*1.6 kg (3 lb 4 oz) beef eye fillet
120 ml (4 fl oz) oil
1 small carrot, chopped
1 small onion, chopped
1 small leek, chopped
50 ml (1³⁄4 fl oz) dry Madeira
or sherry
500 ml (16 fl oz) brown stock
(see page 518)
50 g (1³⁄4 oz) unsalted butter
2 French shallots, finely chopped
1 clove garlic, finely chopped
500 g (1 lb) button mushrooms,
finely chopped
800 g (1 lb 10 oz) puff pastry (see
page 542)
10 slices Parma ham
1 egg, beaten*

One Preheat the oven to hot 220°C (425°F/Gas 7). Remove and reserve the thin muscle from the side of the main beef fillet. Remove and discard the shiny surface membrane and tie the fillet with string at 2 cm (³⁄4 inch) intervals.

Two Roughly chop the beef trimmings. Heat 1 tablespoon of the oil in a shallow pan, then add the beef trimmings and chopped carrot, onion and leek. Gently fry until the mixture browns. Stir in the Madeira, scraping up the sticky juices from the base of the pan, then simmer for a few minutes, or until reduced to a syrup. Stir in the stock. Bring to the boil, then reduce the heat and simmer for 1 hour to reduce to a syrupy sauce while you prepare the Beef Wellington.

Three Place an ovenproof pan over high heat and add the remaining oil. When very hot, add the beef fillet and brown quickly all over. Season well, then transfer to the oven and roast for about 5 minutes for medium rare, 10 minutes for medium and 15 minutes for well done. (The actual cooking time will depend on the thickness of the fillet.) Remove from the pan to cool.

Four Melt the butter in a saucepan and gently cook the shallots for 1–2 minutes, or until soft but not browned. Add the garlic and mushrooms and cook gently until the pan looks dry when scraped with a wooden spoon. The mixture should be barely moist. Set aside.

Five On a lightly floured work surface, roll the pastry 5 mm (¹⁄4 inch) thick, into a rectangle 35 x 60 cm (14 x 24 inches). Transfer to a baking tray, cover with plastic wrap and place in the refrigerator to chill for 15 minutes.

Six Transfer the pastry to the work surface. To reduce excess overlap, cut away each corner, reserving the pastry trimmings and leaving the centre large enough for the fillet—the pastry will resemble a cross. Flatten each flap of pastry with a rolling pin.

Seven Lay the ham slices on the pastry and spread thinly with half the mushrooms. Untie the fillet, season well, place it on the pastry and spread with the remaining mushrooms. Fold the edges of the ham over the fillet. Brush the pastry edges with beaten egg and fold over each other to enclose the fillet.

Eight Put the parcels on a lightly buttered baking tray, seam side down. Cut the excess pastry into strips and crisscross a lattice pattern over the top. Brush with more beaten egg, then pierce small slits in the tops for a crisp finish. Place in the oven for 5 minutes to set, then lower the heat to moderately hot 200°C (400°F/Gas 6) and bake for 20 minutes. Leave to rest for 10 minutes before slicing.

Nine Skim any froth from the simmering sauce, then strain into a sauce boat. Serve with the Beef Wellington.

Beef stroganoff

This well-known and easy-to-make dish consists of strips of beef fillet, shallots and mushrooms sautéed in butter and served in a sour cream sauce.

Preparation time 20 minutes
Total cooking time 30 minutes
Serves 4

3 tablespoons olive oil
600 g (1¼ lb) beef eye fillet, cut into
5 x 1 cm (2 x ½ inch) strips
30 g (1 oz) unsalted butter
3 large shallots, finely chopped
1 tablespoon paprika
50 g (1¾ oz) mushrooms, thinly sliced
25 ml (¾ fl oz) white wine vinegar
50 ml (1¾ fl oz) brandy
250 ml (8 fl oz) chicken stock
(see page 519)
200 ml (6½ fl oz) sour cream
20 g (¾ oz) cornichon or pickled
gherkins, cut into julienne strips
(see Chef's tip)
20 g (¾ oz) cooked beetroot,
cut into julienne strips

One Heat the oil in a frying pan over high heat until very hot. Fry the meat in batches for 3–5 minutes, stirring until lightly browned. Remove from the pan, set aside and keep warm.

Two Melt the butter in the pan, add the shallots and cook for 2 minutes or until soft but not coloured. Stir in the paprika for 45 seconds, then add the mushrooms and cook over high heat until dry. Add the vinegar and cook for 1 minute, or until the pan is nearly dry. Add the brandy, cook until the liquid is reduced to half, then add the stock and reduce to half again. Finally, add half the sour cream and return the meat to the pan to reheat. Serve with some steamed rice or a rice pilaf, dot with the remaining sour cream and garnish with the gherkins and beetroot.

CHEF'S TIP *Julienne strips are vegetables cut to the size and shape of matchsticks.*

Estouffade of beef with green and black olives

*An estouffade is a type of stew where the ingredients are slowly simmered.
It is usually made with beef, wine, carrots and onions. The addition
of ripe olives here gives the recipe its Provençal flavour.*

Preparation time 40 minutes
Total cooking time 2 hours 30 minutes
Serves 4–6

2 kg (4 lb) chuck steak,
cut into cubes
2 carrots, chopped
1 large onion, chopped
2 tablespoons plain flour
2 tablespoons tomato paste (purée)
750 ml (24 fl oz) white wine
1 litre brown stock (see page 518)
3 fresh tomatoes, halved, seeded
and chopped (see page 534)
3 cloves garlic, chopped
1 bouquet garni (see page 520)
200 g (6½ oz) mushrooms,
thinly sliced
425 g (13½ oz) can chopped tomatoes
200 g (6½ oz) slab or sliced
bacon, rind removed and
cut into batons
80 g (2¾ oz) green olives,
pitted and chopped
80 g (2¾ oz) black olives,
pitted and chopped
2 tablespoons chopped
fresh parsley

One Preheat the oven to moderate 180°C (350°F/Gas 4). Season the beef with salt and freshly ground black pepper. Heat a 2.5 cm (1 inch) depth of olive oil in a large flameproof casserole dish. Add the beef, in batches, brown on all sides, then remove from the pan. Add the carrot and onion and cook until lightly golden. Lower the heat, then sprinkle over the flour and cook, stirring, for 2 minutes. Stir in the tomato paste and cook for 1 minute. Pour on the wine and blend in until smooth, then stir to the boil and simmer for 3–4 minutes. Stir in the stock, fresh tomatoes, the garlic and

bouquet garni. Return the meat to the pan, bring just to the boil, then cover and transfer to the oven and cook for about 1 hour 45 minutes, or until the meat is tender.

Two Heat a little oil in a frying pan and fry the mushrooms over high heat for 3–4 minutes, or until dry. Season the mushrooms, remove from the oil and set aside. Clean the pan, add a few drops of olive oil, warm, then add the canned tomatoes and boil until thick and the liquid has evaporated; set aside. Place

the bacon in a pan of cold water, bring to the boil, then drain, rinse the bacon with cold water and dry. Fry the bacon in a little oil until golden, drain on paper towels and set aside.

Three Once the beef is tender when pierced with a fork, remove it and strain the sauce. Discard the vegetables and bouquet garni, then return the meat and sauce to the cleaned casserole with the mushrooms, tomato, bacon and olives. Bring to the boil and check the seasoning. Serve sprinkled with the chopped parsley.

Boeuf bourguignon

The Burgundy region of France is famous for its fine wines and sophisticated cuisine.
Dishes 'à la bourguignonne' generally include a sauce made of red wine
and a garnish of small onions, mushrooms and pieces of bacon.

Preparation time 1 hour
+ marinating overnight
Total cooking time 2 hours 30 minutes
Serves 4

MARINADE
1 large carrot, cut into 1 cm
(1/2 inch) pieces
1 onion, cut into 1 cm (1/2 inch) pieces
1 celery stick, cut into 1 cm
(1/2 inch) pieces
2 cloves garlic
1 bouquet garni (see page 520)
3 tablespoons brandy
10 black peppercorns
1.5 litres good-quality red wine
2 tablespoons oil

1 kg (2 lb) chuck steak, trimmed and
cut into 4 cm (1½ inch) cubes
1 heaped tablespoon tomato
paste (purée)
2 level tablespoons plain flour
400 ml (12¾ fl oz) brown stock
(see page 518)
32 pearl or pickling onions, peeled
1 tablespoon unsalted butter
1/2 tablespoon sugar
150 g (5 oz) mushrooms,
cut into quarters
2 tablespoons chopped garlic
240 g (7½ oz) slab or sliced smoked
bacon, cut into cubes
or short batons
2 slices white bread, crusts removed
and cut into triangles
2 tablespoons chopped fresh parsley

One Place all the ingredients for the marinade in a bowl with the cubes of beef. Cover and refrigerate overnight.

Two Preheat the oven to moderately hot 200°C (400°F/Gas 6). Strain the marinade into a saucepan, remove the beef and set aside, and keep the vegetables and bouquet garni separate. Bring the marinade to the boil, skim off the foam and cook for 6–8 minutes. Strain through a fine sieve.

Three In a large, heavy-based flameproof casserole dish, heat a little oil and butter. Pat dry the meat and brown on all sides in batches, then remove and keep to one side. Add the well-drained vegetables from the marinade, lower the heat slightly and cook, stirring occasionally, until lightly browned. Return the meat to the dish with the tomato paste and stir over medium heat for 3 minutes. Sprinkle with the flour, place in the oven for 6–8 minutes, then remove and mix in the flour. Place over medium heat, add the marinade and bring to the boil, stirring continuously, then add the brown stock and bouquet garni. Return to the boil, cover and cook in the oven for 1 hour 30 minutes, or until the meat is tender.

Four Place the onions, butter, sugar and some salt in a pan and pour in enough water to cover. Cook over medium heat until the water has almost evaporated and swirl the pan until the onions are golden. Fry the mushrooms in a little sizzling butter until golden, then season, drain and add to the onions. Fry the garlic and bacon in a little oil, drain and add to the onions and mushrooms.

Five Brush the bread with melted butter and bake in the oven for 3–5 minutes, or until brown.

Six Once the beef is cooked, skim off excess fat. Remove the beef to a clean flameproof casserole or serving dish, cover and keep warm. Strain the sauce and return it to the pan, discarding the vegetables and bouquet garni. Bring the sauce to the boil and simmer for 15 minutes, or until the sauce coats the back of a spoon, skimming frequently. Season, strain over the meat and simmer or return to the oven for 5 minutes. Add the onions, mushrooms and bacon. Dip a corner of each bread crouton in the sauce, then into the parsley. Sprinkle the remaining parsley over the beef and serve with the croutons on the edge of the dish or on the side.

about beef...

For long, slow-cooked dishes such as boeuf bourguignon it is important that you use cuts of meat such as chuck steak or topside, which will become very tender as they cook. These cuts contain a certain amount of fat and connective tissue which melts into the dish and gives a rich, smooth quality to the sauce.

LE CORDON BLEU ✠ COMPLETE COOK

Roast beef and Yorkshire puddings

*What could be more tantalising and traditional than roast beef served
with crisp, golden Yorkshire puddings and lightly tangy horseradish cream?
Carve the beef at the table for the greatest effect.*

*Preparation time 40 minutes
+ 30 minutes resting
Total cooking time 1 hour 40 minutes
Serves 4–6*

YORKSHIRE PUDDINGS
*175 ml (5¾ fl oz) milk
175 g (5¾ oz) plain flour
2 eggs*

*oil, for cooking
1.5 kg (3 lb) sirloin of beef,
rolled and tied*

HORSERADISH CREAM
*120 ml (4 fl oz) cream, for whipping
40 g (1¼ oz) grated fresh horseradish
a few drops of lemon juice*

JUS
*1 carrot, chopped
1 onion, chopped
1 celery stick, chopped
1 leek, chopped
1 bay leaf
2 sprigs of fresh thyme
3 peppercorns
500 ml (16 fl oz) brown stock
(see page 518)*

One Preheat the oven to hot 220°C (425°F/Gas 7). To make the Yorkshire puddings, combine the milk with 125 ml (4 fl oz) water. Sift the flour and some salt into a bowl and make a well in the centre. Add the eggs and begin to whisk. As the mixture thickens, gradually add the milk and water, whisking until a smooth batter forms. Pour into a jug, cover and stand for 30 minutes.

Two On the stove top, heat 3 tablespoons of oil in a roasting pan over high heat. Add the beef, fat side down, and brown all over, turning with tongs. Transfer the beef to the oven and, turning and basting every 15 minutes, roast for 30 minutes for rare, 45 minutes for medium-rare, and 1 hour for well done.

Three To make the horseradish cream, lightly whip the cream until soft peaks form. Gently fold in the grated horseradish and season to taste with salt, freshly ground pepper and the lemon juice. Do not overfold or the mixture will become too thick. Transfer to a serving bowl, cover and chill.

Four Transfer the beef to a plate, cover lightly with foil and allow to rest for 10–15 minutes before carving. Leaving a tablespoon of fat in the roasting pan, drain the excess fat and use it to brush a deep, 12-hole patty tin or 6-hole Yorkshire pudding tin.

Five Heat the tin in the oven for about 2–3 minutes until lightly smoking. Divide the Yorkshire pudding batter among the holes and bake for about 15 minutes, or until the puddings are puffed and golden.

Six To make the jus, heat the remaining fat in the roasting pan over the stove top. Add the vegetables and gently fry over medium heat for 5 minutes, or until golden, stirring constantly. Drain the pan of any excess fat; add the bay leaf, thyme, peppercorns and a little hot stock, scraping the base of the pan with a wooden spoon. Add the remaining hot stock and simmer to reduce by half, skimming off any foam or fat. Strain into a saucepan, discarding the vegetables and seasonings. Skim again, season to taste, then cover and keep warm. (Pour into a warm sauce boat just before serving.)

Seven Serve the beef and puddings on warm plates, with the jus and horseradish cream on the side. Green vegetables and roast potatoes are traditional accompaniments.

CHEF'S TIP *Resting a roast makes the meat easier to carve and helps prevent the juices running. Any juices from the resting can be poured over the meat, but do not add them to the jus: they will spoil its texture.*

Carbonade à la flamande

Although the word carbonade comes from the Italian for 'charcoal cooked', the beef is not grilled but browned in a pan then transferred to the casserole. This dish first appeared in the Flemish area of northern France, where beef and onions were cooked in beer.

Preparation time 30 minutes
Total cooking time 2 hours 30 minutes
Serves 4

3 tablespoons lard or oil
1 kg (2 lb) chuck steak or topside
of beef, cut into eight 1 cm
(¹/2 inch) slices
4 small onions, thinly sliced
3 tablespoons plain flour
1 tablespoon tomato paste (purée)
1 litre brown ale
1 bouquet garni (see page 520)
3 juniper berries
1 tablespoon soft brown sugar
1.25 litres brown stock (see page 518)

One Preheat the oven to moderate 180°C (350°F/Gas 4). Heat the lard or oil in a heavy-based pan and add the beef in batches. Over high heat, quickly fry to seal and brown. Remove and set aside. Lower the heat, add the onion and cook for 10 minutes, or until soft and golden.

Two Transfer the onion to a 6-litre flameproof dish, stir in the flour and cook over low heat for 2 minutes. Add the tomato paste and cook for 1–2 minutes. Add the brown ale, bouquet garni, juniper berries and sugar and stir to the boil. Add the stock, bring back to the boil, then add the beef and

simmer for 5 minutes, skimming off any foam. Season with salt and pepper, cover and bake for 1 hour 45 minutes.

Three The beef should be tender when pierced with a fork, if not, return to the oven. Once cooked, remove the beef to a serving dish. On top of the stove, bring the sauce to the boil, skimming off any foam, and cook for 10 minutes, or until it is thick enough to coat the back of a spoon. Pour the sauce over the beef and serve.

LE CORDON BLEU ✠ COMPLETE COOK

Steak au poivre

*This is a simple method to make a traditional French pepper steak.
The dish has quite controversial origins—at least four chefs claim to have
invented steak au poivre at various times between 1905 and 1930.*

Preparation time 10 minutes
Total cooking time 30 minutes
Serves 4

800 ml (26 fl oz) brown stock
(see page 518)
4 fillet or rump steaks
100 g (3¼ oz) clarified butter (see
page 520) or oil
50 g (1¾ oz) onion or French shallot,
finely chopped
10 g (¼ oz) crushed black peppercorns
50 ml (1¾ fl oz) white wine
50 ml (1¾ fl oz) brandy
sprigs of fresh parsley, to garnish

One Simmer the stock in a pan until it has reduced to 400 ml (13 fl oz). Season the steaks with salt. In a shallow frying pan big enough to fit the four steaks, heat the clarified butter until it is very hot. Add the steaks and brown for 3–4 minutes on each side for medium rare, and a little longer for medium. Remove from the pan and cover with foil to keep warm. For well-done steak, brown on each side for 3 minutes, then transfer to an ovenproof dish and bake for 8–10 minutes at 200°C (400°F/ Gas 6). Remove and cover with foil.

Two Add the onion to the frying pan and cook for 3–4 minutes, until lightly coloured. Add the peppercorns. Add the wine and half the brandy, stir to scrape up the juices and simmer for 1 minute until syrupy. Stir in the stock and bring to the boil. Cook for 7 minutes, or until syrupy, then add the remaining brandy.

Three Return the steaks to the sauce and reheat for 3–4 minutes, without allowing the sauce to boil. Garnish with the parsley to serve.

Beef casserole with herb scones

Just below the well-risen, golden brown scones is a rich,
tender beef and mushroom casserole, which is
guaranteed to liven up a cold winter's day.

Preparation time 30 minutes
Total cooking time 2 hours
Serves 4–6

2 tablespoons olive oil
750 g (1½ lb) chuck, braising or
stewing steak, cut into 2.5 cm
(1 inch) cubes
2 onions, thinly sliced
1 clove garlic, crushed
1 tablespoon plain flour
200 ml (6½ fl oz) red wine
1 teaspoon tomato paste (purée)
250 g (8 oz) flat mushrooms,
quartered

HERB SCONES
250 g (8 oz) self-raising flour
¼ teaspoon salt
60 g (2 oz) unsalted butter, cut into
cubes and chilled
1 tablespoon chopped fresh herbs,
such as parsley, rosemary or thyme
115 ml (3¾ fl oz) buttermilk
(see Chef's tip)
1 egg, beaten

One Preheat the oven to slow 150°C (300°F/Gas 2). Heat the oil in a flameproof casserole dish until it is very hot, then brown the meat in batches, taking care not to overcrowd the pan, for 3–4 minutes each side. Remove from the dish and set aside.

Two Add the onion to the dish with the garlic and cook for 2 minutes. Sprinkle the flour on top and stir in with a wooden spoon, scraping the base of the dish. Cook for about 1 minute, stirring continuously, until the mixture is golden brown. Gradually stir in the wine, 200 ml (6½ fl oz) water and the tomato paste, and season with salt and freshly ground black pepper. Continue stirring until the mixture begins to thicken, then return the meat to the pan, add the mushrooms and stir to the boil. Cover and either cook gently on the stove or in the oven for 1½ hours.

Three Begin preparing the herb scones no more than about 10 minutes before the beef has finished cooking. Sift the flour and salt into a wide bowl, then add the butter and rub in with a flicking action of the thumb across the tips of the fingers. When the mixture resembles fine breadcrumbs, add the herbs. Stir in the buttermilk, using a round-bladed knife, until the flour has disappeared and the mixture is in large lumps, then draw together quickly into a rough ball. Place on a lightly floured surface and knead quickly until just smooth. Roll or pat out the dough with the palm of your hand to a 1.5 cm (5/8 inch) thickness, then cut out about ten circles using a 5 cm (2 inch) cutter.

Four Remove the casserole from the oven, then increase the temperature to moderately hot 200°C (400°F/Gas 6). Arrange the scones on the surface of the casserole and brush the tops with the egg. Place the casserole at the top of the oven, uncovered, and cook for 12 minutes, or until the scones have risen and turned golden brown.

CHEF'S TIP *If you can't buy buttermilk, add 1 teaspoon of lemon juice to fresh milk to achieve a similar result.*

Braised beef in dill sauce

Slowly braised beef served with a creamy dill sauce makes a welcome change from the more traditional recipes for beef. Delicious served with crisp green vegetables and new potatoes.

Preparation time 25 minutes
Total cooking time 2 hours 15 minutes
Serves 4

1 kg (2 lb) tied joint of topside,
top rump or silverside of beef
1 large carrot, quartered and cut into
4 cm (1½ inch) lengths
3 onions, quartered
1 stick celery, cut into 4 cm
(1½ inch) lengths
1 large clove garlic, quartered
600 ml (20 fl oz) brown stock
(see page 518)
1 small bay leaf
35 g (1¼ oz) unsalted butter
30 g (1 oz) plain flour
150 g (5 oz) sour cream
(see Chef's tips)
10 g (¼ oz) chopped fresh dill
or 3 g (⅛ oz) dried dill

One Preheat the oven to moderate 180°C (350°F/Gas 4). On the top of a stove, heat a little oil in a 2.5 litre capacity flameproof casserole dish until the oil is very hot.

Two Place the joint of beef in the casserole dish and brown quickly on all sides, including the ends, then transfer to a plate. Reduce the heat, add the carrot, onion and celery and cook until golden brown, turning frequently. Add the garlic, place the meat on the vegetables and pour in the stock—it will come about halfway up the meat. Season with salt and freshly ground black pepper and add the bay leaf. Bring to the boil, reduce the heat and cover with greaseproof paper and the lid. Simmer on top of the stove or bake in the oven for 1½ hours, turning the meat every 30 minutes. After 1½ hours, check for tenderness by piercing with a sharp knife—cook for a further 15–30 minutes if necessary.

Three To make the sauce, melt the butter in a pan, add the flour and cook over low heat until the mixture turns from butter yellow to a pale straw colour. Remove from the heat and allow the mixture to cool.

Four Lift the meat out of the casserole dish onto a plate and cover with the greaseproof paper to keep moist. Strain 600 ml (20 fl oz) of the cooking liquid into a jug, discard the vegetables and bay leaf. Skim the fat from the surface.

Five Gradually add most of the measured liquid to the butter and flour mixture and whisk until blended and smooth. Return to the stove, heat gently until lightly thickened, then increase the heat and bring to the boil, stirring. Cook, bubbling, for about 3 minutes, or until the sauce is reduced and lightly syrupy. Stir in the sour cream and reduce for a further 3 minutes, or until it lightly coats the back of a spoon. Stir in the dill, add more seasoning as necessary and cover.

Six Remove the string and slice the beef into 5 mm (¼ inch) thick slices, then drizzle over the remaining cooking liquid to keep it moist. Pour a light coating of the sauce into a clean casserole or shallow serving dish. Place the meat in the dish and coat with the sauce. Cover and keep warm for 5 minutes before serving.

CHEF'S TIPS *For a lighter sauce, use crème fraîche instead of sour cream.*

To prepare this dish in advance, leave the sliced meat in a little cooking liquid and press a piece of buttered greaseproof paper onto the surface. To serve, warm the meat in its liquid and reheat the sauce.

Pot-au-feu

Pot-au-feu literally means 'pot on the fire', and the long, slow cooking of this classic French dish will fill your kitchen with sumptuous aromas as it gently simmers to perfection. The traditional vegetables used in this recipe could be changed to suit the season or your personal taste.

Preparation time 30 minutes
Total cooking time 2 hours 45 minutes
Serves 6–8

2 small leeks
1 celery stick or ½ small celeriac
8–10 black peppercorns
5–6 coriander seeds
½ small green or white cabbage,
cut into quarters
250 g (8 oz) oxtail, cut into
small pieces
750 g (1½ lb) beef ribs
1 small veal knuckle
25 g (¾ oz) salt
1 small onion, studded
with 2 cloves
1 clove garlic
1 bouquet garni (see page 520)
2 carrots, cut into 5 cm (2 inch) pieces
1 turnip or swede, peeled
and quartered

One Tie the leek and celery or celeriac into a bundle. Place the peppercorns and coriander seeds in a small piece of muslin, tie up and set aside. Place the cabbage in a large pan and cover with cold water. Bring to the boil, cook for 3 minutes, then drain and rinse in cold water and set aside.

Two Rinse all the meat and bones, place them in a large pot and cover with cold water. Bring to the boil, then remove from the heat and drain. Rinse the meat again, return to the pot and cover with 3.5 litres cold water. Add the salt and bring to the boil. Skim off the foam and any fat that rises to the surface. Add the onion, garlic, bouquet garni and the sachet of peppercorns and coriander seeds. Simmer over low heat for at least 1 hour 45 minutes.

Three Add the carrot, turnip, cabbage and the leek and celery bundle. Cook for another 30 minutes, or until the meat is tender. Remove and discard the bouquet garni and the sachet of spices. Strain the meat and vegetables, reserving the bouillon. Arrange the meat on a large platter, place the vegetables around the meat, and serve the bouillon separately in a soup tureen.

CHEF'S TIPS *This dish is traditionally served with cornichon pickles or cocktail gherkins, and salt for the meat.*

Boiled potatoes can also be added to the bouillon.

246

Venetian-style liver

*Tender calves' liver, rich in iron, protein and vitamin A,
has a mild flavour that is perfectly enhanced by the soft
caramelised onions in this Venetian recipe.*

Preparation time *20 minutes*
Total cooking time *30 minutes*
Serves 4

500 g (1 lb) calves' liver
vegetable oil, for cooking
250 g (8 oz) onions, thinly sliced

One Make sure the liver is completely free of veins and remove any of the thin skin that may still be attached. Slice the liver into thin strips.

Two Heat 2–3 tablespoons of the oil in a large non-stick frying pan and add the onion and a large pinch of salt. Cook over medium heat for 20–30 minutes, or until the onion is completely soft and golden brown. Remove the onion with a slotted spoon, leaving the oil in the pan.

Three Add a little more oil to the pan if necessary and heat until lightly smoking. Fry the liver in small batches, just enough to cover the base of the pan, for 1 minute, or until it has changed colour from pink to brown. Toss and cook for a moment more. Transfer each batch to a warm plate and season with salt and black pepper.

Four Return all the liver to the pan, add the cooked onion and toss to combine, but not to cook further. Transfer to a warm serving plate and serve immediately with steamed English spinach and a simple risotto.

CHEF'S TIP *The liver must fry quickly to retain its succulence, therefore it is important that the pan is hot or the liver will stick and fry for too long. Don't try to rush by cooking the liver in large batches—too much meat will overcrowd the pan, making the temperature drop and the liver stew rather than fry.*

Blanquette de veau

A blanquette is a classic French 'bourgeois' dish, which derives its name from 'blanc', the French word for white. It is always made from white meat cooked in a white stock or water, then enriched with cream.

Preparation time 20 minutes
Total cooking time 2 hours 10 minutes
Serves 4

1.4 kg (2 lb 12 oz) veal stewing meat,
    such as shoulder
1 carrot, quartered
1 small onion, quartered
1 stick celery, quartered
1 bouquet garni (see page 520)
1 teaspoon salt
10–12 peppercorns
150 g (5 oz) pearl or
    pickling onions
250 g (8 oz) button mushrooms, sliced
1 teaspoon lemon juice
55 g (1¾ oz) unsalted butter
30 g (1 oz) plain flour
300 ml (10 fl oz) thick (double) cream

One Remove excess fat from the veal and cut into 3 cm (1¼ inch) cubes. Place in a large flameproof casserole dish with the carrot, onion, celery, bouquet garni, salt and peppercorns. Cover with 500 ml (16 fl oz) cold water and bring to the boil on the stove top, skimming off any foam that comes to the surface. Reduce the heat and simmer for 1½ hours, or until tender, skimming regularly. Add boiling water if necessary to keep the meat covered in liquid.

Two Cook the onions for 10 minutes in boiling salted water, drain well and set aside. Cook the mushrooms for about 5 minutes in 2–3 tablespoons boiling salted water with the lemon juice and just under half of the butter. Drain well and set aside.

Three After 1½ hours, check if the meat is cooked by piercing it with a fork—it should not resist and should slip easily from the fork. Remove the veal from the cooking liquid. Strain the liquid, discarding the solids, return to the heat and cook for 30 minutes, or until it has reduced by two-thirds of its volume, skimming off excess fat. Cool slightly. Melt the remaining butter in a large pan, add the flour and cook for 1 minute. Stir in the reduced liquid and cook over low heat, whisking constantly, until the sauce has thickened. Add the cream, mix until smooth and season to taste.

Four Add the meat, onions and mushrooms to the pan and simmer for 5 minutes. Serve in a deep serving dish.

Veal chops grand-mère

This hearty dish makes a nourishing and succulent meal with the combination of fried bacon, mushrooms and small potato balls that melt in the mouth.

Preparation time 30 minutes
Total cooking time 1 hour 15 minutes
Serves 4

80 ml (2³/4 fl oz) oil
30 g (1 oz) unsalted butter
4 veal chops, about 200 g
(6¹/2 oz) each
250 g (8 oz) slab bacon, finely diced
300 g (10 oz) button mushrooms
300 g (10 oz) pearl or
pickling onions
1 teaspoon sugar
800 g (1 lb 10 oz) potatoes
30 ml (1 fl oz) white wine
100 ml (3¹/4 fl oz) brown stock
(see page 518)

One Preheat the oven to warm 170°C (325°F/Gas 3). In a large flameproof casserole dish, heat 1 tablespoon of the oil, then add the butter. Cook the chops for 2–3 minutes each side, or until well browned. Remove from the dish and set aside. Add the bacon and cook until browned, remove from the dish and set aside. Add the mushrooms and cook, stirring occasionally, for 2 minutes. Remove from the dish and set aside. Add the onions to a small pan with the sugar and cook, stirring occasionally, until lightly golden. Remove and set aside.

Two Peel the potatoes and scoop out small balls with a melon baller. Heat the remaining oil in a frying pan and cook the potatoes until golden brown, then drain on paper towels.

Three Pour the white wine into the dish and stir well, scraping the bottom of the pan until the pan juices have dissolved. Cook until the wine has reduced by three-quarters. Add the stock and 100 ml (3¹/4 fl oz) water, bring to the boil and cook until reduced by half.

Four Return the meat and vegetables to the casserole dish and toss to coat in the liquid. Season with salt and freshly ground black pepper. Cover and bake for about 30–40 minutes, or until the chops are tender and cooked through. Serve immediately.

Veal chops with Chablis en cocotte

A cocotte is a round or oval cooking pan with two handles and a tight-fitting cover that was traditionally used to cook slow-cooking dishes. Now 'en cocotte' refers to braised dishes in which the meat is first browned and then cooked in a liquid at a low simmer either in the oven or on the stove.

***Preparation time** 15 minutes*
***Total cooking time** 50 minutes*
Serves 4

4 veal chops, about 200 g
(6¹/2 oz) each
60 g (2 oz) unsalted butter
300 g (10 oz) veal trimmings or bones,
finely chopped (ask your butcher)
250 ml (8 fl oz) Chablis
1 bouquet garni (see page 520)
70 g (2¹/4 oz) slab bacon,
finely diced
1 small onion, finely chopped
1 carrot, finely diced
1 turnip, finely diced
1 tablespoon chopped fresh parsley

One Season the veal chops with salt and pepper. In a large frying pan over medium heat, melt two-thirds of the butter and brown the veal for 2–3 minutes on both sides. Once browned, transfer the chops to a plate. Add the trimmings to the pan and brown, then return the veal chops to the pan. Cover, reduce the heat and cook slowly for 4 minutes on each side. Transfer the chops and trimmings back to the plate and set aside. Increase the heat to medium-high and cook the meat juices, stirring constantly, for 3–4 minutes, or until they have caramelised onto the bottom of the pan. Strain the trimmings to remove the excess fat and return to the pan. Add the Chablis and stir well, scraping the bottom, until the cooking juices have dissolved. Cook for about 5 minutes, or until the wine has reduced in volume by three-quarters. Add 500 ml (16 fl oz) water and the bouquet garni and simmer for 30 minutes. Strain the sauce into a jug and discard the veal trimmings and bouquet garni.

Two Meanwhile, melt the remaining butter in another frying pan and brown the bacon for 2–3 minutes. Add the onion and carrot and cook for a further 2 minutes before adding the turnip. Reduce the heat, cover the pan and cook for 8 minutes.

Three Add the sauce, bring to the boil and cook for 10 minutes. Transfer the veal chops into the hot sauce, reduce the heat and leave to simmer for about 5 minutes, or until the veal is heated through. Serve sprinkled with the chopped parsley.

Osso buco

A speciality of Milan, this dish is best made using veal shanks from the hind leg.
The pieces should be cut no thicker than suggested, to ensure tenderness.
Savour the bone marrow by scooping it out with a spoon.

Preparation time 45 minutes
Total cooking time 2 hours 30 minutes
Serves 4

4 veal shanks, cut into 4 cm (1½ inch)
pieces (osso buco)
plain flour, seasoned
oil, for cooking
40 g (1¼ oz) unsalted butter
1 carrot, sliced
1 celery stick, sliced
1 onion, sliced
4 cloves garlic, chopped
8 tomatoes, peeled, seeded
and chopped (see page 534)
250 ml (8 fl oz) white wine
1 bouquet garni (see page 520)
l litre beef stock or water
2 tablespoons chopped fresh parsley
rind of ¼ orange,
finely chopped
rind of ¼ lemon, finely chopped

One Preheat the oven to moderate 180°C (350°F/Gas 4). Trim the meat of sinew and lightly coat with the seasoned flour. Heat a little oil in a small non-stick frying pan and brown the veal on both sides, in batches if necessary. Set aside.

Two Melt the butter in a flameproof casserole dish and cook the carrot, celery and onion over medium heat for 3 minutes. Add the garlic and mix well, then add the chopped tomatoes and cook for 5 minutes. Add the white wine and bouquet garni and cook for another 5 minutes. Add the stock and the browned meat, bring to a simmer, season, cover and place in the oven for 1½ hours, or until the meat is tender.

Three Transfer the meat to a serving platter, cover and keep warm. Heat the

cooking liquid and vegetables and bring to the boil. Skim off any fat or foam on the surface and cook for 20–25 minutes, or until the sauce has thickened and coats the back of a spoon. Stir in the parsley, orange and lemon rind and season with salt and pepper. Simmer for another 5 minutes, then pour over the meat and serve immediately.

CHEF'S TIP *If you prefer a milder citrus flavour, blanch the rind before using. Place it in a small pan and cover with cold water, bring to the boil for about 30 seconds, then strain and refresh. Use as instructed in the recipe.*

Veal parmigiana

This dish from northern Italy successfully combines the delicacy of veal with the strong, tangy flavour of Parmesan cheese.

Preparation time 45 minutes
Total cooking time 1 hour 40 minutes
Serves 4

15 g (¹/₂ oz) fresh basil
1 bay leaf
2 sprigs of fresh thyme
olive oil, for cooking
1 onion, finely chopped
1 kg (2 lb) large ripe tomatoes, peeled,
seeded and diced (see page 534)
3 cloves garlic, finely chopped
4 veal escalopes, about 120 g
(4 oz) each
plain flour, seasoned
2 eggs, lightly beaten
155 g (5 oz) fresh breadcrumbs
30 g (1 oz) Parmesan cheese, grated
1 tablespoon finely chopped
fresh parsley
120 g (4 oz) unsalted butter
250 g (8 oz) mozzarella cheese,
sliced

One Pull the basil leaves from their stems. Tie the stems with the bay leaf and thyme to make a bouquet garni. Heat 4 tablespoons of the olive oil in a pan and slowly cook the onion for 5 minutes without colouring. Add the tomato, garlic and bouquet garni. Season with salt and pepper, and simmer, covered, for 20 minutes, then uncovered for 45 minutes. Remove the bouquet garni and adjust the seasoning to taste.

Two Pound the veal with a meat mallet until 2 mm (¹/₈ inch) thick. Coat in the flour, patting off the excess. Toss the coated veal in the beaten egg.

Three Mix together the breadcrumbs, Parmesan and parsley in a shallow dish. Drain any excess egg from the veal and then coat with the breadcrumb mixture, pressing well with your fingers to make it stick.

Four Preheat the oven to moderately hot 200°C (400°F/Gas 6). Heat about 125 ml (4 fl oz) of the oil in a large non-stick frying pan. Add half the butter and, when it is foaming, cook two pieces of veal for about 3 minutes, or until golden brown, turning once. Drain on paper towels. Discard any leftover oil and butter from the pan and cook the remaining veal in fresh oil and butter. Arrange the veal in an ovenproof dish, cover with the mozzarella and bake for 10 minutes, or until the cheese has melted. Before serving, pour the tomato sauce on top and garnish with the fresh basil leaves.

Veal with lemon and capers

*The capers and lemon provide a sharp contrast
to the buttery sauce in this classic Italian dish.*

Preparation time 20 minutes
Total cooking time 25 minutes
Serves 4

*4 veal escalopes, about 125 g
(4 oz) each
plain flour, seasoned
2 eggs, beaten
2 tablespoons oil
40 g (1¼ oz) unsalted butter
250 ml (8 fl oz) white wine
3 tablespoons capers
250 ml (8 fl oz) chicken (see page 519)
or veal stock (see page 518)
1–2 tablespoons lemon juice
125 g (4 oz) unsalted butter, cut into
cubes and chilled*

One Pound the meat with a mallet until
it is 3 mm (⅛ inch) thick, then cut into
thirds and coat with the seasoned flour.
Put the beaten egg in a bowl and mix
together with 2 tablespoons water. Toss
the veal in the egg mixture, shaking off
any excess.

Two Heat the oil and butter in a non-
stick frying pan. Cook the veal, in
batches, for 3–5 minutes, until golden
brown on both sides. Drain on paper
towels, cover and keep warm while
cooking the other veal slices.

Three Pour off the oil from the pan, add
the wine and capers and cook for about

8 minutes, or until almost dry. Add the
stock and cook for 5 minutes, or until
reduced by half. Add 1 tablespoon
lemon juice, then transfer the sauce to a
small pan (keeping the frying pan on one
side). Whisk in the cubes of butter,
without allowing the sauce to boil.
Adjust the seasoning, adding more
lemon juice if necessary. Transfer the
veal to the frying pan, pour over the
sauce, cover and leave for 2 minutes
before serving.

Veal kidneys sautéed in white wine

A simple and delicious dish of veal kidneys cooked with wine, shallots and herbs.
The recipe may be adjusted according to personal preference by adding mustard or cream.
Use these variations to transform this one recipe into three different meals.

Preparation time 25 minutes
Total cooking time 25 minutes
Serves 4

3 veal kidneys, outer fat removed
60 g (2 oz) unsalted butter
4 French shallots, finely chopped
250 ml (8 fl oz) white wine
500 ml (16 fl oz) brown stock
(see page 518)
1 tablespoon chopped
fresh parsley

One Remove the fat and fine membrane from around the kidneys, then lay them flat, hold in place with one hand and cut each through sideways with a sharp knife. Using the tip of a sharp knife or scissors, trim away the core from the cut side of each kidney half. Cut the kidneys into bite-sized pieces. Melt two-thirds of the butter in a flameproof casserole dish over high heat and brown the kidneys in batches for 2–3 minutes—taking care not to overcook. Remove the kidneys, set aside and keep warm.

Two Reduce the heat to medium and, using the same dish, melt the remaining butter. Add the shallots and cook for 1 minute, without colouring, then add the wine and cook for about 5 minutes, or until it is almost completely evaporated. Add the stock and cook for a further 8–10 minutes, or until the sauce is thick enough to coat the back of a spoon. Season to taste with salt and black pepper. Add the kidneys and heat through for 1 minute without boiling. Remove from the heat, stir in the parsley and serve.

CHEF'S TIP *For a richer dish, the stock can be replaced with cream.*

LE CORDON BLEU COMPLETE COOK

Rack of lamb with a herb crust

The French Mediterranean region of Provence is known for its sunny climate and wonderful fresh vegetables and herbs. The herb crust in this Provençal dish features aromatic thyme, found growing wild in the hills.

Preparation time 1 hour
Total cooking time 1 hour 30 minutes
Serves 4

2 x 6-chop racks of lamb (best end of neck), trimmed and cleaned and with the bones and trimmings retained (see Chef's tip)
2 tablespoons oil

LAMB JUS
½ onion, chopped
3 cloves garlic, coarsely chopped

HERB CRUST
120 g (4 oz) fresh breadcrumbs
5 cloves garlic, finely chopped
4 tablespoons finely chopped fresh parsley
1 tablespoon fresh thyme leaves
80 g (2¾ oz) unsalted butter, softened

One Preheat the oven to moderately hot 200°C (400°F/Gas 6). Score the fat on the outside of the racks in a crisscross pattern. Heat the oil in a frying pan over medium–high heat, season the lamb, place in the pan and cook quickly to seal and brown the surface. Remove the lamb from the pan and set aside. Place the bones and lean trimmings in a roasting tin and roast in the oven for 20–30 minutes, then remove to cool. Increase the oven temperature to very hot 250°C (500°F/Gas 10).

Two To make the lamb jus, remove the bones and trimmings from the roasting tin, leaving the fat behind, and place them in a pan with the onion, garlic and 400 ml (12¾ fl oz) water. Bring to a simmer and cook for 30 minutes.

Three To make the herb crust, mix together the fresh breadcrumbs, chopped garlic, parsley and thyme leaves in a large bowl. Season and mix in the softened butter to form a paste.

Four Press a layer of the herb crust onto the fat side of the racks, leaving the bones and the bottom clean. Place the crusted racks in a roasting tin and lightly brown in the oven for 20–25 minutes. Set aside and keep warm.

Five Strain the jus into another pan and cook until reduced in volume by three quarters, skimming off the fat or any impurities that float to the surface. Serve on the side in a sauce boat.

CHEF'S TIP *Ask your butcher to trim and clean the lamb racks for you. You can also do it yourself by cutting away the fat and meat to expose the bones, then scraping the bones until they are perfectly clean.*

Lamb cutlets with pea fritters and garlic cream sauce

Lean pink lamb cutlets served with bright green pea fritters and a creamy garlic sauce make an unusual, appetising and colourful summer meal.

Preparation time 35 minutes
+ 40 minutes refrigeration
Total cooking time 1 hour
Serves 4

1 teaspoon salt
800 g (1 lb 10 oz) peas, fresh or frozen
10 g (1/4 oz) unsalted butter
1 egg yolk
2 teaspoons finely chopped fresh mint leaves
plain flour, seasoned
2 eggs
60 g (2 oz) blanched almonds, finely chopped
60 g (2 oz) dried breadcrumbs
oil, for deep-frying
12 lamb cutlets, trimmed of excess fat
30 g (1 oz) unsalted butter, melted

GARLIC CREAM SAUCE
10 cloves garlic, halved
100 ml (3 1/4 fl oz) white wine (not too dry)
300 ml (10 fl oz) thick (double) cream

One Half-fill a pan with water and bring to the boil. Add the salt and peas, return to the boil, then reduce the heat and simmer for 3 minutes, or until the peas are tender. Drain, then purée the peas in a food processor. Push the purée through a fine sieve to remove the skins.

Two Melt the butter in a small pan, add the pea purée and cook over low heat for about 7 minutes, or until the mixture is dry. Remove from the heat, stir in the egg yolk and chopped mint, and season with salt and freshly ground pepper. Leave to cool, then refrigerate for about 20 minutes, or until firm.

Three Put the flour on a sheet of grease-proof paper. Beat the eggs in a shallow bowl. Mix together the almonds and breadcrumbs and place them on another sheet of paper. Divide the pea mixture into 12 portions and roll each portion into a ball, or shape into a patty Coat the fritters with the flour, dip in the egg and then roll in the almond mixture. Refrigerate for 20 minutes.

Four To make the garlic cream sauce, place the garlic in a small saucepan, cover with cold water and bring to the boil. Reduce the heat and simmer for 3 minutes, then drain. Return the garlic to the pan, add the white wine and cream, then cover and simmer gently for about 25 minutes, or until the garlic is soft. Pour the garlic mixture into a food processor or blender and process until smooth. Transfer to a clean pan to keep warm and season to taste. Preheat the grill to high, and set the oven to its lowest setting.

Five Deep-fry the fritters in small batches at 180°C (350°F), following the method in the Chef's techniques on page 537 and stirring gently to ensure even browning. When they are golden, drain on crumpled paper towels. Place on a wire rack and keep warm in the oven.

Six Brush the lamb cutlets with the melted butter and season with salt and freshly ground pepper. Grill the cutlets for 3 minutes on each side for pink, or longer if preferred.

Seven Divide the lamb cutlets and fritters among warm serving plates and serve with a little garlic cream sauce.

about garlic...

Garlic has different strengths according to how fresh it is and how it is prepared and cooked. Fresh, young garlic has a much less harsh flavour than older garlic. The strongest garlic flavour is gained by crushing the garlic as this breaks down the majority of the cell walls. However, finely chopped garlic will also be strongly flavoured. Sliced garlic will give a milder flavour and cooked whole cloves of garlic, either roasted or simmered, will be sweet rather than strong.

LE CORDON BLEU COMPLETE COOK

Devilled kidneys with sage polenta discs

*These herb and polenta discs are an unusual
alternative to toast when serving
devilled kidneys for breakfast or brunch.*

*Preparation time 40 minutes
+ 1 hour resting
Total cooking time 25 minutes
Serves 4–6*

SAGE POLENTA DISCS
*600 ml (20 fl oz) milk
25 g (3/4 oz) unsalted butter
175 g (53/4 oz) instant polenta
50 g (13/4 oz) Parmesan cheese, grated
30 g (1 oz) fresh sage, finely chopped*

oil, for deep-frying

DEVILLED KIDNEYS
*8 lambs' kidneys
11/2 tablespoons tomato chutney
1/2 teaspoon mustard
dash of Worcestershire sauce
small pinch of cayenne pepper
60 g (2 oz) unsalted butter
1 French shallot, chopped
2–3 tablespoons beef (see page 518)
or vegetable stock*

One To make the polenta discs, heat the milk and butter in a large pan until nearly boiling. Using a whisk, briskly beat in the cornmeal and stir over medium heat for 2–3 minutes, or until thick. Remove and cool for 1 minute. Add the Parmesan and sage, season well and cool for another 5 minutes. Lightly flour the work surface and roll or press out the polenta to a thickness of 1 cm (1/2 inch). Leave to cool and firm for about 1 hour. Using a 5 cm (2 inch) plain cutter, cut out 25–30 discs. Place the discs in a single layer on two trays lined with baking paper and cover.

Two To prepare the devilled kidneys, remove the fat and fine membrane from around the kidneys, then lay them flat, hold in place with one hand and cut each through sideways with a sharp knife. Using the tip of a sharp knife or scissors, trim away the core from the cut side of each kidney half. In a small bowl, stir together the tomato chutney, mustard, Worcestershire sauce and the cayenne pepper. In a wide frying pan, melt half the butter and, over medium heat, cook the shallot for 3–4 minutes, or until golden. Transfer the shallot to a plate, wipe out the pan with paper towels and set aside.

Three Heat the oven to very slow 120°C (250°F/Gas 1/2). Deep-fry the polenta discs in small batches for 2–3 minutes at 180°C (350°F), following the method in the Chef's techniques on page 537. Drain on crumpled paper towels. Transfer to a wire rack and keep the discs warm in the oven, uncovered to retain their crispness.

Four Melt the remaining butter in the frying pan. When sizzling hot, add the kidneys, skin side down first. Cook over high heat for 20 seconds, turn over and cook for another 20 seconds. Remove to the plate with the shallot. Lower the heat, add the mustard mixture from the bowl to the pan and stir for a moment to blend. Return the kidneys and the shallot to the pan and toss for about 1–2 minutes, or until cooked through. Put four or five polenta discs on each plate and divide the kidneys among them. Add the stock to the pan and cook for 1 minute, stirring to blend in the kidney juices. Pour the sauce over the kidneys and serve immediately.

CHEF'S TIP *Devilled kidneys can also be served on toast. The sage and polenta discs can be served with scrambled or fried eggs, grilled tomatoes or sausages.*

Lamb fillets with coriander gravy

*Roasted pine nuts add a wonderful texture to these medallions
of pink lamb, presented on a bed of English spinach,
with a syrupy sauce of shallots, coriander and mint.*

Preparation time 30 minutes
Total cooking time 30 minutes
Serves 4

2 x 6-chop racks of lamb (best end
of neck)
1 tablespoon clarified butter (see
page 520) or oil
2 large French shallots, chopped
500 ml (16 fl oz) lamb stock
(see page 518) or light beef stock
25 g (¾ oz) fresh coriander leaves,
chopped
1 tablespoon chopped fresh mint
1 tablespoon hazelnut oil
1.5 kg (3 lb) English spinach leaves
2 large tomatoes, peeled, seeded and
diced (see page 534)
100 g (3¼ oz) pine nuts, toasted

One Remove the 'eye' or long round
fillet of meat at the thick end of each
rack by running a small, sharp knife
between the meat and the bone.

Two Heat the clarified butter in a
shallow pan. Season the fillets with salt,
then fry over gentle heat, turning now
and then, for 10–12 minutes, or until
still just pink inside and browned
outside. Remove, cover and keep warm.

Three Drain the pan of excess fat, add
the shallots and cook for 2 minutes, or
until lightly coloured. Add the stock,
bring to the boil, then reduce the heat
and simmer for 10 minutes, or until
syrupy. Remove from the heat, adjust
the seasoning, then stir in the coriander
and mint. Cover and keep warm.

Four In another frying pan, heat the
hazelnut oil and cook the spinach leaves
over high heat until just wilted. Drain

and season to taste. Pack the spinach
into four flat 250 ml (4 fl oz) moulds or
ramekins, then turn each mould out
onto the centre of a warm plate.

Five Carve the lamb fillets into medallions
about 5 mm (¼ inch) thick. Arrange on

the spinach and swirl the sauce around.
Sprinkle with tomato and pine nuts.

CHEF'S TIP *Ask your butcher to remove
the fillets from the racks of lamb for you.*

LE CORDON BLEU 🛡 COMPLETE COOK

Navarin of lamb

This traditional French lamb and potato stew has existed for over 180 years and is said to have been named after one of the main ingredients, 'navet', the French word for turnip. Other vegetables may also be added to the stew if desired, as in this recipe.

Preparation time 45 minutes
Total cooking time 2 hours
Serves 4

1 kg (2 lb) lamb shoulder, boned
80 ml (2¾ fl oz) oil
40 g (1¼ oz) unsalted butter
1 large onion, finely chopped
1 tablespoon tomato paste (purée)
2 large tomatoes, peeled, seeded and chopped (see page 534)
3 cloves garlic, chopped
1 tablespoon plain flour
1 bouquet garni (see page 520)
150 g (5 oz) peas
1 large carrot, cut into 5 cm (2 inch) pieces
2 turnips, peeled and quartered
12 new or baby potatoes
1 tablespoon chopped fresh parsley

One Preheat the oven to moderately hot 200°C (400°F/Gas 6). Trim off any excess fat from the meat and cut into 2.5 cm (1 inch) cubes. Heat the oil in a frying pan and cook the lamb in batches until brown. Remove from the pan, drain off the oil, and set aside.

Two Place a 3 litre flameproof casserole dish on top of the stove and melt the butter. Gently cook the onion for 5 minutes, without colouring. Add the tomato paste and cook over medium heat for 2 minutes. Add the tomatoes and cook for a further 3 minutes. Add the garlic and mix. Add the lamb and any juices and sprinkle the top with flour. Without mixing in the flour, place the dish in the oven for 5 minutes.

Three Remove the casserole from the oven and place over medium heat. Mix in the flour, then gradually add 1.5 litres boiling water. Mix well by scraping down the sides and bottom of the dish. Simmer for a few minutes, skimming off the foam, then add the bouquet garni, season with salt and black pepper, cover and return to the oven. Cook for 1 hour. Bring a large pan of salted water to the boil and cook the peas for 3 minutes. Drain, refresh with cold water, drain again, then set aside.

Four Remove the casserole from the oven and place over medium heat. Add the carrot, turnip and potatoes and cook for 15 minutes, then add the peas. Cook for a further 10–15 minutes, or until the meat and potatoes are tender. Remove the bouquet garni and discard, then season to taste with salt and black pepper. Stir in the chopped parsley just before serving.

Roasted lamb with vegetables

This memorable roast is served with a classic French garnish of bacon, mushrooms, glazed pearl onions and golden brown potatoes. It makes a special dish for a Sunday lunch with all the family.

Preparation time 1 hour 15 minutes
Total cooking time 1 hour
Serves 6

100 ml (3¼ fl oz) oil
1 lamb shoulder, about 1.5 kg (3 lb), deboned (ask your butcher to tie the lamb, chop the bones and reserve the trimmings)
1 carrot, chopped
1 onion, chopped
½ celery stick, chopped
2 cloves garlic, crushed
1 sprig of fresh thyme or ¼ teaspoon dried thyme
1 bay leaf
300 g (10 oz) bacon
300 g (10 oz) pearl onions or large-bulb spring onions, peeled
70 g (2¼ oz) unsalted butter
1 tablespoon sugar
300 g (10 oz) button mushrooms
1 kg (2 lb) potatoes, peeled
375 ml (12 fl oz) chicken stock (see page 519)
2 tablespoons chopped fresh parsley

One Preheat the oven to moderately hot 200°C (400°F/ Gas 6). Heat half the oil in a large ovenproof frying pan over high heat. Season the lamb and brown on all sides in the hot oil. Remove and set aside. Add the bones and trimmings to the pan and brown all over.

Two Add the carrot, onion, celery, garlic, thyme and bay leaf to the pan. Rest the lamb on the bones, then transfer to the oven and roast for 40 minutes for rare, or 1 hour for medium, basting two or three times.

Three Cut the bacon into 3 mm (⅛ inch) pieces. In a pan, lightly brown the bacon, then drain. Place the pearl onions in a medium saucepan over high heat with a tablespoon of the butter, the sugar, 50 ml (1¾ fl oz) water, and salt and freshly ground pepper to taste. Cook until the water has evaporated and the onions are a light blonde colour.

Four Cut the mushrooms into quarters, then sauté them in a tablespoon of the butter over high heat until browned. Season to taste and drain.

Five Using a melon-baller, carve the potatoes into balls, placing them in cold water to prevent browning, then transfer

to a pan of cold water. Bring to the boil, boil for 1 minute, then drain.

Six Heat the remaining oil in an ovenproof pan over high heat. When the oil is hot, add the potatoes, tossing to coat them evenly with oil. Cook for 2–3 minutes, or until the potatoes are well coloured, then transfer to the oven and bake for 20 minutes, or until tender. Drain off the excess oil, toss the potato balls in a tablespoon of the butter and season to taste.

Seven Remove the lamb from the oven and place on a wire rack to rest. Drain the pan of excess fat, remove the bones and trimmings, and place the pan on the stovetop over medium-high heat. Cook for 2–3 minutes, or until the vegetables have coloured, then add the stock and stir to dissolve the cooking juices. Cook for about 10 minutes, or until reduced in volume by a third. Strain through a sieve and season to taste.

Eight Toss together the pearl onions, potatoes, mushrooms and bacon and reheat if necessary. Sprinkle with the chopped parsley. Carve the lamb into slices about 1 cm (½ inch) thick; serve with the vegetables and bacon arranged around, and the sauce on the side.

about lamb...

The flavour of lamb varies according to where it was raised and how young it is. Milk-fed lamb has a milder flavour than hill or mountain-raised lamb. Most supermarket lamb is relatively mild in flavour so, if you prefer a stronger taste, ask your butcher for slightly older lamb which has been hung for a week or so.

Lancashire hot pot

A traditional regional British casserole, the exceptional taste of this dish comes from the meat cooked on the bone adding to the flavour of the stock as it cooks.

Preparation time 30 minutes
Total cooking time 2 hours 20 minutes
Serves 4

1 kg (2 lb) middle neck of lamb chops
20 g (3/4 oz) unsalted butter
900 g (1 lb 13 oz) potatoes, peeled
2 large onions, finely sliced
2 carrots, sliced into 2 mm (1/8 inch)
thick rounds
1/2 teaspoon chopped fresh thyme
1 bay leaf
400 ml (123/4 fl oz) brown stock
(see page 518)
60 g (2 oz) unsalted butter,
melted

One Preheat the oven to moderate 180°C (350°F/Gas 4). Brush a 3.5 litre oven-proof casserole dish with butter. Trim off the excess fat from the lamb, melt the butter in a frying pan and, over high heat, quickly fry the chops until lightly browned and just sealed, but not cooked through. Remove from the pan and transfer the chops to a plate.

Two Slice the potatoes into 2 mm (1/8 inch) thick rounds and cover the base of the casserole dish with about a third of the slices. Season lightly with salt and pepper. Place the chops neatly on the potato, scatter with the onion, carrot and thyme, season lightly and add the bay leaf. Put the remaining potato slices into the dish, neatly overlapping the very top layer. Pour on enough of the stock to come up to just under the top layer by pouring the stock down one side of the dish so that the top layer is not wet. Brush well with melted butter and season lightly with salt and pepper. Cover and cook on the middle shelf of the oven for 1 1/2 hours.

Three Remove the lid, then add a little more stock or water if the liquid has been taken up by the potato and you would like it to be moister. Return the dish to the oven for about 45 minutes, uncovered, or until the meat is cooked and the potato top is crisp and brown. Serve hot with green vegetables.

CHEF'S TIPS *Do not slice the peeled potato until required or it will discolour. Also, do not keep sliced potato in cold water, as the starch that is needed to help thicken the hot pot will only be washed out.*

If you wish, you can add one lamb's kidney, halved, trimmed of its core and cut into 1 cm (1/2 inch) pieces. Scatter it raw onto the lamb as it goes into the casserole dish.

Braised lamb with tomato sauce

*A simple yet delicious lamb stew, flavoured with garlic,
bacon and tomatoes, which can be served with rice or fresh pasta.*

Preparation time 25 minutes
Total cooking time 1 hour 45 minutes
Serves 4

*1.2 kg (2 lb 6½ oz) lamb shoulder,
boned, trimmed and cut into
small pieces*
2 tablespoons oil
40 g (1¼ oz) unsalted butter
60 g (2 oz) slab bacon, diced
1 small onion, chopped
1 small carrot, chopped
2 tablespoons tomato paste (purée)
1 tablespoon plain flour
*500 g (1 lb) tomatoes, peeled, seeded
and chopped (see page 534)*
1 bouquet garni (see page 520)
4 cloves garlic, chopped
*500 ml (16 fl oz) brown stock
(see page 518) or water*
*1 tablespoon chopped fresh parsley
or basil*

One Preheat the oven to moderate 180°C (350°F/Gas 4). Season the lamb with salt and pepper. Heat the oil in a heavy-based frying pan over medium–high heat, add the lamb and brown it, in batches, for about 6–8 minutes, or until well coloured on all sides. Drain on paper towels.

Two Melt the butter in a large flame-proof casserole dish over medium heat. Add the bacon and cook until golden brown. Add the onion and carrot and cook for about 3 minutes. Stir in the tomato paste and cook for a further 2 minutes. Sprinkle with the flour and bake for 5 minutes. Remove from the oven and mix in the flour. Add the tomatoes, bouquet garni and garlic. Place on the heat and cook for 5 minutes, stirring constantly, then add the stock or water. Bring to the boil, stirring constantly. Add the lamb, cover and bake for 1 hour, or until the meat is tender when pierced with the tip of a sharp knife.

Three Remove the meat from the sauce, cover and keep warm. Strain the sauce through a fine sieve, pressing to extract as much liquid as possible. Discard the solids. Pour the sauce into a pan.

Four Bring the sauce back to the boil, skimming if necessary. Simmer for about 10 minutes, or until the sauce is thick enough to coat the back of a spoon. Add the lamb and stir until heated through. Season with salt and pepper. Sprinkle with the parsley or basil and serve.

Cassoulet

Haricot beans are the essential ingredient in this dish from the Languedoc region of France and give the cassoulet its creaminess. Some sort of meat, depending on the region, and a gratin topping are added near the end of cooking. The word cassoulet comes from 'cassole', an earthenware pot traditionally used for cooking this dish.

*Preparation time 1 hour 30 minutes
+ soaking overnight*
Total cooking time 4 hours 30 minutes
Serves 4–6

*250 g (8 oz) dried haricot beans
(navy beans), soaked overnight
in cold water*
100 g (3¼ oz) fresh pork rind
100 g (3¼ oz) slab bacon
½ carrot
½ onion, studded with a clove
2 bouquets garnis (see page 520)
1 clove garlic
*40 g (1¼ oz) goose fat, duck fat
or lard*
*200 g (6½ oz) boneless lamb shoulder,
cut into 8 pieces*
*200 g (6½ oz) boneless pork shoulder,
cut into 8 pieces*
1 small onion, chopped
*2 tomatoes, peeled, seeded and diced
(see page 534) or 1 tablespoon
tomato paste (purée)*
1 clove garlic, crushed
*300 g (10 oz) fresh garlic sausage,
sliced*
*4 small fresh Toulouse
or pork sausages*
*2 legs duck or goose confit or
1 cooked duck maryland (leg
quarter), about 360 g (11½ oz)
altogether, cut into 2 pieces*
90 g (3 oz) fresh breadcrumbs

One Preheat the oven to moderate 180°C (350°F/Gas 4). Rinse the soaked beans and cover generously with fresh cold water in a large pan. Add the pork rind and slab bacon and bring to the boil. As soon as it reaches the boil, remove from the heat, strain and refresh in cold water. Cover once more with fresh water, return to the heat and add the carrot, onion and clove, 1 bouquet garni and the garlic. Simmer for about 1½ hours (do not add salt, as this will interfere with the cooking of the beans and make them tough).

Two While the beans are simmering, melt 25 g (¾ oz) of the goose fat, duck fat or lard in a large flameproof casserole dish. Season the lamb shoulder and pork shoulder and brown in the casserole dish. Remove and set aside. In the same dish, cook the chopped onion until soft but not coloured. Add the tomato or tomato purée, crushed garlic and the second bouquet garni. Heat until bubbling, return the meat to the casserole dish, cover and place in the oven for 1 hour to 1½ hours, or until the meat is tender. Remove the meat from the casserole.

Three Reduce the oven temperature to warm 160°C (315°F/Gas 2–3). Add the garlic sausage, Toulouse sausages and confit to the casserole, bring to a simmer on the stove, then cook in the oven for 20 minutes. Transfer the confit and the sausages to a bowl and keep warm. Set the sauce aside. Reduce oven temperature to slow 150°C (300°F/Gas 2).

Four When the beans are almost cooked (they should be tender with a slight resistance), drain and add the beans' cooking liquid to the reserved sauce in the casserole dish. Remove and discard the vegetables and bouquet garni. Remove the slab bacon and pork rind and set aside to cool. Keeping the bacon and pork separate, cut them into bite-sized pieces.

Five Warm a large, ovenproof serving dish. Cover the bottom with some of the pork rind and then cover with a layer of beans. Add the lamb shoulder, pork shoulder, sausages, confit and about 250–375 ml (8–12 fl oz) of the reserved liquid. Cover with another layer of beans and top with the pieces of bacon, the remaining pork rind and liquid. Sprinkle the breadcrumbs over the top and then drizzle them with the remaining melted goose fat. Bake for 1 hour, or until the breadcrumbs are lightly coloured, then serve.

---

about cassoulet...

The ingredients used in cassoulet vary depending on where it is made. Several different cities in Languedoc have their own version. You can vary the types of sausage if you prefer or use just lamb or pork rather than both.

Country-style terrine

This coarsely textured pâté derives its name from the deep rectangular dish in which it is cooked. Meat terrines often contain a high proportion of pork, and some pork fat, to prevent the meat from becoming dry.

Preparation time 30 minutes
+ 2 nights refrigeration
Total cooking time 50 minutes
Serves 6–8

20 g (3/4 oz) unsalted butter
2 cloves garlic, chopped
2 French shallots, chopped
3 sprigs of fresh thyme
1 small bay leaf
200 g (6½ oz) pork fat,
finely diced
150 g (5 oz) calf, lamb or ox liver,
finely diced
400 g (12¾ oz) pork loin, finely diced
40 ml (1¼ fl oz) brandy
50 ml (1¾ fl oz) white wine
½ teaspoon salt
¼ teaspoon ground nutmeg
50 g (1¾ oz) fresh breadcrumbs
1 tablespoon milk
1 egg, beaten
20 rashers streaky bacon

One Melt the butter in a pan over low heat. Warm the garlic, shallots, thyme and bay leaf with the pork fat, liver and pork loin. Gently cook for 3–5 minutes. Add the brandy, wine, salt, nutmeg and some pepper, stirring well to coat the meat—the mixture should be warm, not hot. Leave the mixture to cool, then refrigerate overnight.

Two Preheat the oven to moderate 180°C (350°F/Gas 4). Wrap a small piece of wood or stiff cardboard (the same size as the top of a 1 litre terrine) in aluminium foil. Soak the breadcrumbs in milk.

Three Remove the thyme and bay leaf from the terrine mixture. Process the meat in a food processor in short bursts until roughly chopped, then transfer to a bowl. Mix together the breadcrumbs and egg and add to the meat. Mix well.

Four Line a greased terrine mould with bacon, letting the rashers hang over the sides. Add the meat mixture, fold the rashers over and cover with a layer of bacon, then a sheet of greased baking paper. Place the terrine in a roasting tin and pour enough boiling water into the tin to come halfway up the side of the terrine. Bake for about 30–40 minutes. To check the temperature, insert the tip of a small knife into the centre of the terrine for a few seconds. If the blade comes out hot, the terrine is cooked; if not, cook for another 5 minutes, or until the knife comes out hot.

Five Remove from the oven and allow to cool for 20 minutes. Place the wood or cardboard across the top, then weigh it down with a heavy can. Refrigerate overnight. Leave the terrine at room temperature for at least 30 minutes before serving. The terrine can be served in the mould, or turned out onto a board or plate.

White bean stew with fennel sausages

*Dried cannellini beans—full of protein, calcium and iron—
are cooked with aniseed-flavoured Italian sausages in a
creamy herb sauce, making this stew a complete meal.*

Preparation time 25 minutes
Total cooking time 1 hour 30 minutes
Serves 4

375 g (12 oz) dried cannellini beans
1 small onion, diced
1 small carrot, diced
1 small celery stick, diced
sprig of fresh thyme
sprig of fresh rosemary
1 teaspoon black peppercorns
4 Italian-style sausages with fennel
60 ml (2 fl oz) thick (double) cream
chopped fresh parsley, to garnish

HERB BUTTER
1 clove garlic, roughly chopped
1 tablespoon chopped fresh parsley
1 tablespoon fresh rosemary leaves
1 tablespoon fresh thyme leaves
120 g (4 oz) unsalted butter, softened

One Place the beans and vegetables in a large flameproof casserole dish with the sprigs of thyme and rosemary. Wrap the peppercorns in a piece of muslin and add to the dish. Cover with 1.5 litres cold water. Place on the stove and bring to the boil, then reduce the heat to low and simmer for 55 minutes.

Two To make the herb butter, use a mortar and pestle or a blender to purée the garlic, parsley, rosemary, thyme and butter until smooth. Season to taste with salt and pepper and set aside.

Three Preheat the oven to moderate 180°C (350°F/Gas 4). Heat a little oil in a frying pan and brown the sausages. Cut diagonally into four pieces and add to the beans after they have finished simmering. Cover and bake in the oven for 30 minutes, or until the beans are

tender. There should be just enough liquid left to cover the beans. If not, add more water.

Four Remove the sausages and set aside. Remove the sachet of peppercorns and the sprigs of herbs and discard. Mix in the herb butter and the cream and season to taste. Arrange the sausages on top, sprinkle with some chopped parsley and serve.

LE CORDON BLEU COMPLETE COOK

Loin of pork with prunes and Armagnac

This recipe for roast pork has a strong Christmas flavour to it,
with a stuffing of sweet prunes and French brandy.
Loin of pork is a cut that is easy to carve into neat slices.

Preparation time 30 minutes
+ 1 hour soaking
Total cooking time 1 hour 50 minutes
Serves 4–6

60 g (2 oz) pitted prunes
1½ tablespoons Armagnac
1.5 kg (3 lb) boned loin of pork, with
a long rib flap if possible
2 teaspoons oil
15 g (½ oz) unsalted butter

HERB SAUCE
35 g (1¼ oz) unsalted butter
2 large French shallots, chopped
500 ml (16 fl oz) chicken stock
(see page 519)
225 ml (7¼ fl oz) cream
1½ tablespoons finely chopped
fresh sage
1½ tablespoons finely chopped
fresh parsley

One Put the prunes in a bowl and pour in the Armagnac. Cover and soak for at least 1 hour.

Two Preheat the oven to moderately hot 200°C (400°F/Gas 6). Remove the skin and excess sinew from the pork, leaving a thin layer of fat. Turn the loin over and open it out flat (one side, where the muscle is, will be thicker). Cut a long slit down the length of the muscle to halfway through the meat. Remove the prunes from the Armagnac, reserving the Armagnac, and gently push them into the slit, then close and roll the flatter meat around the muscle. Tie pieces of string 2.5 cm (1 inch) apart along the loin to hold it together.

Three Heat the oil in a frying pan, add the butter and heat until frothy. Add the pork and fry over medium–high heat for 5–8 minutes, or until sealed and browned all over. Transfer to an oven-proof dish or roasting pan and bake for 1–1¼ hours, or until the juices run clear when pierced with a skewer.

Four To make the herb sauce, melt the butter in a pan, add the shallots and cook, covered, over low heat for about 5 minutes, or until soft and translucent. Add the reserved Armagnac and cook, uncovered, until reduced to about 1 tablespoon. Pour in the stock and simmer for 15–20 minutes, or until reduced to ¼ cup (60 ml/2 fl oz), then stir in the cream and simmer until the sauce lightly coats the back of a spoon. Remove from the heat, cover the surface with plastic wrap and keep warm.

Five Remove the pork from the oven and transfer it to a plate. Leave to rest for 5 minutes, then place on a chopping board. Gently reheat the sauce, but do not allow it to bubble for more than 1 minute. Add the sage and parsley and season with salt and black pepper just before serving. Remove the string from the meat and, using a thin, sharp knife, cut the pork into slices. Arrange the slices on plates and pour the sauce around. Serve with a green salad or vegetables and potatoes.

about prunes...

Prunes are dried plums. The plums are usually dried and then rehydrated by different degrees to produce semi-dried or dried prunes. The semi-dried variety are softer and do not need to be soaked for as long. Some of the best are prunes d'Agen from Aquitaine in France. However, all types are suitable for this recipe.

Honey-glazed spiced ham

A whole ham is perfect for feeding a large gathering. This version is served hot with a mustard cream sauce, but any leftovers make a delicious cold lunch with a green salad and pickles.

Preparation time *30 minutes*
+ overnight soaking
Total cooking time *6 hours*
Serves 20

7 kg (14 lb) uncooked leg of ham,
smoked or unsmoked
2 onions
2 celery sticks
3 carrots
3–4 bay leaves
3 sprigs fresh thyme
1 clove
4 allspice

HONEY GLAZE
125 g (4 oz) soft brown
or demerara sugar
105 g (3¹/₂ oz) honey
1¹/₂ teaspoons ground mixed spice
1 tablespoon English mustard
cloves, for decoration

MUSTARD CREAM SAUCE
500 ml (16 fl oz) thick (double) cream
75 g (2¹/₂ oz) English mustard
25 g (³/₄ oz) whole mustard seeds,
soaked in water

One Soak the ham overnight in cold water, changing the water once or twice.

Two Preheat the oven to warm 160°C (315°F/Gas 2–3). Tip off the soaking liquid from the ham and rinse the ham under cold water. Pat dry, place in a large roasting pan and distribute the vegetables, herbs and spices around it. Pour 500 ml (16 fl oz) cold water into the pan and cover the pan with foil. Bake for 20 minutes per 500 g (1 lb), then cook for an extra 20 minutes.

Three Remove the ham from the oven and lift it out of the liquid. Reserve the cooking liquid and discard the vegetables. To prepare the ham, follow the method in the Chef's techniques on page 531. Raise the oven temperature to moderate 180°C (350°F/Gas 4).

Four To make the honey glaze, mix all the ingredients except the cloves together in a bowl and spread over the ham with a palette knife. Push a clove into the centre of each diamond. Place, fat-side-up, on a rack over a roasting pan into which 1 cm (¹/₂ inch) water has been poured (this will make the pan easier to clean later on). Bake the ham for 20 minutes, or until the surface is lightly caramelised. Rest for 30 minutes before carving.

Five To make the mustard cream sauce, boil the ham's cooking liquid in a pan over high heat for 30 minutes, or until reduced to a light syrup. Add the cream and return to the boil, then remove from the heat and stir in the mustard and drained mustard seeds. Do not reboil or the mustard will lose its fresh flavour. Taste and season if necessary.

Six To carve the ham, follow the method in the Chef's techniques on page 531. Serve the ham with the hot mustard cream sauce, some new potatoes and a selection of vegetables.

CHEF'S TIPS *If you want to serve the ham cold, allow it to cool after removing from the oven. Rather than serving the ham with the hot mustard cream sauce, you can mix 250 g (8 oz) mayonnaise with 30 g (1 oz) wholegrain mustard to accompany the ham. Serve with hot new potatoes, mixed salad leaves and pickles or chutneys.*

If a whole ham is too big, use a half ham or piece of boned gammon. Cook in the same way, calculating the cooking time at 30 minutes per 500 g (1 lb).

Saucisson de Lyon with warm potato salad

Lyon is renowned for its hearty dishes, often featuring onions, potatoes and charcuterie. The Lyonnais sausages used in this recipe need to be carefully poached to prevent them from bursting, and can be bought or made with or without pistachios.

Preparation time 35 minutes
Total cooking time 55 minutes
Serves 4

COURT-BOUILLON
1 carrot, thinly sliced
2 onions, thinly sliced
2 celery sticks, thinly sliced
2 small leeks, white part only,
thinly sliced
3 sprigs of fresh thyme
1 bay leaf
10 black peppercorns
1 teaspooon salt
500 ml (16 fl oz) white wine

4 large potatoes, about 800 g
(1 lb 10 oz)
500 g (1 lb) Lyonnais or pure pork
sausages (see Chef's tip)

MUSTARD DRESSING
4 tablespoons Dijon mustard
4 tablespoons finely chopped
French shallots
250 ml (8 fl oz) oil
2 tablespoons chopped
fresh parsley

One To make the court-bouillon, place the carrot, onion, celery, leek, seasonings and white wine in a large pan and bring to the boil for 5 minutes over high heat. Remove the pan from the heat and set aside to cool.

Two Place the potatoes in a large pan of salted water. Bring to the boil, then reduce the heat and simmer for about 20–30 minutes, or until tender to the point of a knife. Drain, rinse lightly with cold water and peel, then slice into 5 mm (1/4 inch) thick slices. Cover and keep warm.

Three Meanwhile, place the sausages in the cooled court-bouillon. Pour in about 2 litres water to completely cover the sausages, bring to a simmer and poach for 20 minutes. Do not allow to boil or the sausages will burst. Remove from the heat and set aside.

Four To make the mustard dressing, mix the mustard and shallots in a bowl, slowly whisk in the oil until smooth and thick, then stir in the parsley. Season the warm potato slices with salt and black pepper and mix with the dressing.

Five Transfer the warm potatoes to a large platter. Remove the sausages from

the court bouillon, dry with paper towels and cut into 16 equal slices. Arrange the slices around the potato salad and serve.

CHEF'S TIP *To make the Lyonnais sausages from scratch, finely mince 450 g (14 oz) pork loin and 150 g (5 oz) lean veal shoulder and mix them together in a bowl with 160 g (5 1/4 oz) pork fat (lard), salt and pepper. Add 100 g (3 1/4 oz) shelled and skinned pistachios and mix together well. Using a large sausage funnel, fill a large sausage casing with the sausage mixture to make a 30–35 cm (12–14 inch) long sausage. Tie off the ends with kitchen string.*

Venison casserole

Venison is the most common large game and has a distinctive strong flavour. In this recipe, the venison is slowly cooked to perfection with onions, mushrooms and garlic in red wine. It is then combined with redcurrant jelly and juniper berries to produce a truly memorable dish.

Preparation time 30 minutes
Total cooking time 2 hours
Serves 4

750 g (1½ lb) braising venison, off the
bone, or 2 kg (4 lb) venison cutlets
185 g (6 oz) pearl or pickling onions
2 tablespoons olive oil
250 g (8 oz) button mushrooms
1 clove garlic, crushed
1 tablespoon plain flour
250 ml (8 fl oz) red wine
1 tablespoon redcurrant jelly
6 juniper berries, crushed

One Preheat the oven to warm 170°C (325°F/Gas 3). If using venison off the bone, cut into 4 cm (1½ inch) pieces.

Two Place the onions in a small pan with just enough cold water to cover them. Bring to the boil, reduce the heat, simmer for 2 minutes, then drain. Heat the oil in a 2.5 litre flameproof casserole over high heat. When very hot, add the meat in batches and fry for 1–2 minutes each side, or until brown on all sides. Remove from the dish and keep warm.

Three Add the onions to the casserole and toss gently until beginning to colour. Add the mushrooms and garlic and cook for about 1 minute. Sprinkle with flour and cook, stirring, for 1 minute. Stir in the wine, 250 ml (8 fl oz) water and some salt and bring to the boil. Return the meat to the dish, cover and bake for 1½ hours.

Four Remove the casserole from the oven and strain off the liquid into a small pan. Bring to the boil and cook for 1 minute to reduce the liquid. Stir in the redcurrant jelly, add the juniper berries and return to the boil. Season to taste, then pour the liquid over the casserole. Return to the oven and cook for a further 15 minutes to heat through. Serve piping hot with a potato and celeriac purée.

Sautéed rabbit with mushrooms

Rabbit meat is very lean, which makes this tasty dish even more attractive. Combined with mushrooms, shallots and tomatoes, slowly cooked in white wine and enhanced with the flavour of fresh herbs, this rabbit casserole is perfect for a special occasion.

Preparation time 25 minutes
Total cooking time 1 hour 20 minutes
Serves 4

1.8 kg (3 lb 10 oz) rabbit,
cut into 8 pieces
80 g (2¾ oz) unsalted butter
130 g (4¼ oz) mushrooms, sliced
2 French shallots, chopped
250 ml (8 fl oz) white wine
3 large tomatoes, peeled, seeded
and chopped (see page 534)
500 ml (16 fl oz) brown stock
(see page 518)
1 bouquet garni (see page 520)
1–2 teaspoons chopped
fresh tarragon
1 tablespoon chopped fresh chervil

One Season the rabbit pieces with salt and pepper and preheat the oven to moderate 180°C (350°F/Gas 4). Melt half the butter in a large flameproof casserole dish over medium heat and brown the rabbit in batches. Remove the meat from the dish and set aside. Discard the butter left in the dish, then return the dish to the heat and add the remaining butter. Add the mushrooms and cook for 3 minutes, then add the shallot and cook for 3 minutes. Add the wine and continue cooking for 3 minutes, or until almost all the liquid has evaporated.

Two Add the tomato and mix well. Bring to the boil, reduce the heat and simmer for 10 minutes. Add the stock and bouquet garni and return to the boil. Allow to boil for 5 minutes, skimming off any foam or fat from the surface.

Three Return the rabbit to the dish and bring to a simmer. Cover and bake for 20–25 minutes, or until the rabbit is tender. To test the meat, pierce a thick piece with a fork and lift it up. If tender, it should slide easily from the bone. Transfer the rabbit to a serving platter, cover and keep warm. Place the casserole dish on the stove top and remove the bouquet garni. Bring to the boil and cook for about 5–10 minutes, skimming as necessary. Adjust the seasoning and check the consistency of the sauce. If the sauce is not thick enough, continue to boil for 5 minutes, or until it is the desired consistency.

Four Stir in the chopped tarragon and chervil and pour the sauce over the rabbit. Serve immediately.

Rabbit and marjoram cobbler with herb scones

Rabbit, with its light and tender flesh, is a favourite game meat in Italy. Here it is teamed with fresh herbs, both in the stew and in the scones placed on top to soak up the flavoursome juices.

Preparation time 40 *minutes*
Total cooking time 1 *hour* 30 *minutes*
Serves 4

1 rabbit, weighing 1.25 kg (2 lb 8 oz),
cut into 8 pieces
plain flour, seasoned
butter or oil, for cooking
1 onion, finely chopped
150 g (5 oz) button mushrooms, sliced
1 teaspoon tomato paste (purée)
1 clove garlic, chopped
500 ml (16 fl oz) chicken stock (see
page 519)
8 ripe tomatoes, peeled, seeded
and chopped (see page 534)
1 tablespoon chopped fresh rosemary
2 tablespoons chopped fresh marjoram
1 tablespoon chopped fresh parsley

HERB SCONES
250 g (8 oz) self-raising flour
60 g (2 oz) unsalted butter, cut into
cubes and chilled
1 tablespoon chopped fresh herbs,
such as parsley, rosemary, thyme
or marjoram
120 ml (4 fl oz) buttermilk
1 egg, beaten

One Coat the rabbit in the flour. Heat a little butter or oil in a frying pan, brown the rabbit on all sides, then drain on paper towels. Add the onion to the pan and cook over low heat until soft. Add the mushrooms, increase the heat and stir in the tomato paste and garlic. Transfer to a flameproof casserole, add the rabbit and season well.

Two Pour in the stock (it should be enough to barely cover the rabbit) and simmer gently for 30 minutes. Add the tomatoes and cook for 10 minutes. Add

the rosemary, marjoram and parsley. Check that the meat is tender.

Three To make the scones, preheat the oven to moderately hot 200°C (400°F/ Gas 6). Sift the flour and a good pinch of salt into a large bowl, add the butter and rub in until crumbly. Toss in the herbs, then stir in the milk with a knife until the dry flour has disappeared and the mixture is in large lumps. Turn out

onto a lightly floured surface and gather into a smooth ball. Roll or pat out to 1.5 cm (5/8 inch) thick. Work quickly— you want the dough to rise in the oven, not waste its rising power while it's being rolled. Cut into 4 cm (1½ inch) rounds, brush the tops with the egg and arrange immediately over the rabbit casserole. Place the dish near the top of the oven and bake for 12 minutes, or until the scones are golden.

pasta and rice

Pesto with spaghetti

*This recipe for the classic, uncooked basil, Parmesan and pine nut sauce (pictured top right)
makes enough for about 25 servings. It is usually served over pasta
but also doubles as a sauce with chicken or chargrilled vegetables.*

Preparation time 15 minutes
Total cooking time Nil
Makes approximately 800 ml (26 fl oz)

80 g (2³/4 oz) fresh basil
100 g (3¹/2 oz) Parmesan cheese
2 cloves garlic
50 g (1³/4 oz) pine nuts
100 ml (3¹/4 fl oz) olive oil
spaghetti, to serve

One Tear the basil leaves from the stalks, discarding the stalks. Wash the basil leaves well and dry thoroughly in a salad spinner or gently pat dry with a tea towel.

Two Grate the Parmesan, then process it in a food processor until it resembles fine breadcrumbs. Add the garlic and pine nuts and process briefly to roughly combine the ingredients. Add the basil at this point and process to combine.

Three While the machine is still running, slowly add the olive oil until a paste is formed. Season with salt and freshly ground black pepper, then continue to add the oil until it reaches a spoonable consistency. Cook about 115 g (4 oz) spaghetti per person according to the manufacturer's instructions and stir the pesto through. The remaining pesto can be stored covered in the refrigerator for up to 3 days.

CHEF'S TIP *If you wish to store the pesto for a longer period, transfer it to a sterilised jar, cover the surface with olive oil and store the jar in the refrigerator. Once you have opened it, the pesto must be used within 2–3 days. Each time you use some, add a little more oil to the jar to keep the surface covered.*

Tomato concassé with ravioli

*This is a classic vegetable preparation. The term 'concassé'
is also used to describe finely diced tomato used as
a garnish (pictured bottom right).*

Preparation time 15 minutes
Total cooking time 15 minutes
Serves 4

*olive oil or good vegetable oil,
for cooking*
2 large French shallots, finely chopped
1 clove garlic, finely chopped
*1 tablespoon tomato paste (purée),
optional*
*500 g (1 lb) ripe tomatoes, peeled,
seeded and chopped (see page 534)*
1 bouquet garni (see page 520)
500 g fresh ravioli (see page 533)

One Heat a little oil in a shallow pan and add the shallot and garlic. Cook gently until softened, but not brown. Stir in the tomato purée if the fresh tomatoes are not particularly ripe.

Two Add the chopped tomato to the pan with the bouquet garni and cook rapidly, stirring with a wooden spoon, for about 7 minutes, or until the mixture is dry. Remove the bouquet garni and season, to taste, with salt and black pepper.

Three Cook the ravioli in a large pan of boiling water for 5 minutes, or until it floats to the surface. Drain and serve the sauce over the top.

Tortellini with creamy mushroom sauce

Fresh tortellini, small pasta parcels containing meat, cheese or vegetable fillings, are now available in most supermarkets and delicatessens, making this delicious dish very easy to put together.

Preparation time 15 minutes
Total cooking time 35 minutes
Serves 4

40 g (1¼ oz) unsalted butter
2 French shallots,
finely chopped
500 g (1 lb) cap or button mushrooms,
thinly sliced
1 tablespoon lemon juice
2 tablespoons port
500 ml (16 fl oz) thick (double) cream
500 g (1 lb) fresh tortellini

One Over low heat, melt the butter in a frying pan and cook the shallots with a pinch of salt for 3–5 minutes without colouring. Toss the mushrooms in the lemon juice, add to the pan with another pinch of salt and cook over medium heat for about 10–15 minutes, or until the mushrooms are dry and all the liquid has evaporated. Add the port and cook for 2–3 minutes, or until almost dry, being careful to not let the mixture scorch. Stir in the cream and simmer for about 5–10 minutes, or until the sauce is thick enough to coat the back of a spoon. Check for seasoning.

Two Meanwhile, bring a large pan of salted water to the boil. Add a splash of oil to stop the pasta sticking and cook the tortellini according to the manufacturer's instructions. Drain well and divide the tortellini among four warm plates. Spoon the sauce over the top and serve with some freshly ground black pepper.

CHEF'S TIP *For a stronger flavour, mix some soaked dried mushrooms, such as porcini or shiitake, with the cap or button mushrooms.*

Ziti Amatriciana

The ziti used in this recipe are very long thin tubes.
If unavailable, use macaroni or penne.

Preparation time *15 minutes*
Total cooking time *50 minutes*
Serves 4–6

2 tablespoons olive oil
400 g (12³/4 oz) pancetta or
bacon, cut into 5 mm (1/4 inch)
thick pieces
1 onion, thinly sliced
2–3 red chillies, finely sliced,
or 1/2 teaspoon dried chilli flakes
2 x 425 g (13¹/2 oz) cans chopped
Italian tomatoes or 1.75 kg (3¹/2 lb)
tomatoes, peeled and chopped (see
page 534)
500 g (1 lb) ziti
grated Parmesan cheese, to serve

One In a heavy-based saucepan, heat half the oil and slowly brown the pancetta or bacon for 5 minutes, then drain and set aside on paper towels. Add the onion and lightly brown for about 3 minutes, then add the chilli and cook for 2 minutes. Add the pancetta or bacon and the tomatoes, cover and cook over medium heat for about 20 minutes, then cook uncovered for a further 10–15 minutes, or until thick.

Two Bring a large pan of salted water to the boil. Add a splash of oil to stop the pasta sticking and cook the ziti according to the manufacturer's instructions. Drain well.

Three Divide the pasta among the serving bowls and serve with the sauce and freshly grated Parmesan.

CHEF'S TIP *The degree of spiciness depends on the chillies available. Remember that most of the heat is in the seeds and membranes. Be careful when handling the chillies and keep your fingers away from your face.*

Spaghetti Bolognese

Spaghetti Bolognese (pictured top right) reflects the rich style of the cooking of Bologna in northern Italy and is undoubtedly one of the best-known and most well-loved Italian pasta dishes.

Preparation time 50 minutes
Total cooking time 1 hour 10 minutes
Serves 6–8

125 ml (4 fl oz) olive oil
1 kg (2 lb) lean beef mince
1 large onion, finely chopped
2 tablespoons tomato paste (purée)
80 ml (2¾ fl oz) red wine
8 cloves garlic, finely chopped
2.5 kg (5 lb) fresh tomatoes, peeled, seeded (see page 534) and puréed in a food mill
4 sprigs of fresh thyme
1 bay leaf
750 g (1½ lb) spaghetti
grated Parmesan cheese, to serve

One In a large pot, heat half the oil until very hot. Add the beef mince, season with salt and black pepper, and brown for 10 minutes, or until the liquid from the meat has evaporated. Strain off the fat and set the meat aside.

Two Heat the remaining oil in the pot, add the onion and cook for 5 minutes, without colouring. Add the tomato purée and cook for 1–2 minutes, then add the wine and cook for 5 minutes. Transfer the meat back to the pan, add the garlic, tomatoes, thyme and bay leaf and simmer for 45 minutes, or until the liquid has reduced by half. Remove the thyme and bay leaf.

Three Meanwhile, bring a large pan of salted water to the boil. Add a splash of oil to stop the pasta sticking and cook the spaghetti according to the manufacturer's instructions. Drain well and transfer to individual plates. Spoon the sauce on top and serve with the grated Parmesan.

Fettuccine Alfredo

A delicious creamy dish (pictured bottom right) that is simple and quick to make. For good results, however, it is essential to use freshly grated Parmesan, as shop-bought ground Parmesan is usually a poor substitute.

Preparation time 5 minutes
Total cooking time 15 minutes
Serves 4

400 ml (12¾ fl oz) thick (double) cream
220 g (7 oz) Parmesan cheese, grated
3 tablespoons chopped fresh flat-leaf parsley
500 g (1 lb) fettuccine
grated Parmesan cheese, to serve

One Place the cream in a heavy-based pan and bring to the boil. Gradually whisk in the Parmesan. Add the parsley, season with salt and freshly ground black pepper, then stir until the sauce is well combined.

Two Meanwhile, bring a large pan of salted water to the boil. Add a splash of oil to stop the pasta sticking and cook the fettuccine according to the manufacturer's instructions. Drain well and toss in the cream sauce.

Three Serve in individual bowls with freshly grated Parmesan on the side.

Pumpkin ravioli with basil butter

The delicate flavour of the pumpkin and herb ravioli filling is perfectly complemented by the basil and garlic butter. When making ravioli, it is important to try to roll the pasta as thinly as possible, while also making sure that it won't tear when handled.

Preparation time 1 hour 30 minutes
Total cooking time 1 hour 20 minutes
Serves 6–8

400 g (12³/₄ oz) pumpkin or butternut
squash
30 ml (1 fl oz) olive oil
75 g (2¹/₂ oz) Parma ham, finely
chopped
50 g (1³/₄ oz) Parmesan cheese, grated
2 tablespoons chopped fresh basil
3 tablespoons chopped fresh sage
1 egg yolk
30 ml (1 fl oz) thick (double) cream
pinch of nutmeg

PASTA
400 g (12³/₄ oz) plain flour
1 teaspoon salt
40 ml (1¹/₄ fl oz) olive oil
4 eggs, lightly beaten

HERB BUTTER
160 g (5¹/₄ oz) unsalted
butter or olive oil
6 cloves garlic, halved
30 g (1 oz) fresh basil

One Preheat the oven to moderately hot 190°C (375°F/Gas 5). Place the pumpkin on a lightly oiled baking tray and brush with the olive oil. Bake for about 1 hour, or until the flesh is soft when pressed lightly with a spoon. Set aside.

Two To make the pasta, follow the method in the Chef's techniques on page 532, dividing the dough into four pieces before passing it through the pasta machine. Pass the pieces through the thinnest setting on the machine, making sure they are at least 16 cm (6¹/₂ inches) wide, then cut into 12 cm (5 inch) wide strips.

Three Scrape out the pumpkin flesh and mash. Stir in the Parma ham, Parmesan, basil, sage, egg yolk and cream. Season with the nutmeg, salt and pepper. Cover.

Four Spoon heaped teaspoons of the pumpkin mixture at 6 cm (2¹/₂ inch) intervals along the pasta strips, following the method in the Chef's techniques on page 533. Lightly brush with water around the edges of the pumpkin. Lay another sheet of pasta on top and press around each mound to expel any air and to seal. Cut out the ravioli with a 6 cm (2¹/₂ inch) biscuit cutter, then flour lightly. Place in a single layer between sheets of baking paper and refrigerate until ready to use.

Five Bring a large pan of salted water to the boil. Add a splash of oil to stop the pasta sticking and cook the ravioli in batches for 5–6 minutes, or until they float. Drain well.

Six To make the herb butter, melt the butter over low heat in a small pan, then add the garlic and leave to infuse for a few minutes, without letting the garlic brown. Take the pan off the heat and remove the garlic with a slotted spoon. Tear the basil and add to the sauce. Add the ravioli and toss to coat well.

CHEF'S TIP *Bake some shelled pumpkin seeds until golden brown and then lightly salt. Toss over the ravioli.*

Classic lasagne

Although you can make this very popular classic Italian dish with shop-bought lasagne sheets, the flavour and texture of thinly rolled fresh pasta is quite unique and well worth the effort.

Preparation time 1 hour
+ 20 minutes resting
Total cooking time 2 hours 15 minutes
Serves 10–12

olive oil, for cooking
1 kg (2 lb) beef mince
1 large onion, finely chopped
8 cloves garlic, finely chopped
4 x 425 g (13½ oz) cans peeled Italian tomatoes, undrained and puréed in a food mill or processor
125 ml (4 fl oz) red wine
3 tablespoons tomato paste (purée)
4 sprigs of fresh thyme
1 bay leaf
650 g (1 lb 5 oz) ricotta cheese
100 ml (3¼ fl oz) thick (double) cream
4 eggs
400 g (12¾ oz) mozzarella cheese, thinly sliced
50 g (1¾ oz) Parmesan cheese, grated

PASTA
400 g (12¾ oz) plain flour
1 teaspoon salt
2 tablespoons olive oil
4 eggs

One Heat 2 tablespoons of the oil in a large pan until very hot. Add the beef mince and brown for 10 minutes, or until the liquid has almost evaporated. Strain off the fat and set the meat aside. Reduce the heat to low, heat a little more oil and cook the onion for 5 minutes, without colouring. Add the garlic, tomatoes, wine, tomato paste, thyme, bay leaf and beef and simmer for 45 minutes to 1 hour, or until the liquid has reduced by half.

Two To make the pasta, follow the method in the Chef's techniques on page 532, dividing the dough into four pieces before passing through the pasta machine. Drain the ricotta in a sieve, then mix with the cream and eggs in a large bowl. Season, cover and set aside. Preheat the oven to moderately hot 190°C (375°F/Gas 5).

Three Roll out the pasta dough to about 1–2 mm (¹⁄₁₆ to ⅛ inch) thick and cut into 10 x 12 cm (4 x 5 inch) rectangles. Blanch two or three sheets at a time briefly in boiling salted water, then drain on tea towels.

Four Spread about 200 ml (6½ fl oz) of the meat sauce in a 3.5 litre ovenproof dish. Arrange a layer of pasta on top and cover with a third of the cheese mixture, then another layer of meat sauce. Repeat the layers twice more and finish with a layer of pasta covered with meat sauce. Cover with mozzarella and sprinkle with Parmesan. Bake for 45 minutes, or until golden brown. Leave to rest for 20 minutes before cutting.

Pasta with prosciutto and Parmesan

This simple pasta dish makes the most of two of Italy's most famous ingredients—prosciutto, a salt-cured ham, and the rich, grainy Parmesan. As both of these ingredients are salty, particular care should be taken when seasoning this dish.

Preparation time 20 minutes
Total cooking time 20 minutes
Serves 4

3 tablespoons olive oil
400 g (12³/4 oz) farfalle (pasta bows)
1 large onion, thinly sliced
200 g (6¹/2 oz) button mushrooms,
thinly sliced
3 zucchini (courgettes), cut into batons
1 large clove garlic, chopped
150 g (5 oz) prosciutto, cut into strips
300 ml (10 fl oz) crème fraîche
100 g (3¹/4 oz) Parmesan cheese,
grated
fresh basil leaves, to garnish

One Bring a large pan two-thirds full of water to the boil. Add a good pinch of salt and 1 tablespoon of the olive oil. Add the farfalle to the water, stir with a fork and cook according to the manufacturer's instructions until the pasta is *al dente*. Pour into a colander and refresh under plenty of cold running water. Leave to drain until needed.

Two Heat a pan over high heat and add the remaining olive oil. When the oil is hot, add the onion, mushrooms, zucchini and garlic and fry for about 2 minutes, or until the vegetables are lightly coloured. Reduce the heat, add the prosciutto strips and fry for 2–3 minutes. Stir in the crème fraîche and heat the mixture for another 2 minutes. Stir in the grated Parmesan and season with salt and black pepper.

Three Add the pasta to the pan, stir, then cook briefly to ensure the pasta is heated. Serve immediately with the fresh basil leaves sprinkled over the pasta.

Linguine vongole

*Linguine, the Italian word for 'little tongues', are long flat noodles.
Here they are teamed with fresh clams in a creamy white wine and parsley
sauce. A little time-consuming to make, but well worth the effort.*

*Preparation time 25 minutes
+ 1 hour soaking
Total cooking time 50 minutes
Serves 4–6*

2 kg (4 lb) clams
100 g (3¼ oz) unsalted butter
1 large onion, finely chopped
1 large stick celery, finely sliced
2 sprigs of fresh thyme
1 bay leaf
8 stems of fresh flat-leaf parsley
8 cloves garlic, chopped
100 g (3¼ oz) cap or button
mushrooms, sliced
750 ml (24 fl oz) dry white wine
500 g (1 lb) linguine
2 tablespoons plain flour
400 ml (12¾ fl oz) thick (double)
cream
4 tablespoons chopped fresh
flat-leaf parsley

One Wash the clams, then soak for 1 hour in cold water, changing the water several times. While the clams are soaking, melt 80 g (2¾ oz) of the butter in a large pot. Add the onion and cook over low heat for 5 minutes, then add the celery, thyme, bay leaf, parsley stems, garlic, mushrooms and wine. Bring to the boil and cook for 5 minutes. Add the drained clams to the boiling liquid and cook, covered, for 5–8 minutes (15–20 minutes for large clams), or until they open. Remove the clams with a slotted spoon, discarding any that are unopened, and set aside to cool. Remove the meat from half the clam shells, rinse under cold water, drain and coarsely chop. Boil the sauce for another 10 minutes, then strain through a sieve lined with a muslin. Measure out 400 ml (12¾ fl oz) of the liquid.

Two Bring a large pan of salted water to the boil. Add a splash of oil to stop the pasta sticking and cook the linguine according to the manufacturer's instructions. Drain well, toss with a little olive oil and keep warm.

Three Over low heat, melt the remaining butter in a saucepan. Stir in the flour and cook for 2 minutes. Remove from the heat and gradually whisk in the reserved cooking liquid. Return to the

heat and bring to the boil, stirring constantly. Reduce the heat to low and simmer for 5 minutes, or until thickened. Whisk in the cream and simmer for another 5 minutes. Add the whole and chopped clams, parsley and some salt and black pepper. Cook for 30 seconds and serve over the linguine.

CHEF'S TIP *Use the smallest clams you can find—they are less tough than the large variety.*

LE CORDON BLEU ✿ COMPLETE COOK

Spaghetti alla diavola

Diavola, meaning devil in Italian, refers to any dish that has been enlivened with chillies and garlic. Sometimes simple is better, so here is a recipe (pictured top left) that is simply spicy, garlicky and good.

Preparation time 15 minutes
Total cooking time 15 minutes
Serves 4

500 g (1 lb) spaghetti
250 ml (8 fl oz) olive oil
2 heads of garlic, sliced
½–1 teaspoon dried chilli flakes, or to taste
chopped fresh flat-leaf parsley, to serve
freshly grated Parmesan cheese, to serve

One Bring a large pan of salted water to the boil. Add a splash of oil to stop the pasta sticking together and cook the spaghetti according to the manufacturer's instructions.

Two While the pasta is cooking, heat the oil in a pan over medium heat. Add the garlic and chilli flakes and cook for 10–15 minutes, or until the garlic starts to brown slightly. Drain the pasta and toss in the hot sauce. Season to taste.

Three Sprinkle with chopped parsley and serve with the freshly grated Parmesan.

CHEF'S TIP *Use the dried chilli flakes with discretion—some are much hotter than others.*

Linguine with Gorgonzola sauce

This dish (pictured bottom left) can be made with other cheeses if Gorgonzola is unavailable. Any mild blue cheese can be used in its place.

Preparation time 10 minutes
Total cooking time 15 minutes
Serves 4–6

500 g (1 lb) linguine
300 ml (10 fl oz) thick (double) cream, at room temperature
300 g (10 oz) Gorgonzola or similar blue cheese, cut into cubes

One Bring a large pan of salted water to the boil. Add a splash of oil to the pan to stop the pasta from sticking and cook the linguine according to the manufacturer's instructions.

Two Meanwhile, in a heavy-based saucepan, bring the cream to the boil. Remove from the heat and whisk in the cheese until smooth. Strain through a fine sieve.

Three Drain the pasta and toss in the hot sauce. Serve immediately.

Mushroom ravioli in rosemary garlic cream

*Ideal as a first course or for a light lunch,
the creamy sauce in this dish perfectly complements
the ravioli with its tasty mushroom filling.*

Preparation time *1 hour
+ 20 minutes cooling*
Total cooking time *45 minutes*
Serves 4 as a starter

PASTA
*100 g (3¼ oz) plain flour
pinch of salt
1 teaspoon oil
1 egg, lightly beaten*

MUSHROOM FILLING
*olive oil, for cooking
2 French shallots, finely chopped
150 g (5 oz) button or wild
mushrooms, chopped
2 tablespoons fresh breadcrumbs
10 g (¼ oz) each of chopped
fresh chervil, thyme, flat-leaf
parsley and basil*

*500 ml (16 fl oz) chicken stock (see
page 519)
8 cloves garlic, roughly chopped
sprig of fresh rosemary, cut into pieces
500 ml (16 fl oz) thick (double) cream*

*beaten egg, to glaze
shavings of Parmesan cheese, to
garnish*

One Make the pasta, following the method in the Chef's techniques on page 532. Divide the dough into two pieces before passing it through the machine.

Two To make the filling, heat a little oil over low heat and cook the shallots for 3 minutes. Add the mushrooms and a good pinch of salt. Cook, stirring, for 10 minutes, or until the mushrooms are dry. Season, to taste, then mix in the breadcrumbs, herbs and enough olive oil to just bind the mixture. Set aside.

Three To make the sauce, cook the chicken stock and chopped garlic in a saucepan over high heat for 20 minutes, or until the mixture is syrupy. Remove from the heat, add the sprig of rosemary and leave to cool for about 20 minutes. Remove the rosemary, transfer the sauce to a blender or food processor and blend until the mixture is smooth. Strain into a small saucepan, add the cream and simmer over low heat for 5 minutes, or until the sauce is thick enough to coat the back of a spoon. Season, to taste, and keep warm.

Four Mark one strip of pasta with a round 4 cm (1½ inch) pastry cutter and make the ravioli following the method in the Chef's techniques on page 533.

Five Bring a large saucepan of salted water to the boil. Cook the ravioli for 2–3 minutes, or until it floats. Strain, then serve with the sauce and Parmesan.

Italian meatballs

Tasty meatballs cooked in a rich tomato sauce and served with spaghetti make a warming winter dish. The meatballs can be made from beef mince or a combination of beef and pork mince if preferred.

Preparation time 50 minutes
Total cooking time 1 hour 25 minutes
Serves 4

4 tablespoons olive oil
1 onion, finely chopped
2 cloves garlic, finely chopped
¼ teaspoon chopped fresh oregano
500 g (1 lb) lean beef mince
1 egg, lightly beaten
500 g (1 lb) spaghetti
grated Parmesan cheese, to serve

SAUCE
2 tablespoons olive oil
1 large onion, finely chopped
4 x 425 g (13½ oz) cans whole peeled
Italian tomatoes, undrained
and puréed in a food mill
or food processor
5 cloves garlic, finely chopped
1 bay leaf
2 sprigs of fresh thyme

One Heat half the oil over gentle heat and cook the onion for 5–7 minutes, or until soft. Off the heat, add the garlic and oregano and stir well. Strain off any excess oil and set aside to cool. Once cooled, add to the meat and mix well. Season and add enough of the egg to bring the mixture together.

Two Divide the meat into eight portions and roll into smooth balls. Heat the remaining olive oil in a frying pan and cook the meatballs until browned. Drain on a plate lined with paper towels.

Three To make the sauce, heat the olive oil and slowly cook the onion for 5 minutes, without colouring. Add the tomatoes, garlic, bay leaf, thyme and the meatballs and simmer, covered, over

low heat, for 20 minutes. Uncover and simmer for 30–40 minutes, skimming as needed. Remove the bay leaf and thyme and season to taste with salt and pepper

Four Bring a large pan of salted water to the boil. Add a splash of oil to stop the

pasta sticking together and cook the spaghetti according to the instructions.

Five Drain well and transfer the pasta to a large platter or individual plates. Top with the sauce and meatballs. Serve with the Parmesan on the side.

Vegetable lasagne

Try this deliciously different lasagne with its crunchy vegetables and cheese sauce with a hint of nutmeg. Making your own pasta is both enjoyable and satisfying.

Preparation time 1 hour
+ 30 minutes resting
Total cooking time 1 hour 30 minutes
Serves 6

PASTA DOUGH
300 g (10 oz) plain flour
1 teaspoon salt
30 ml (1 fl oz) olive oil
3 eggs, lightly beaten

CHEESE SAUCE
25 g (3/4 oz) unsalted butter
25 g (3/4 oz) plain flour
500 ml (16 fl oz) milk
1/4 teaspoon ground nutmeg
75 ml (2 1/2 fl oz) cream
100 g (3 1/4 oz) Gruyère cheese, grated

25 g (3/4 oz) unsalted butter
1 small onion, sliced
4 ripe tomatoes, peeled, seeded and chopped (see page 534)
1 sprig of fresh thyme
1 bay leaf
200 g (6 1/2 oz) carrots, diced
250 g (8 oz) small broccoli florets
1/2 cauliflower, cut into florets
80 g (2 3/4 oz) Gruyère cheese, grated

One Make the pasta following the method in the Chef's techniques on page 532. Wrap in plastic wrap and rest for 20 minutes.

Two To make the cheese sauce, melt the butter in a pan, stir in the flour with a wooden spoon and cook gently for 3 minutes, stirring continuously. Remove from the heat and whisk in the cold milk. Blend thoroughly, season to taste with salt and freshly ground black pepper and add the nutmeg. Return to the heat and bring slowly to the boil, stirring continuously. Lower the heat and cook for 7 minutes, stirring occasionally. Stir in the cream and cheese. Set aside, covered with buttered greaseproof paper.

Three Heat the butter in a pan and cook the onion slowly without browning. Add the tomato, thyme and bay leaf. Season to taste with salt and pepper. Simmer for 15 minutes, or until pulpy. Discard the bay leaf and thyme.

Four Bring a large pan of salted water to the boil. Add the carrot, reduce the heat and simmer for 4 minutes. Add the broccoli and cauliflower and simmer for 3 minutes. Drain and refresh with cold water to stop the cooking process. Drain well and set aside.

Five Preheat the oven to moderately hot 190°C (375°F/Gas 5). On a lightly floured surface, roll out the pasta dough to 1 mm (1/16 inch) thick. Cut with a sharp knife into long strips 8 x 15 cm (3 x 6 inches) and cook a few strips at a time, in a large saucepan of boiling salted water with a dash of oil, for 2–3 minutes, or until *al dente*. Transfer to a bowl of cold water, drain and put between layers of tea towel.

Six Mix the cheese and tomato sauces and simmer for 15 minutes. Add the vegetables to the sauce. Season to taste.

Seven Butter a 2 litre ovenproof dish and layer with sheets of pasta and the vegetable mixture, finishing with a sheet of pasta. Sprinkle cheese over the top and bake for 35 minutes.

Ricotta shells

The extensive cooking time for this dish may seem alarming at first glance, however, it is worth noting that in fact both the rich tomato sauce and the finished cheese and herb stuffed pasta shells spend much time cooking in the oven, leaving you free to do other things.

Preparation time 1 hour
Total cooking time 2 hours 30 minutes
Serves 4

40 g (1¼ oz) unsalted butter
60 g (2 oz) slab bacon, diced
1 small onion, chopped
1 small carrot, chopped
2 tablespoons tomato
paste (purée)
1 tablespoon plain flour
500 g (1 lb) tomatoes, peeled,
seeded and chopped (see page 534)
1 bouquet garni (see page 520)
4 cloves garlic, chopped
500 ml (16 fl oz) chicken stock (see
page 519) or water
32–40 large pasta shells
500 g (1 lb) ricotta cheese
25 g (¾ oz) Parmesan cheese, grated
2 eggs
1 tablespoon chopped fresh parsley
1 tablespoon chopped fresh basil
¼ teaspoon grated nutmeg
250 g (8 oz) fresh mozzarella cheese or
bocconcini, sliced or grated

One Preheat the oven to moderate 180°C (350°F/Gas 4). To make the tomato sauce, melt the butter over medium heat in a large ovenproof pan (with a lid). Add the bacon and cook until golden brown. Add the onion and carrot and cook for 3 minutes. Add the tomato paste, stir well and cook for another 2 minutes. Sprinkle with the flour and place in the oven for 5 minutes. Remove and stir well until the flour disappears, then add the tomatoes, bouquet garni and garlic. Cook on the stove for 5 minutes, stirring well, then add the stock and bring to the boil, stirring. Cook for 2 minutes, then cover and bake for 1 hour.

Two Bring a large pan of salted water to the boil. Add a little oil to stop the pasta sticking and cook the shells according to the manufacturer's instructions. Drain and drizzle with a little olive oil. Arrange on a damp tea towel.

Three Lightly oil the inside of a large ovenproof dish. Combine the ricotta, Parmesan, eggs, herbs and nutmeg and season, then spoon into a piping bag with a plain nozzle. Fill each shell and arrange in a single layer in the dish.

Four Strain the tomato sauce through a sieve, pressing well to extract as much liquid as possible. Discard the solids. Bring back to the boil and skim if necessary. Simmer for 20 minutes, or until the sauce thickens. Pour over the stuffed shells. Sprinkle the mozzarella cheese over the sauce and bake for 30–40 minutes, or until the cheese is melted and browned.

vegetables

Vegetable tian

Layers of vegetables with added flavour from herbs and garlic are delicious baked in a shallow dish that can be presented at the table. Suitable for lunch or dinner.

Preparation time 30 minutes
Total cooking time 1 hour
Serves 4

olive oil, for cooking
1 small onion, thinly sliced
750 g (1½ lb) tomatoes, peeled, seeded and diced (see page 534)
400 g (13 oz) large mushrooms, sliced
400 g (13 oz) potatoes, thinly sliced
2 cloves garlic, finely chopped
500 g (1 lb) English spinach leaves
1 sprig of fresh rosemary
3 tablespoons chopped fresh parsley

One Preheat the oven to moderately hot 190°C (375°F/Gas 5). Heat a little olive oil in a heavy-based pan and gently cook the onion with a pinch of salt for 3 minutes, without colouring. Add the tomato and cook gently for 7 minutes. Season to taste and set aside.

Two Pan-fry the mushrooms in a little olive oil over high heat for 3–4 minutes. Drain off any excess moisture. Season to taste and set aside.

Three Fry the potato in batches in olive oil over medium–low heat for 3 minutes. Return all the potato to the pan, add the garlic and cook for 1 minute. Season and drain on paper towels.

Four Arrange a layer of potato in a 2 litre ovenproof dish and cover with a layer of the mushrooms, a layer of spinach, then a layer of tomato. Cover with greaseproof paper and bake for 30–45 minutes. Sprinkle with rosemary and parsley to serve.

CHEF'S TIP *Top with grated Parmesan or crumbled feta cheese before baking.*

Mixed glazed vegetables

The initial shaping of the vegetables with a melon baller may be a little fiddly but for a special occasion you will find this beautifully presented dish well-worth the trouble.

Preparation time 40 minutes
Total cooking time 30 minutes
Serves 4

20 pearl onions
2 zucchini (courgettes)
3 turnips
3 carrots
60 g (2 oz) unsalted butter
3 teaspoons sugar

One Soak the pearl onions in a bowl of warm water for 5 minutes, to make peeling easier. Lightly trim the root end, being careful not to cut off too much, since it is the root end that will keep the pearl onions intact.

Two Using a standard 2 cm (³⁄₄ inch) melon baller, make 20 balls each of the zucchini, turnip and carrot. Cook the zucchini balls for 1 minute in boiling salted water and refresh in iced water. Drain and transfer to a small saucepan. Add one third of the butter, 1 teaspoon of the sugar, ¹⁄₂ teaspoon salt and 30 ml (1 fl oz) water and cook until the water has evaporated and a syrupy glaze remains. Check to see if the vegetables are tender. If not, add some water and cook a little longer. Roll the vegetables around to evenly coat, then set aside and keep warm.

Three Put the turnip and carrot balls in a pan with half of the remaining butter, 1 teaspoon of the sugar, ¹⁄₂ teaspoon salt and enough water to just cover. Cook in the same way as the zucchini, then set aside and keep warm. Repeat with the peeled pearl onions.

Four Reheat by combining the vegetables in a pan, placing the pan over medium heat and rolling the vegetables around to prevent them from browning, for about 3–5 minutes. Transfer to a serving dish.

CHEF'S TIPS *Leave the vegetables at room temperature for about 1 hour before preparing.*

If you can't get pearl onions, use small pickling onions and remove a few outer layers.

Roast potatoes

Roasted meats are never quite the same without crisp,
golden roast potatoes. Use the best quality ingredients—potatoes,
olive oil and salt—to further enchance the flavour.

Preparation time *15 minutes*
Total cooking time *50 minutes*
Serves 4

1 kg (2 lb) floury potatoes
oil, for cooking

One Preheat the oven to moderately hot 190°C (375°F/ Gas 5). Peel the potatoes and cut them into similar-sized pieces for even cooking, by halving or quartering, depending on their size. Put in a pan, cover with cold water and add a large pinch of salt. Bring to the boil, lower the heat and simmer for 5 minutes. Drain, then while the potatoes are still hot, hold each one in a cloth and lightly scratch the surface with a fork. Return to the pan and cover to keep hot.

Two Preheat a roasting tin over high heat and add oil to a depth of about 1 cm (½ inch). As the oil just starts to smoke, add the potatoes in a single layer. Roll them in the hot oil to seal all sides. Bake for 40 minutes, or until the potatoes are golden, turning and basting frequently with the oil. Drain on crumpled paper towels, sprinkle with salt and serve while still hot.

CHEF'S TIPS *King Edward, spunta and sebago potatoes are perfect for roasting.*

Boiling potatoes prior to roasting removes excess sticky starch from the surface, leaving them dry and crisp. Scratching the surface gives texture to that crispness. Rolling hot potatoes in hot oil will then seal them, leaving the centres floury and oil free.

If the potatoes are to accompany a roasted meat, instead of cooking them in a separate pan, place them in the hot fat around the meat as it cooks to pick up the flavour.

For special occasions, shave off the square edges. The rounded potatoes will roll easily in the pan for all-over colour and crispness: the secret of the perfect roast potato.

LE CORDON BLEU ✤ COMPLETE COOK

Potato and spinach croquettes

The flavours of spinach and Parmesan enliven the potato in these croquettes. They are great for a light lunch or supper but also work well as picnic food.

Preparation time 30 minutes
Total cooking time 45 minutes
Makes 14 croquettes

500 g (1 lb) floury potatoes
pinch of ground nutmeg
20 g (3/4 oz) unsalted butter
1 egg yolk
oil, for deep- or shallow-frying
40 g (1 1/4 oz) Parmesan cheese, grated
50 g (1 3/4 oz) cooked English spinach, finely chopped
60 g (2 oz) plain flour, seasoned
3 eggs, beaten
1 tablespoon peanut (groundnut) oil
150 g (5 oz) dry breadcrumbs

One Peel the potatoes and cut them into similar-sized pieces for even cooking, by halving or quartering, depending on their size. Put in a pan, cover with cold water and add a large pinch of salt. Bring to the boil, lower the heat and simmer for about 20 minutes, or until quite tender.

Two Drain the potatoes and dry them by shaking them in the pan over low heat for 2 minutes. Purée the potatoes, following the method in the Chef's techniques on page 536, or mash them until smooth. Season with salt and pepper, to taste, and nutmeg. Add the butter and egg yolk. Spread out on a tray to cool. Preheat the oil in a deep-fryer or large pan, to moderate 180°C (350°F), following the method in the Chef's techniques on page 537.

Three Mix the Parmesan with the very well-drained spinach in a bowl. Add the potato, salt and black pepper to the mixture and stir to combine. On a floured surface, and using floured hands, roll the mixture beneath a flat hand to form cylinders about 6 x 2 cm (2 1/2 x 3/4 inches). Even up and flatten the ends.

Four Put the flour on a tray. Combine the eggs and oil in a bowl and put the breadcrumbs on a large piece of greaseproof paper. Roll the croquettes carefully through the flour and pat off the excess. Dip them in the egg to coat well, drain off the excess and roll in breadcrumbs, lifting the edges of the paper to make it easier. It may be necessary to coat the croquettes twice in egg and crumbs if your mixture is a little too soft to hold its shape well. Fry in batches until evenly browned and lift out, shaking off any excess oil. Drain on crumpled paper towels.

CHEF'S TIPS *The potato must not be too wet or the croquettes will split and absorb the oil.*

Shake off or press on excess bread-crumbs or they will burn and cling to the croquettes as dark specks.

Gratin of root vegetables

Root vegetables go well with roast meats and this gratin (pictured top right) baked with a golden Gruyère topping is a perfect match for a simple roast.

Preparation time 30 minutes
Total cooking time 45 minutes
Serves 4

30 g (1 oz) unsalted butter
1 clove garlic, finely chopped
250 ml (8 fl oz) milk
250 ml (8 fl oz) cream
1 large waxy potato, thinly sliced
pinch of grated nutmeg
1 small carrot, thinly sliced
1 small swede, thinly sliced
½ parsnip, thinly sliced
1 small turnip, thinly sliced
110 g (3½ oz) Gruyère cheese, grated

One Melt the butter in a pan, add the garlic and cook over low heat for 1 minute. Add the milk, cream, potato, nutmeg, a pinch of salt and some black pepper. Bring to the boil and cook, covered, for 5 minutes. Add the carrot and cook for 3 minutes, then add the swede and cook for 3 minutes. Add the parsnip and cook for another 3 minutes, then finally add the turnip and cook for 2 minutes. The vegetables should be tender, but still have a little resistance when tested with the point of a sharp knife. Strain the cooking liquid from the vegetables and reserve.

Two Preheat the oven to moderate 180°C (350°F/Gas 4). Butter a 1.5 litre shallow gratin or ovenproof dish. Layer the vegetables in the prepared dish and pour over some of the reserved cooking liquid to just cover. Sprinkle with the cheese and bake for 20–25 minutes, or until the vegetables are tender and the surface is golden. Leave to stand for 10 minutes before serving.

Pumpkin purée

A purée works beautifully with meat dishes that have a lot of sauce to soak up. You could use parsnip or swede instead of the pumpkin (pictured bottom right).

Preparation time 10 minutes
Total cooking time 30 minutes
Serves 4

1 kg (2 lb) butternut pumpkin, peeled and chopped into 5 cm (2 inch) cubes
50 g (1¾ oz) unsalted butter, cut into cubes and chilled
60 ml (2 fl oz) thick (double) cream
pinch of grated nutmeg

One Bring a large saucepan of salted water to the boil, add the pumpkin cubes, then reduce the heat and simmer for 15–20 minutes, or until the pumpkin is tender to the point of a sharp knife. Drain well and return to the pan. Shake the pan over low heat for about 1 minute to dry out the pumpkin.

Two Pass the pumpkin through a mouli sieve or mix in a food processor to a fine purée, then return to a clean pan and, over low heat, beat in the butter followed by the cream. Season with the nutmeg and some salt and freshly ground black pepper and serve with meat, fish or poultry.

Cauliflower cheese

Perfect partners, cauliflower and cheese baked in this way make a hearty winter dish. If you don't like the strong taste of Gruyère cheese, you can always use Cheddar instead.

Preparation time 10 minutes
Total cooking time 30 minutes
Serves 4–6

1 cauliflower, about 500 g (1 lb)
30 g (1 oz) unsalted butter
30 g (1 oz) plain flour
500 ml (16 fl oz) milk
pinch of ground nutmeg
100 ml (3¼ fl oz) cream
130 g (4¼ oz) Gruyère cheese, grated
2 egg yolks

One Preheat the oven to moderate 180°C (350°F/Gas 4). Remove the outer leaves of the cauliflower and break the head into small serving-sized pieces. Place in cold salted water, bring slowly to the boil, reduce the heat and simmer for about 10 minutes, or until the cauliflower is cooked, but still slightly firm. Drain, refresh in cold water, then drain again.

Two To make the cheese sauce, melt the butter in a pan, stir in the flour with a wooden spoon or whisk and cook over low heat for 3 minutes. Remove from the heat and gradually stir in the cold milk. Return to the heat and bring to the boil, stirring continuously. Add the nutmeg and season with salt and pepper. Stir in the cream. Remove from the heat and add 100 g (3¼ oz) of cheese and the egg yolks. Set aside. Cover the surface with plastic wrap or damp greaseproof paper to prevent a skin from forming.

Three Lightly brush an ovenproof dish with butter. Pour a thin layer of the sauce onto the base, arrange the cauliflower over the sauce and pour over the remaining sauce so that it coats the cauliflower. Sprinkle with the remaining cheese and some pepper and nutmeg and bake for 15 minutes, or until the cheese is golden brown.

CHEF'S TIPS *If the sauce looks lumpy before the cream has been added to it, simply whisk it until it is smooth. It is important to do this before the cheese is added to prevent strands of cheese from sticking to the whisk.*

Gruyère is quite a strong cheese—if you use a milder variety add a little mustard to bring out the flavours.

LE CORDON BLEU ❧ COMPLETE COOK

Green beans with bacon

This dish is very popular as a vegetable on the side, served with grilled or baked meats or chicken. The salty flavour of bacon blends perfectly with green beans.

Preparation time 10 minutes
Total cooking time 15 minutes
Serves 4–6

500 g (1 lb) green beans
1 teaspoon salt
300 g (10 oz) smoked bacon
50 g (1³/4 oz) unsalted butter
3 tablespoons finely chopped
fresh parsley

One Top and tail the beans. Bring a large pan of water to the boil. Add the salt and beans and simmer for 10 minutes, or until tender. Refresh with cold water. Drain well.

Two Remove the rind from the bacon. Cut the bacon into small, short strips. Heat a dry frying pan, add the bacon and fry over medium heat. Remove and drain on paper towels.

Three Drain the bacon fat from the pan, clean the pan with paper towels and add the butter. Toss the beans in the butter, add the bacon and season to taste. As soon as they are warmed through, transfer to a dish, sprinkle with parsley and serve immediately.

CHEF'S TIPS *To maintain the green colour of the beans, add the salt and beans to the boiling water at the same time. This creates a fast bubble, which helps to fix the chlorophyll.*

As a variation, substitute two or three tinned anchovy fillets for the bacon. Prepare them first by soaking in milk, draining and drying them with paper towels. Chop and toss in the butter.

Sautéed potatoes

This is such a simple way to prepare potatoes, yet it remains a firm family favourite (pictured top left).

Preparation time 20 minutes
Total cooking time 20 minutes
Serves 4

3 floury potatoes
3 tablespoons oil, for frying
40 g (1¼ oz) unsalted butter

One Peel the potatoes and cut into 1.5 cm (⅝ inch) cubes. Place in a bowl of cold water until ready to use.

Two Drain the potato cubes and pat them dry—this will remove any excess starch that may make the potatoes stick to the frying pan.

Three Heat a large non-stick frying pan over medium-high heat. Add the oil. When the oil is hot, add the potato cubes and stir or toss to evenly coat them with the oil. Tossing regularly, cook for 10–15 minutes, or until the potatoes are well coloured all over and cooked through. Pour them into a sieve to drain off the oil.

Four Melt the butter in the same frying pan, then add the potato cubes once again. Toss them in the pan until evenly coated with the butter, then season to taste with salt and black pepper.

Mashed potatoes

There are as many versions of mashed potato as there are cooks. This mash (pictured bottom left) is wonderfully creamy.

Preparation time 10 minutes
Total cooking time 35 minutes
Serves 4

4 floury potatoes
250 ml (8 fl oz) milk or cream
20 g (¾ oz) unsalted butter

One Peel the potatoes, cut into quarters and place in a large pan of salted water. Bring to the boil, then reduce the heat and simmer for 30–35 minutes, or until tender to the point of a knife.

Two Heat the milk or cream to boiling point, then remove from the heat and leave to set aside.

Three Drain the potatoes and transfer to a large heat-resistant bowl. Mash with a large fork or potato masher, gradually mixing in enough butter and hot milk to give a good consistency, ensuring there are no lumps. Season to taste with salt and freshly ground black pepper.

CHEF'S TIP *To vary the flavour, steep your favourite herbs in the hot milk or cream for a few minutes, then strain out. Or purée and mix in other root vegetables, like parsnip or carrot. Olive oil can replace the butter.*

Anna potatoes

*Traditionally cooked in a copper two-handled baking
dish that conducts heat to give the potatoes an even brown crust,
this classic French dish is a type of potato 'cake'.*

Preparation time 45 minutes
Total cooking time 45 minutes
Serves 4–6

1 kg (2 lb) potatoes
250 g (8 oz) clarified butter
(see page 520)

One Preheat the oven to hot 220°C (425°F/Gas 7). Peel and trim the potatoes, then thinly slice them with a sharp knife or a mandolin set at 2 mm (⅛ inch), following the method in the Chef's techniques on page 536. Place the slices in water until ready to cook.

Two Rinse the potato slices in cold water and pat dry with a paper towel. Heat 60 g (2 oz) of the butter in a large, non-stick frying pan over medium heat. Add some potato slices—not too many: they should be able to move around easily in the pan—and roll them in the butter for a few minutes until well coated and hot. Strain the potatoes, return the excess butter to the pan and repeat in batches until all the potato slices are done. Set aside for about 5 minutes, or until cool enough to handle.

Three Coat the base of an ovenproof frying pan with 60 g (2 oz) of the butter. Leaving the pan over low heat, add some of the potato slices, arranging them in slightly overlapping circles. Season with salt and pepper, then arrange a second layer of potato slices on top, this time overlapping the slices in the opposite direction. Repeat until all the slices have been used, seasoning well after each layer.

Four Drizzle the remaining butter over the top, then transfer to the oven and bake for 30 minutes, or until tender to the point of a sharp knife.

Five To unmould, pour off any excess butter. Place a plate or platter over the frying pan and, in a single motion, turn it over. Serve immediately.

LE CORDON BLEU ❦ COMPLETE COOK

Provençal stuffed tomatoes

Olive oil, garlic, parsley and tomato predominate in the cuisine of the Provence region of France, reflecting its close proximity to the Mediterranean.

Preparation time 30 minutes
+ 20 minutes draining
Total cooking time 15 minutes
Serves 4

4 tomatoes
60 ml (2 fl oz) extra virgin olive oil
4 cloves garlic, finely chopped
1 tablespoon chopped
fresh thyme
2 tablespoons chopped fresh parsley
60 g (2 oz) fresh breadcrumbs

One Preheat the oven to moderately hot 190°C (375°F/Gas 5). Remove the stem ends from the tomatoes. Place the tomatoes stem side down (to make the tomatoes more secure) and cut in half. Carefully remove the seeds with a teaspoon. Season with some salt and leave, cut side down, on paper towels to drain for about 20 minutes.

Two Gently heat the olive oil until warm. Remove from the heat and add the garlic, thyme, parsley and breadcrumbs.

Season with salt and pepper and mix well with a wooden spoon. Season the tomato halves with pepper and fill with the bread stuffing, making a slight dome on top of each tomato half. Place in an oiled ovenproof dish and drizzle with extra olive oil. Bake for 5–10 minutes, or until the stuffing is golden.

CHEF'S TIP *This recipe would also work successfully using eight small tomatoes with the tops cut off and the seeds scooped out.*

Vichy carrots

The water used for cooking this dish should really be Vichy water, a natural and healthy mineral water from the springs at Vichy in France. These carrots are a colourful accompaniment to veal and chicken dishes.

Preparation time 15–20 minutes
Total cooking time 20–30 minutes
Serves 4

600 g (1¼ lb) carrots
30 g (1 oz) sugar
60 g (2 oz) unsalted butter
30 g (1 oz) chopped fresh parsley

One Peel the carrots, slice thinly and put in a pan with enough water to barely cover. Add a pinch of salt as well as the sugar and butter and cover with a paper lid made from a round of greaseproof paper (see Chef's tips).

Two Cook over high heat until almost all the water has evaporated and the juices are syrupy. The carrots should be tender. If not, add a little more water (about 60 ml/2 fl oz) and continue to cook. Toss the carrots to evenly coat them. Sprinkle with the chopped fresh parsley and serve in a deep dish.

CHEF'S TIPS *A paper lid or cartouche serves to slow the process of steam escaping, allowing foods to remain moist and preventing them cooking too quickly. To make a paper lid, prepare a piece of greaseproof paper larger than the diameter of the pan. Fold in half, then into quarters and fold once again into a fan shape. To measure the diameter of the pan, place the point in the centre of the pan and cut at the point the folded paper reaches the edge of the pan. Snip the point and unfold. The paper should now be a circle about the same diameter as the pan with a small hole in the centre.*

Baked eggplant

The pronounced flavour of the eggplant is often combined with tomato, garlic and herbs. These stuffed eggplant originated in Turkey as 'imam bayildi'.

Preparation time 40 minutes
Total cooking time 1 hour
Serves 4

olive oil, for cooking
2 large French shallots, finely chopped
800 g (1 lb 10 oz) tomatoes,
peeled, seeded and
diced (see page 534)
6 cloves garlic, finely chopped
small pinch of cayenne pepper
60 g (2 oz) fresh basil leaves, chopped
2 small eggplant (aubergines)
4 small tomatoes, stems removed
100 g (3¼ oz) Gruyère cheese, grated

One Preheat the oven to slow 150°C (300°F/Gas 2). In a heavy-based frying pan, heat a little oil over medium heat, add the French shallots and cook for 2–3 minutes, without colouring. Add the diced tomato and garlic, season with salt and cayenne pepper and simmer for 15 minutes, or until thick. Mix in the chopped basil, set aside and keep warm.

Two Meanwhile, cut the eggplant in half lengthways. Score the flesh, being careful not to cut through the skin. Rub the surface with olive oil and season with salt. Place the eggplant cut side down in an ovenproof dish or roasting tin and bake for 15 minutes, or until soft. Allow to cool. Increase the oven to moderately hot 200°C (400°F/Gas 6).

Three Cut the small tomatoes in half from top to bottom and thinly slice into semi-circles. Set aside.

Four Scoop out the flesh of the cooked eggplant. Set the empty skins aside. Chop up the pulp and remove some of the liquid by cooking in a frying pan for

5–10 minutes over low heat. Transfer the pulp to a bowl and mix in half the cooked tomato. Season and then spoon the mixture into the eggplant skins. Place in an ovenproof dish and arrange the tomato slices on top. Sprinkle with the cheese and bake until golden brown.

Five Purée the remaining cooked tomato in a blender. Thin out if necessary with some water or chicken stock. Place in a small saucepan and heat through, checking the seasoning. To serve, spoon some of the tomato sauce onto the plate and arrange the eggplant on top.

Carrot purée

For this method of cooking, the carrots should be sliced very thinly so they will cook quickly and evenly (pictured top right).

Preparation time 10 minutes
Total cooking time 20 minutes
Serves 4–6

40 g (1¼ oz) unsalted butter
450 g (14¼ oz) carrots, thinly sliced
pinch of nutmeg or ground coriander

One Melt the butter in a large shallow frying pan, add the carrot and season with salt and pepper. Add the nutmeg or coriander. Cover the pan with a sheet of greaseproof paper and a lid. It is important to cover to prevent loss of steam made by the carrots as they cook, or they will dry and turn brown.

Two Cook over low heat for 15 minutes, or until very soft and tender enough to be mashed with a fork, then remove the paper and lid. Cook, uncovered, over high heat to reduce any excess moisture, then cool slightly. Purée in a food processor until smooth. Return to the pan, adjust the seasoning to taste and reheat to serve. Serve in a neat mound or use two dessertspoons to shape the purée into oval quenelles.

CHEF'S TIP *The purée can be reheated in the microwave as long as it is in a suitable container.*

Broccoli purée with blue cheese

Puréed broccoli (pictured bottom right) goes well with almost any dish. Add the cheese only moments before serving.

Preparation time 10 minutes
Total cooking time 20 minutes
Serves 4–6

450 g (14¼ oz) broccoli
40 g (1¼ oz) unsalted butter
45 g (1½ oz) blue cheese, grated or finely crumbled

One Trim the individual broccoli stalks from the main stem, discard the stem and check that about 220 g (7 oz) of broccoli remains. Wash thoroughly and drain, then trim and slice the stalks very thinly, reserving the flower heads.

Two Melt the butter in a medium pan, add the sliced stalks, cover with greaseproof paper and a lid. Cook very gently for 10 minutes until tender, but not coloured. Finely chop the florets and add to the pan with 125 ml (4 fl oz) water. Cook, uncovered, for 5 minutes until tender, but still bright green. Drain well, transfer to a food processor and blend until smooth. Return to the pan, reheat and remove from the heat to stir in the cheese. Season, to taste, with salt and black pepper.

Three Serve in a neat mound or use two dessertspoons to shape the purée into oval quenelles.

CHEF'S TIP *A great accompaniment to meat, fish or poultry, and especially good with steak. Do not add the cheese until just before serving or it may become stringy with overheating.*

Tortilla

This thick potato omelette is offered in slices in tapas bars and cafés all over Spain, and each region has its own variations. The original, although seemingly plain, is delicious. This is a quick recipe that can be jazzed up with a variety of extra ingredients.

Preparation time 15 minutes
+ 25 minutes standing
Total cooking time 25 minutes
Serves 4–6

125 ml (4 fl oz) olive oil
3–4 potatoes, peeled and
cut into 1 cm (1/2 inch) cubes
1 large onion, thinly sliced
8 eggs

One Heat the oil in a 20 cm (8 inch) ovenproof frying pan. Add the potato cubes and cook over medium heat, without colouring, for 7 minutes, or until tender.

Two Add the onion and cook for 7–8 minutes without colouring. Season to taste with salt and black pepper, then strain and reserve the oil. Place the potato and onion mixture in a bowl to cool for 10 minutes.

Three Beat the eggs, season to taste with salt and freshly ground black pepper, pour over the potato and onion mixture and mix until well coated. Leave to stand for 15 minutes. Preheat the oven to moderately hot 200°C (400°F/Gas 6).

Four In the same pan, heat 1 tablespoon of the strained oil over medium heat. Pour in the potato and egg mixture, spreading the potato evenly in the pan. Cook for about 2 minutes, then transfer the pan to the oven and cook for 4–6 minutes, or until the egg sets around the edges, yet is still soft in the centre.

Five Take the pan from the oven and shake it to loosen the tortilla. To turn the tortilla over, carefully slide it onto a plate. Place the pan over the tortilla, then flip the pan and plate over: the cooked side of the tortilla should be nicely coloured. Cook over medium heat for 2 minutes, then bake in the oven for 2 minutes more. Remove from the oven and slide onto a clean, warm plate. Slice the tortilla into wedges and serve hot, or at room temperature.

CHEF'S TIP *For a dash of extra flavour, sauté some bacon or sausage with the potatoes. Alternatively, add some sautéed vegetables or a little grated cheese.*

Grilled marinated vegetables

*Served cold with a vinaigrette or hot straight from
the grill, these vegetables make a delicious
light dish, full of colour and flavour.*

Preparation time 20 minutes
+ 2 hours marinating
Total cooking time 40 minutes
Serves 6

1 eggplant (aubergine),
about 200 g (6¹/2 oz)
250 g (8 oz) zucchini (courgettes)
200 g (6¹/2 oz) carrots
3 large red capsicums (peppers)
70 g (2¹/4 oz) button mushrooms
2 sprigs of fresh thyme, finely chopped
2 sprigs of fresh parsley, finely
chopped
170 ml (5¹/2 fl oz) olive oil
1 tablespoon lemon juice
3 tablespoons chopped fresh basil
2¹/2 tablespoons balsamic vinegar

One Cut the eggplant, zucchini and
carrots lengthways into 1 cm (¹/2 inch)
thick, long slices. Halve the capsicums,
remove the seeds and cut into quarters.
Remove the mushroom stalks.

Two Spread the vegetables on a tray,
sprinkle with salt, pepper, thyme and
parsley. Reserve 2 tablespoons of the
olive oil and combine the rest with the
lemon juice. Pour over the vegetables
and sprinkle with the basil. Marinate for
2 hours.

Three Heat a grill or barbecue and brush
with the remaining oil. Slowly grill the
vegetables on both sides until tender. (If
you prefer less crunchy carrots, grill
them for a few minutes before adding
the other vegetables.)

Four Arrange the vegetables on a dish
and drizzle with the balsamic vinegar.

Braised red cabbage

*Chou rouge à la flamande is a traditional dish of northern France
and an excellent accompaniment to roast pork or game
Slow-cooking produces a wonderful result.*

Preparation time 20 minutes
Total cooking time 1 hour 45 minutes
Serves 8

1 red cabbage
45 g (1½ oz) unsalted butter
1 onion, sliced
2 cooking apples
2 tablespoons white wine vinegar
1 tablespoon sugar
1½ tablespoons plain flour

One Preheat the oven to warm 170°C (325°F/Gas 3). Quarter the cabbage, cut out the stalk and shred the cabbage finely. Put the cabbage in a large saucepan of boiling salted water (there should be enough water to more than cover the cabbage), bring back to the boil and drain. The cabbage will now have taken on an inky blue colour. This is normal, and it will regain its colour later. You may have to do this in batches, depending on the size of the saucepan.

Two Melt 15 g (½ oz) of the butter in a large casserole, add the onion, cover and cook gently until transparent. Peel, quarter, core and slice the apples finely before adding them to the onion. Cook for a few minutes, remove the mixture from the dish and set aside.

Three Add the cabbage to the casserole, layering with the onion and apple mixture and sprinkling with the vinegar, sugar and 2 tablespoons of water. Season. You will see the red colour return as the vinegar is added. Cover with thickly buttered paper and the lid and bake for about 1½ hours, or until very tender. Stir occasionally and moisten with a little extra water if necessary.

Four Soften the remaining butter in a bowl and mix in the flour. Push the cabbage to one side of the pan. There will be some liquid at the bottom of the casserole. Add one quarter of the butter and flour and stir in. The liquid will thicken slightly. Repeat on the other side. Toss together and only add more butter and flour if any watery liquid is present. A lot of flavour and seasoning is in the liquid, so it is just thickened to cling to the cabbage. Do not thicken too much. Taste and season. The cabbage should be gently sweet and sour. It may be necessary to add a little more sugar or vinegar, to taste.

Mixed beans in sweet and sour tomato

A delicious medley of fresh green beans and pulses in a piquant tomato dressing. This salad can be served warm or cold and is ideal as a light lunch with some bread and cheese.

Preparation time 25 minutes
Total cooking time 25 minutes
Serves 4

375 g (12 oz) French beans, trimmed
120 ml (4 fl oz) olive oil
2 French shallots, finely chopped
2 teaspoons dark brown sugar
1 clove garlic, crushed
3 tablespoons white wine vinegar
2 red chillies, seeded and diced
250 g (8 oz) ripe tomatoes, peeled,
  seeded and diced (see page 534)
150 g (5 oz) canned chickpeas, rinsed
  and drained
150 g (5 oz) canned red kidney beans,
  rinsed and drained
15 g (1/2 oz) fresh coriander, chopped
15 g (1/2 oz) fresh parsley, chopped

One Bring a pan of salted water to the boil and cook the French beans for 5 minutes, or until just tender but still a little crisp. Refresh in cold water and drain well.

Two In a large, heavy-based frying pan, heat 2 tablespoons of the olive oil and cook the shallots over medium heat until they have softened. Stir in the brown sugar, garlic, white wine vinegar and red chillies and continue to cook, stirring, for 3–4 minutes, or until the sugar is beginning to caramelise. Add the tomato, season and cover the pan. Lower the heat and simmer for about 10 minutes, stirring once or twice.

Three Mix together all the beans and pulses with all but 1 tablespoon of the chopped herbs, and season well. Add the tomato mixture and remaining olive oil, stir gently and sprinkle with the remaining herbs. Serve warm or cold.

Vegetable gateaux

These pretty layered vegetable bakes make a good accompaniment to a festive dinner, or can be prepared in advance and served on Christmas Day, with a rich tomato sauce or pesto, for any vegetarian guests.

Preparation time 25 minutes
+ 30 minutes standing
Total cooking time 35 minutes
Serves 4

1 small thin eggplant (aubergine), cut
into 3 mm (¹/8 inch) slices
30 g (1 oz) rock salt
2–3 zucchini (courgettes), cut
into 5 mm (¹/4 inch)
diagonal slices
80 ml (2³/4 fl oz) olive oil
1 teaspoon chopped fresh thyme
1 fennel bulb
1 red onion, finely sliced

One Layer the eggplant slices in a colander, sprinkling rock salt between the layers as they go in. Top with a plate smaller than the colander to press the slices lightly, stand in a bowl and leave for 30 minutes.

Two Place the zucchini in a bowl, add half the oil and the thyme and toss to coat. With a small sharp knife, remove the woody stalks at the top of the fennel bulb. With a large knife, cut the bulb in half from the top and down through the root. Cut away the root from each half then cut the fennel into 5 mm (¹/4 inch) slices.

Three Preheat the oven to moderately hot 200°C (400°F/ Gas 6). In the colander, rinse the eggplant, then dry well on paper towels. Heat a heavy-based frying pan, lightly brush with some of the remaining oil and cook the eggplant for 10 minutes, or until tender. Remove from the pan and place in a bowl. Add a little more oil if necessary, then cook the onion for 2 minutes, or until tender and remove to a separate bowl. Cook the fennel in batches for about 10 minutes, or until tender and remove to a bowl. Finally, cook the zucchini for about 5 minutes, or until tender.

Four Place four metal rings, 10 x 3.5 cm (4 x 1¹/4 inches), or four 150 ml (5 fl oz) ramekins on a baking tray. If using ramekins, cut a disc of foil or baking paper and place in the base of each.

Five Beginning and ending with eggplant, fill the rings or ramekins neatly with layers of the vegetables, draining off any excess oil and seasoning with salt and black pepper between the layers. Bake for about 6–8 minutes to heat through.

Six If using rings, lift the gateaux onto a plate and carefully remove the hot metal rings. If in ramekins, turn out onto a serving plate. Serve as a side dish or as a main-course dish with a thick tomato sauce or pesto.

CHEF'S TIPS *These gateaux can be prepared in advance and simply heated through in the oven when required.*

They are also excellent served hot as a first course with a beurre blanc, hollandaise sauce or a red capsicum coulis. Alternatively, serve cold with a herb mayonnaise and crusty bread.

Roasted parsnips with honey and ginger

*A very popular vegetable in Ancient Greece and
during the Middle Ages and the Renaissance,
the parsnip has a lovely sweet flavour.*

Preparation time 10 minutes
Total cooking time 20 minutes
Serves 6

750 g (1½ lb) parsnips, peeled
60 ml (2 fl oz) oil
15 g (½ oz) unsalted butter
1 tablespoon clear honey
1 tablespoon finely grated
or chopped fresh ginger

One Preheat the oven to hot 220°C (425°F/Gas 7). Cut the peeled parsnips in half lengthways, or quarters if they are large, to make pieces about 8 cm (3 inches) long and 2.5 cm (1 inch) thick. Remove any woody cores. Place in a large saucepan and cover with enough water. Add a pinch of salt and bring to the boil over high heat. Boil for 1 minute before draining. Return the cooked parsnips to the saucepan and dry well by shaking the pan over low heat for about 1 minute.

Two Heat the oil in a roasting tin on the stove top. Add the parsnips and cook quickly over high heat, turning to colour evenly. Add the butter to the pan, transfer to the oven for 10 minutes. Spoon or tip out the excess oil.

Three Add the honey and ginger, turning the parsnips to coat evenly, and roast for another 5 minutes.

Four Lift the parsnips out of the pan and serve hot with pork or chicken.

LE CORDON BLEU COMPLETE COOK

Braised witlof

This is a vegetable that is wonderful braised, even though it is often thought of as being a salad ingredient. Witlof is also found under the name Belgian endive.

Preparation time 15 minutes
Total cooking time 1 hour 30 minutes
Serves 4

60 g (2 oz) unsalted butter
4 witlof (chicory)
500 ml (16 fl oz) chicken stock
(see page 519) or water
1 tablespoon lemon juice
1/2 teaspoon sugar
1 teaspoon chopped fresh parsley

One Preheat the oven to moderate 180°C (350°F/Gas 4). Grease a baking dish with one third of the butter. Remove any blemished outer leaves of the witlof and trim and core the root end. This removes some of the bitterness. Wash and place them in the prepared dish.

Two Add the chicken stock or water with the lemon juice to the dish. Season lightly with salt, pepper and the sugar. Bring to the boil on the stove top. Remove and cover with buttered greaseproof paper and then foil. Transfer to the oven and bake for about 1–1¼ hours, or until the witlof are tender. Remove the witlof and place on a rack to drain, reserving the cooking liquid. Cook the liquid over high heat until syrupy. Set aside and keep warm.

Three Once the witlof are cooled, lightly tie in the middle with some kitchen string. Heat the remaining butter in a non-stick frying pan and brown the witlof until they are nicely coloured. Remove the string, place the witlof in a serving dish and cover with the reduced cooking liquid. Sprinkle with the parsley.

CHEF'S TIP *Before tying with the string, wrap a slice of bacon around the middle.*

Ratatouille

*This is a classic dish from the sunny French region of Provence
using the freshest tomatoes, zucchini, eggplant, capsicums
and onions, sautéed in olive oil with herbs.*

Preparation time *40 minutes*
Total cooking time *1 hour*
Serves 4

1 onion, diced
80 ml (2¾ fl oz) olive oil,
for cooking
250 g (8 oz) tomatoes, peeled,
seeded and diced (see page 534)
2 cloves garlic, chopped
1 red capsicum (pepper), seeded
and cut into short strips
1 bouquet garni (see page 520)
250 g (8 oz) zucchini (courgettes),
cut into batons
250 g (8 oz) eggplant (aubergine), cut
into batons
60 g (2 oz) chopped fresh basil leaves

One Preheat the oven to moderate 180°C
(350°F/Gas 4). In an ovenproof frying
pan, cook the onion in a little of the
olive oil, over medium–low heat, for
3–5 minutes, or until soft, being careful
not to let the onion colour. Add the
tomato and garlic and cook for
15 minutes, stirring occasionally.

Two In another frying pan, sauté the
capsicum in oil for 2–3 minutes over
medium–high heat. Strain off the excess
oil and add to the tomato mixture with
the bouquet garni.

Three Sauté the zucchini and eggplant
separately in oil, for 3–4 minutes. Add
to the tomato mixture. Season to taste,
cover and bake for 30 minutes. Just
before serving, remove the bouquet
garni and stir in the basil.

CHEF'S TIP *This dish can be made on
the stove top instead of being baked.
Cook over low heat, stirring often.*

Gratin dauphinois

*This potato dish has many versions, some with onion or other vegetables added,
some with stock and different herbs. Seasoning, cheese, cream and garlic are the key
to making this particular version successful. Experiment to suit your own taste.*

Preparation time 30 minutes
Total cooking time 1 hour
Serves 4–6

500 g (1 lb) potatoes
500 ml (16 fl oz) milk
pinch of grated nutmeg
100 ml (3¼ fl oz) thick
(double) cream
1 clove garlic, chopped or minced
100 g (3¼ oz) Gruyère cheese, grated

One Preheat the oven to warm 170°C
(325°F/Gas 3). Thinly slice the potatoes.
Place in a saucepan, cover with the milk
and season with some salt, freshly
ground black pepper and grated nutmeg.

Two Bring to a simmer over medium-low
heat and simmer until the potato is
almost cooked but still firm. Strain and
set the milk aside.

Three Rub a 20 x 16 cm (8 x 6½ inch)
ovenproof dish with some butter.
Arrange the potato slices in even layers
in the dish.

Four Reheat the milk and allow to
simmer for a few minutes. Add the
cream and garlic, bring back to a simmer
and check the seasoning. Simmer for a
few minutes, then pour over the potato.
Sprinkle with the grated cheese and bake
for 35–45 minutes, or until the potato is
tender and the top is lightly browned.

CHEF'S TIP *When making a sauce to
accompany a bland vegetable such as
potatoes, be sure to season it well.*

· LE CORDON BLEU ·

sauces

White sauce

Create a variety of sauces by adding flavours such as herbs or grated cheese to this basic sauce, pictured (top right) with broccoli and cauliflower.

Preparation time 5 minutes
Total cooking time 10 minutes
Makes approximately 550 ml (18 fl oz)

30 g (1 oz) unsalted butter
30 g (1 oz) plain flour
500 ml (16 fl oz) milk
small pinch of ground nutmeg

One Melt the butter in a heavy-based pan over low–medium heat. Sprinkle the flour over the butter and cook for 1–2 minutes without allowing it to colour, stirring continuously with a wooden spoon.

Two Remove the pan from the heat and slowly add the milk, whisking to avoid lumps. Return to medium heat and bring to the boil, stirring constantly. Cook for 3–4 minutes, or until the sauce coats the back of a spoon. If the sauce has lumps, pass it through a fine sieve and reheat in a clean pan. Season with salt, pepper and nutmeg. Serve hot.

CHEF'S TIP *Flavour the sauce by adding an onion studded with cloves to the milk, then warming the milk through.*

Mornay sauce

A white sauce enriched with cheese and egg yolks makes a perfect topping for scallops (pictured bottom right). To finish, simply flash under the grill until golden brown.

Preparation time 10 minutes
Total cooking time 15 minutes
Makes approximately 550 ml (18 fl oz)

30 g (1 oz) unsalted butter
30 g (1 oz) plain flour
500 ml (16 fl oz) milk
2 egg yolks
100 g (3¼ oz) Gruyère cheese, grated
pinch of ground nutmeg

One Melt the butter in a heavy-based pan over low-medium heat. Sprinkle the flour over the butter and cook for 1–2 minutes without allowing it to colour, stirring continuously with a wooden spoon.

Two Remove the pan from the heat and slowly add the milk, whisking to avoid lumps. Return to medium heat and bring to the boil, stirring constantly. Cook for 3–4 minutes, or until the sauce coats the back of a spoon. If the sauce has lumps, pass it through a fine sieve and reheat in a clean pan.

Three Remove from the stove, add the yolks and cheese off the heat and mix. Season with salt, pepper and nutmeg.

LE CORDON BLEU COMPLETE COOK

Mayonnaise

Mayonnaise can be used as a sauce or a salad dressing. It is served
here with hard-boiled eggs, pumpernickel, olives, capers and gherkins (pictured top left).
See page 521 for step-by-step instructions to accompany this recipe.

Preparation time 10 minutes
Total cooking time Nil
Makes approximately 400 ml
(12³/4 fl oz)

2 egg yolks
50 g (1³/4 oz) Dijon mustard,
or 1 heaped teaspoon dried
mustard powder
275 ml (9 fl oz) peanut (groundnut)
or olive oil
1 tablespoon white wine vinegar

One Bring all the ingredients to room temperature. Stand a large deep bowl on a tea towel to make it stable. Whisk the egg yolks, mustard, ground white pepper, to taste, and 1 teaspoon salt with a balloon whisk or with electric beaters until evenly combined.

Two Whisk in the oil a drop at a time until the mixture starts to thicken, then add the oil in a thin stream while you whisk constantly. If the oil is added too quickly, the mayonnaise will separate. Stop whisking occasionally to allow each addition to emulsify to a thick, creamy mixture. Continue until 100 ml (3¹/4 fl oz) of oil has been added.

Three The mayonnaise should have begun to thicken well at this stage. Whisk in the vinegar. Whisk in the remaining oil gradually.

Four Adjust the flavour of the mayonnaise with a touch more vinegar or salt and whisk in 1–2 tablespoons of boiling water if it curdles or separates.

Five The mayonnaise can be stored for up to a week in the refrigerator. Use it as a base for a number of sauces such as Thousand Island and tartare.

Thousand Island dressing

This creamy dressing is full of flavour and often served over a salad. Shown here (bottom left)
with salad leaves and prawns, you could also use it in sandwiches or with burgers.

Preparation time 10 minutes
+ 20 minutes refrigeration
Total cooking time Nil
Makes approximately 350 ml (11 fl oz)

250 g (8 oz) mayonnaise
80 g (2³/4 oz) tomato sauce
80 g (2³/4 oz) chilli relish
or chilli sauce
1 small onion, grated
1 red or green capsicum (pepper),
seeded and finely chopped
1 teaspoon Worcestershire sauce,
or to taste
1 teaspoon Tabasco, or to taste
1 teaspoon brandy, or to taste

One In a bowl, stir the mayonnaise, tomato sauce and chilli relish until combined. Stir in the onion, green pepper, Worcestershire sauce, Tabasco and brandy, each to taste.

Two Cover the bowl with plastic wrap and refrigerate until needed. Make the dressing at least 20 minutes ahead of serving, cover and refrigerate to allow the flavours to develop.

CHEF'S TIP *Try serving this dressing on a crisp salad of iceberg lettuce. To turn the salad into a meal, add chilled cooked prawns and large garlic croutons.*

Jus

*A jus is made from the sticky caramelised juices left in the
tin after roasting veal, poultry, lamb or beef. We have shown it with
roast rack of lamb and steamed Asian greens (pictured top right).*

Preparation time 15 minutes
Total cooking time 30 minutes
Makes approximately 250 ml (8 fl oz)

*500 g (1 lb) roasted joint of meat or
poultry*
*500 ml (16 fl oz) brown stock for dark
meats or chicken stock for lighter
meats (see pages 518–19)*
1 carrot, chopped
1 onion, chopped
1 celery stick, chopped
1 leek, chopped
1 bay leaf
2 sprigs of fresh thyme
3 peppercorns

One When the meat or poultry is
cooked, remove it from the tin and allow
to rest for 20 minutes. If there is a lot of
fat in the tin, tip off most of it, leaving
enough to fry the vegetables. In a
separate pan, heat the stock over
medium heat.

Two Add the carrot, onion, celery and
leek to the roasting tin and cook gently
on top of the stove for 5 minutes,
stirring constantly with a wooden spoon
to prevent burning, until golden brown.

Tip the excess fat from the tin and add
the bay leaf, thyme and peppercorns. Stir
in some of the hot stock, scraping the
base of the pan with a wooden spoon
constantly until it boils.

Three Pour in the remaining stock and
bring to the boil. Reduce the heat to a
simmer and cook for 5–10 minutes, or
until reduced by half, skimming the
surface of foam or fat throughout
cooking. Strain the jus into a jug.
Season, to taste, with salt and pepper.

Thickened roast gravy

*Gravy is made by adding flour to the juices left from roasting meats
such as beef or chicken. It is shown here with roast beef, Yorkshire pudding,
roast potatoes and vegetables (pictured bottom right).*

Preparation time 15 minutes
*Total cooking time 1–2 hours, depending
on meat chosen*
Makes approximately 300 ml (10 fl oz)

oil, for cooking
meat of your choice, for roasting
1/2 onion, cut into large cubes
1 small carrot, cut into large cubes
1/2 celery stick, cut into large pieces
2 cloves garlic, lightly crushed
1 bay leaf
2 sprigs of fresh thyme
30 g (1 oz) plain flour
*500 ml (16 fl oz) brown stock for dark
meats or chicken stock for lighter
meats (see pages 518–19)*

One Heat 5 mm (1/4 inch) of oil in a
roasting tin on top of the stove. Add the
meat and turn and baste for about
5 minutes to seal all sides. Remove the
meat from the tin. Put the vegetables,
garlic and herbs on the base of the tin.
Lay the meat over the vegetables and
roast at the temperature appropriate for
the meat.

Two When the meat is cooked, remove
and keep it warm. Drain off any fat,
leaving the juices and sediment behind
with the vegetables. If necessary, add

more colour to the vegetables by frying
on top of the stove in the roasting tin or
returning to the oven.

Three Stir in the flour and cook for
1 minute over low heat. Remove from
the heat and slowly add the stock,
stirring to prevent lumps forming.
Return to medium heat and stir until
boiling. Lower the heat and simmer for
20 minutes, skimming froth and fat
occasionally, then strain and season to
taste with salt and freshly ground black
pepper. Serve hot.

Mousseline sauce

A simple but delicious sauce, shown here (top right)
with steamed beans and poached white fish fillet.

Preparation time 15 minutes
Total cooking time 5 minutes
Makes approximately 500 ml (16 fl oz)

200 g (6¹/2 oz) clarified butter
(see page 520)
3 egg yolks
small pinch of cayenne pepper, to taste
juice of ¹/2 lemon
30 ml (1 fl oz) cream, for whipping

One Half-fill a pan with water and heat until simmering. Have ready a heatproof bowl that will fit over the pan without actually touching the water.

Two To make the sauce, melt the butter in a separate pan. Place the egg yolks and 3 tablespoons water in the heatproof bowl and whisk until foamy. Place over the simmering water and whisk over low heat until thick and the mixture leaves a trail on the surface when the whisk is lifted. Remove from the heat and gradually add the melted butter, whisking constantly. When all the butter is incorporated, season with cayenne pepper, lemon juice and salt. Keep the sauce warm over the pan of warm water.

Three Half whip the cream until the trail made by the whisk can be seen, but if the bowl is tipped the cream just runs thickly. Add it to the sauce and fold very carefully. This sauce is excellent with poached fish or asparagus. Mousseline sauce is always served warm.

CHEF'S TIP *At no time must this sauce be allowed to get too hot or the yolks will cook and separate from the butter. If this starts to happen, remove the pan from the water bath and try adding a few drops of cold water or a block of ice and whisking vigorously.*

Béarnaise sauce

This creamy, tangy sauce is pictured (bottom right) with
beef fillet, roast potatoes and baby cauliflower.

Preparation time 20 minutes
Total cooking time 10 minutes
Makes approximately 375 ml (12 fl oz)

260 g (8¹/4 oz) clarified butter
(see page 520)
2 tablespoons fresh tarragon,
roughly chopped
2 tablespoons fresh chervil,
roughly chopped
1 French shallot, finely chopped
4 peppercorns, crushed
100 ml (3¹/4 fl oz) white wine
vinegar
6 egg yolks
pinch of cayenne pepper

One Half fill a medium pan with water and heat until simmering. Have ready a heatproof bowl that will fit over the pan without actually touching the water.

Two Melt the butter in a separate pan. Set aside 1 tablespoon tarragon and ¹/2 tablespoon chervil. Place the shallots and peppercorns in a small saucepan with the vinegar and remaining tarragon and chervil. Bring to the boil and simmer for 4–6 minutes, or until the liquid has reduced by three quarters. Transfer to the heatproof bowl and place over the simmering water over very low heat. Add the egg yolks and whisk until thick and the mixture leaves a trail on the surface when the whisk is lifted.

Three Remove from the heat and gradually pour in the butter, whisking continuously, until all the butter is incorporated. Strain through a sieve and season with salt and cayenne pepper. Add the reserved tarragon and chervil just before serving. Serve lukewarm, don't overheat. If the sauce separates, whisk in a few drops of cold water or blocks of ice to restore consistency. The sauce may be kept warm in a clean bowl or small pan, covered with plastic wrap, and set over the pan of warm water.

LE CORDON BLEU COMPLETE COOK

White wine sauce

*This elegant sauce is shown here (top left) with
poached white fish and vegetables.*

Preparation time 10 minutes
Total cooking time 40 minutes
Makes approximately 300 ml (10 fl oz)

15 g (1/2 oz) unsalted butter
3 French shallots, finely chopped
300 ml (10 fl oz) white wine
*300 ml (10 fl oz) chicken or fish stock
(see page 519)*
*400 ml (123/4 fl oz) thick (double)
cream*

One Melt the butter in a heavy-based pan over low heat. Gently cook the shallots in the pan, without colouring, until they are soft and transparent.

Two Pour in the white wine, scraping the base of the pan with a wooden spoon. Turn up the heat and boil until the liquid has reduced by half. Add the stock and boil until reduced to 100 ml (31/4 fl oz).

Three Stir in the cream and continue to reduce the sauce until it is thick enough to coat the back of a spoon.

Four Pass the sauce through a fine sieve if you wish. Season and serve warm. The sauce can be kept warm over a pan of simmering water for up to half an hour before serving. Do not let the water boil at this stage or the sauce may split. This sauce is best served with fish or chicken.

CHEF'S TIPS *Use a stock to complement the dish you are accompanying, for example, fish stock with poached fish.*

To prevent a skin forming on the sauce while you are keeping it warm, cover the surface with plastic wrap.

Green peppercorn sauce

*This pungent peppery sauce, laced with brandy,
is pictured (bottom left) with steak and new potatoes.*

Preparation time 10 minutes
Total cooking time 15 minutes
Makes approximately 200 ml (61/2 fl oz)

30 g (1 oz) green peppercorns, drained
100 ml (31/4 oz) brandy
*300 ml (10 fl oz) brown or lamb stock
(see page 518)*
*100 ml (31/4 fl oz) thick (double)
cream*

One Place the peppercorns in a heavy-based pan and, at a very low heat, warm through for 1–2 minutes, until dry, being careful not to burn them. Roughly break the peppercorns against the side of the pan with the back of a wooden spoon.

Two Pour the brandy into the pan, increase the heat and quickly boil for 1–2 minutes, or until the brandy has evaporated. Stir in the stock, bring to the boil and boil for about 5 minutes, or until reduced by one quarter.

Three Add the cream and cook over high heat until the sauce coats the back of the spoon. Season and serve immediately, with grilled or pan-fried red meat.

CHEF'S TIP *This sauce has a strong peppery taste because the green peppercorns are cooked in the sauce from the beginning. If you prefer, reduce the stock and cream in a separate pan, then add to the peppercorns and brandy. Stir and season to taste. The flavour will not be quite as strong.*

Beurre fondu

*This classic sauce can be varied by the liquid used to suit the
dish with which it is served. It can be served with vegetables, chicken
or fish. We have pictured it (top right) with a selection of vegetables.*

Preparation time 5–7 minutes
Total cooking time 10 minutes
Makes approximately 250 ml (8 fl oz)

*50 ml (1¾ fl oz) water, dry white wine
or chicken stock (see page 519)
200 g (6½ oz) unsalted butter,
cut into small cubes and chilled
lemon juice, to taste*

One Place the liquid (water, dry white
wine or chicken stock) in a small
saucepan and bring to the boil.

Two While the liquid is simmering, use
an electric whisk to whisk in the cubes
of butter, a few at a time, to obtain a
smooth consistency. Remove the pan
from the heat and season, to taste, with
some lemon juice, salt and pepper. Serve
the sauce immediately, or keep it warm
(not hot), covered with plastic wrap,
over a pan of warm water, for up to
30 minutes before use.

CHEF'S TIP *If the sauce becomes too
cold, it will set. Warm it by stirring over
a pan of hot water. If it becomes too hot,
it will separate. If this starts to happen,
quickly remove the bowl from the water
and stir in an ice cube or a few drops of
cold water.*

Beurre blanc

*Another exquisite classic, seasoned with French shallots,
which is ideal to serve with fish such as the poached
salmon cutlet shown in the picture (bottom right).*

Preparation time 10 minutes
Total cooking time 25 minutes
Makes approximately 250 ml (8 fl oz)

*2 large French shallots, very
finely chopped
100 ml (3¼ fl oz) white wine vinegar
100 ml (3¼ fl oz) dry white wine
200 g (6½ oz) unsalted butter, cut into
small cubes and chilled*

One Add the shallots, white wine vinegar
and white wine to a small wide-based
pan and heat over medium heat until the
liquid has evaporated to 2 tablespoons.

Two As soon as the liquid boils, reduce
the heat to very low and whisk in the
butter, piece by piece. Whisk continuously
to achieve a smooth and pale sauce.
Season to taste with salt and ground
white pepper. Serve immediately, or
transfer the sauce to a bowl, cover with
plastic wrap and sit over a pan of warm
water until you are ready to serve. You
may wish to sieve the sauce for a
smoother consistency. Serve with fish or
chicken dishes.

CHEF'S TIP *Try adding a pinch of
saffron threads with the wine. Also, try
adding finely grated orange, lime or
lemon rind or a small amount of
chopped herbs such as tarragon, chives
or dill.*

Bread sauce

*A classic accompaniment to roast chicken, turkey or game,
this delicately flavoured sauce is a favourite for serving with Christmas dinner.
It is shown here (top left) with turkey and vegetables.*

*Preparation time 5 minutes +
15 minutes standing
Total cooking time 15 minutes
Makes approximately 400 ml (12¾ fl oz)*

*400 ml (12¾ fl oz) milk
8 cloves
1 small onion
or 2 large French shallots
2 bay leaves
120 g (4 oz) fresh white breadcrumbs*

One Pour the milk into a saucepan and set over medium heat. Push the pointed ends of the cloves into the onion and add the onion to the milk with the bay leaves. Bring slowly to the boil. Remove from the heat, cover and set aside for 15 minutes to allow the flavours to infuse into the milk.

Two Strain the milk through a fine sieve and discard the flavouring ingredients. Gradually add the breadcrumbs to the milk, whisking continuously, until the sauce has thickened to a thick pouring consistency. Season, to taste, with salt and pepper.

Three The sauce may be made a day in advance, although some additional milk should be added before serving as the breadcrumbs will have absorbed more milk overnight. Serve the sauce warm from a sauce boat.

CHEF'S TIP *You can also add a pinch of nutmeg or infuse the milk with other flavours such as peppercorns. Stir in a little cream or a large nut of butter at the end for a richer sauce.*

Rouille

*This is the delicious traditional accompaniment
for the bouillabaisse shown here (bottom left).*

*Preparation time 20 minutes
Total cooking time 1 hour 20 minutes
Makes approximately 300 ml (10 fl oz)*

*1 floury potato
1 red capsicum (pepper)
1 egg yolk
1 teaspoon tomato paste (purée)
1 clove garlic, peeled
120 ml (4 fl oz) olive oil
pinch of cayenne*

One Preheat the oven to moderate 180°C (350°F/Gas 4). Set the potato on a baking tray and prick it several times with a fork. Bake for 1 hour, or until tender when tested with the point of a small knife. Alternatively, prick the potato all over, wrap in paper towel and microwave on high for 4–6 minutes, turning halfway through cooking. When cool enough to handle, cut in half and scoop out the flesh into a food processor.

Two Cut the capsicum in half and remove the seeds and membrane. Lightly oil the skin and cook under a preheated grill, skin side up, until the skin is blistered and blackened, following the

Chef's technique on page 535. Alternatively, bake for 15 minutes. Place in a plastic bag and, when cool, peel away the skin. Add the flesh to the food processor with the egg yolk, tomato paste and garlic. Blend until smooth.

Three While the machine is running, gradually pour in the oil in a thin steady stream, until well incorporated. Season, to taste, with salt, pepper and cayenne pepper, remembering that the rouille should be quite fiery. Serve in a bowl or spread onto crisp bread croûtes. If serving as an accompaniment to a bouillabaisse, place a spoonful in the centre of the soup.

Bordelaise sauce

A sauce from the Bordeaux region of France, this is traditionally made with wine, shallots and bone marrow. The bone marrow in this particular recipe however is optional as the sauce is also delicious without it. It is pictured here with grilled steak (top right).

Preparation time 10 minutes
Total cooking time 20 minutes
Makes approximately 250 ml (8 fl oz)

300 g (10 oz) beef shin bone with marrow, cut into 10 cm (4 inch) lengths, optional
4 French shallots, very finely chopped
6 peppercorns
1 sprig of fresh thyme
1/2 bay leaf
400 ml (12 3/4 fl oz) red wine
400 ml (12 3/4 fl oz) brown veal stock (see page 518)
15 g (1/2 oz) unsalted butter, cut into cubes and chilled

One If using the shin bone, prepare it by placing the pieces of bone in enough cold water to cover, then simmer for about 5 minutes, or until the marrow slips out easily. Thinly slice the marrow.

Two Place the shallots in a wide-based pan with the peppercorns, thyme and bay leaf. Stir in the red wine and bring to the boil. Reduce by simmering briskly for about 3 minutes, or until the liquid has evaporated and the pan is almost dry.

Three Stir in the veal stock, scraping the base of the pan with a wooden spoon, and return to the boil. Reduce the heat and simmer for 10 minutes, or until the sauce is reduced to 250 ml (8 fl oz). Skim the surface occasionally. Season with salt and pepper. Strain through a fine sieve before whisking in the butter, piece by piece, until the sauce has thickened slightly. Finish by adding the bone marrow, reheated by simmering in water or tossing in a hot pan. Serve hot.

Shellfish sauce

With similar ingredients to those used in a bisque, this sauce is perfect with all types of shellfish, especially lobster as shown (bottom right).

Preparation time 20 minutes
Total cooking time 1 hour
Makes approximately 350 ml (11 fl oz)

vegetable oil, for cooking
2 cloves garlic, lightly crushed
1/2 onion, roughly diced
1 small carrot, roughly diced
1 celery stick, chopped
1 bay leaf
2 sprigs of fresh thyme
500 g (1 lb) seafood trimmings such as crab, lobster or prawn shells
100 ml (3 1/4 fl oz) white wine
50 ml (1 3/4 fl oz) brandy
30 g (1 oz) plain flour
2 tablespoons tomato paste (purée)
100 g (3 1/4 oz) tomatoes, halved and seeded
1 litre fish stock (see page 519)
50 ml (1 3/4 fl oz) thick (double) cream, optional

One Heat the oil and garlic gently in a large deep pan. Add the vegetables and cook, stirring occasionally, until the vegetables are soft and lightly coloured.

Two Stir in the bay leaf, thyme and prawn shells. Pour in the wine and brandy, scraping the base of the pan to lift all the juices. Cook until the pan is dry. Sprinkle the flour in and stir in the tomato paste and tomato. Add the stock and stir until boiling. Reduce the heat and simmer for about 30–40 minutes, stirring occasionally.

Three Strain into a clean pan and keep warm. Season with salt and pepper and stir in the cream, if using. Serve hot.

Sauce verte

This colourful, mayonnaise-based sauce complements dishes such as the poached salmon fillet shown here (top left).

Preparation time 20 minutes
Total cooking time 15 minutes
Makes approximately 375 ml (12 fl oz)

50 g (1¾ oz) English spinach leaves
50 g (1¾ oz) fresh tarragon
1 teaspoon chopped fresh chives
50 g (1¾ oz) fresh chervil or parsley
50 g (1¾ oz) watercress, trimmed
1 clove garlic, roughly chopped
250 g (8 oz) mayonnaise

One Wash the spinach leaves thoroughly in cold water until all traces of sand or dirt are removed. Drain. Wash the herbs thoroughly and drain.

Two Combine all the greenery in a food processor, along with the garlic and 30 ml (1 fl oz) water. Purée until fine.

Three Pour the mixture into a heavy-based pan, heat gently to simmering and cook until the mixture appears to be dry and looks slightly separated. Strain immediately through a muslin-lined sieve. Cool a little until you can draw the muslin ends together and twist to squeeze out any remaining moisture. Discard the liquid.

Four In a bowl, combine a small amount of the mayonnaise with the dry purée to loosen it. Add to the remainder of the mayonnaise to make a bright green sauce. Taste and season. Serve cold with salads, cold poached poultry and fish, soups and terrines.

Marie Rose sauce

Adjust the flavourings in this sauce to your own taste and serve with your favourite seafood, such as the grilled scallops and prawns pictured (bottom left).

Preparation time 5 minutes
Total cooking time Nil
Makes approximately 350 ml (11 fl oz)

250 g (8 oz) mayonnaise
80 g (2¾ oz) tomato sauce
Worcestershire sauce, to taste
Tabasco, to taste
brandy, to taste

One Stir the mayonnaise and tomato sauce together in a small bowl. Add a few drops each of Worcestershire sauce, Tabasco and brandy and stir to combine.

Two Cover the surface of the sauce with plastic wrap and leave to chill in the refrigerator. Serve with seafood.

Rémoulade sauce

This sauce, which is the traditional accompaniment to grated celeriac, is also delicious with cold meats such as the ham, turkey and beef pictured here (top right).

Preparation time 10 minutes
+ 10 minutes refrigeration
+ 15 minutes soaking
Total cooking time Nil
Makes approximately 325 ml (10 fl oz)

3 anchovy fillets
60 ml (2 fl oz) milk
250 g (8 oz) mayonnaise
2 teaspoons Dijon mustard
25 g (³/4 oz) capers, drained
and chopped
50 g (1³/4 oz) cornichons or gherkins,
drained and chopped

One Place the anchovy fillets in a small bowl, soak in the milk for 15 minutes, then drain. Discard the milk and finely chop the anchovies.

Two Stir the mayonnaise in a small bowl with the chopped anchovies and mustard until combined. Mix the capers and the cornichons into the sauce.

Three Cover with plastic wrap and chill in the refrigerator for 10 minutes, or until required for serving. Serve the rémoulade sauce with grilled fish, grated celeriac or cold meats.

Classic vinaigrette

A classic vinaigrette can be used to add a tang to all types of salads or vegetables. Here it is shown simply with mixed salad leaves (bottom right).

Preparation time 5 minutes
Total cooking time Nil
Makes approximately 250 ml (8 fl oz)

2 tablespoons Dijon mustard
50 ml (1³/4 fl oz) white wine vinegar
200 ml (6¹/2 fl oz) olive oil
or good-quality salad oil

One Whisk together the mustard and vinegar in a bowl, with salt and pepper, to taste.

Two Slowly drizzle in the oil, whisking continuously. This will result in an emulsification, giving a thick smooth texture, rather than the oil separating and sitting on top. If the vinaigrette is too sharp for your taste, add a little more oil.

Three The vinaigrette can be kept at room temperature, in a sealed container and out of direct sunlight, for up to 1 week before serving.

CHEF'S TIP *As a rule of thumb, the guide for vinaigrettes is one part acid (wine vinegar or lemon juice) to four parts oil.*

Tomato sauce

*This excellent tomato sauce, full of flavour, is shown
here with deep-fried battered fish (top left), but it would
also be delicious with meat or pasta.*

Preparation time 20 minutes
Total cooking time 45 minutes
Makes approximately 410 ml (13 fl oz)

2 tablespoons olive oil
2 tablespoons tomato paste (purée)
100 g (3¼ oz) carrots, diced
100 g (3¼ oz) onions, diced
100 g (3¼ oz) bacon, diced
*2 kg (4 lb) very ripe tomatoes, peeled,
seeded and diced (see page 534)
or 4 x 425 g (13½ oz) cans
tomatoes, drained and
roughly chopped*
4 sprigs of fresh thyme
2 bay leaves
small pinch of cayenne pepper

One Heat the olive oil in a pan over medium heat. Stir the tomato paste into the oil and cook for 30 seconds, stirring continuously with a wooden spoon to avoid burning. Stir in the diced carrot, onion and bacon and continue to cook gently, without colouring, for another 10 minutes, or until all the vegetables are tender.

Two Add the tomato, thyme and bay leaves to the pan and gently cook for 30 minutes (longer if using canned tomatoes), stirring occasionally.

Three Strain through a coarse sieve, pressing with a wooden spoon to extract as much liquid and pulp as possible. Discard the ingredients in the sieve. Season with salt and cayenne pepper and serve hot.

Apple sauce

*The tartness of this sauce is the perfect accompaniment to roast pork,
(pictured bottom left), and other rich and fatty meats, such as duck or goose.*

Preparation time 15 minutes
Total cooking time 15 minutes
Makes approximately 500 ml (16 fl oz)

*4 cooking apples,
peeled and cut into small cubes*
pinch of cinnamon or cumin
2 teaspoons caster sugar

One To make in a saucepan, combine the apple cubes, cinnamon or cumin and sugar in a pan and add enough water to barely cover the base of the pan. Cover with greaseproof paper and a lid and cook the apples over low-medium heat for 10–15 minutes, or until the apples have broken down to a purée. You may need to mash the apple with a fork or push it through a sieve to remove lumps.

Two If a runnier consistency is required, add some water towards the end of cooking. Also, you may adjust the sweetness with more sugar to taste. Serve hot or cold.

Three To make in the microwave, place the apples in a large microwave-proof dish with the cinnamon or cumin and sugar. Microwave on high for about 4 minutes, or until the apples break down to a purée when pressed against the side of the dish with a fork.

Hollandaise sauce

This smooth, butter-based basic sauce is famed for serving with asparagus, as shown. See page 521 for step-by-step instructions to accompany this recipe.

Preparation time 10 minutes
Total cooking time 10 minutes
Makes approximately 500 ml (16 fl oz)

HOLLANDAISE SAUCE
3 egg yolks
200 g (6½ oz) clarified butter,
melted (see page 520)
juice of ½ lemon
small pinch of cayenne pepper

One To make the hollandaise sauce, whisk the egg yolks with 3 tablespoons of water in a heatproof bowl until foamy. Place the bowl over a pan half-filled with simmering water and whisk until thick. The bowl should not touch the water.

Two Gradually add the melted butter, whisking constantly over very low heat. The sauce must not be allowed to get too hot, or it may curdle. The sauce should leave a trail on the surface when the whisk is lifted. Once all the butter has been incorporated, strain the sauce into a clean bowl. Stir in the lemon juice and season with salt, pepper and the

cayenne. Keep the sauce warm over a pan of warm water.

Two You can use a food processor to make the sauce: whisk the egg yolks and water and, with the motor running, add the melted warm butter in a thin stream.

CHEF'S TIPS *Once made, the sauce should be kept lukewarm. If it is over-heated, it will separate. If this should happen, the sauce can be repaired by adding a little cold water and whisking.*

Measure out small amounts of cayenne pepper with the tip of a knife. Avoid using your fingertips in case you rub your eyes or lips afterwards.

Crème anglaise

This rich custard sauce, traditionally flavoured with vanilla, has a light consistency. Serve hot or cold to accompany all manner of desserts, such as the poached peach shown in the picture.

Preparation time *5 minutes*
Total cooking time *20 minutes*
Makes approximately *350 ml (11 fl oz)*

250 ml (8 fl oz) milk
1 vanilla pod, split lengthways
3 egg yolks
30 g (1 oz) caster sugar

One Pour the milk into a deep, heavy-based saucepan over medium heat. Scrape the seeds from the vanilla pod and add to the milk with the pod. Slowly bring to the boil to allow the flavour of the vanilla to infuse into the milk. Remove from the heat.

Two In a bowl, using a wooden spoon, whisk together the egg yolks and the sugar until pale and thick. Pour the hot milk onto the yolks and mix well. Pour the mixture back into a clean saucepan and cook over extremely gentle heat, stirring continuously, for 5 minutes, or until it begins to thicken and coats the back of a spoon. If the mixture is getting too hot, remove the pan from the heat for a few seconds and continue to stir. Do not allow it to boil. Strain into a bowl and discard the vanilla pod. If serving cold, allow the custard to cool before chilling in the refrigerator. To reheat the sauce, transfer to a heatproof bowl or deep dish and set over a pan of hand-hot water, stirring continuously and taking care not to overheat.

CHEF'S TIPS *This custard sauce can be kept in the refrigerator for up to 3 days in an airtight container.*

Take extra care when cooking the basic mixture. If the heat is too high, the mixture will cook too quickly around the sides of the pan and curdle or separate as the egg yolks become overcooked and 'scramble' in the milk. The sauce can be saved by adding a dash of cold milk and rapidly whisking, which releases the heat as quickly as possible to reduce any further curdling. If the sauce has curdled and been saved in this way, it may be slightly lumpy and need to be passed through a sieve before using.

Fruit coulis

Make this fabulous fruit sauce using whatever berries are in season. Ideal for serving with any dessert, ice cream or sorbet (pictured top right).

Preparation time 5 minutes
Total cooking time 5 minutes
Makes approximately 250 ml (8 fl oz)

250 g (8 oz) firm ripe raspberries
125 g (4 oz) caster sugar
juice of ½ lemon
alcohol or liqueur of your choice (see Chef's tips)

One Prepare the fruit by removing any that is bruised or overripe.

Two Combine the raspberries in a saucepan with the caster sugar and lemon juice and bring to the boil to soften the berries slightly. Remove from the heat and allow to cool.

Three Transfer to a food processor and blend to a smooth purée. Pass through a fine sieve to remove the seeds. At this stage your favourite alcohol can be added, to taste. This fruit sauce can be stored in an airtight container in the refrigerator for up to 1 week and should be served cold.

CHEF'S TIPS *Try Kirsch, Calvados, eau de vie de poivre, or Cointreau.*

When fresh berries are not available, use frozen ones instead. Thaw them before use. You may need to adjust the sugar content accordingly.

A quick, non-cook method is suitable if the fruit is very soft and will purée easily. To process the fruit with icing sugar instead of caster sugar, sieve as described in the recipe and then stir in the lemon juice.

Orange and Grand Marnier sauce

Crêpes or ice cream can be dressed up with this sophisticated tangy sauce (pictured bottom right).

Preparation time 10–15 minutes
Total cooking time 20 minutes
Makes approximately 300 ml (10 fl oz)

250 ml (8 fl oz) fresh orange juice
25 g (¾ oz) sugar
1 teaspoon finely grated orange rind
200 g (6½ oz) unsalted butter, cut into small cubes and chilled
60 ml (2 fl oz) Grand Marnier, Cognac or Cointreau

One Bring the orange juice, sugar and grated orange rind slowly to the boil in a saucepan. Continue to boil, stirring occasionally, until the orange liquid becomes syrupy.

Two Whisk the butter into the boiling liquid, piece by piece, until a smooth consistency is obtained. Remove the pan from the heat and add the liqueur, to taste. Serve the sauce immediately or keep it warm (not hot) for no more than about 30 minutes before use.

CHEF'S TIP *If the sauce becomes too cold, it will set. If it is too hot, it will separate. To rescue the sauce from both these problems, melt the former to a lukewarm heat and cool the latter to the same temperature. You can do this by bringing to the boil a small amount of water or orange juice, then adding a small amount of hard butter and whisking it in to obtain a smooth consistency. Slowly add either of the problem sauces to this mixture, whisking continuously.*

Chocolate sauce

This is a favourite accompaniment for many desserts and fruits, such as the poached pear and vanilla ice cream shown here (pictured top left).

Preparation time 10 minutes
Total cooking time 20 minutes
Makes approximately 315 ml (10 fl oz)

225 g (7¼ oz) caster sugar
100 g (3¼ oz) dark chocolate, chopped
25 g (¾ oz) good-quality cocoa powder, sifted

One Combine 300 ml (10 fl oz) of water with the sugar and chopped chocolate in a medium saucepan and slowly bring to the boil, stirring continuously. Remove from the heat.

Two In a bowl, mix the cocoa powder and 50 ml (1¾ fl oz) water to a smooth paste. Pour this into the saucepan over medium heat and bring back to the boil, whisking vigorously and continuously. Simmer, uncovered, for 5–10 minutes, until the sauce coats the back of a spoon. Do not allow the sauce to boil over. Strain and allow to cool a little.

CHEF'S TIP *This sauce may be served hot or cold and keeps well for up to 1 week if stored in an airtight container in the refrigerator.*

Butterscotch sauce

A very rich sauce ideal to serve hot with ice cream. It also works particularly well with waffles (pictured bottom left).

Preparation time 5 minutes
Total cooking time 15 minutes
Makes approximately 315 ml (10 fl oz)

1 vanilla pod, split lengthways
450 ml (14¼ fl oz) cream
200 g (6½ oz) caster sugar

One Scrape the seeds from the vanilla pod and add with the pod to a saucepan with the cream. Bring slowly to the boil, remove from the heat and allow the flavours to infuse into the cream, then strain and discard the vanilla pod.

Two In a separate saucepan and using a wooden spoon, stir half the sugar continuously over medium heat, until the sugar has melted. Add the remaining sugar and cook until the sugar is fluid and light golden.

Three Remove from the heat and add the cream in a slow steady stream, stirring continuously. Be careful as the sugar will splatter when the liquid is added. When all the cream has been incorporated, return to the boil and cook, stirring, until the sauce coats the back of the spoon. If you have a few lumps of sugar left in the bottom of the pan simply pass the liquid through a wire sieve. This sauce may be served either hot or cold.

CHEF'S TIP *For an adult version of the sauce, try adding a little malt whisky, to taste. You could also add a little espresso coffee, to taste.*

Whisky sauce

*This is a great sauce for Christmas puddings and desserts,
flavoured with fresh vanilla and whisky (pictured in jug, right).*

Preparation time 15 minutes
Total cooking time 25 minutes
Makes 600 ml (20 fl oz)

600 ml (20 fl oz) milk
large pinch of ground nutmeg
1 vanilla pod, split lengthways
30 g (1 oz) unsalted butter
30 g (1 oz) plain flour
2 tablespoons sugar
2 egg yolks
2 tablespoons cream or milk
3 tablespoons whisky

One Place the milk in a pan with the nutmeg. Scrape the seeds from the vanilla pod and add to the milk with the pod. Heat gently until small bubbles appear around the edge of the pan. Set aside to cool, then strain the milk, discard the pod and wipe out the pan.

Two Melt the butter in the pan over low heat. Sprinkle the flour over the butter and cook, stirring continuously with a wooden spoon, for 1–2 minutes, without allowing it to colour.

Three Remove from the heat and slowly add the vanilla milk, whisking or beating vigorously to avoid lumps. Return to low heat and bring slowly to the boil, stirring constantly. Add the sugar, then simmer for 3–4 minutes.

Four In a heatproof bowl, stir together the egg yolks and cream or milk, then pour on a quarter of the hot sauce, stir together to blend and return the mixture to the remaining sauce in the pan. Add the whisky to the mixture and stir constantly over low heat to heat through, without allowing the sauce to boil. Stir in more sugar or whisky, to taste, and strain the sauce. Serve the sauce warm.

Brandy butter

*The classic partner for Christmas pudding, brandy butter also
tastes wonderful with fruit mince pies (pictured in bowl, right).*

Preparation time 20 minutes
Total cooking time Nil
Makes 250 ml (8 fl oz)

120 g (4 oz) unsalted butter,
at room temperature
120 g (4 oz) soft brown sugar
2–3 tablespoons brandy

One Place the butter in a bowl and whisk using electric beaters or beat with a wooden spoon until soft and creamy. Add the brown sugar a tablespoon at a time, whisking well between additions, until the mixture is light and creamy.

Two Whisk in the brandy, half a tablespoon at a time. Do not add the brandy too quickly or the mixture will separate. Place in a serving bowl, cover with plastic wrap and refrigerate until needed. Return to room temperature before serving.

CHEF'S TIPS *For a variation, add a little grated orange rind, or use caster sugar for a lighter flavour.*

If you want to make the brandy butter well in advance, you could try placing the butter in a piping bag with a star-shaped nozzle and piping small rosettes onto baking trays lined with greaseproof paper. Freeze until hard and store in a bag in the freezer until needed.

desserts

Hot chocolate soufflés

A well-risen, feather-light soufflé is one of the hallmarks of a great chef. The real skill lies in transporting the soufflé to the table before it begins to cool and collapse.

Preparation time *20 minutes*
Total cooking time *20–25 minutes*
Serves 6

50 g (1³/₄ oz) good-quality dark
chocolate, roughly chopped
250 ml (8 fl oz) milk
60 g (2 oz) unsalted butter
3 tablespoons plain flour
caster sugar, to coat dishes
4 eggs, separated
2¹/₂ tablespoons caster sugar
1 tablespoon cocoa powder, sifted
icing sugar, to dust

One Preheat the oven to moderate 180°C (350°F/Gas 4). Put the chocolate in a bowl. Heat the milk in a saucepan until just at boiling point. Pour onto the chocolate and stir until the chocolate has melted. Melt the butter in a saucepan and add the flour. Cook over low heat for 1 minute. Add the chocolate milk gradually, stirring continuously with a wooden spoon. Bring to the boil and then remove immediately from the heat. Set aside to cool completely.

Two Brush six 250 ml (8 fl oz) soufflé dishes with butter, working the brush from the bottom upwards. Refrigerate until the butter is firm, then repeat. Half fill one of the dishes with caster sugar and, without placing your fingers inside the mould, rotate so that a layer of sugar sticks to the butter. Tap out the excess sugar and use to coat the other moulds.

Three Stir the yolks into the chocolate mixture. In a separate bowl, whisk the egg whites with electric beaters until soft peaks form. Add the sugar and whisk for 30 seconds. Fold in the cocoa powder. Lightly beat a third of the egg-white mixture into the chocolate mixture to just blend. Add the rest of the egg-white mixture and fold in very gently but quickly. Do not overmix or the mixture will lose its volume.

Four Spoon in the mixture to fill each dish completely and level the top with a palette knife. Sprinkle with sifted icing sugar and then run your thumb just inside the top of each soufflé dish to create a ridge and help the soufflé rise evenly, following the method in the Chef's technique on page 539. Bake for 15 minutes, or until the soufflés are well risen and a light crust has formed. The soufflés should feel just set when pressed lightly with your fingers. Dust the tops lightly with sifted icing sugar and serve immediately.

LE CORDON BLEU ❖ COMPLETE COOK

Crèmes brûlées

The literal translation of this rich dessert is 'burnt cream'. Just before serving, chilled custard is sprinkled with sugar, which is quickly caramelised under a grill to form a brittle topping, creating a delicious contrast in flavour and texture to the smooth, creamy custard beneath.

***Preparation time** 20 minutes*
+ overnight refrigeration
***Total cooking time** 55 minutes*
Serves 6

4 egg yolks
2¹/₂ tablespoons caster sugar
300 ml (10 fl oz) thick (double) cream
300 ml (10 fl oz) cream
vanilla extract or essence
3 tablespoons sugar

One Preheat the oven to slow 150°C (300°F/Gas 2). Have six 100 ml (3¹/₄ fl oz) ramekins ready.

Two Whisk the egg yolks and sugar in a large heatproof bowl. Set aside. Bring all the cream and a few drops of vanilla to the boil in a heavy-based pan, then reduce the heat and simmer for about 8 minutes. Remove the pan from the heat and slowly pour the cream onto the egg mixture, whisking vigorously so the eggs do not scramble. Strain the custard into a jug, then pour into the ramekins.

Three Put the ramekins in a roasting tin. Pour enough boiling water into the tin to reach 1 cm (¹/₂ inch) below the tops of the ramekins. Bake the custards for 40–45 minutes, or until just firm to the touch. Remove from the oven and cool, then cover and refrigerate overnight.

Four To make the caramel, evenly sprinkle some sugar over the top of each custard with a teaspoon. Without piercing the skin of the custard, spread the sugar out very gently using a finger or the spoon, then repeat to form a second layer of sugar. Remove any sugar from the inside edges of the ramekins as it will burn on the dish. Place the ramekins on a metal tray and glaze under a very hot grill for 2–3 minutes, or until the sugar has melted and has formed a layer of caramel. Allow the glaze to set or harden before serving.

CHEF'S TIPS *This wonderful dessert is enhanced by fruit. Before pouring the custard into the ramekins, arrange a few berries (strawberries or raspberries are ideal) in the bottom of the dish, or prunes presoaked in Armagnac.*

You can also use a blowtorch to brown the sugar on top of the custards.

Apple strudel

In Vienna it is said that to make a perfect apple strudel the dough must be stretched so finely that a love letter can be read through it.

Preparation time 40 minutes
+ 30 minutes resting
Total cooking time 50 minutes
Serves 6–8

185 g (6 oz) strong or plain flour
1 egg, lightly beaten
120 g (4 oz) unsalted butter
90 g (3 oz) fresh breadcrumbs
3 tablespoons caster sugar
2 teaspoons ground cinnamon
600 g (1¼ lb) cooking or very sharp dessert apples
60 g (2 oz) sultanas
icing sugar, for dusting

One Sift the flour and a pinch of salt into a large bowl. Make a well in the centre, add the beaten egg and 75 ml (2½ fl oz) warm water, and mix with your hands to a smooth dough. With the bowl tipped to one side, and with open fingers, beat the dough, rotating your wrist. The dough is ready when it pulls away from the bowl and is difficult to beat. Place the dough in a clean, lightly floured bowl, cover and leave in a warm place for 15 minutes.

Two Melt half of the butter in a pan. Slowly fry the breadcrumbs until golden brown, then set aside to cool in a bowl. Mix the sugar and cinnamon in a small bowl. Preheat the oven to moderate 180°C (350°F/Gas 4).

Three Thoroughly flour one side of a large clean tea towel, place the pastry on top and, with your fingers, gently stretch the dough to a large rectangle measuring about 50 x 60 cm (20 x 24 inches); cover with a clean tea towel and set aside for 15 minutes. Melt the remaining butter and set aside.

Four Peel, quarter, core and finely slice the apples, and combine with the breadcrumbs, cinnamon mixture and sultanas. Brush the dough liberally with the melted butter, then sprinkle the apple mixture all over the dough. Trim away the thick edge with a pair of scissors.

Five Pick up the tea towel from the shorter side, and push away and down from you to lightly roll the strudel up like a swiss roll. Tip the strudel carefully onto a tray, seam-side down or to one side. Leave the strudel straight, or curve it lightly into the traditional 'crescent'. Brush the pastry well with any remaining butter.

Six Bake for 35–45 minutes, or until crisp and golden. Cool slightly, sprinkle with icing sugar and serve warm with vanilla custard, ice cream or whipped cream.

Clafoutis

This classic dessert is based on a dish originating in the French country region of Limousin, where clafoutis is enjoyed when sweet, dark cherries are ripe. Cherries are the favoured fruit for this dessert, although plums or pears can also be used.

Preparation time 40 minutes
Total cooking time 45 minutes
Serves 4

1 fresh peach or 2 tinned peach halves,
drained of syrup
250 g (8 oz) cherries
500 ml (16 fl oz) thick (double) cream
1 vanilla pod, split lengthways
6 egg yolks
1 egg
1 tablespoon custard powder
2½ tablespoons plain flour
25 ml (³/4 fl oz) Cointreau
icing sugar, for dusting

One Preheat the oven to slow 150°C (300°F/Gas 2). If you are using a fresh peach, plunge it into boiling water for 10–20 seconds, then transfer to a bowl of iced water.

Two Peel the peach and cut around the fruit towards the stone. Gently twist the halves in opposite directions to expose the stone, then lift out the stone with a knife. If the peach is too slippery, simply cut the flesh from the stone. Process or sieve one peach half and measure out 50 ml (1³/4 fl oz) of purée. Slice the remaining peach half into neat segments and set aside. Carefully pit the cherries and set aside.

Three Place the cream in a heavy-based pan with the vanilla pod, then heat until scalding—this is when bubbles form around the edge of the cream surface, yet the cream is not boiling. Remove the vanilla pod.

Four Whisk the egg yolks and the whole egg together in a large bowl. Beat in the custard powder and flour, then stir in the peach purée. Whisk the scalding cream into the egg mixture. Add the Cointreau and stir.

Five Lightly grease a 2 litre shallow ovenproof dish with softened butter. Place all the fruit in the dish. Pour the custard over the top and bake for about 40 minutes, or until a skewer inserted into the centre of the dessert comes out clean. Immediately sift the icing sugar over the top. Serve hot.

378   LE CORDON BLEU ✤ COMPLETE COOK

Crêpes Suzette

*In this illustrious dessert, very fine pancakes are warmed in
a lightly caramelised orange butter sauce, then doused with
Cointreau and ignited to flaming glory at the table.*

*Preparation time 30 minutes
+ 30 minutes resting
Total cooking time 45 minutes
Makes 12 crepes*

CREPE BATTER
*90 g (3 oz) plain flour
1 teaspoon caster sugar
2 eggs, plus 1 egg yolk, lightly beaten
170 ml (5½ fl oz) milk
25 g (¾ oz) clarified butter, melted
(see page 520)*

*clarified butter, for cooking
(see page 520)*

SAUCE
*4 white sugar cubes
800 g (1 lb 10 oz) oranges
40 g (1¼ oz) clarified butter, melted
(see page 520)
3 tablespoons caster sugar
45 ml (1½ fl oz) Cointreau
30 ml (1 fl oz) brandy*

One To make the batter, sift the flour into a bowl with a pinch of salt and the sugar. Make a well in the centre, then add the eggs and extra egg yolk. Mix well with a wooden spoon or whisk, gradually incorporating the flour. Combine the milk with 60 ml (2 fl oz) water and gradually add to the batter. Add the clarified butter and beat until smooth. Cover. Set aside for 30 minutes.

Two Melt a little clarified butter in a shallow heavy-based or non-stick pan measuring 15–17 cm (6–7 inches) across the base. When a haze forms, cook the crepes, following the method in the Chef's techniques on page 538.

Three To make the sauce, rub all the sugar cube sides over the rind of an orange to soak up the aromatic oil, then crush the cubes with the back of a wooden spoon. Juice the oranges to produce 315 ml (10 fl oz) liquid. Over gentle heat, melt the clarified butter in a wide shallow pan or frying pan. Dissolve the crushed sugar in the butter, then add the caster sugar. Cook, stirring, for 2 minutes. Slowly add the orange juice,

keeping well clear of the pan as the mixture may spit. Increase the heat to medium and simmer until reduced by one third.

Four Fold the crepes in half, then into triangles. Place them in the orange sauce, slightly overlapping, with their points showing. Tilt the pan, scoop up the sauce and pour it over the crepes to moisten them well.

Five Cook over low heat for 2 minutes. Turn off the heat and have a saucepan lid ready in case you need to put out the flame. Pour the Cointreau and brandy over the sauce in the pan without stirring. Immediately light the sauce with a match, standing well back from the pan. Serve the crepes on warmed plates. Fresh vanilla ice cream is a lovely accompaniment.

CHEF'S TIP *Any leftover crepes can be stacked with sheets of greaseproof paper between them, wrapped in foil and frozen in an airtight bag. To defrost, refrigerate overnight, then peel off to use. They are a very versatile stand-by.*

about crêpe pans...

If you make crepes or omelettes on a regular basis, it is a good idea to invest in a special pan which you use only for these two things. A non-stick pan is perfect for both crepes and omelettes, though you can season a cast iron pan yourself.

Tarte Tatin

This delicious 'upside down' tart was invented by the Tatin sisters, who ran a hotel-restaurant in the Sologne region at the turn of the century. It was first served in Paris at Maxim's, where it is still a house speciality.

*Preparation time 50 minutes
+ 20 minutes chilling
Total cooking time 1 hour 20 minutes
Serves 6–8*

PASTRY

*125 g (4 oz) unsalted butter,
at room temperature
50 g (1¾ oz) caster sugar
1 egg, beaten
1–2 drops vanilla extract or essence,
optional
200 g (6½ oz) plain flour*

*60 g (2 oz) sugar
90 g (3 oz) unsalted butter
about 10 Pink Ladies, Fuji
or Cox apples, about 220 g (7 oz)
each, peeled, cored and halved and
tossed in 1 teaspoon lemon juice*

One To make the pastry, cream the butter and sugar in a bowl, using a wooden spoon or electric beaters. Add the egg and vanilla in two or three stages, mixing well before each addition. Sift the flour with a pinch of salt, add to the mixture and stir until smooth. Draw the dough together with your hands to form a rough ball, flatten with the palm of your hand to 1 cm (½ inch) thickness. Wrap in plastic wrap. Chill for 20 minutes.

Two Preheat the oven to moderate 180°C (350°F/Gas 4). Roll out the chilled dough to a circle, 3 mm (⅛ inch) thick, place on a lined tray and refrigerate.

Three In a 20 cm (8 inch) ovenproof frying pan (with sloping sides), place the sugar and butter together. Cook over medium heat, stirring constantly, for 10 minutes, or until it begins to bubble and colour slightly.

Four Cook the apples and add the pastry following the method in the Chef's techniques on page 538. Make a few small incisions in the pastry to allow steam to escape, then place the pan on a tray and bake for about 15–20 minutes, or until the pastry is nicely coloured.

Five Remove from the oven and allow to sit for 2 minutes. Place a serving platter over the pan and tilt to allow any juices to flow out into a bowl. In one swift motion, flip the pan over, giving it a good shake to ensure the apples loosen. Carefully lift the pan. If there is any extra liquid, drizzle it over the apples. Serve warm.

CHEF'S TIPS *It is important to have a big enough pan to allow you to baste the apples. You also need to be careful of caramel catching on the bottom of the pan.*

The apples will give off liquid, so the caramel must be well reduced before the pastry goes on.

Gratin of summer berries

*Beneath a luscious froth of sabayon, quickly grilled
until golden brown, lies an assortment of fresh sweet
berries for a delectable summer dessert.*

Preparation time 20 minutes
Total cooking time 20 minutes
Serves 4

*600 g (1¼ lb) mixed berries,
such as strawberries, blueberries,
raspberries and blackberries
2 eggs
2 egg yolks
80 g (2¾ oz) caster sugar
1 tablespoon Kirsch*

One Wash the strawberries, dry well,
discard the stalks and cut each
strawberry in half. Sort the remaining
berries to ensure they are all fresh.
Arrange the fruit on four ovenproof
plates or individual shallow dishes.

Two Half-fill a large pan with water and
heat until simmering. Have ready a
heatproof bowl that will fit over the pan
without actually touching the water.

Three To make the sabayon, place the
eggs, egg yolks, sugar and Kirsch in the
bowl, then place the bowl over the pan
of simmering water, ensuring the base of
the bowl is not touching the water.
Whisk for 10–15 minutes, or until the
mixture is thick and creamy and leaves a
trail as it falls from the whisk.

Four Preheat the grill to high. Spoon the
sabayon over the berries and quickly
grill until the sabayon is brown all over.
Serve immediately.

CHEF'S TIP *The plates of fruit can be
arranged in advance. Cover the plates
with plastic wrap so the berries do not
dry out.*

Hot Cointreau and orange soufflés

A beautifully risen, hot soufflé is always a sight to behold. This spectacular dessert, flavoured simply with the sweetness of sun-drenched orange, will create a sensation among even the most discerning dinner guests.

Preparation time 35 minutes
Total cooking time 20 minutes
Serves 6

softened butter, for greasing
110 g (3³/4 oz) caster sugar, and extra for lining
2 tablespoons orange juice
2 teaspoons grated orange rind
1 tablespoon Cointreau
250 ml (8 fl oz) milk
¹/2 vanilla pod, split lengthways
4 eggs, separated
1 tablespoon plain flour
1 tablespoon cornflour
sifted icing sugar, to dust

One Preheat the oven to moderate 180°C (350°F/Gas 4). Brush the insides of six 180 ml (6 fl oz) soufflé dishes with melted butter, working the brush from the bottom upwards. Refrigerate to set and repeat.

Two Half-fill a soufflé dish with some sugar, and without placing your fingers inside the dish, rotate it so that a layer of sugar adheres to the butter. Tap out the excess sugar and repeat with the remaining soufflé dishes.

Three Place the orange juice and grated rind in a small pan over medium–high heat. Simmer for 3–5 minutes to reduce the volume by three quarters—the mixture should be quite syrupy. Pour in the Cointreau, scraping the base of the pan with a wooden spoon. Remove from the heat and allow to cool.

Four Bring the milk and vanilla pod slowly to the boil. In a bowl, and using a wooden spoon, mix together 75 g (2¹/2 oz) of the caster sugar and two of the egg yolks, then mix in the flour and cornflour. Remove the vanilla pod from the boiling milk; stir a little of the milk into the egg mixture, then add all the mixture to the milk in the pan. Beat rapidly with the wooden spoon over medium heat until the mixture thickens and comes to the boil. Boil gently for 1 minute to cook the flour, stirring continuously to prevent sticking.

Five Pour the mixture into a clean bowl, stir to cool it slightly, then beat in the reduced orange sauce. Stir in the remaining two egg yolks and run a small piece of butter over the surface to melt and prevent a skin forming. (If you prefer, place a sheet of baking paper on the surface instead.)

Six In a clean, dry bowl, whisk the egg whites until they form soft peaks. Add the remaining sugar and whisk for 30 seconds. Add a third of the egg whites to the milk mixture and lightly beat in until just combined. Using a large metal spoon, fold in the remaining egg whites gently but quickly. Do not overmix, as this will cause the mixture to lose volume and become heavy.

Seven Set the soufflé dishes on a baking tray. Spoon in the mixture to completely fill each dish, smooth the surface of each soufflé and sprinkle with sifted icing sugar. Run your thumb just inside the top of each soufflé dish to create a ridge and help the soufflé rise evenly, following the method in the Chef's technique on page 539. Bake for 12 minutes, or until well risen with a light crust. The soufflés should feel just set when pressed lightly with a fingertip. Serve at once.

CHEF'S TIP *This soufflé, up to the end of step 4, can be prepared a few hours in advance.*

Rhubarb crumble

This simple pudding is a great way to use up a glut of ripe, in-season fruit. In this version, tangy rhubarb perfectly complements the buttery, short topping.

Preparation time *30 minutes*
Total cooking time *40 minutes*
Serves 6

2 tablespoons strawberry jam
650 g (1 lb 5 oz) trimmed rhubarb,
cut in 2.5 cm (1 inch) lengths
2 tablespoons demerara sugar
60 g (2 oz) wholemeal flour
60 g (2 oz) plain flour
90 g (3 oz) unsalted butter,
cut into cubes and chilled
105 g (3½ oz) caster sugar
or demerara sugar
1 tablespoon pumpkin seeds,
toasted
1 tablespoon hazelnuts, toasted
and roughly chopped

One Place the strawberry jam in a wide, shallow pan with 2 tablespoons water, then add the rhubarb in a single layer with the 2 tablespoons of demerara sugar. Bring to the boil, then immediately lower the heat to a simmer, cover tightly with a lid or piece of foil and cook for about 5 minutes. The acidity of rhubarb does vary, so taste at the end of cooking time and stir in more sugar if necessary.

Two Transfer the rhubarb into a 1.25 litre ovenproof dish, about 20 cm (8 inches) in diameter and fairly deep. Spread out evenly, then pour over enough rhubarb juice to come halfway up the rhubarb. Set aside to cool. Preheat the oven to moderate 180°C (350°F/Gas 4).

Three Sieve the wholemeal and plain flours together into a bowl, tipping the bits from the wholemeal flour back into the bowl. Rub the butter into the flour using your fingertips until the mixture resembles fine breadcrumbs. Continue to rub in the butter until small lumps begin to form, then add the sugar, pumpkin seeds and hazelnuts and toss to incorporate completely.

Four Scatter the crumble mixture evenly over the rhubarb in the dish without pressing it down and then bake for 20–30 minutes, or until the topping is golden brown. Dust the pudding with a little extra sugar and serve warm or cold with cream.

Treacle pudding

*This family favourite is rich with golden syrup and is
served with a delicious cinnamon-flavoured syrup that
should be poured over just before serving.*

Preparation time 35 minutes
Total cooking time 2 hours
Serves 6

*240 g (7¹/2 oz) unsalted butter,
at room temperature*
240 g (7¹/2 oz) caster sugar
4 eggs, beaten
1/2 teaspoon vanilla extract or essence
finely grated rind of 2 lemons
240 g (7¹/2 oz) self-raising flour
120 g (4 oz) golden syrup

GOLDEN SYRUP SAUCE
1 cinnamon stick
¹/4 vanilla pod
150 g (5 oz) golden syrup
grated rind and juice of 1 lemon

One Prepare a 2 litre pudding basin for
steaming (see Chef's techniques, page 539).

Two Place the butter and sugar in a bowl
and, using a wooden spoon or electric
beaters, beat together until light and
creamy. Add the beaten egg in six
additions, beating well between each
addition, then mix in the vanilla and
lemon rind. Sieve the flour onto the
mixture and fold in using a large metal
spoon or plastic spatula.

Three Place the golden syrup in the base
of the pudding basin and spoon the
sponge mixture on top. Cover and steam
for 1 hour 40 minutes, following
the steaming method in the Chef's

techniques on page 539. To test when
the pudding is done, pierce with a
skewer. If it comes out clean, the
pudding is cooked (though it may still
look a bit sticky from the syrup).

Four To make the golden syrup sauce,
place the cinnamon, vanilla, golden syrup,
lemon juice and rind and 300 ml (10 fl oz)
water into a pan and bring to the boil.
Simmer for about 15 minutes to reduce
by one-third, then remove and discard
the cinnamon stick and vanilla pod.

Five Allow the cooked pudding to stand
for 10 minutes before removing the
string, foil and paper. Serve with the
golden syrup sauce.

Steamed orange pudding

*Hot, light and full of flavour, this pudding will brighten
the gloom of a winter's day like a burst of summer sunshine.
Serve with orange sauce or custard.*

Preparation time 30 minutes
Total cooking time 1 hour 45 minutes
Serves 6

100 g (3¼ oz) thin-cut marmalade
2 large oranges, peel and
pith removed
125 g (4 oz) unsalted butter,
at room temperature
125 g (4 oz) caster sugar
finely grated rind of 1 orange
2 large eggs, beaten
185 g (6 oz) self-raising flour
milk, for mixing

ORANGE SAUCE
320 ml (10¼ fl oz) orange juice
2 egg yolks
½ teaspoon cornflour
45 g (1½ oz) caster sugar
1 teaspoon Grand Marnier
or Cointreau

One Prepare a 1.25 litre pudding basin for steaming, following the method in the Chef's techniques on page 539.

Two Spoon the marmalade into the pudding basin. Finely slice the oranges, then line the basin with the orange slices, from the marmalade base to the top of the bowl.

Three In a bowl, beat the butter with a wooden spoon or electric whisk to soften. Slowly add the sugar, beating until light and fluffy. Mix in the orange rind. Add the egg in four additions, beating well between each addition. Sift in the flour and quickly fold into the mixture using a large metal spoon or plastic spatula. As the last traces of flour are mixed in, add a little milk to form a soft consistency: the mixture should drop from the spoon with a flick of the wrist.

Four Immediately transfer the mixture to the pudding basin and steam, following the method in the Chef's techniques on page 539, for 1½–1¾ hours, or until the pudding is springy to the light touch of a finger.

Five When cooked, carefully remove the pudding from the steamer. Remove the foil and paper, place a warm plate over the pudding basin and carefully turn the pudding over and remove the bowl. (If you are not serving the pudding immediately, place the bowl back over the pudding to prevent it from drying out and keep it warm.)

Six To make the orange sauce, bring the orange juice to the boil in a small pan. In a bowl, beat the egg yolks, cornflour and sugar until thick and light. Pour the hot orange juice into the bowl, mix until blended, then return to the pan. Cook over medium heat, stirring constantly with a wooden spoon, until the mixture coats the back of the spoon and the sauce does not close over when a line is drawn across the spoon with a finger.

Seven Remove from the heat, strain into a bowl, then stir in the Grand Marnier or Cointreau. If you are not using the sauce straight away, dust the surface lightly with caster sugar to prevent a skin forming. The sugar can be stirred in just before serving. Serve the sauce warm or cold with the pudding.

Bread and butter pudding with panettone

If you have a yearning for comfort food, bread and butter pudding is hard to beat.
For special occasions, this humble and economical dish can be transformed into something really
marvellous with glacé fruits, a dash of rum, some brioche or, as in this case, Italian panettone.

Preparation time 20 minutes
Total cooking time 50 minutes
Serves 4

3 tablespoons sultanas
2 tablespoons rum, brandy
or amaretto
250 g (8 oz) panettone
3 eggs
3 tablespoons caster sugar
500 ml (16 fl oz) milk
1 vanilla pod, split lengthways
1 tablespoon apricot jam, warmed
icing sugar, to dust

One Preheat the oven to warm 160°C (315°F/Gas 2–3). Place the sultanas in a 23 cm (9 inch) oval pie dish and pour the alcohol over the top.

Two Cut the panettone to make two or three round slices about 1 cm (1/2 inch) thick, then remove the crust. Cut each slice into four quarters (almost triangles). Neatly overlap them in the base of the pie dish.

Three Whisk the eggs and sugar in a heatproof bowl. Place the milk and vanilla pod in a pan, bring to the boil, then slowly whisk the scalding milk into the egg and sugar mixture.

Four Pour the mixture through a fine strainer into the pie dish, over the panettone. Put the dish in a roasting tin and pour enough boiling water into the tin to come halfway up the side of the dish. Bake for 40–45 minutes, or until the custard has set and is golden brown.

Five Remove the pie dish from the oven and, while the pudding is still warm, brush the surface with the warm apricot jam. Lightly dust with icing sugar and serve either hot or cold.

CHEF'S TIPS *If the panettone is not a sweet one, simply increase the sugar to taste.*

Fruit loaf is a perfect alternative to panettone as it already has a loaf shape. Simply cut off the crusts, slice the bread and cut each slice in half diagonally to form triangles.

LE CORDON BLEU COMPLETE COOK

Pears poached in red wine

A light yet satisfying end to a meal, this colourful dessert can be dressed up even further by adding some prunes to poach with the pears in the spiced wine sauce. Use a full-bodied red wine.

Preparation time 45 minutes
Total cooking time 50 minutes
Serves 4

1.5 litres red wine
425 g (13½ oz) sugar
2 cinnamon sticks
1 vanilla pod
1 clove
rind of 1 lemon
rind of 1 orange
4 pears
2 tablespoons redcurrant jelly
2 oranges
fresh mint leaves,
to garnish
fresh raspberries or redcurrants,
to garnish

One In a flameproof casserole dish, bring the wine, 300 g (10 oz) of the sugar, the spices, lemon rind and orange rind to the boil.

Two Peel the pears, leaving the stems intact, and remove the blossom end using the tip of a vegetable peeler or a small knife. Place the pears in the hot wine, cover with a round of aluminium foil or baking paper, and simmer over low heat for about 20 minutes, or until tender to the point of a sharp knife, turning or basting the pears if the liquid does not cover them completely. (The actual cooking time will depend on their ripeness.) Remove the pears from the wine and set aside to cool.

Three Bring the wine back to the boil, then reduce the heat to low and simmer for 15 minutes, or until reduced in volume by one third. Add the redcurrant jelly and allow it to melt completely, then strain and set aside to cool.

Four Thinly peel the oranges with a vegetable peeler, avoiding the bitter white pith. Cut the peel into very fine strips and place in a small pan with cold water. Bring to the boil, then drain and rinse well in cold water. Drain the peel and set aside.

Five In the same pan, mix the remaining sugar with 250 ml (8 fl oz) water and boil until the sugar dissolves. Add the drained peel, reduce the heat and simmer for 2–3 minutes, or until the syrup thickens and the peel has absorbed the sugar and appears translucent.

Six Arrange the pears in a serving dish and cover with the sauce. Sprinkle with the orange peel, garnish with mint and decorate with raspberries or redcurrants.

CHEF'S TIP *To give the pears a rich dark colour, soak them in the poaching liquid overnight.*

Fruit cobbler

The name 'cobbler' came from America in the nineteenth century and refers to a fruit pie with a scone topping. This cobbler has a golden hazelnut and apricot topping over summer's late fruit.

Preparation time 1 hour
+ 20 minutes refrigeration
Total cooking time 40 minutes
Serves 6

COBBLER TOPPING
310 g (10 oz) plain flour
2 teaspoons baking powder
75 g (2½ oz) unsalted butter,
cut into cubes and chilled
45 g (1½ oz) caster sugar
2 eggs, beaten
3 tablespoons milk
100 g (3¼ oz) hazelnuts,
finely chopped
75 g (2½ oz) dried apricots,
finely chopped

FRUIT COMPOTE
55 g (1¾ oz) caster sugar
25 g (¾ oz) unsalted butter
2 cloves
1 cinnamon stick
½ vanilla pod, split lengthways
2 dessert apples, peeled, cored
and cut into eighths
2 ripe pears, peeled, cored and cut
into 2 cm (¾ inch) pieces
3 fresh apricots, halved and stoned,
or 6 canned apricot halves
2 fresh peaches, halved, stoned
and cut into eighths, or 4 canned
peach halves, sliced
3 fresh plums, halved and stoned,
or 3 canned and stoned
dark plums, halved
finely grated rind of 1 lemon
finely grated rind of ½ orange
pinch of ground mixed spice
pinch of ground cinnamon

1 egg yolk
icing sugar, for dusting

One Brush a round 21 cm (8½ inch) diameter and 4 cm (1½ inch) deep ovenproof dish with melted butter.

Two To make the cobbler topping, sieve the flour and baking powder into a bowl. Rub the butter into the flour using your fingertips until the mixture resembles fine breadcrumbs. Lightly stir in the sugar, make a well in the centre and add the eggs and milk. Bring the mixture roughly together using a palette knife. Add the hazelnuts and apricots and bring everything together to form a dough, shape into a ball and flatten slightly. Wrap in plastic wrap and place in the refrigerator for about 20 minutes.

Three To make the fruit compote, first prepare a caramel using the caster sugar and 3 tablespoons water, following the method in the Chef's techniques on page 540. When the caramel has stopped cooking, return to the heat and remelt the caramel gently, then mix in the butter, cloves, cinnamon stick, vanilla and apple and cook, covered, for 5 minutes. Add the pear, apricot, peach and fresh plum, cover and gently cook for about 5 minutes, stirring occasionally. (If using canned plums, add at the end of the 5 minutes cooking time or they will break up.) Discard the flavourings, stir in the lemon and orange rind and the ground spices, and pour the compote into the prepared dish.

Four Preheat the oven to hot 210°C (415°F/Gas 6–7). On a lightly floured surface, roll out the topping dough to 1.5 cm (⅝ inch) thick, then cut out circles using a 6 cm (2½ inch) plain cutter. Arrange the circles, slightly overlapping, on top of the hot compote.

Five Beat the egg yolk and 1 teaspoon water together to make an egg wash and brush over the top of the cobbler. Do not brush the cut sides or the egg will set and prevent rising. Bake for 15 minutes, or until well risen and golden brown. Cool for 5–10 minutes before serving, then dust with the sifted icing sugar and serve with cream or ice cream.

Sticky toffee puddings

These puddings are also known as sticky date puddings, as dates are the secret ingredient that keeps the puddings moist and delicious. The toffee sauce ensures they remain famously sticky.

Preparation time 40 minutes
+ 1 hour soaking
Total cooking time 40 minutes
Serves 10

200 g (6½ oz) dates, pitted
and chopped
45 g (1½ oz) raisins
grated rind of ½ lemon
1 teaspoon bicarbonate of soda
2 tablespoons coffee essence
or 1 tablespoon instant coffee mixed
with 2 tablespoons boiling water
115 g (3¾ oz) unsalted butter,
at room temperature
180 g (5¾ oz) soft light brown sugar
4 eggs, beaten
240 g (7½ oz) self-raising flour

TOFFEE SAUCE
1 vanilla pod, split lengthways
60 g (2 oz) unsalted butter
150 g (5 oz) demerara sugar
150 ml (5 fl oz) thick (double) cream

One Brush ten 175 ml (5¾ fl oz) pudding moulds or ramekins with melted butter and chill before brushing again, then dust with flour and tap out the excess. Preheat the oven to moderate 180°C (350°F/Gas 4).

Two Place the dates, raisins and lemon rind in a bowl. Sprinkle with the bicarbonate of soda and coffee essence, pour on 300 ml (10 fl oz) boiling water, cover and set aside to soak for one hour.

Three Place the butter and sugar in a bowl and, using a wooden spoon or electric beaters, beat until light and creamy. Add the beaten eggs in six additions, beating well after each addition. Sieve the flour and a pinch of

salt onto the mixture and fold in with a large metal spoon or plastic spatula. Add the date and raisin mixture with its liquid and stir gently to make a loose batter.

Four Spoon the mixture into the moulds to three-quarters full. Make a slight hollow in the centre of the mixture and bake for about 20–30 minutes, or until springy to the touch.

Five To make the toffee sauce, scrape the vanilla seeds into the pan and add the pod, butter, sugar and cream and stir for about 3 minutes to dissolve the sugar, then simmer over low–medium heat,

without stirring, until smooth and golden brown. Remove and discard the vanilla pod, set the sauce aside and keep it warm.

Six When the puddings are cooked, allow to stand for 10 minutes, then turn out. Serve warm with the toffee sauce and whipped cream.

CHEF'S TIP *If 10 puddings are too many, you could either halve the recipe or freeze the extra puddings. When you are ready to use the frozen puddings, defrost, then wrap in foil and reheat in a moderate 180°C (350°F/Gas 4) oven for about 20 minutes.*

Traditional rice pudding

*This classic favourite, so simple to prepare, cooks slowly
and gently in the oven, allowing the rice time to absorb all the liquid.
The result is delightfully soft and creamy.*

*Preparation time 5 minutes
+ 30 minutes standing
Total cooking time 2 hours
Serves 4*

750 ml (24 fl oz) milk
20 g (3/4 oz) caster sugar
2–3 drops vanilla extract or essence
75 g (2 1/2 oz) short-grain rice
unsalted butter, for topping
freshly grated nutmeg, to taste

One Combine the milk, sugar, vanilla
and rice in a 1 litre pie or ovenproof dish
and leave to stand for 30 minutes.
Preheat the oven to moderate 180°C
(350°F/Gas 4).

Two Dot the butter over the mixture,
sprinkle some nutmeg over the top and
cover with foil. Place the dish on the
middle shelf of the oven and bake for
1 hour, stirring once or twice with a fork.

Three Remove the foil and reduce the
oven temperature to slow 150°C
(300°F/Gas 2). If serving the pudding
cold, bake for another 45 minutes, leave
to cool, then refrigerate until ready to
serve. If serving hot, cook for 1 hour, or
until a brown skin forms and the interior
of the pudding is soft and creamy. Serve
hot with a teaspoon of strawberry jam or
cold with berries or poached red plums.

CHEF'S TIPS *If the rice pudding is too
dry, adjust the consistency before serving
by lifting the skin to one side and adding
a little cold milk.*

*To vary the flavour, use cinnamon
in place of the vanilla and nutmeg,
or sprinkle some sultanas or chopped
mixed fruit peel in with the rice
before cooking.*

Baked apple and fruit charlotte

*As legend has it, this famous moulded dessert was named
after the wife of George III, England's famous 'mad' king.
It is traditionally set in a tall, bucket-shaped mould.*

*Preparation time 30 minutes
+ 1 hour cooling
Total cooking time 1 hour 20 minutes
Serves 6*

*14 thin slices of white bread,
trimmed of crusts
175 g (5¾ oz) unsalted butter
500 g (1 lb) Granny Smith apples,
peeled, cored and finely chopped
500 g (1 lb) cooking apples, peeled,
cored and finely chopped
90 g (3 oz) soft brown sugar
pinch of ground cinnamon
½ teaspoon ground nutmeg
50 g (1¾ oz) walnuts, finely chopped
50 g (1¾ oz) sultanas or other
dried fruits
2 tablespoons marmalade (optional)
grated lemon rind (optional)
3 tablespoons apricot jam
(see Chef's tips)*

One Brush a 1.25 litre charlotte mould with softened butter. Cut six slices of bread in half to form rectangles; cut five slices in half at a diagonal to form triangles. Reserve the remaining three slices of bread.

Two Turn the mould upside down and place the bread triangles on top, overlapping the edges to completely cover the top of the mould. Hold the triangles in place and, using the mould as a guide, trim the excess edges with scissors so the triangles will fit inside the base of the mould exactly.

Three Melt 150 g (5 oz) of the butter, dip the trimmed triangles in, then line the base of the mould. Dip the rectangles in butter and arrange around the sides, overlapping the edges until the mould is completely covered, filling any gaps with the bread trimmings. Dip the reserved slices of bread in the butter and set aside.

Four To make the filling, melt the remaining butter in a large pan. Add the apples, cover the pan with baking paper and then a lid. Cook the apples over low heat for 15–20 minutes, or until they are soft and have the consistency of apple sauce. Add the sugar and stir over high heat for about 5 minutes, or until the mixture falls from the side of the spoon in wide drops. Stir in the cinnamon, nutmeg, walnuts and sultanas. Remove from the heat. Add the marmalade, and perhaps a little grated lemon rind. Set aside to cool.

Five Preheat the oven to moderately hot 190°C (375°F/ Gas 5). Ladle the filling into the mould until half full. Cover the filling with half the reserved bread slices, press down firmly, then add the remaining filling. If the filling is not level with the mould lining, trim the bread carefully with the tip of a small knife or scissors. Cover with the remaining reserved bread, taking care to fill any gaps. Press in gently and cover with foil.

Six Place the charlotte on a baking tray and bake for 45 minutes to 1 hour, or until golden and firm. Leave to cool completely before turning out onto a serving plate: this should take about 1 hour.

Seven Warm the apricot jam and 25 ml (¾ fl oz) water in a small pan over low heat until melted. Brush the mixture over the surface of the charlotte to give a light glaze.

CHEF'S TIPS *A heatproof soufflé dish or cake tin can be used instead of a charlotte mould.*

If the jam is very fruity, it will be easier to brush onto the charlotte if it has been strained after warming. An inexpensive jam is fine for this purpose.

For extra zest, replace the sultanas with 1–2 tablespoons chopped glacé ginger and the nutmeg with ground ginger.

For an indulgent accompaniment, whip 150 ml (5 fl oz) whipping cream with 50 g (1¾ oz) sugar, then stir in 2 tablespoons of Calvados.

Eve's pudding

As the name of this English pudding suggests, it should be made with apples, which take on a tempting caramelised sweetness under the light sponge and golden almonds.

Preparation time 25 minutes
Total cooking time 45 minutes
Serves 6

APPLE COMPOTE
55 g (1³/4 oz) unsalted butter, softened
75 g (2¹/2 oz) caster sugar
2 cloves
¹/2 teaspoon ground cinnamon
1 vanilla pod, split lengthways
750 g (1¹/2 lb) Golden Delicious
apples, peeled, cored and
cut into eighths

ALMOND TOPPING
120 g (4 oz) unsalted butter, at
room temperature
120 g (4 oz) caster sugar
finely grated rind of 1 lemon
¹/2 teaspoon vanilla extract or essence
3 eggs, beaten
25 g (³/4 oz) plain flour
120 g (4 oz) ground almonds, sieved
75 g (2¹/2 oz) flaked almonds

2 tablespoons apricot jam
icing sugar, for dusting

One Brush a 1.5 litre ovenproof dish, 2 cm (³/4 inch) deep, with melted butter.

Two To make the apple compote, place the butter and sugar in a large pan and stir over low heat to melt the butter and dissolve the sugar. Add the cloves, cinnamon and vanilla pod to the pan, then add the apple and mix to coat with the butter. Cover and cook very gently for 5 minutes, or until the apple is just starting to soften. Discard the flavourings and spread the mixture evenly over the base of the prepared dish. Set aside to cool. Preheat the oven to moderate 180°C (350°F/Gas 4).

Three To make the almond topping, place the butter, sugar, lemon rind and vanilla in a bowl and, using a wooden spoon or electric beaters, beat until light and creamy. Add the beaten egg in six additions, beating well between each addition. Sieve the flour and a pinch of salt onto the mixture, scatter on the ground almonds and, using a large metal spoon or spatula, fold in gently to combine. Spoon over the apple mixture, smooth the top and sprinkle with the flaked almonds. Bake for about 30–35 minutes, or until the topping is firm to the touch.

Four In a small pan, heat the apricot jam with 2 teaspoons of water. When the mixture has melted and begins to boil, sieve it into a small bowl and, while still hot, brush it all over the surface of the pudding. Leave for 1 minute, then dust with the sifted icing sugar. Serve with cream.

Oeufs à la neige

*In English, this amazing dessert is better known as 'floating islands',
or more literally 'snow eggs'. A rich custard (crème anglaise) is topped
with meltingly soft meringues and drizzled with caramel.*

Preparation time 40 minutes
Total cooking time 40 minutes
Serves 6–8

SYRUP
185 g (6 oz) sugar

CREME ANGLAISE
500 ml (16 fl oz) milk
1 vanilla pod
6 egg yolks
125 g (4 oz) caster sugar

MERINGUES
6 egg whites
125 g (4 oz) caster sugar

CARAMEL
100 g (3¼ oz) sugar
50 ml (1¾ fl oz) water
lemon juice, to taste

One To make the syrup, dissolve the sugar in 2 litres water over low heat. Bring to the boil, then reduce the heat and leave to simmer gently.

Two To make the crème anglaise, prepare a large bowl of ice or iced water and place a smaller bowl inside. Place the milk and vanilla pod in a heavy-based pan, and just bring to the boil. Make the custard following the Chef's techniques on page 541, then strain it into the prepared bowl in the ice. Leave to cool, stirring occasionally.

Three To make the meringues, beat the egg whites in a clean, dry bowl until stiff peaks form. Add the sugar and beat until smooth and glossy. Shape into 'eggs' using two large spoons dipped in water, then poach in the gently simmering syrup for 3 minutes, taking care not to crowd the pan. Turn using a slotted spoon and poach for 3 more minutes. Drain on a tea towel, and leave to cool.

Four Make the caramel, following the method in the Chef's techniques on page 540. Stop the cooking immediately by plunging the saucepan into a large, heatproof bowl of iced water. Remove the saucepan from the water and keep the caramel warm or it will harden.

Five To serve, fill a shallow bowl with crème anglaise and top with poached meringues. Drizzle the caramel over the top and serve the remaining sauce in a sauce boat.

Traditional Christmas pudding

This richest of fruit puddings needs no introduction. We have given two traditional methods—boiling and steaming—and both are easy to make in advance and can be reheated easily on Christmas day.

Preparation time 45 minutes
+ overnight marinating
Total cooking time 10–12 hours
Serves 8

MARINATED FRUITS
250 g (8 oz) sultanas
250 g (8 oz) raisins
315 g (10 oz) currants
60 g (2 oz) glacé cherries
60 g (2 oz) candied mixed peel
60 g (2 oz) dates, stoned and chopped
1 1/2 teaspoons mixed spice
1 teaspoon ground cinnamon
1 teaspoon ground nutmeg
1/4 teaspoon ground ginger
grated rind of 2 oranges and juice
of 1 orange
grated rind of 1 lemon
105 ml (3 1/2 fl oz) stout
125 ml (4 fl oz) brandy

PUDDING
150 g (5 oz) apples, peeled, cored
and grated
150 g (5 oz) plain flour
105 g (3 1/2 oz) ground almonds
200 g (6 1/2 oz) suet, shredded
150 g (5 oz) dark brown sugar
200 g (6 1/2 oz) fresh white
breadcrumbs
2 eggs, beaten
2 tablespoons treacle

3 tablespoons brandy

One To make the marinated fruits, place all the ingredients in a large bowl and mix together well. Cover with plastic wrap and leave overnight in a cool place.

Two The next day, prepare the pudding by placing all the ingredients in a bowl and making a well in the centre. Add the marinated fruits and mix to a soft batter.

Three To boil the pudding, place a 70 cm (28 inch) square of calico or a tea towel in a pan of water and bring to the boil. Drain, then squeeze out wearing rubber gloves. Lay the cloth out flat and dust generously with flour. Using your hand, smooth the flour evenly onto the cloth. Place the pudding mixture in the centre of the cloth. Gather the cloth tightly around the mixture and twist it as tightly as you can to force the mixture into a round ball shape. Tie string around the twisted cloth, as tightly and as close to the pudding as possible.

Four Bring a pan of water to the boil, large enough for the pudding to move around in and with a saucer or trivet at the bottom. Place the pudding in the pan, cover and boil for 10–12 hours.

Five Remove the pudding from the pan and remove the string. Leave for 5 minutes, then loosen the cloth, turn the pudding out onto a plate and gently peel away the cloth.

Six To steam the pudding, prepare a 2.5 litre pudding basin, following the method in the Chef's techniques on page 538. Spoon the mixture into the basin, cover and steam for 10 hours. Leave the pudding to stand in the basin for 15 minutes, then remove the string, foil and paper and turn out.

Seven In a small pan, warm the brandy, then at the table pour it over the pudding and ignite it at arm's length. Serve with cream or brandy butter.

CHEF'S TIP *To prepare ahead of time, steam or boil the pudding for 8 hours, then leave to cool (for the boiled pudding, hang up to dry overnight). Remove the cloth or paper and check the surface is completely dry. Re-cover with dry cloth or new paper and store somewhere cool. To reheat, cook the pudding for 2 hours, then leave for 15 minutes before serving.*

Sherry trifle

This famous British dessert is a Christmas tradition, with its sherry-soaked sponge, red fruit and rich custard. You can use fresh or frozen berries. If you prefer a non-alcoholic version, substitute orange juice for the sherry.

Preparation time 55 minutes
+ 1 hour 20 minutes chilling
Total cooking time 30 minutes
Serves 8

SPONGE
3 eggs
90 g (3 oz) caster sugar
55 g (1³/4 oz) plain flour
150 g (5 oz) raspberry jam

2–3 tablespoons sweet sherry
150 g (5 oz) raspberries
150 g (5 oz) blackberries
500 ml (16 fl oz) cream
25 g (³/4 oz) icing sugar
¹/4 teaspoon vanilla extract or essence
2 tablespoons pistachio nuts, chopped
8 strawberries, halved

CUSTARD
500 ml (16 fl oz) milk
35 g (1¹/4 oz) custard powder
75 g (2¹/2 oz) caster sugar
165 ml (5¹/2 fl oz) cream

One Preheat the oven to hot 220°C (425°F/Gas 7). Brush a 25 x 30 cm (10 x 12 inch) swiss roll tin with melted butter, line the base with baking paper and brush again with melted butter.

Two To make the sponge, bring a pan half full of water to the boil, then remove from the heat. Have ready a heatproof bowl that will fit over the pan without actually touching the water. Place the eggs and sugar in the bowl, then place over the pan of simmering water. Beat for 4 minutes, or until pale, trebled in volume and when lifted on the beaters, the mixture falls back to leave a ribbon-like trail. Remove the bowl from the pan and continue beating for 2 minutes, or until the mixture is cold. Sieve the flour onto the mixture and, using a large metal spoon, fold in until just combined. Pour into the prepared tin, lightly level with a palette knife and bake for 6 minutes, or until pale golden and springy to the touch of a finger. Slide in its paper onto a rack and leave to cool, then turn over onto a clean piece of greaseproof paper and remove the paper on which it was baked. Spread the sponge thinly with jam and, using the paper, roll up from one long side into a swiss roll. Wrap in greaseproof paper and chill for 20 minutes.

Three Discard the paper and, using a serrated or sharp knife, cut into 5 mm (¹/4 inch) slices. Arrange the slices across the base and up the side of a large glass bowl with a wide, flat base. Fill the centre with any remaining slices, then drizzle the sherry over the sponge and add the raspberries and blackberries, levelling the top. Cover the bowl with plastic wrap and chill until required.

Four To make the custard, bring the milk almost to the boil in a deep, heavy-based pan. Place the custard powder and sugar in a bowl, add the cream and quickly whisk to blend and prevent lumps. Whisk in about one third of the hot milk, then pour the mixture back into the pan. Bring to the boil over low-medium heat, whisking vigorously, then remove from the heat. Continue to gently whisk for about 5 minutes while the custard cools to a warm but still flowing mixture, then pour onto the fruit. Cover the surface with plastic wrap and chill for at least 1 hour.

Five Whisk together in a bowl the cream, icing sugar and vanilla until soft peaks form. Decorate the trifle with this cream mixture and decorate with the nuts and strawberries. Refrigerate until ready to serve.

Pavlovas with fragrant fruit

*These dramatic, feather-light mounds of pillowy meringue
are a treat when combined with champagne-steeped
fruit and creamy Greek yoghurt.*

Preparation time 20 minutes
Total cooking time 2 hours 10 minutes
Makes 6

PAVLOVAS
6 egg whites
220 g (7 oz) caster sugar
1 teaspoon white wine vinegar
2 teaspoons boiling water

60 g (2 oz) caster sugar
1/2 vanilla pod, split lengthways
*250 ml (8 fl oz) sparkling wine
or champagne*
*1 kg (2 lb) mixed soft fruit, such as
strawberries, raspberries, stoned
black cherries and blackberries*
280 ml (9 fl oz) thick (double) cream
1 1/2 tablespoons icing sugar
185 ml (6 fl oz) Greek yoghurt
1 1/2 tablespoons Kirsch

One Preheat the oven to very slow 120°C
(250°F/Gas 1/2). Line two large baking
trays with baking paper.

Two To make the pavlovas, place the egg
whites in a clean dry bowl and beat
them with a balloon whisk or electric
beaters until soft peaks form. Gradually
add the sugar, vinegar and boiling water
and whisk continuously until the
meringue is thick and glossy. Using two
large wet metal spoons, divide and shape
the meringue into six ovals and place on
the prepared baking trays. Cook for
about 1 1/2–2 hours, or until the pavlovas
are pale and crisp on the outside with
soft, chewy centres.

Three To prepare the fruit, place the
sugar in a large pan with the vanilla pod
and sparkling wine and heat gently until
simmering. Simmer for 5 minutes, then

remove from the heat. Add the fruit and
set aside to cool, during which time the
soft fruit will poach in the liquid. Remove
the vanilla pod just before serving.

Four Using a balloon whisk, whip the
cream until it just forms soft peaks, then
sift in the icing sugar and fold in with
the yoghurt and Kirsch.

Five To serve the dessert, place the
pavlovas on plates and top with a

generous spoon of the Kirsch-flavoured
cream. Place two tablespoons of the fruit
on top of each pavlova, allowing the
juice to drizzle down the sides, and serve
some of the remaining fruit around the
bases of the desserts or serve in a
separate bowl.

CHEF'S TIP *If you prefer to make a
neater shape for the pavlovas, pipe six
rounds, using a piping bag with a plain
2 cm (3/4 inch) nozzle.*

Chocolate and Cointreau mousse

Mousse in French literally means froth or foam. This melt-in-the-mouth mousse marries the classic flavours of chocolate and orange, is simple to prepare, and makes a magical finale to any meal.

Preparation time *40 minutes*
+ 1 hour refrigeration
Total cooking time *5 minutes*
Serves 4–6

125 g (4 oz) dark chocolate
50 g (1¾ oz) unsalted butter
70 ml (2¼ fl oz) orange juice
2½ tablespoons cocoa powder
2 eggs, separated
25 ml (¾ fl oz) Cointreau
100 ml (3¼ fl oz) cream, for whipping
1 egg white, extra
1½ tablespoons caster sugar
orange segments and whipped cream,
to serve

One Place the chocolate, butter and orange juice in a heatproof bowl over a pan of just-simmering water. When the chocolate and butter have melted, stir in the cocoa powder. Remove from the heat and whisk in the egg yolks and Cointreau. Leave to cool.

Two In a chilled bowl, beat the cream until soft peaks form. Cover and refrigerate until ready to use.

Three Beat all the egg whites in a clean, dry bowl until soft peaks form. Add the sugar; beat until smooth and glossy.

Four Using a large metal spoon, gently fold the egg whites into the cooled chocolate mixture. Before they are completely incorporated, fold in the whipped cream. Transfer the mixture into individual serving dishes or a large serving bowl and refrigerate for at least 1 hour. Serve with orange segments and whipped cream.

Gooseberry fool

England is the home of this old-fashioned but delicious dessert made of cooked, strained and puréed fruit, chilled and folded into custard and whipped cream. Traditionally, fool is made from gooseberries, although any fruit may be used.

Preparation time 40 minutes
+ 2 hours refrigeration
Total cooking time 25 minutes
Serves 4–6

GOOSEBERRY PURÉE
120 g (4 oz) caster sugar
500 g (1 lb) fresh gooseberries,
topped and tailed
1 leaf gelatine
or ½ teaspoon gelatine powder

1½ tablespoons cornflour
3 tablespoons caster sugar
125 ml (4 fl oz) milk
125 ml (4 fl oz) Greek or plain
thick yoghurt
75 ml (2½ fl oz) cream, for whipping
1 egg white
100 ml (3¼ fl oz) whipped cream,
to serve
4–6 macaroon biscuits, to serve

One To make the purée, reserve 1 tablespoon of sugar and place the rest in a heavy-based pan with 250 ml (8 fl oz) water. Stir over low heat until the sugar dissolves. Bring to the boil, add the fruit, reduce the heat and simmer for 10 minutes, or until tender. Strain the liquid. Purée the fruit in a food processor, then stir in the reserved sugar.

Two Soak the gelatine leaf or powder, following the Chef's techniques on page 541.

Three In a separate heatproof bowl, combine the cornflour and 1 tablespoon of the sugar. Add 50 ml (1¾ fl oz) of the milk and stir until smooth. Bring the remaining milk almost to the boil, then whisk it into the cornflour and sugar. Place in a clean pan and whisk over low heat until the mixture boils and thickens. Remove from the heat.

Four Stir the soaked gelatine into the hot custard until dissolved, then cover with baking paper and leave to cool. Stir in the fruit purée and yoghurt, mixing well.

Five Whip the cream until soft peaks form, then fold into the custard. Whisk the egg white in a clean, dry bowl until stiff, then whisk in the remaining sugar and fold into the custard. Pipe or spoon the fool into tall glasses, ensuring there are no air pockets. Chill for 2 hours to set. Serve with freshly whipped cream and macaroons.

CHEF'S TIP *If the gooseberries are tart, sweeten them with a little sugar. Frozen gooseberries can be used in this recipe if fresh ones are not available.*

Iced raspberry soufflé

This chilled raspberry soufflé always looks wonderful and is a great conversation piece. It can also be made days—if not weeks—ahead, leaving more time for you to spend with your guests.

Preparation time 45 minutes + 6 hours freezing + 30 minutes standing
Total cooking time 10 minutes
Serves 4–6

550 g (1 lb 2 oz) raspberries
250 g (8 oz) caster sugar
5 egg whites
400 ml (12³/4 fl oz) cream,
for whipping
200 ml (6¹/2 fl oz) cream,
for whipping, extra
fresh raspberries,
to garnish
sprigs of fresh mint,
to garnish

One Purée the raspberries in a food processor, then press through a fine sieve to eliminate the seeds. Weigh out 300 g (10 oz) of raspberry purée and set aside.

Two Cut out a piece of greaseproof or baking paper to measure 25 x 9 cm (10 x 3¹/2 inches). Wrap the paper around the outside of a 1 litre, 18 cm (7 inch) soufflé dish to make a collar. Secure the overlapping paper in place with tape or kitchen string, keeping the paper free of creases.

Three Place the caster sugar and 60 ml (2 fl oz) water in a medium heavy-based pan and heat gently to dissolve the sugar. Bring the syrup to the boil, then follow the Chef's techniques for making Italian meringue on page 539.

Four In a separate bowl, whip the first quantity of cream to soft peaks.

Five Using a metal spoon, gently fold the meringue into the reserved raspberry purée until thoroughly mixed, then fold in the cream until the streaks disappear. Be careful not to overmix, as this will cause the cream to thicken and separate and make the soufflé look grainy.

Six Spoon the mixture into the soufflé dish right up to the edge of the paper collar, then gently smooth the surface of the soufflé. Freeze the soufflé for a minimum of 6 hours.

Seven Just before serving, peel off the paper collar and allow the soufflé to stand for 30 minutes to soften. Whip the extra cream and use it to decorate the soufflé. Serve the soufflé topped with the fresh raspberries and sprigs of mint.

Cherry brandy snap baskets

*You can make the brandy snap baskets and the ice cream
for this pretty and unusual dessert in advance, then
just fill the baskets when you're ready to serve.*

Preparation time 20 minutes
+ 30 minutes chilling
Total cooking time 15 minutes
Makes 6

BRANDY SNAP BASKETS
60 g (2 oz) unsalted butter
60 g (2 oz) light brown sugar
2 tablespoons golden syrup
60 g (2 oz) plain flour
*few drops of vanilla extract
or essence*

*500 ml (16 fl oz) vanilla ice cream,
preferably home-made*
*425 g (13½ oz) morello cherries,
stoned, drained and
finely chopped*
2 tablespoons port
sprigs of fresh mint, to decorate

One To make the brandy snap baskets, place the butter, sugar and golden syrup in a small pan and heat gently until the sugar has dissolved. Cool for 1 minute, then stir in the flour and vanilla extract. Transfer to a small bowl and chill for 30 minutes. Preheat the oven to moderate 180°C (350°F/Gas 4).

Two Remove the ice cream from the freezer and leave it to slightly soften for 10 minutes, without allowing to melt. Mix the cherries and port into the softened ice cream. Cover and return to the freezer to firm up.

Three Line two baking trays with baking paper. Divide the brandy snap dough into six even-sized pieces and roll into round balls. Place three on each tray, leaving plenty of space between them, and flatten into a circle with moistened fingertips. Bake for 5–6 minutes.

Four Have ready six teacups upside down on the work surface. Allow the biscuits to rest for 1 minute after baking, then use a palette knife to drape one over each cup, pressing it into a basket shape. Leave until cold and then set into shape.

Five Set a brandy snap basket in the centre of each plate and fill with two scoops of the prepared cherry ice cream.

Six Serve the cherry brandy snap baskets immediately, decorated with a sprig of fresh mint.

Coffee granita with panna cotta

*A coffee-flavoured granita teamed with a silky
Italian custard makes a refreshing start to the day.*

*Preparation time 1 hour
+ overnight chilling
Total cooking time 20 minutes
Serves 4*

*235 g (7¼ oz) caster sugar
15 g (½ oz) instant dark roast
coffee powder
30 ml (1 fl oz) coffee liqueur,
optional
4 leaves gelatine or 2 teaspoons
powdered gelatine
2 vanilla pods, split lengthways
250 ml (8 fl oz) milk
250 ml (8 fl oz) thick (double) cream*

One Simmer 175 ml (5¾ fl oz) water and 175 g (5¾ oz) of the sugar in a pan for 10 minutes. Mix the coffee with a little water to form a paste and stir in. Leave to cool.

Two Add 500 ml (16 fl oz) water and the liqueur. Pour the granita into a shallow plastic or metal container and freeze the granita overnight.

Three Soak the gelatine leaves, following the instructions in the Chef's techniques on page 541, or dissolve the powder in 2 tablespoons hot water. Scrape the vanilla seeds into a pan and add the pods, milk, cream and remaining sugar. Bring to the boil, strain into a bowl and discard the pods.

Four Add the gelatine to the hot milk mixture (if you are using leaves, squeeze out any excess water first), then stir to melt. Place the bowl inside a bowl of ice water and stir until the gelatine begins to set (as the spoon is drawn through it, you will see a line across the base of the bowl). Pour into four 100 ml (3¼ fl oz) moulds or ramekins. Leave to chill overnight.

Five Half an hour before serving, refrigerate four plates. Release the panna cotta from the moulds by wrapping each in a hot cloth and turning it over. Scoop out the granita in flakes by drawing the side of a metal spoon across its surface. Serve on the chilled plates with the panna cotta.

Chocolate profiteroles

*The name profiterole is derived from the French word 'profit',
and originally meant a small gift, which is just what these
chocolate-smothered pastry balls are.*

Preparation time 30 minutes
Total cooking time 30 minutes
Serves 6

*2 quantities choux pastry (see
page 545)
1 egg, lightly beaten and strained,
to glaze*

FILLING
*350 ml (11 fl oz) cream, for whipping
1¹/₂ tablespoons caster sugar
1–2 drops vanilla extract
or essence*

*icing sugar, to dust
chocolate sauce, to serve (see
page 369)*

One To make the profiteroles, preheat the oven to moderately hot 200°C (400°F/Gas 6). Brush a baking tray with melted butter and refrigerate until needed. Spoon the choux pastry into a piping bag fitted with a 9 mm (³/₈ inch) plain nozzle.

Two With the nozzle about 1 cm (¹/₂ inch) above the tray, pipe well-spaced 2.5 cm (1 inch) diameter balls, then stop the pressure on the bag and quickly pull away. Brush the top of each ball with the strained egg, making sure that it does not run down the sides or it will burn during cooking. Lightly press down the top of each ball with your finger to even the top. Bake for 15–20 minutes, or until well risen and golden brown. The profiteroles should sound hollow when the bases are tapped. Make a small hole in the base of each profiterole with the point of a small knife. Transfer the profiteroles to a wire rack to cool thoroughly.

Three To make the filling, whisk the cream, sugar and vanilla together until stiff peaks form. Spoon into a piping bag fitted with a small round nozzle and pipe into the base of each profiterole.

Four To serve, stack the profiteroles in a pyramid in a glass bowl or on individual plates. Dust with sugar and serve with the warm chocolate sauce.

Vanilla ice cream

No commercial ice cream can ever compare with the creamy, decadent richness of the home-made variety. This classic favourite is peppered with fine black specks: the tiny seeds of the vanilla pod, which release a fabulous flavour. For a light, smooth result every time, with minimal fuss, an ice-cream churn is highly recommended.

Preparation time 20 minutes
+ churning or beating + freezing
Total cooking time 10 minutes
Serves 4

5 egg yolks
100 g (3 1/4 oz) caster sugar
375 ml (12 fl oz) milk
1 vanilla pod, split lengthways
125 ml (4 fl oz) thick (double) cream

One Whisk the egg yolks and sugar in a heatproof bowl until thick, creamy and almost white. Bring the milk and vanilla pod slowly to the boil in a heavy-based pan. Gradually whisk the boiling milk into the eggs and sugar, then transfer the mixture to a clean pan. Stir constantly with a wooden spoon over low heat for about 3–5 minutes, or until the custard thickly coats the back of the spoon. Ensure that the mixture does not boil, as this will cause it to separate.

Two Pour through a fine strainer into a clean bowl. Place the bowl in some iced water to cool. When the custard is very cold, stir in the cream, then pour the mixture into an ice-cream churn and churn for 10–20 minutes, or until the paddle leaves a trail in the ice cream, or the ice cream holds its own shape. Remove from the churn and freeze in an airtight, stainless steel container for 3–4 hours or overnight.

Three Alternatively, freeze the custard and cream mixture in a 1 litre container for 3 hours, or until firm. Scoop into a large bowl and beat with electric beaters for 1–2 minutes, or until thick and creamy. Return the mixture to the container and freeze for 3 hours. Repeat the beating and freezing twice, then freeze overnight.

CHEF'S TIP *This ice cream can take on a range of flavours. A little coffee extract may be added to the custard at the end of step 1, or 50–100 g (1 3/4–3 1/4 oz) chopped chocolate may be added to the milk before boiling. Another delicious option is to fold amaretto or crushed biscuits into the frozen ice cream before it is stored.*

Zabaglione with sponge fingers

This deliciously light Zabaglione must be eaten immediately after it is made. It takes only a few minutes to whisk and serve and is perfect for unexpected guests.

Preparation time 15 minutes
Total cooking time 20 minutes
Serves 4–5

SPONGE FINGERS
2 eggs, separated
50 g (1³/4 oz) caster sugar
50 g (1³/4 oz) plain flour
icing sugar, to dust

ZABAGLIONE
4 egg yolks
100 g (3¹/4 oz) caster sugar
75 ml (2¹/2 fl oz) Marsala

One Preheat the oven to moderately hot 200°C (400°F/ Gas 6). Line a baking tray with greaseproof paper. Fit a piping bag with a 1 cm (¹/2 inch) plain nozzle.

Two To make the sponge fingers, whisk the egg yolks and sugar in a bowl until creamy and almost white. In a separate bowl, whisk the egg whites until stiff peaks form as the whisk is lifted away. With a large metal spoon or plastic spatula, fold a third of the egg white into the yolk mixture. Sift half the flour into the yolk mixture and carefully fold in, then add another portion of egg white. Repeat with the remaining flour and egg white, taking care not to overmix. Spoon the mixture into the piping bag and pipe 8 cm (3 inch) lengths slightly apart on the baking tray. Dust liberally with the sifted icing sugar, then leave at room temperature for 5 minutes to dissolve the sugar and create a pearl effect. Bake for 10 minutes, or until golden brown. Remove the sponge fingers from the tray by lifting the greaseproof paper with the biscuits, then placing them upside-down on the work surface. Sprinkle the back of the paper with water to make it easy to peel away. Turn the biscuits over and cool on a wire rack.

Three To make the zabaglione, bring a pan half-full of water to the boil, then turn the heat as low as possible. Whisk the egg yolks and sugar in a heatproof bowl until almost white. Mix in the Marsala. Place the bowl over the barely steaming water and whisk until the mixture increases to four times its volume and is firm and frothy. Pour into four large wine glasses and serve immediately with the sponge fingers.

CHEF'S TIP *Zabaglione is an excellent standby dessert for unexpected guests. If you do not have any of the traditional Italian Marsala, you can use some Madeira instead.*

Lemon delicious

*Also known as 'Lemon surprise' or just 'Lemon pudding',
this wonderful pudding separates as it cooks into a light soufflé
sponge topping with a tart lemon sauce hidden beneath.*

Preparation time *25 minutes*
Total cooking time *40 minutes*
Serves 4

*60 g (2 oz) unsalted butter,
at room temperature*
95 g (3¼ oz) caster sugar
finely grated rind of 1 lemon
2 large eggs, separated
2 tablespoons plain flour
3 tablespoons lemon juice
250 ml (8 fl oz) milk
icing sugar, for dusting

One Preheat the oven to moderate 180°C (350°F/Gas 4). Brush a 20 x 15 x 5 cm (8 x 6 x 2 inch) ovenproof dish with melted butter.

Two Using a wooden spoon or electric beaters, beat the butter to soften it, then beat in the sugar in small additions. Continue beating until the mixture is light and creamy, then mix in the lemon rind and egg yolks until well blended. Gently fold in the flour, followed by the lemon juice.

Three In a small pan, warm the milk until tepid. Fold into the lemon mixture.

Four Place the egg whites in a large clean dry bowl, add a pinch of salt and beat them with a balloon whisk or electric beaters until soft peaks form. Using a plastic spatula or a large metal spoon, mix 1 tablespoon of the egg white into the lemon mixture to loosen it, then gently fold in the remaining egg white, being careful not to stir the air out of the mixture and so lose volume.

Five Pour the mixture into the prepared dish, then put the dish in a roasting tin and pour enough boiling water into the tin to come halfway up the side of the dish. Bake for 30–35 minutes, or until the top is a pale golden brown and firm to the light touch of a finger. Serve the pudding hot or chilled. If you are serving it cold, dust with a little sifted icing sugar before serving.

CHEF'S TIP *When the lemon juice meets the butter, the mixture may curdle. However, when you add the milk, the mixture should become smooth again (make sure the milk is barely warm—if it is too hot, the flour and yolks will cook at this stage and the pudding may become too heavy).*

Summer puddings

Perfect for entertaining, these pretty puddings need to be prepared the day before to allow the fruit juices to flavour and stain the bread its distinctive vivid pink colour. Use day-old bread that holds together.

Preparation time *30 minutes + overnight refrigeration*
Total cooking time *5 minutes*
Serves 6

18 thin slices stale white bread
1 kg (2 lb) mixed soft fruits, such as blackberries, raspberries, strawberries and blackcurrants, fresh or frozen and hulled
90 g (3 oz) caster sugar, depending on the sweetness of the fruit

One Cut the crusts from the bread and discard. Reserving two or three slices for the top, cut circles and strips out of the remaining slices to line the base and sides of six 155 ml (5 fl oz) ramekins or pudding moulds, or a 1 litre pudding basin. Make sure the ramekins or basin are completely lined and that there are no spaces between the slices of bread.

Two Halve or quarter the strawberries if large, then place all the fruit in a large pan with 2 tablespoons water and the sugar, to taste. Cover and cook over low heat for about 5 minutes, or until the juices are running from the fruit and they are just tender but still whole.

Three Ladle the fruit and juices into the bread-lined ramekins or basin until it reaches almost to the top of the bread, reserving any excess. Cover with the reserved slices of bread, trimming to fit snugly onto the surface of the fruit. Place on a tray to catch any excess juices and cover with a plate and a weight of about 1 kg (2 lb) if using the pudding basin, or smaller weights if using the ramekins (you can use cans). Leave overnight on the tray in the refrigerator for the juices to stain and flavour the bread.

Four When ready to serve, remove the weights and carefully turn out the puddings. Serve cold with the extra fruit and juice spooned over and a sorbet, ice cream or cream.

CHEF'S TIP *For the best colour and texture, use fewer strawberries than the other softer and darker fruit.*

Chocolate roulade

Whipped cream and fresh raspberries fill this delicate chocolate sponge. It is also delicious with other fresh fruits, such as strawberries or peaches.

*Preparation time 25 minutes
+ 20 minutes refrigeration
Total cooking time 8–10 minutes
Serves 6*

CHOCOLATE SPONGE
*2 eggs
3 tablespoons caster sugar
4 tablespoons plain flour
2 teaspoons cocoa powder*

FILLING
*150 ml (5 fl oz) cream, for whipping
2 1/2 tablespoons icing sugar
200 g (6 1/2 oz) fresh raspberries*

cocoa powder and icing sugar, to dust

One To make the sponge, preheat the oven to moderately hot 200°C (400°F/ Gas 6). Line a 23 x 30 cm (9 x 12 inch) swiss roll tin with baking paper. Put the eggs and sugar in a large bowl. Half fill a saucepan with water and bring to the boil. Remove from the heat and place the bowl over the saucepan, making sure it is not touching the water. The water should be steaming. Using electric beaters, whisk for 5–7 minutes, or until the mixture becomes thick and creamy, has doubled in volume and leaves a trail as it falls from the beaters. The temperature of the mixture should never be hot, only warm. Remove the bowl from the water and continue to whisk until the mixture is cold.

Two Sift the flour and cocoa powder together and, using a large metal spoon, carefully fold into the whisked mixture. Stop folding as soon as the flour and cocoa powder are just combined or the mixture will lose its volume. Pour the mixture into the tin and spread it evenly

using a palette knife. Bake for 6–8 minutes, or until springy to the light touch of a finger. Remove the sponge from the tin while still hot by sliding it, with the paper on, to a wire rack to cool. Leave to cool, then turn over onto a large piece of greaseproof paper or clean cloth and remove the paper that was used for baking.

Three To make the filling, whip the cream with the icing sugar until firm

peaks form. Spread the cream onto the chocolate sponge and sprinkle with the raspberries. Roll up by picking up the paper or cloth at one of the longer ends and pushing it down and away from you while rolling, finishing with the seam underneath. Trim each end and refrigerate for 20 minutes.

Four Sprinkle a little sifted cocoa powder and icing sugar onto the roulade.

Fruit terrine

This luscious dessert yields a truly fruit-filled flavour with every tingling mouthful. The secret is to use two loaf tins instead of one, sitting one on top of the other to prevent the fruit floating to the top before the jelly has set.

Preparation time 40 minutes
+ 1–2 nights refrigeration
Total cooking time 5–10 minutes
Serves 8

100 g (3¼ oz) blackcurrants
120 g (4 oz) redcurrants
110 g (3¾ oz) blueberries
350 g (11¼ oz) strawberries
225 g (7¼ oz) raspberries
4 leaves gelatine
or 2 teaspoons gelatine powder
250 ml (8 fl oz) rosé wine
2 tablespoons caster sugar
1 tablespoon lemon juice
75 ml (2½ fl oz) sieved
raspberry purée
(see Chef's tips)

One Sort through all the fruit and remove any stalks, then gently mix the fruit together, taking care not to bruise or damage any. Soak the gelatine leaves , following the Chef's techniques on page 541, or dissolve the gelatine powder in 2 tablespoons of water.

Two Carefully arrange the fruit into a 1 kg (2 lb) loaf tin, placing the smaller fruits on the bottom.

Three In a small pan, heat half the wine until it begins to simmer. Remove the pan from the heat and add the sugar, gelatine and lemon juice. Stir to dissolve. Add the remaining wine and the raspberry purée. Reserve 150 ml (5 fl oz) of the liquid and pour the rest over the fruit. Cover with plastic wrap. Place a lightly weighted 1 kg (2 lb) loaf tin on top, then refrigerate for at least 1 hour, or overnight if possible, until the terrine has set. Remove the top loaf tin and plastic wrap.

Four Gently warm the reserved wine-liquid and pour over the surface of the terrine. Cover again with plastic wrap and refrigerate overnight to set.

Five Just before serving, turn out the terrine by dipping the base of the tin very briefly in hot water and inverting it onto a plate. Slice the terrine, decorate with some extra fresh berries, and serve with crème fraîche.

CHEF'S TIPS *Sieving 150 g (5 oz) of raspberries will produce the required quantity of raspberry purée.*

Do not rinse the raspberries, and only rinse the other fruit if it is sandy.

Small strawberries give the best results in this fruit terrine, but if they are not available, you could use larger strawberries, cut in half.

Bavarian vanilla cream

*A bavarois is an egg-based custard folded through with
whipped cream and flavoured with chocolate, coffee, praline
or even fruit. This bavarois is simply laced with real vanilla.*

Preparation time 1 hour
+ 1 hour refrigeration
Total cooking time 10 minutes
Serves 4

3 leaves gelatine or 1½ teaspoons
gelatine powder
2 eggs, separated
3 tablespoons caster sugar
250 ml (8 fl oz) milk
1 vanilla pod, split lengthways
125 ml (4 fl oz) thick (double) cream,
lightly whipped

One Lightly grease four 250 ml (8 fl oz)
moulds (you can use any shape moulds
for these desserts), and prepare the
gelatine leaves, following the Chef's
techniques on page 541, or dissolve the
powder in 2 tablespoons water.

Two Beat the egg yolks and sugar in a
bowl until thick, creamy and almost
white. Slowly bring the milk and vanilla
pod to the boil.

Three Follow the method for making
custard in the Chef's techniques on page
541. Stir the soaked gelatine into the hot
custard, ensuring the gelatine dissolves
completely. Strain into a clean bowl,
then leave over a bowl of ice until
almost at the point of setting, stirring
occasionally, and checking often.

Four Whisk the egg whites until stiff—
they should stand in shiny peaks when
the whisk is lifted. Using a metal spoon,
fold the lightly whipped cream into the
cold custard, then carefully fold in the
egg whites.

Five Spoon the mixture into the moulds
and refrigerate for at least 1 hour, or
until set. Unmould by gently shaking at
an angle of 45°, or dipping the base of
the mould briefly in boiling water and
tapping onto a serving dish.

CHEF'S TIPS *The egg whites should not
be whisked in advance or the volume
will drop and the texture be dry and
granular. Add a pinch of sugar while the
egg whites are lightly foaming to
stabilise and help them stiffen.*

*Ensure the custard is cold before
adding the cream: if the cream melts, the
dessert will lose volume.*

LE CORDON BLEU COMPLETE COOK

Lemon meringue pie

This time-honoured favourite—a shortcrust pastry case smothered by a creamy lemon filling and a layer of meringue—should be baked and served on the same day.

Preparation time 45 minutes
+ 40 minutes refrigeration
Total cooking time 45 minutes
Serves 6

1 quantity shortcrust pastry (see page 544)

LEMON FILLING
3 egg yolks
150 g (5 oz) caster sugar
2 teaspoons finely grated lemon rind
juice of 3 lemons
30 g (1 oz) unsalted butter

200 g (6½ oz) caster sugar
4 egg whites
1 tablespoon icing sugar, for dusting

One Preheat the oven to moderate 180°C (350°F/Gas 4). Gently roll the pastry between two sheets of baking paper to about 2.5 mm (⅛ inch) thick, then ease into a lightly greased 22 cm (9 inch) loose-bottomed fluted flan tin. Blind bake for 10 minutes, following the method in the Chef's techniques on page 547. Remove the baking beads or rice and the paper. Bake for 10 more minutes, or until the centre begins to colour. Remove from the oven and cool on a wire rack.

Two To prepare the filling, heat a pan of water until gently simmering. Whisk or beat the egg yolks and sugar in a large heatproof bowl until light and creamy. Add the lemon rind, juice and then the butter. Sit the bowl over the pan of barely simmering water and whisk continuously for 15–20 minutes, or until thickened. When ready, the mixture will leave a 'ribbon' when drizzled from the whisk. While the filling is still hot, pour into the cool, prebaked flan case.

Three Place the sugar and 50 ml (1¾ fl oz) water in a heavy-based pan and heat gently to dissolve the sugar. Bring to the boil to make Italian meringue, following the Chef's technique on page 539.

Four Place the meringue in a piping bag fitted with a 1 cm (½ inch) star nozzle. Starting in the centre, pipe the meringue in continuous concentric circles covering the entire flan, keeping the meringue inside the pastry edge. Dust the surface with icing sugar. Bake for 5 minutes, or until the meringue is lightly coloured. Leave to cool and then refrigerate for 20 minutes, or until the filling is set.

CHEF'S TIP *If possible, refrigerate the pastry dough overnight. This helps prevent the pastry shrinking during the cooking process.*

about lemons...

Lemons vary in acidity and sweetness according to their variety. Taste the lemon juice and adjust the sugar accordingly if you need to. Lemons give up their juice much more easily when they are warm and you can heat them for a couple of seconds in the microwave to warm them a little.

Chocolate and chestnut terrine

*This rich, chilled terrine freezes well for up to 3 months.
With its yuletide chestnut flavouring, it makes a great
centrepiece for a Christmas party. It is rich, so serve thinly sliced.*

Preparation time 20 minutes
+ 12 hours refrigeration
Total cooking time 10 minutes
Serves 10–12

185 g (6 oz) good-quality dark
chocolate, chopped
90 g (3 oz) unsalted butter,
at room temperature
90 g (3 oz) caster sugar
400 g (12³/4 oz) can unsweetened
chestnut purée
1/4 teaspoon vanilla extract
or essence
1/4 teaspoon coffee granules, dissolved
in 1 teaspoon hot water
30 ml (1 fl oz) rum
good-quality dark chocolate,
for shaving
fresh berries or orange segments,
to garnish

One Grease a 7.5 x 17 x 7.5 cm (3 x 7 x 3 inch) loaf tin. Line the base with baking paper, then oil the paper.

Two Place the chocolate in a heatproof bowl over a pan half-full of boiling water. Remove the pan from the heat, stir the chocolate until melted, then remove the bowl from the pan and leave to cool for 5 minutes.

Three In a separate bowl, beat the butter to soften, then add the sugar and beat until pale and light. Whisk in the chestnut purée until softened, then whisk in the melted chocolate until thoroughly blended. Mix in the vanilla, coffee and rum.

Four Transfer the mixture to the loaf tin, smooth the top, cover with plastic wrap or foil and refrigerate for 12 hours.

Five To serve, loosen the sides of the loaf tin with a small palette or round-bladed knife; turn out the terrine and remove the paper. Using a vegetable peeler, shave off curls from the edge of the dark chocolate bar and use these to garnish the terrine. Slice and serve with fresh berries or orange segments.

LE CORDON BLEU ❖ COMPLETE COOK

Touraine crémets with raspberry coulis

A speciality of the French towns of Angers and Saumur, these simple yet delicious crémets can be served with a raspberry coulis or fresh berries. Traditionally they are made without the icing sugar and served with fresh cream and plenty of white sugar.

Preparation time 20 minutes
+ 1 hour setting time
Serves 4

200 ml (6½ fl oz) cream, for whipping
300 g (10 oz) fromage frais or cream cheese (see Chef's tip)
50 g (1¾ oz) icing sugar
fresh mint sprigs, to garnish
red berries, to garnish

RASPBERRY COULIS
400 g (12¾ oz) fresh raspberries
80 g (2¾ oz) icing sugar
few drops of lemon juice

One Line four 9 cm (3½ inch) wide ramekins with pieces of muslin large enough to hang over the top of the moulds. Pour the cream into a bowl, place the bowl into a bowl filled with ice cubes and a little water and lightly whip the cream until it leaves a trail, but just runs if the bowl is tipped. Add the fromage frais or cream cheese and whip until creamy. Stir in the icing sugar and pour the mixture into the ramekin dishes. Fold the excess muslin over to cover the mixture and place in the refrigerator for at least 1 hour.

Two To make the raspberry coulis, blend the raspberries in a food processor, add the sugar and lemon juice to taste and then pass the purée through a fine sieve. For a deep red coulis, do not blend the purée for too long—this incorporates air and will cause it to turn pink.

Three Turn the muslin back over the top edge of the moulds, then turn the moulds over carefully onto individual plates and remove the moulds then the muslin. Pour some of the raspberry coulis around each crémet and decorate with the mint and red berries.

CHEF'S TIP *For a very light and refreshing dessert, use fromage frais, and for a richer dessert, use cream cheese.*

Orange flower crème caramel

*A refreshing and elegant dessert that can
be prepared a day before if you wish, making
it an ideal sweet finish to a dinner party.*

*Preparation time 25 minutes
+ 4 hours chilling
Total cooking time 55 minutes
Makes 6*

220 g (7 oz) caster sugar
500 ml (16 fl oz) milk
1/2 vanilla pod, split lengthways
grated rind of 1 orange
3 eggs, beaten
2 egg yolks
1 teaspoon orange flower water

One Preheat the oven to slow 150°C
(300°F/Gas 2).

Two Prepare a caramel using 90 g (3 oz)
of the sugar and a tablespoon of water,
following the method in the Chef's
techniques on page 540. After the
caramel has stopped cooking, reheat
over a low heat if set, then pour into six
125 ml (4 fl oz) ramekins. Tip a little to
coat the sides and bottom of the
ramekins, holding them in a cloth to
protect your hands.

Three Bring the milk, vanilla pod and
orange rind to the boil slowly in a small
pan. In a bowl, whisk together the eggs,
egg yolks, remaining sugar and the
orange flower water until creamy, then
whisk in the boiling milk and pour

through a sieve into a jug, discarding the
vanilla pod and rind.

Four Pour the mixture onto the caramel
in the ramekins and place them in
a roasting tin. Pour enough boiling
water into the tin to come halfway up
the sides of the ramekins and bake for
about 30–35 minutes, or until just set.
Remove the ramekins from the roasting
tin and chill for at least 4 hours or
overnight.

Five To serve, carefully run the blade
of a palette knife around the edge of
each crème caramel, then hold the centre
of a dessert plate over the ramekin and
invert onto the plate, carefully lifting off
the ramekin and letting the liquid
caramel run over the dessert.

Petits pots au chocolat

These dainty little chocolate custards are prepared and cooked in a very similar way to crème caramel, except that they are much richer, with a fine, smooth texture that melts in the mouth.

Preparation time 10 minutes
+ refrigeration
Total cooking time 45 minutes
Serves 6

375 ml (12 fl oz) milk
150 ml (5 fl oz) cream
50 g (1¾ oz) good-quality dark
chocolate, chopped
½ vanilla pod, split lengthways
1 egg
3 egg yolks
100 g (3¼ oz) caster sugar
whipped cream and grated chocolate,
to serve

One Preheat the oven to warm 170°C (325°F/Gas 3). Place the milk, cream, chocolate and vanilla pod in a heavy-based pan and bring to the boil. Using a wooden spoon, cream the egg, egg yolks and sugar together until thick and light. Pour in the melted chocolate mixture and stir to blend. Strain into a jug and discard the vanilla pod. Remove any froth by skimming across the top with a metal spoon.

Two Pour the mixture into six 100 ml (3¼ fl oz) ramekins, filling them up to the top. Place the ramekins in a roasting tin and pour enough boiling water into the tin to come to 1 cm (½ inch) below their rims. Bake for 30 minutes, or until the surface of the custard feels elastic when touched and your finger comes away clean. If this is not the case, cook for a little while longer. Remove the ramekins from the water bath and allow to cool. When cold, place the whipped cream in a piping bag fitted with a star-shaped nozzle. Pipe rosettes of cream on the tops of the ramekins. Sprinkle with grated chocolate.

Tiramisù

Layers of sponge biscuits soaked in coffee and Kahlua,
rich mascarpone cream and a generous dusting of cocoa powder
have contributed to the enormous success of this dessert today.

Preparation time 35 minutes + chilling
Total cooking time Nil
Serves 4–6

3 egg yolks
120 g (4 oz) caster sugar
180 g (5¾ oz) mascarpone
300 ml (10 fl oz) cream,
for whipping
3 tablespoons Kahlua
500 ml (16 fl oz) strong coffee,
cooled
36 sponge finger biscuits
cocoa powder, for dusting

One Beat the egg yolks with the sugar until the sugar has dissolved and the mixture is light. Add the mascarpone and mix well. Beat the cream into stiff peaks and gently fold into the mascarpone mixture, then spread a thin layer of the mascarpone cream over the base of a deep 35 cm (14 inch) oval dish.

Two Add the Kahlua to the coffee. Dip the sponge fingers into the coffee, soaking them well. Depending on the freshness of the biscuits, they may require more or less soaking, but be careful not to oversoak. Arrange a layer of sponge fingers close together in the dish—you may need to break them to fit the shape of your dish. Cover with another layer of the mascarpone cream, then another layer of sponge fingers, arranging them in the opposite direction to the first layer. Repeat the layers, finishing with mascarpone cream. Smooth the top and keep chilled until ready to serve. Generously dust with cocoa powder just before serving.

CHEF'S TIP *Tiramisù is best made several hours in advance so that the flavours have time to blend.*

LE CORDON BLEU ✠ COMPLETE COOK

Individual lemon cheesecakes

Refreshingly lemony with a gingernut base,
the ever-popular cheesecake is here served in
individual portions with a red grape jelly top.

Preparation time 20 minutes + 1 hour
chilling + overnight chilling
Total cooking time 5 minutes
Makes 6

155 g (5 oz) gingernut biscuits
60 g (2 oz) unsalted butter, melted
300 g (10 oz) full-fat cream cheese
grated rind and juice of 3 lemons
375 g (12 oz) condensed milk
155 g (5 oz) Greek or plain thick
yoghurt
2 level teaspoons gelatine powder
185 ml (6 fl oz) red grape juice

One Put the biscuits in a plastic bag and crush with a rolling pin, then mix with the melted butter. Alternatively, place in a food processor and use the pulse button to produce fine crumbs. Drizzle over the melted butter and pulse again until thoroughly mixed into the crumbs.

Two Set six 8 x 7 cm (3 x 2³⁄₄ inch) baking rings (see Chef's tips) on a small tray lined with baking paper and divide the crumbs between them. Press into the base of the rings with the bottom of a glass. Chill while you make the filling.

Three Use electric beaters or a food processor to combine the cream cheese, lemon rind and juice and condensed milk until completely smooth. Add the yoghurt and blend for a few seconds just to combine. Divide the cheese mixture among the rings, leaving a small gap at the top for the jelly, then place in the refrigerator overnight to set.

Four In a small pan, sprinkle the gelatine over half the grape juice and leave to stand until spongy. Place over a low heat and whisk until the gelatine has completely dissolved. Remove from the heat, stir in the remaining grape juice and cool to room temperature. Carefully spoon a layer of grape jelly over each cheesecake, then chill in the refrigerator for 1 hour.

Five To serve, hold a hot cloth momentarily around the cheesecakes to help slide off the rings, then transfer to serving plates using a palette knife.

CHEF'S TIPS *Small tin cans with the top and bottom removed make a good substitute for the ring moulds. Wash thoroughly and line with a strip of baking paper before use.*

If your baking rings are not tall enough, line them with a collar of baking paper to give added height.

Stewed rhubarb with ginger

*This tangy rhubarb compote (pictured bottom right) is enhanced
by the colour and flavour of the redcurrant
jelly and enlivened by the ginger.*

Preparation time 10 minutes
Total cooking time 20 minutes
Serves 4

3 tablespoons redcurrant jelly
1 kg (2 lb) rhubarb
30 g (1 oz) crystallized or glacé ginger,
finely chopped
a little caster or demerara sugar

One In a small bowl, beat the redcurrant jelly with a spoon until smooth. Pour into a wide pan and add 4 tablespoons water.

Two Trim and discard the leaves and the base of the stalks from the rhubarb. Cut the rhubarb into 2.5 cm (1 inch) lengths and add to the pan in a single layer.

Three Bring to the boil and immediately turn the heat down to a bare simmer. Cover tightly with a lid or foil and cook for 10–15 minutes, or until tender. The rhubarb should still hold its shape. Be careful to cook very gently or you will end up with a purée.

Four Transfer to a bowl, add the ginger and taste. You may require a little caster or demerara sugar sprinkled over at this stage, depending on the acidity of the rhubarb. Leave to cool slightly and serve warm or, if you prefer, prepare the day before and chill overnight.

CHEF'S TIP *The acidity of the rhubarb will vary considerably so the recipe is only a guide as to sweetness. Add as much sugar as you require. Serve the rhubarb by itself or with thick yoghurt.*

Eastern rice pudding

*The cardamom adds a distinctly Eastern flavour
to this creamy rice pudding (pictured top right).*

Preparation time 5 minutes
Total cooking time 25 minutes
Serves 4

seeds of 4 cardamom pods, crushed
400 ml (12¾ fl oz) cream
400 ml (12¾ fl oz) milk
75 g (2½ oz) caster sugar
75 g (2½ oz) short-grain rice

One Combine the crushed cardamom pods, the cream and the milk in a medium saucepan. Bring to the boil, then remove from the heat, cool slightly and stir in the sugar and rice. At this stage, the rice mixture can be refrigerated overnight or it can be cooked immediately.

Two Bring the rice mixture to the boil, lower the heat and cook, stirring constantly as it begins to thicken, for 20–25 minutes, or until the rice is just soft and the liquid has become creamy. The pudding should have a soft, flowing consistency and when a spoon is drawn through, the base of the pan should be seen and the pudding flow quickly to fill the parting behind it. (Remember that the rice will continue to thicken slightly when removed from the heat.) Serve with dried fruits or a fruit conserve.

patisserie

LE CORDON BLEU COMPLETE COOK

Croissants

*Croissants require time and effort to produce, but the rich buttery
results will astound friends and family. For step-by-step guidance
on how to make croissants, see page 548.*

For step-by-step guidance on how to make croissants, see page 548.

*Preparation time 3 hours + resting
+ chilling overnight*
Total cooking time 20 minutes
Makes 12–16

500 g (1 lb) plain flour
1 teaspoon salt
50 g (1¾ oz) caster sugar
320 ml (10 fl oz) milk
15 g (½ oz) fresh yeast
or 7 g (¼ oz) dried yeast
340 g (11 oz) unsalted butter,
at room temperature
2 egg yolks, lightly beaten
whole almonds, to decorate

ALMOND CREAM
60 g (2 oz) unsalted butter, softened
60 g (2 oz) caster sugar
1 egg, beaten
60 g (2 oz) ground almonds
15 g (½ oz) plain flour
rind of ½ lemon

One Sift the flour, salt and sugar into a large bowl and make a well in the centre. Heat the milk to warm, stir in the yeast and 1 tablespoon of the flour until dissolved, then leave to stand until bubbles form. Add to the dry ingredients and bring together to form a soft dough, then tip out onto a floured work surface and knead for 5 minutes, or until smooth and elastic. Transfer the dough to a floured bowl and cover. Set aside in a warm area for about 1 hour, or until doubled in volume.

Two Meanwhile, put the butter between two sheets of plastic wrap and roll into a rectangle measuring about 20 x 10 cm (8 x 4 inches).

Three Once the dough has risen, punch it down and transfer to a floured work surface. Roll into a rectangle about 40 x 12 cm (16 x 5 inches). The dough should be just over twice as long as the butter and a little bit wider. Place the butter on the lower half of the dough and fold the dough over to completely enclose the butter. Seal the edges with your fingertips. Turn the dough so that the fold is on the right-hand side and lightly roll the dough into a large rectangle twice as long as it is wide. Brush off excess flour and fold the dough into even thirds like a letter, with the bottom third up and the top third down. Chill in plastic wrap for 20 minutes.

Four To make the almond cream, beat the butter and sugar together using a wooden spoon or electric beaters, until light and creamy. Gradually add the egg, a third at a time, beating well after each addition. Stir in the ground almonds, flour and lemon rind.

Five Remove the dough from the refrigerator and cut it in half. On a well-floured surface, roll each piece of dough into a large rectangle, and trim it to 22 x 36 cm (8¾ x 4½ inches). Using a triangular template with a base of 18 cm (7 inches) and sides of 14 cm (5½ inches), cut the rectangles into six triangles (you should be left with two end triangles). Along the wide end of the triangle, pull down to form a longer triangle and spoon a little almond cream onto the wide base. Roll the dough up, starting from the wide end, to form crescents, tucking the triangular point underneath the dough. Place the croissants on baking trays and lightly brush with the egg yolk. Cover with plastic wrap and refrigerate overnight.

Six Remove the croissants from the refrigerator and set aside to rise for 30–45 minutes, or until they have doubled in size. Do not hurry this process by putting the croissants anywhere too warm, or the butter in the dough will melt. Preheat the oven to moderately hot 200°C (400°F/Gas 6). Toast the almonds under a medium grill until golden.

Seven Once the croissants have doubled in size, gently brush with a second layer of egg and decorate with the almonds. Bake for 15–20 minutes, or until golden.

Brioche

Brioche, a light yeast dough enriched with butter and eggs, is wonderful with butter and jam or as an accompaniment to stewed fruit. There are many different ways to mould brioche dough—this recipe is shaped in the traditional 'brioche à tête', where the small ball on the top represents the 'head' of the brioche.

Preparation time 30 minutes
+ 4 hours rising
Total cooking time 25 minutes
Makes 1 large loaf or 4 small loaves

2 tablespoons warm milk
15 g (½ oz) fresh yeast
or 7 g (¼ oz) dried yeast
375 g (12 oz) strong or plain flour
55 g (1¾ oz) caster sugar
1 teaspoon salt
6 eggs, lightly beaten
175 g (5¾ oz) unsalted butter,
softened
1 egg, beaten and mixed
with 2 tablespoons of water,
for glazing

One Pour the milk into a bowl and dissolve the yeast in it. Add 1 tablespoon of the flour, cover and set aside until bubbles start to appear. Sift the remaining flour, sugar and salt into a large bowl, make a well in the centre and add the beaten eggs and yeast mixture. Draw the flour into the wet ingredients to make a sticky dough, then transfer to a floured surface.

Two Lift and throw the dough down on the work surface with floured hands for 20 minutes, or until the dough forms a smooth ball. Place in an oiled bowl and turn the dough over to coat with the oil. Cover and leave to rise at room temperature for 2–2½ hours, or until doubled in volume.

Three Turn out the dough, punch down, cover and leave to rest for 5 minutes, then transfer to the work surface again. Place the soft butter on top of the dough and pinch and squeeze the two of them together until they are well combined.

Knead for 5 more minutes, or until the dough is smooth again. Cover and let rest for 5 minutes.

Four Brush a 1.2 litre brioche mould or four small 425 ml (15 fl oz) brioche moulds liberally with melted butter. If using the small moulds, divide the dough in four. Set aside a quarter of each piece of dough. Form the large pieces into balls and drop them into the moulds seam side down. Make a hole in the top of each ball with your finger and form the reserved pieces into tear-drop shapes to fit into the holes. Press down to seal.

Cover and leave to rise for 1–1½ hours, or until the moulds are half to three-quarters full.

Five Preheat the oven to moderately hot 200°C (400°F/Gas 6). Lightly brush with egg glaze and bake for 20–25 minutes, or until a nice golden brown. Turn out and cool on a wire rack.

CHEF'S TIP *For raisin brioche, soak 2 tablespoons raisins in some rum to plump them up. Drain well and add to the dough after all the butter has been incorporated.*

Fruit tartlets

These traditional pastries are at their best when there is a summer glut of red fruit and berries. You can also make one large tart, which would be the perfect end to a summer picnic.

Preparation time 45 minutes
+ 30 minutes chilling
Total cooking time 30 minutes
Makes 6

PASTRY CREAM
315 ml (10 fl oz) milk
90 ml (3 fl oz) lemon juice
grated rind of 2 lemons
4 egg yolks
100 g (3 1/4 oz) caster sugar
2 tablespoons plain flour
2 tablespoons cornflour

1 quantity sweet pastry (see page 546)
400 g (12 3/4 oz) mixed berries
100 g (3 1/4 oz) apricot jam

One Brush six 8 x 2 cm (3 x 3/4 inch) loose-bottomed tartlet tins with melted butter. Preheat the oven to moderately hot 200°C (400°F/Gas 6).

Two To make the pastry cream, place the milk, lemon juice and rind in a pan and bring slowly to the boil. In a bowl, whisk the egg yolks with the sugar until light in colour. Sift in the flour and cornflour and whisk until combined. Pour half the boiling milk into the yolk mixture, whisk well and return to the pan with the remaining milk. Bring to the boil, stirring constantly, and boil for 1 minute to completely cook the flour. Remove from the heat and spread the pastry cream onto a tray to cool quickly. Cover the surface with baking paper to prevent a skin forming and leave to cool. When cool, whisk until smooth.

Three Roll out the pastry on a floured surface to a 3 mm (1/8 inch) thickness. Cut six 12 cm (5 inch) circles of pastry to fit the tins, then ease into the tins,

prick the bases with a fork and chill for 20 minutes. Cut six circles of baking paper slightly larger than the tartlet tins and place into the pastry cases. Fill with baking beans or rice. Bake for about 10 minutes. Remove the baking beans or rice and paper from the pastry cases and return to the oven for a further 5 minutes, or until golden. Remove the fruit tartlets from the oven, rest for 2 minutes, then remove from their tins and place on a wire rack to cool.

Four Pipe or spoon the pastry cream into the cases to three quarters-full, levelling the surface, then pile the berries on top so that the tarts look generously filled.

Five In a small saucepan, heat the apricot jam with 3 tablespoons water. When the mixture begins to boil, sieve into a small bowl and, while still hot, brush a thin layer of the jam glaze over the cooled tartlets. Serve warm or at room temperature.

Melting moments

*As their name suggests, these melt-in-the-mouth biscuits
with their soft butter cream and jam filling are simply irresistible.*

Preparation time 45 minutes
Total cooking time 20 minutes per tray
Makes about 30

250 g (8 oz) unsalted butter,
at room temperature
100 g (3¼ oz) icing sugar, sifted
1 teaspoon finely grated lemon rind
2 egg yolks
300 g (10 oz) plain flour
2 tablespoons raspberry jam, beaten
icing sugar, to dust

BUTTER CREAM
80 g (2¾ oz) caster sugar
1 egg white
80 g (2¾ oz) unsalted butter,
at room temperature

One Preheat the oven to moderate 180°C (350°F/Gas 4). Brush two baking trays with melted butter. Using a wooden spoon or an electric whisk, cream together the butter, icing sugar and lemon rind until light and fluffy.

Two Add the egg yolks and mix thoroughly. Sift in the flour and work with a wooden spoon until the mixture comes together to form a smooth soft paste. Spoon into a piping bag with an 8 mm (⅓ inch) star nozzle.

Three Pipe enough 1.5–2 cm (⁵/₈–¾ inch) rosettes to fill the prepared baking trays, spacing well apart (see Chef's techniques, page 555). Bake for 10–12 minutes, or until the edges are golden. Cool on a wire rack. Repeat with the remaining mixture, preparing the trays as instructed in step 1.

Four To make the butter cream, in a small saucepan, over low heat, dissolve 60 g (2 oz) of the sugar in 1 tablespoon water, stirring occasionally. Increase the heat and bring to the boil. Simmer, without stirring, for 3–5 minutes. To prevent crystals of sugar forming, wipe down the sides of the pan with a brush dipped in water. Meanwhile, whisk the egg white until stiff. Add the remaining caster sugar and whisk until stiff and shiny and peaks form when the whisk is lifted. While whisking the meringue, pour on the bubbling syrup in a thin steady stream, aiming between the bowl and the whisk. Continue to whisk until the mixture is cold. Gradually add the soft butter.

Five Divide the biscuits into pairs and spread jam on the flat side of one of each pair. Using a plain 4 mm (¼ inch) nozzle, pipe a little of the butter cream mixture onto the other biscuit, sandwich the two together and dust lightly with sifted icing sugar.

Florentines

Accredited to Austrian bakers, this wonderful mixture of sugar, butter, cream, nuts and fruit has its origins in Italy. Crisp to eat, they have the added allure of a chocolate base, which is traditional but optional.

Preparation time 20 minutes
+ 10 minutes standing
Total cooking time 15 minutes per tray
Makes 25–30

120 g (4 oz) unsalted butter
125 g (4 oz) caster sugar
100 g (3 1/4 oz) candied orange peel,
finely chopped or mixed peel
30 g (1 oz) glacé cherries, cut into
8 pieces
60 g (2 oz) blanched flaked almonds
120 g (4 oz) blanched almonds,
chopped
30 ml (1 fl oz) thick (double) cream
250 g (8 oz) good-quality dark
chocolate, chopped

One Preheat the oven to moderate 180°C (350°F/Gas 4). Brush two baking trays with melted butter.

Two Melt the butter in a small saucepan, stir in the sugar, slowly bring to the boil and remove from the heat. Add the candied peel, cherries, the flaked and chopped almonds and mix well. Whisk the cream until it is thick and gently stir it into the warm mixture. Set aside for about 10 minutes, or until cool and thick.

Three Using a heaped teaspoon of mixture for each florentine, spoon on enough mounds of the mixture to fill the two baking trays (see Chef's techniques, page 555). Space well apart as the biscuits will spread. Bake for about 5 minutes, or until lightly set. Using a large cutter or a cup, shape the spread mixture into neat rounds by pulling in the edges. Return to the oven for 4 minutes. Reshape with the cutter and leave to cool for 3 minutes, or until firm enough to remove from the tray.

Carefully lift them with a palette knife and cool on a wire rack. Repeat with the remaining mixture, preparing the trays as instructed in step 1. Warm the mixture a little if it has cooled too much to spoon easily.

Four Bring a saucepan half-full of water to the boil, then remove from the heat. Place the chocolate in a heatproof bowl and place over the pan of steaming water, without the base touching the water. Stir occasionally until the chocolate has melted then leave to cool to room temperature. Using a palette knife, spread on to the smooth underside of the florentines. Return to the rack until the chocolate is just setting. Run a fork through the chocolate to make wavy lines and leave to set at room temperature.

CHEF'S TIP *Florentines make excellent petits fours if made with 1/2 teaspoon of mixture. They will store in an airtight container for up to 1 week. Any extra biscuit mixture can be stored in the refrigerator for 1 week.*

Almond and hazelnut macaroons

*These nutty macaroons (pictured far right) are crisp
on the outside with a meltingly soft inside.*

Preparation time 20 minutes
Total cooking time 25 minutes
Makes 36

30 g (1 oz) hazelnuts
30 g (1 oz) ground almonds
125 g (4 oz) icing sugar
2 egg whites
pinch of caster sugar

One Preheat the oven to moderate 180°C (350°F/Gas 4).

Two Place two baking trays on top of each other, then line the top tray with baking paper (this will prevent the bottom of the macaroons overbrowning during baking).

Three Toast the hazelnuts by placing on a baking tray and toasting for 3–5 minutes, taking care not to let the hazelnuts burn. Leave to cool, then place in a food processor and pulse until the nuts finely ground.

Four Reduce the oven temperature to warm 160°C (315°F/Gas 2–3). Sift the almonds, hazelnuts and icing sugar into a bowl, then sift again to make sure that they are thoroughly mixed. In a separate bowl, whisk the egg whites with the pinch of sugar until stiff and shiny and the mixture forms stiff peaks when the whisk is lifted.

Five Using a metal spoon, carefully fold the dry ingredients into the egg whites, trying not to lose any air. The mixture should be shiny and soft, not liquid.

Six Spoon into a piping bag with a 7.5 mm (1/3 inch) nozzle. Pipe 2 cm (3/4 inch) wide rounds onto the prepared trays, leaving room for expansion. Bake, in two batches if necessary, for 15–20 minutes, or until golden and crisp, checking the macaroons frequently. Cool on the tray for a few minutes, then remove to a wire rack.

Palmiers

*These supremely simple biscuits (pictured right) show off
perfect home-made puff pastry to its best effect.*

Preparation time 20 minutes
Total cooking time 20 minutes
Makes 15

60 g (2 oz) sugar
2 level teaspoons ground cinnamon

1/2 quantity puff pastry
(see page 542)

One Preheat the oven to hot 220°C (425°F/Gas 7) and brush a baking tray with melted butter.

Two Mix the sugar and cinnamon together in a bowl and use instead of flour to dust the work surface. Quickly roll the dough out to a 5 mm (1/4 inch) thick rectangle and sprinkle generously with the sugar and cinnamon. Fold the short sides in three times to meet in the centre, sprinkle with more sugar and cinnamon, then fold in half as if you were closing a book. Cut horizontally across the pastry into 1 cm (1/2 inch) slices and place onto the prepared tray with a cut side uppermost. Flatten gently with a rolling pin and sprinkle with more sugar. Bake for 10 minutes, then turn the palmiers over and bake for a further 10 minutes, or until richly caramelised. Cool on a wire rack.

CHEF'S TIP *For a quick dessert, sandwich the palmiers together with 280 ml (9 fl oz) cream whipped together with 1 tablespoon icing sugar and 1 tablespoon brandy.*

Madeleines

These well-known individual, shell-shaped sponges are traditionally served plain, with coffee or tea. They are also a perfect accompaniment to desserts such as pears poached in red wine.

Preparation time 15 minutes
+ 10 minutes standing
Total cooking time 10 minutes
Makes 12

2 eggs
50 g (1³/4 oz) caster sugar
2 teaspoons demerara sugar
1¹/2 teaspoons clear honey
90 g (3 oz) plain flour
1 teaspoon baking powder
60 g (2 oz) unsalted butter,
melted and cooled
icing sugar, for dusting

One Preheat the oven to moderate 180°C (350°F/Gas 4). Butter a 12-hole madeleine tin, chill in the refrigerator until set, butter lightly a second time and chill. Dust with flour and tap out the excess to leave a fine coating.

Two Separate the eggs. Set aside the egg whites in a bowl. Combine the egg yolks in a bowl with half the caster sugar, the demerara sugar and honey, and whisk until trebled in volume and pale in colour. With a clean whisk, beat the egg whites until stiff, then add the remaining caster sugar. Whisk until a stiff, shiny textured meringue is formed. Fold one third of the meringue into the yolk mixture.

Three Sift the flour, baking powder and a small pinch of salt together into a bowl. Fold half the dry ingredients into the yolk mixture, using a large metal spoon or plastic spatula, followed by one third of the meringue, then add the remaining dry ingredients. Fold in the final one third of meringue and, just as it disappears, pour in the butter and very carefully fold in until just combined. Do not overfold at any stage. Pipe, using a bag fitted with a 4 mm (¹/4 inch) plain nozzle, or spoon carefully into the tins until they are two-thirds full. Set aside to rest for 10 minutes.

Four Bake in the upper half of the oven for about 8–10 minutes, or until pale golden brown and springy when lightly touched, or until a fine skewer comes out clean when inserted into the centre. Turn the madeleines out of the tin and set aside to cool completely on a wire rack. Serve with the shell side up, dusted with sifted icing sugar.

CHEF'S TIP *You could vary the flavour of the madeleines by adding the finely grated rind of half a lemon or orange to the egg mixture.*

Saint-Honoré

During the Middle Ages, most pastries were produced by the clergy,
hence the religious names or connotations they still have today.
Saint Honoré is the patron saint of pastry-makers.

Preparation time 1 hour
+ 30 minutes chilling
Total cooking time 1 hour 30 minutes
Serves 6–8

½ quantity sweet pastry
(see page 546)
1 quantity choux pastry (see page 545)
1 egg, beaten
250 g (8 oz) caster sugar

CHANTILLY CREAM
200 ml (6½ fl oz) cream, for
whipping, chilled
50 g (1¾ oz) icing sugar
1 teaspoon vanilla extract or essence

One Preheat the oven to moderate 180°C (350°F/Gas 4). Grease two baking trays with melted butter and chill. Lightly flour the work surface and roll the sweet pastry out to 3 mm (⅛ inch) thick. Cut out a circle 20 cm (8 inches) in diameter for the base of the Saint-Honoré. Place on one of the baking sheets, prick with a fork and brush lightly with beaten egg.

Two Spoon the choux pastry into a piping bag fitted with a large 1 cm (½ inch) pastry nozzle and pipe a band of choux pastry around the edge of the sweet pastry, about the same thickness as the sweet pastry. Pipe another band inside the first one, touching the outer band, and brush with the beaten egg. Bake for 40 minutes, or until the pastry is well browned and the choux well puffed. Do not open the oven door for the first 15 minutes or the choux pastry will collapse. Cool on a wire rack.

Three On the other chilled baking sheet, pipe small balls of choux pastry, the size of walnuts, leaving at least 5 cm (2 inches) between them. Brush with the beaten egg and smooth the tops. Bake for 40 minutes, or until well browned and puffed. Cool on a wire rack.

Four To make the caramel, fill a shallow pan with cold water and set it next to the stove. Place the caster sugar and 3 tablespoons water in a heavy-based saucepan and make caramel, following the method in the Chef's techniques on page 540. Carefully dip one side of each choux ball into the caramel and allow to cool on a buttered baking tray for 2 minutes. Then dip the choux balls in again, on their other sides, and quickly stick them, at regular intervals, around the edge of the Saint-Honoré base.

Five To make the Chantilly cream, pour the cream into a bowl and add the sugar and vanilla. Using a balloon whisk or electric beaters, whip the cream mixture until it forms soft peaks and holds in the whisk when lifted from the bowl.

Six Place the cream in a pastry bag fitted with a large star nozzle, then fill the centre of the base. Refrigerate for at least 30 minutes before serving.

Thin apple tart

This spectacular tart—Tarte fine aux pommes—has a crisp shortcrust base spread with almond cream and topped with glazed apples. The pastry is finer than the usual shortcrust, but if you don't have time to make your own you could use ready-made shortcrust.

Preparation time 1 hour
+ 40 minutes refrigeration
Total cooking time 1 hour
Serves 6–8

SHORTCRUST PASTRY
100 g (3¼ oz) plain flour
50 g (1¾ oz) icing sugar
50 g (1¾ oz) unsalted butter
1 egg yolk
vanilla extract or essence

ALMOND CREAM
3 tablespoons icing sugar
30 g (1 oz) unsalted butter, softened
1 teaspoon vanilla extract or essence
1 egg yolk
3 tablespoons ground almonds

500 g (1 lb) Golden Delicious apples
juice of 1 lemon
apricot jam, for glazing

One To make the pastry, sift the flour and icing sugar into a bowl, then rub in the butter until the mixture resembles breadcrumbs. Make a well in the centre and add the egg yolk, a few drops of vanilla, a pinch of salt and enough cold water to help form a dough. Turn out onto a floured surface and gather the dough together to make a smooth ball. Cover with plastic wrap and refrigerate for 30 minutes, or until just firm.

Two Preheat the oven to moderate 180°C (350°F/Gas 4). Remove the plastic wrap from the chilled pastry, then very gently roll out the pastry between two sheets of greaseproof or baking paper to a thickness of 2.5 mm (⅛ inch). Carefully ease the pastry into a greased, shallow loose-bottomed flan tin, 22 cm (8¾ inches) across the base.

Three Blind bake the pastry for 20 minutes, following the Chef's techniques on page 547. Remove the baking beads and paper, then bake for a further 10 minutes, covering the pastry with foil if it looks like burning. Remove from the oven and allow to cool.

Four To make the almond cream, beat together the icing sugar, butter and vanilla until light and creamy. Add the egg yolk and beat well, then add the ground almonds. Spread the mixture in an even layer over the cooled pastry shell.

Five Peel, quarter and core the apples and sprinkle with lemon juice. Thinly slice the apples and arrange in overlapping circles over the almond cream. Bake for 20–25 minutes, or until the apples are cooked. Cool on a wire rack.

Six When the tart has cooled, place some apricot jam in a small pan and bring to the boil. (Add a spoonful of water if the jam becomes too thick for spreading.) Sieve the jam and, using a pastry brush, lightly dab the surface of the tart with the jam to make the apples shine.

CHEF'S TIPS *Handle the pastry as little as possible, working quickly and lightly.*

Make sure the tart has cooled before brushing it with the jam. If the tart is still hot, the fruit will simply soak up the jam and the tart will lose its shine when it cools.

about apples...

Golden Delicious apples are used for this recipe (as for Tarte Tatin) because they hold their shape when cooked, without becoming mushy. Other suitable varieties would be Pink Lady or Fuji.

Chocolate éclairs

*In French, éclair means literally 'lightning'. The name
of these filled choux pastry buns is possibly
due to the fact that they rarely last long on the plate!*

Preparation time 1 hour
Total cooking time 1 hour 15 minutes
Makes 12

1 quantity choux pastry
(see page 545)
1 egg, lightly beaten

PASTRY CREAM
250 ml (8 fl oz) milk
1 teaspoon vanilla extract or essence
2 egg yolks
60 g (2 oz) caster sugar
1½ tablespoons plain flour
1½ tablespoons cornflour

CHOCOLATE GANACHE
75 g (2½ oz) chocolate, chopped
into small pieces
75 g (2½ oz) cream

One Preheat the oven to moderate 180°C (350°F/Gas 4). Grease a baking tray with softened butter and place in the refrigerator to chill.

Two Fill a piping bag fitted with a medium plain nozzle with the choux pastry. Pipe the mixture to form 8–10 cm (3–4 inch) logs on the baking tray. Lightly brush with the beaten egg. Take care not to let any of the egg drip down the sides as this may prevent the dough from rising evenly. Press gently with a fork. Bake for 30–35 minutes, or until crisp and golden. Immediately remove from the baking sheet and place on a wire rack to cool.

Three To make the pastry cream, place the milk and vanilla in a saucepan and bring slowly to the boil. In a bowl, whisk the egg yolks with the caster sugar until light in colour. Sift in the plain flour and cornflour and whisk until well combined. Pour half the boiling milk into the yolk mixture, whisk well and return to the saucepan with the remaining milk. Bring to the boil, stirring constantly, and boil for 1 minute to completely cook the flour. Remove from the heat and spread the pastry cream on a tray to cool quickly. Cover the surface with baking paper to prevent a skin forming on the surface. Leave to cool completely.

Four To make the chocolate ganache, place the chocolate pieces in a small bowl. Bring the cream to the boil in a small saucepan, then pour it over the chocolate. Wait a few seconds, then gently stir until the chocolate is completely melted and smooth.

Five Using a small knife, make a small hole at one end on the underside of each éclair. Place the cooled pastry cream in a bowl and whisk until smooth, then spoon the cream into a piping bag with a small nozzle. Push the tip into one of the holes and fill the entire cavity with the pastry cream. Hold the éclair in the palm of your hand and stop filling just at the moment you feel it expanding. A little of the cream will ooze out once the piping bag nozzle is removed; wipe it off.

Six Using a small knife or spatula, carefully spread the chocolate ganache over the tops of the éclairs. Leave in a cool place until the ganache sets.

LE CORDON BLEU ✦ COMPLETE COOK

Millefeuille

Millefeuille, meaning 'a thousand leaves', refers to the layers of puff pastry used in this recipe. Filled with a delicious vanilla cream, a millefeuille may be served as one large pastry or cut into individual portions.

*Preparation time 1 hour
+ 15 minutes resting
Total cooking time 40 minutes
Serves 6*

**1 quantity puff pastry
(see pages 542–3)
strawberries, to garnish
icing sugar, to dust**

**PASTRY CREAM
750 ml (24 fl oz) milk
1 vanilla pod, split lengthways
9 egg yolks
185 g (6 oz) caster sugar
75 g (2½ oz) plain flour
50 g (1¾ oz) cornflour**

One Preheat the oven to hot 210°C (415°F/Gas 6–7). Divide the dough in two and roll each piece into a square, 2–3 mm (⅛ inch) thick. Place one square on a buttered baking tray lined with baking paper, and prick all over with a fork to stop the dough from rising too much. Allow the pastry to rest in the refrigerator for 15 minutes. Before baking, cover the pastry with a second sheet of baking paper and another baking tray. Bake for 10–15 minutes. Flip the pastry over and return to the oven for 10 minutes, or until lightly golden all over. Remove the top baking tray and paper and leave on a wire rack to cool. Repeat with the other square.

Two To make the pastry cream, place the milk and vanilla pod in a saucepan and bring to the boil. In a bowl, whisk the egg yolks with the sugar until light in colour. Sift in the flour and cornflour and whisk until well combined. Remove and discard the vanilla pod, then pour half the boiling milk into the yolk mixture, whisk well and return to the saucepan with the remaining milk. Bring to the boil, stirring constantly, and boil for 1 minute to completely cook the flour. Remove from the heat and spread the pastry cream on a tray to cool quickly. Cover the surface with baking paper to prevent a skin forming.

Three Trim the edges of the pastry with a serrated knife and reserve the trimmings, then cut each square in two. Save the neatest piece for the top. Whisk the cooled pastry cream until smooth. Pipe or spoon a third of the cream onto a piece of puff pastry, cover with a second piece of pastry and pipe the second third of the cream on top. Repeat with the third piece of pastry and remaining cream. Place the last piece of pastry on top and press lightly. Smooth any cream that comes out of the sides with a spatula, and fill any holes. Crush the pastry trimmings and press onto the sides. Decorate with the strawberries and dust with sifted icing sugar.

Brioche plum tart

This delicious tart is made from a soft brioche dough and filled with a vanilla cream and fresh ripe plums. Perfect for serving at tea time or the end of a summer party.

Preparation time 45 minutes
+ overnight refrigeration
Total cooking time 45 minutes
Serves 6

BRIOCHE DOUGH
2 teaspoons milk
1½ teaspoons fresh yeast
or 1 teaspoon dried yeast
165 g (5½ oz) strong or plain flour
3 teaspoons caster sugar
½ teaspoon salt
2 eggs, lightly beaten
60 g (2 oz) unsalted butter, softened

PASTRY CREAM
500 ml (16 fl oz) milk
½ vanilla pod, split lengthways
5 egg yolks
125 g (4 oz) caster sugar
2 tablespoons plain flour
2 tablespoons cornflour

250 g (8 oz) plums, halved and stoned
50 g (1¾ oz) apricot jam

One Pour the milk into a bowl and dissolve the yeast in it. Add 1 tablespoon of the flour, cover and set aside until bubbles start to appear. Sift the remaining flour, sugar and salt into a large bowl, make a well in the centre and add the beaten eggs and yeast mixture. Draw the flour into the wet ingredients to make a sticky dough, then transfer to a floured surface.

Two Lift and throw the dough down on the work surface with floured hands for 20 minutes, or until the dough forms a smooth ball. Place in an oiled bowl and turn the dough over to coat with the oil. Cover and leave to rise at room temperature for 2–2½ hours, or until doubled in volume.

Three Turn out the dough, punch down, cover and leave to rest for 5 minutes, then transfer to the work surface again. Place the soft butter on top of the dough and pinch and squeeze the two of them together until they are well combined. Knead for 5 more minutes, or until the dough is smooth again. Cover and leave to rest for 5 minutes.

Four Grease a 20 cm (8 inch) loose-bottomed flan tin with softened butter. Roll out the dough into a 3–4 mm (⅛–¼ inch) thick circle. Line the tin with the dough, following the method in the Chef's techniques on page 547. Chill for 20 minutes. Preheat the oven to warm 165°C (320°F/Gas 2–3).

Five To make the pastry cream, place the milk and vanilla in a saucepan and bring slowly to the boil. In a bowl, whisk the egg yolks with the sugar until light in colour. Sift in the flour and cornflour and whisk until well combined. Remove and discard the vanilla pod, then pour half the boiling milk into the yolk mixture, whisk well and return to the saucepan with the remaining milk. Bring to the boil, stirring constantly, and boil for 1 minute to completely cook the flour. Remove from the heat and spread the pastry cream on a tray to cool quickly. Cover the surface with baking paper to prevent a skin forming and leave to cool. Whisk the pastry cream to smooth to use.

Six Spread the pastry cream over the base of the brioche and arrange the plums, flat side down, on top. Bake for 40 minutes, or until the brioche is crisp and golden. Allow to cool on a wire rack before removing from the tin.

Seven Heat the jam with 1 tablespoon water until melted. Bring to the boil and sieve. Brush over the plums to glaze.

about plums...

You can vary the look of this recipe according to the colour of the plums you use. Some have a yellow flesh whereas others have a deep, dark red flesh. Skin colours also vary. You could also use greengages if you like.

Lemon tart

This lemon tart is the perfect end to any meal, with just the right balance of tangy lemon and sweetness. Try substituting other citrus fruits such as orange or lime, or a combination of two fruits.

Preparation time 30 minutes
+ refrigeration
Total cooking time 50 minutes
Serves 8

1 quantity sweet pastry (see page 546)
icing sugar, to dust

FILLING
150 ml (5 fl oz) thick (double) cream
4 eggs
150 g (5 oz) caster sugar
200 ml (6¹/2 fl oz) lemon juice
finely grated rind of 1 lemon

One Brush a 4 cm (1¹/2 inches) deep loose-bottomed flan tin, 18 or 20 cm (7–8 inches) across the base, with some melted butter.

Two On a lightly floured surface, roll out the sweet pastry into a circle about 3 mm (¹/4 inch) thick and line the flan tin (see Chef's techniques, page 547). Chill in the refrigerator for 30 minutes. Preheat the oven to moderately hot 190°C (375°F/Gas 5). Bake blind for 10 minutes, following the method in the Chef's techniques on page 547, until the pastry is firm. Remove the beads and paper and, if the bottom of the pastry looks wet, return to the oven for an extra 3–4 minutes. Reduce the heat to very slow 140°C (275°F/Gas 1).

Three To make the filling, warm the cream in a small pan over low heat. In a large bowl, whisk together the eggs, sugar and lemon juice. Stir in the warmed cream. Pass the mixture through a fine sieve, then stir in the grated lemon rind and pour into the pastry case. Return to the oven and bake for 35 minutes, or until the filling is just firm to the touch. When the tart comes out of the oven it will appear quite soft in the middle. Allow to cool completely, then remove from the tin and chill in the refrigerator for several hours or overnight, until the filling is firm enough to cut. Dust the top with sifted icing sugar just before serving.

CHEF'S TIP *Keep refrigerated and use within 3 days.*

Pithiviers

This pastry originated in the town of Pithiviers in central France. It becomes the traditional Twelfth Night cake when a bean is added before the cake is sealed. The guest who gets the bean becomes king or queen for the day. During the winter holidays, these cakes can be seen adorned with gold crowns in French patisseries.

Preparation time 45 minutes
+ refrigeration
Total cooking time 40 minutes
Serves 4–6

1 quantity puff pastry
(see pages 542–3)
1 egg, beaten
30 g (1 oz) caster sugar

ALMOND CREAM
50 g (1¾ oz) unsalted butter, softened
50 g (1¾ oz) caster sugar
50 g (1¾ oz) ground almonds
1 egg
½ tablespoon plain flour
2 teaspoons rum

One Preheat the oven to hot 220°C (425°F/ Gas 7). Cut the puff pastry in half and roll into two 20 cm (8 inch) squares. Place on lined baking trays and then refrigerate.

Two To make the almond cream, beat the butter and sugar, add the ground almonds and egg and mix well. Stir in the flour, and then the rum. Cover and place in the refrigerator.

Three Remove one of the baking trays of puff pastry from the refrigerator. Using a plate or large round pastry ring, make a light imprint 14 cm (5½ inches) in diameter. Brush around the imprint with the beaten egg. Place the almond cream in the centre and spread it into a dome, taking care not to touch the part of the dough that was brushed with the beaten egg. Place the second piece of puff pastry over the first and press the edges to seal.

Four Using the tip of a teaspoon, gently press around the edge of the pastry to make small, uniform semicircles— creating a scalloped effect. Refrigerate for 10 minutes, then use a small knife to cut away the pattern marked by the spoon. Preheat the oven to moderately hot 200°C (400°F/Gas 6).

Five Make a syrup by mixing the caster sugar with 30 ml (1 fl oz) water in a small saucepan. Stir with a spoon over medium heat until the sugar has dissolved, then bring to the boil and remove from the heat to cool.

Six Brush the pastry with the beaten egg, without letting any drip down the sides, as this will prevent the pastry from rising properly. Using the tip of a small knife, score the top of the pastry in a spiral pattern. Bake for 10 minutes, then reduce the heat to moderate 180°C (350°F/Gas 4) and bake for another 25 minutes, or until golden brown. Remove from the oven and immediately brush the top with the syrup to give it a shine. Serve the pithiviers warm.

Praline dacquoise

Dramatically striped and flavoured with light praline butter cream,
this dessert can be made up to a day in advance and chilled,
a great advantage when entertaining.

Preparation time 1 hour 30 minutes
+ 20 minutes chilling
Total cooking time 20 minutes
Serves 8

ALMOND SPONGE
140 g (4½ oz) ground almonds
65 g (2¼ oz) plain flour
230 g (7¼ oz) caster sugar
100 ml (3¼ fl oz) milk
9 egg whites

HAZELNUT BUTTER CREAM
125 g (4 oz) caster sugar
2 egg whites
155 g (5 oz) unsalted butter, softened
30 g (1 oz) chocolate hazelnut spread

55 g (1¾ oz) flaked almonds
icing sugar, for decoration
cocoa powder, for decoration

One Preheat the oven to moderately hot 190°C (375°F/Gas 5). Line a 22 x 32 cm (8½ x 13 inch) swiss roll tin with baking paper and brush with melted butter.

Two To make the almond sponge, sieve the ground almonds, flour and 170 g (5½ oz) of the caster sugar together into a bowl. Add the milk and 1 egg white and beat with a wooden spoon until smoothly blended. In a separate clean, dry bowl, whisk the remaining egg whites until stiff peaks form, then gradually whisk in the remaining 60 g (2 oz) caster sugar to form a stiff and shiny meringue. Using a large metal spoon or plastic spatula, carefully fold one third of the meringue into the almond sponge mixture until well incorporated, then gently fold in the remaining meringue in three or four additions. Be careful not to fold too much or the mixture will lose volume.

Three Spread the mixture gently over the prepared tray and bake for 7–10 minutes, or until golden and springy. Loosen the edges with the point of a knife and turn out onto a wire rack covered with baking paper. Do not remove the paper used in baking.

Four To make the hazelnut butter cream, put 90 g (3 oz) of the sugar and 60 ml (2 fl oz) water in a small heavy-based pan. Stir over low heat until the sugar dissolves completely. Using a wet pastry brush, brush any sugar crystals from the side of the pan. Increase the heat and

boil, without stirring, until the syrup reaches the soft-ball stage, which is around 120°C (250°F). If you don't have a sugar thermometer, drop ¼ teaspoon of the syrup into iced water. The ball of syrup should hold its shape but be soft when pressed.

Five Meanwhile, whisk the egg whites until very soft peaks form, then add the remaining sugar and whisk until stiff and glossy. Continue whisking and carefully pour in the hot syrup, pouring between the beaters and the side of the bowl. Whisk until cold. Gradually whisk in the butter and chocolate spread until well combined.

Six Using a serrated knife, trim the edges of the sponge to neaten and cut into three 20 x 10 cm (8 x 4 inch) pieces, discarding the paper. Use one-third of the butter cream to cover the first layer of sponge, cover with the second piece and repeat with another third of butter cream. Top with the remaining sponge. Coat the top and sides with the remaining butter cream and smooth with a palette knife. Chill for 20 minutes, or until set.

Seven Toast the flaked almonds under a medium grill until golden. Dust the cake with icing sugar. Cut 1 cm (½ inch) strips of paper and lay on top of the cake at 1.5 cm (⅝ inch) intervals. Dust with sifted cocoa and remove the paper carefully to show brown and white lines. Press the toasted almonds onto the sides.

Pecan pie

This classic pie originated in America's South and uses corn syrup and dark brown sugar to give a rich nutty taste. Traditionally it is served with a spoonful of whipped cream.

*Preparation time 20 minutes
+ 30 minutes resting
Total cooking time 50 minutes
Serves 6–8*

*3/4 quantity sweet pastry
(see page 546)*

FILLING
*2 eggs
pinch of salt
35 g (1¼ oz) unsalted butter, melted
150 g (5 oz) light corn syrup
125 g (4 oz) dark brown sugar
1 teaspoon vanilla extract or essence
125 g (4 oz) pecans, roughly chopped*

One Preheat the oven to warm 160°C (315°F/Gas 2–3). Roll the dough out to 2.5 mm (1/8 inch) thick and line a loose-bottomed flan tin, 22 cm (8¾ inches) across the base and 2.5 cm (1 inch) deep (see Chef's techniques, page 547).

Two To make the filling, beat the eggs in a bowl. Add the salt, butter, corn syrup, brown sugar and vanilla extract or essence and mix until well combined.

Three Sprinkle the pecans over the bottom of the lined flan tin, then pour over the filling. Bake for 45–50 minutes, or until the filling has just set. If the filling puffs up too much, reduce the oven to slow 150°C (300°F/Gas 2).

Four Leave the tart in the flan tin for 5 minutes, or until cool enough to handle, then remove on to a wire rack and leave to cool completely.

CHEF'S TIP *The pecans can be replaced by almost any nut, such as macadamias, walnuts, hazelnuts or even pine nuts.*

Tartelettes amandines

These small almond cakes are a well-loved patisserie classic and are perfect for eating at tea time. Amandine is the name given to various almond-flavoured French pastries and cakes.

Preparation time 45 minutes
Total cooking time 20 minutes
Makes 18

ALMOND CREAM
115 g (3³/4 oz) unsalted butter, softened
115 g (3³/4 oz) caster sugar
grated rind of 1 lemon
2 eggs, beaten
115 g (3³/4 oz) ground almonds
30 g (1 oz) plain flour
few drops of vanilla extract or essence

1 quantity sweet pastry (see page 546)
125 g (4 oz) seedless raspberry jam
60 g (2 oz) flaked almonds
45 g (1¹/2 oz) apricot jam
45 g (1¹/2 oz) icing sugar, sieved
few drops of pink food colouring

One To make the almond cream, beat the butter, sugar and lemon rind together using a wooden spoon or electric beaters until light and creamy. Gradually add the eggs, a sixth at a time, beating well after each addition. Stir in the ground almonds, flour and vanilla extract. Transfer to a piping bag fitted with a 2 cm (³/4 inch) nozzle and refrigerate.

Two Brush eighteen 6 x 2 cm (2¹/2 x ³/4 inch) loose-bottomed tartlet tins with melted butter. Roll out the pastry on a floured surface to a 2 mm (¹/8 inch) thickness. Cut eighteen 10 cm (4 inch) circles of pastry to fit the tins, then ease them into the tins and prick the bases with a fork. Preheat the oven to moderate 180°C (350°F/Gas 4).

Three Beat the raspberry jam with a spoon until soft and fluid, then place a little in the base of each tartlet. Pipe in

the almond cream until the tartlets are three quarters full and bake for 12–15 minutes, or until golden. Cool the tartlets in the tins on a wire rack. Toast the flaked almonds under a medium grill until golden, taking care not to burn.

Four In a small saucepan, heat the apricot jam with 2 tablespoons water. When the mixture has melted and begins to boil, sieve it into a small bowl and, while still hot, brush it over the tartlets.

Arrange the toasted almonds over one half of each tartlet.

Five In a small bowl, mix the icing sugar, 2 teaspoons of water and a tiny amount of the pink food colouring until the mixture is smooth and just delicately pink. Spoon the icing thinly over the half of the tartlets without almonds.

Opéra

Adapted from a complex French recipe, this dessert is a true work of art. It consists of layers of sponge cake, chocolate ganache, butter cream and coffee syrup, finished with a rich chocolate topping.

Preparation time 1 hour 45 minutes
+ refrigeration
Total cooking time 1 hour
Serves 4–6

ALMOND SPONGE
75 g (2½ oz) icing sugar
2½ tablespoons plain flour
75 g (2½ oz) ground almonds
3 eggs
15 g (½ oz) unsalted butter, melted and cooled
3 egg whites
1 tablespoon caster sugar

CHOCOLATE GANACHE
200 g (6½ oz) good-quality dark chocolate, finely chopped
120 ml (4 fl oz) milk
110 ml (3¾ fl oz) thick (double) cream
50 g (1¾ oz) unsalted butter, softened

COFFEE SYRUP
1½ tablespoons caster sugar
1½ tablespoons instant coffee

BUTTER CREAM
70 g (2¼ oz) caster sugar
1 egg white
1 tablespoon instant coffee
100 g (3¼ oz) unsalted butter, softened

One To make the sponge, preheat the oven to hot 220°C (425°F/Gas 7). Line a 20 x 30 cm (8 x 12 inch) baking tin with baking paper. Sift the icing sugar and flour into a large bowl. Stir in the ground almonds. Add the eggs and whisk until pale. Fold in the melted butter. Whisk the egg whites until stiff, add the sugar and whisk until stiff peaks form. Whisk a third of the egg white mixture into the almond mixture, then carefully fold in the remaining egg white mixture until just combined. Pour onto the tray and gently spread. Bake for 6–7 minutes, or until golden and springy. Loosen the edges with the point of a knife. Turn out onto a wire rack covered with baking paper. Do not remove the paper used in baking.

Two To make the ganache, put the chocolate in a bowl. Heat the milk and 30 ml (1 fl oz) of the cream until just at boiling point. Pour onto the chocolate, add the butter and mix until smooth. Allow to set until spreadable.

Three To make the coffee syrup, put the sugar and 90 ml (3 fl oz) water in a saucepan and stir until dissolved. Bring to the boil and add the coffee.

Four To make the butter cream, put the sugar and 3 teaspoons of water in a small heavy-based saucepan. Make a sugar syrup following the method on page 540. Meanwhile, whisk the egg white into very soft peaks. Whisking continuously, pour in the hot syrup between the beaters and the side of the bowl. Whisk until cold. Dissolve the coffee in a teaspoon of boiling water, cool to room temperature and add to the butter. Beat in half the egg white mixture, then fold in the other half.

Five Cut the sponge into three pieces, each 10 x 20 cm (4 x 8 inches). Soak one piece with a third of the coffee syrup, then spread with half the butter cream. Cover with the second piece of sponge, soak with syrup and spread with half the ganache. Cover with the last piece of sponge, soak with the remaining syrup and top with the remaining butter cream. Smooth the top and refrigerate until the butter cream is firmly set.

Six Melt the remaining ganache over a pan of simmering water. Heat the remaining cream to boiling point and stir into the ganache. Leave to cool, then smooth over the top of the cake.

Fraisier

*This is a wonderful gateau for an elegant picnic, or to end a light
summer meal. If pink marzipan is not available, knead a few drops
of red food colouring through the marzipan until the colour is uniform.*

*Preparation time 1 hour 50 minutes
+ cooling
Total cooking time 40 minutes
Serves 6–8*

GENOESE SPONGE
*3 eggs
1 egg yolk
110 g (3³/4 oz) caster sugar
110 g (3³/4 oz) plain flour
10 g (¹/4 oz) unsalted butter, melted
and cooled*

SYRUP
*90 g (3 oz) sugar
25 ml (³/4 fl oz) Kirsch*

CREME MOUSSELINE
*250 ml (8 fl oz) milk
1 vanilla pod
60 g (2 oz) caster sugar
2 egg yolks
20 g (³/4 oz) plain flour
20 g (³/4 oz) cornflour
1 tablespoon Kirsch
125 g (4 oz) unsalted butter, softened*

*500 g (1 lb) strawberries, hulled
50 g (1³/4 oz) sieved strawberry jam
100 g (3¹/4 oz) pink marzipan*

One Preheat the oven to moderate 180°C (350°F/Gas 4). To make the Genoese sponge, whisk the eggs, egg yolk and sugar in a bowl over a pan or bowl of hot steaming water until it leaves a trail. Remove from the heat and whisk until cold. Sift the flour, fold it into the mixture, then fold in the melted butter. Pour into a lightly greased 20 x 5 cm (8 x 2 inch) springform ring and bake for 20–25 minutes, or until the sponge shrinks in from the side of the pan. Run a knife inside the ring to release the sponge, then cool on a wire rack. Slice the cold sponge lengthways into two halves and set aside.

Two To make the syrup, dissolve the sugar in 65 ml (2¹/4 fl oz) water in a pan over low heat. Bring to the boil and boil for 1 minute, then stir in the Kirsch and allow to cool.

Three To make the crème mousseline, bring the milk and vanilla pod to the boil. In a bowl, whisk the sugar and egg yolks until pale, then stir in the flours. Strain the milk into the yolk mixture, whisking constantly. Return to the pan and beat rapidly over medium heat until thickened, then boil for 1 minute, stirring constantly. Remove from the heat to cool completely. Add the Kirsch and gradually beat in the butter, whisking well between each addition.

Four Set aside a strawberry for decoration. Halve a third of the strawberries and quarter the rest. To assemble the cake, place a sponge-half in the springform ring (make sure the ring is clean), baked side down. Brush with some syrup, spread with a little jam and some of the mousseline. Place the halved strawberries around the outer edge of the cake, the cut sides facing out.

Five Spoon the mousseline into a piping bag fitted with a 1 cm (¹/2 inch) nozzle. Pipe into the gaps between the strawberries. Arrange the remaining strawberries over the sponge, then cover with the remaining mousseline. Smooth the surface and gently press the other sponge on top.

Six Remove the springform ring. Brush on more syrup and thinly spread with jam. Dust a work area with icing sugar, roll out the marzipan to a circle 3 mm (¹/8 inch) thick, and cut a circle with the springform ring. Lift the marzipan onto the cake and smooth the top. Heat the remaining jam, dip in the whole strawberry and place it on top of the cake, in the centre.

Chocolate-dipped fruits

These are a clever idea for petits-fours to serve with coffee after a meal. You can use many different kinds of fruit as long as the surface remains dry.

Preparation time 20 minutes
+ 15 minutes refrigeration
Total cooking time 10–15 minutes
Serves 4–6

540 g (1 lb 1¼ oz) strawberries
2 clementines or mandarin oranges
185 g (6 oz) good-quality dark chocolate, chopped
1 tablespoon white vegetable shortening or cooking oil

One Line a baking tray with greaseproof or baking paper. Clean the strawberries by brushing with a dry pastry brush, or rinsing them very quickly in cold water and drying well on a thick layer of paper towels. Discard any berries with soft spots. Peel the clementines or mandarin oranges and remove as much of the white pith as possible, then break the fruit into individual segments.

Two Put the chocolate in a bowl. Half-fill a saucepan with water and bring to the boil. Remove from the heat and place the bowl over the pan, making sure it is not touching the water. Leave the chocolate to melt slowly. Stir in the shortening or oil, and mix until melted and completely incorporated. Remove the bowl from the pan and place on a folded towel to keep it warm.

Three Holding the berries by their stems or hulls, dip about three-quarters of the way into the chocolate, so that some of the colour of the fruit still shows. Gently wipe off any excess chocolate on the edge of the bowl and place the coated strawberries on their sides on the tray. Repeat with the clementines or mandarins, drying each segment on paper towels before dipping. If the chocolate becomes too thick, reheat the water, remove from the heat and place the bowl over the pan until the chocolate returns to the required consistency.

Four Once all the fruit has been dipped in the chocolate, place in the refrigerator for 15 minutes, or until the chocolate has just set. Remove from the refrigerator and keep in a cool place until ready to serve. Do not serve directly from the refrigerator—the cold temperature will inhibit the full flavour and sweetness of the fruit, and the chocolate will be too hard.

CHEF'S TIPS *Any fruit can be used, but the best results are with ones that can be left whole or have a dry surface.*

If the strawberry stems are too short, use a toothpick to dip them.

Use a small pair of tongs for the clementine or mandarin slices—do not use a toothpick as it will pierce the fruit, and the juices will prevent the chocolate from coating evenly.

LE CORDON BLEU ❦ COMPLETE COOK

White chocolate fudge

Made with creamy white chocolate, this fudge is flavoured with pistachio nuts and is ultra sweet, so eat it in small quantities, if you can.

Preparation time *15 minutes*
+ 2 hours refrigeration
Total cooking time *7 minutes*
Makes about 50 pieces

350 g (11¼ oz) caster sugar
30 g (1 oz) unsalted butter
pinch of salt
125 ml (4 fl oz) evaporated milk
1 vanilla pod
300 g (10 oz) good-quality white chocolate, chopped
80 g (2¾ oz) pistachio nuts

One Grease an 18 cm (7 inch) square cake tin. Put the sugar, butter, salt and evaporated milk in a large saucepan. Split the vanilla pod in half lengthways and scrape the small black seeds into the saucepan with the point of a knife. Add the pod to the saucepan. Bring to the boil over medium heat, stirring continuously with a wooden spoon. Lower the heat and simmer for about 5 minutes, stirring continuously.

Two Remove the saucepan from the heat and lift out the vanilla pod with a fork or slotted spoon. Stir in the chopped chocolate until it has melted completely and the mixture is smooth. Stir in the pistachios and pour into the prepared tin. Refrigerate for about 2 hours, or until firm.

Three Cut into small squares and serve in petit four paper cases. Store in the refrigerator for up to a week.

CHEF'S TIPS *Chopped hazelnuts can be substituted for the pistachios.*

Using a vanilla pod will give a delicious flavour to the fudge, but if you wish to avoid seeing the black seeds, use ½ teaspoon vanilla extract or essence instead.

Amaretti

*Traditionally made with bitter almonds, this recipe
uses the more readily available blanched almonds.*

Preparation time 10 minutes
Total cooking time 15 minutes per tray
Makes about 40

*75 g (2½ oz) blanched almonds,
halved or chopped
75 g (2½ oz) caster sugar
1 egg white
3 teaspoons Amaretto liqueur
2 drops almond essence
icing sugar, to dust*

One Preheat the oven to moderate 180°C
(350°F/Gas 4). Line two baking trays
with baking paper.

Two Place the almonds and the sugar in a
food processor and process to a fine
powder. Add the egg white, Amaretto
and almond essence and process to form
a soft dough.

Three Spoon the mixture into a piping
bag, fitted with a 1.5 cm (⁵/8 inch) plain
nozzle. Pipe enough 2.5 cm (1 inch)
rounds to fill the two prepared baking
trays, spacing the biscuits well apart.
Hold the nozzle 1 cm (½ inch) away
from the tray to form well-rounded

shapes. Bake for 12–15 minutes, or until
golden. Cool on a wire rack. Repeat
with the remaining mixture, preparing
the trays as instructed in step 1. Dust the
the amaretti with sifted icing sugar while
they are still warm.

CHEF'S TIPS *For a good result, ensure
the almonds and sugar are very finely
ground before adding the egg white.*

*To be traditionally Italian, place two
biscuits flatside together and wrap in
coloured tissue paper, twisting the ends.
They look wonderful piled on a serving
plate or given as gifts.*

*For a variation, top each biscuit with
half an almond before baking.*

Chocolate rum truffles

In the true style of truffles, these petits fours are highly decadent and very rich. They are delicious served with coffee as a special after-dinner treat.

Preparation time 40 minutes
+ refrigeration
Total cooking time 10 minutes
Makes 24

300 g (10 oz) good-quality dark
chocolate, finely chopped
100 ml (3¼ fl oz) thick (double)
cream
1 teaspoon vanilla extract
or essence
25 ml (¾ fl oz) dark rum
cocoa powder, to dust

One Put the chopped chocolate in a bowl. Place the cream and vanilla in a small saucepan and heat until it is just at boiling point. Pour the cream directly over the chopped chocolate. Gently mix with a whisk until the mixture is smooth. If there are any lumps, place the bowl over a pan of barely steaming water, off the heat, and lightly stir for a moment to melt any remaining chocolate. Mix in the rum and refrigerate the ganache until it is set.

Two Form the ganache into small balls with a melon baller, or pipe it into small balls using a piping bag fitted with a plain nozzle. Return to the refrigerator to set. Roll the balls between your palms to form a perfect sphere, then roll in the cocoa powder, using a fork to roll them around until evenly coated.

CHEF'S TIP *Since these truffles are not dipped in chocolate before they are rolled in the cocoa powder, they should be eaten within 2–3 days. Store them in an airtight container in the refrigerator. For a perfect finish, roll the truffles in the cocoa powder a second time just before serving.*

LE CORDON BLEU

baking

White bread

Baking fresh bread is one of the most pleasurable ways to feed family and friends and is also a relaxing way to spend an afternoon. Start with this classic white loaf.

Preparation time 20 minutes + proving (about 4 hours 30 minutes)
Total cooking time 40 minutes
Makes 1 x 750 g (1½ lb) loaf

30 g (1 oz) fresh yeast
or 1 tablespoon dried yeast
1 tablespoon sugar
500 g (1 lb) white bread flour
1 teaspoon salt
30 g (1 oz) butter, softened
milk, to glaze

One Prepare the yeast with 300 ml (10 fl oz) water and the sugar following the method in the Chef's techniques on page 550.

Two Sieve the flour and salt into a large mixing bowl and make a well in the centre. Add the yeast mixture and butter to the well and gradually bring the mixture together with your hands, or use an electric mixer fitted with a dough hook on slow speed, until a rough dough is formed. Turn the dough out onto a lightly floured work surface and knead

for about 10 minutes, or until smooth and elastic (see Chef's techniques, page 551). Alternatively, knead the dough in an electric mixer on medium speed for about 5 minutes.

Three Return the dough to a clean, lightly oiled bowl and turn once to coat the surface in oil. Cover with a clean, damp tea towel and allow to prove at room temperature until doubled in size (the proving time will depend on the temperature of your kitchen).

Four Turn the dough out onto a lightly floured work surface and knead gently for 2–3 minutes until smooth. Roll into a 25 x 45 cm (10 x 18 inch) rectangle and shape the loaf by rolling up tightly into a sausage shape (see Chef's techniques, page 551).

Five Butter a baking tray and lift the bread onto the tray, seam side down. Use a very sharp knife to cut diagonal slashes in a crisscross pattern on the top of the loaf (see Chef's techniques, page 552). Cover with a damp tea towel and allow to rise again until nearly doubled in size. Towards the end of this time, preheat the oven to hot 210°C (415°F/ Gas 6–7).

Six Brush the proved loaf with the milk and bake for 35–40 minutes, or until golden brown and hollow sounding when tapped on the base. Remove from the tray and cool on a wire rack.

CHEF'S TIP *To make rolls, divide the dough into sixteen equal pieces and roll each on a lightly floured work surface in the hollow of your hand until it forms a smooth ball. Bake for 15–20 minutes.*

Baguette

*Professional bakers use a special flour for baguettes that is not readily
available to the home cook. However, using a mixture of bread and plain
flours produces an excellent version of this classic French bread.*

Preparation time *45 minutes + proving
(about 3 hours 30 minutes)*
Total cooking time *25 minutes*
Makes 4 x 350 g (11 oz) loaves

30 g (1 oz) fresh yeast
or 1 tablespoon dried yeast
650 g (1 lb 5 oz) white bread flour
350 g (11 oz) plain flour
10 g (¹/4 oz) salt

One Prepare the yeast with 600 ml
(20 fl oz) water following the method in
the Chef's techniques on page 550.

Two Sieve the flours and salt into a large
mixing bowl and make a well in the
centre. Add the yeast mixture to the well
and gradually bring the mixture together
with your hands, or use an electric mixer
fitted with a dough hook on slow speed,
until a rough dough is formed. Turn the
dough out onto a lightly floured work
surface and knead for about 10 minutes,
or until smooth and elastic (see Chef's
techniques, page 551). Alternatively,
knead in an electric mixer on medium
speed for about 5 minutes.

Three Return the dough to a clean,
lightly oiled bowl and turn once to coat
the surface in oil. Cover with a clean,
damp tea towel and allow to prove at
room temperature until doubled in size
(the proving time will depend on the
temperature of your kitchen).

Four Turn the dough out onto a lightly
floured work surface and knead gently
for 2–3 minutes until smooth. Divide the
dough into four pieces, shape each piece
into a rough rectangle about 30 cm
(12 inches) long and roll tightly into
long baguette shapes.

Five Sprinkle flour over a baking tray
and lift the bread onto the tray, allowing
plenty of space between each loaf. Spray
the loaves with a fine mist of water and
sprinkle with flour. Use a very sharp
knife to cut five diagonal slashes on the
top of each loaf, to a depth of about
5 mm (¹/4 inch) (see Chef's techniques,
page 552). Cover with a damp tea towel
and allow to rise again until nearly
doubled in size. Towards the end of this
time, preheat the oven to hot 220°C
(425°F/Gas 7).

Six Bake the baguettes for 20–25 minutes,
or until golden, crisp and hollow sounding
when tapped on the base. Remove from
the tray and cool on a wire rack.

Petits pains au lait

These small rolls are made with an enriched bread dough and milk for a soft texture and golden crust. They are great as dinner rolls to accompany a French meal.

Preparation time 40 minutes
+ proving (about 3–4 hours)
Total cooking time 15 minutes
Makes 16 dinner rolls

30 g (1 oz) fresh yeast
or 1 tablespoon dried yeast
1 tablespoon sugar
500 g (1 lb) white bread flour
1 teaspoon salt
30 g (1 oz) milk powder
30 g (1 oz) butter, softened
milk, to glaze
3 tablespoons nibbed sugar,
to decorate (optional)

One Prepare the yeast with 300 ml (10 fl oz) water and the sugar following the method in the Chef's techniques on page 550.

Two Sieve the flour, salt and milk powder into a large mixing bowl and make a well in the centre. Add the yeast mixture and butter to the well and gradually bring the mixture together with your hands, or use an electric mixer fitted with a dough hook on slow speed, until a rough dough is formed. Turn the dough out onto a lightly floured work surface and knead for about 10 minutes, or until smooth and elastic (see Chef's techniques, page 551). Alternatively, knead in an electric mixer on medium speed for about 5 minutes.

Three Return the dough to a clean, lightly oiled bowl and turn the dough once to coat all over the surface in oil. Cover with a clean, damp tea towel and allow to prove at room temperature until doubled in size (the proving time will depend on the temperature of your kitchen).

Four Turn the dough out onto a lightly floured work surface and knead gently for 2–3 minutes until smooth. Divide the dough into sixteen equal-sized pieces. Roll each piece on a lightly floured work surface in the hollow of your hand until it forms a round and smooth ball, then flatten slightly and roll into miniature loaves with elongated ends.

Five Butter two baking trays and lift the rolls onto the trays, allowing plenty of space between each one. Cover with a damp tea towel and allow to rise again

until nearly doubled in size. Towards the end of this time, preheat the oven to hot 210°C (415°F/Gas 6–7).

Six Brush the proved rolls with the milk and, using scissors, snip into the tops of the rolls along their length to a depth of about 1 cm (1/2 inch) (see Chef's techniques, page 552). Sprinkle with the nibbed sugar, if using, and bake for 10–12 minutes, or until golden brown and hollow sounding when tapped on the base. Remove from the tray and cool on a wire rack.

Granary bread

*Granary flour purchased ready-mixed with a whole
range of grains is added here to thick, honey-like
malt to make a superb, easy loaf.*

*Preparation time 25 minutes + proving
(about 2 hours 30 minutes)
Total cooking time 35 minutes
Makes 1 x 1 kg (2 lb) loaf*

*40 g (1¼ oz) fresh yeast
or 1¼ tablespoons dried yeast
500 g (1 lb) malted grain
or granary flour
1 teaspoon salt
1 teaspoon sugar
30 g (1 oz) butter
2 teaspoons liquid malt
beaten egg, to glaze*

One Prepare the yeast with 300 ml
(10 fl oz) water following the method in
the Chef's techniques on page 550.

Two Place the flour, salt and sugar into a
large mixing bowl, stir to mix and make
a well in the centre. Melt the butter in a
small pan over low heat, add the liquid
malt and stir until smooth. Add this to
the well with the yeast mixture. Using
your hand with fingers slightly apart,
gradually draw the flour into the liquid.
Continue until all the flour has been
incorporated and a soft dough is formed.
Turn the dough out onto a lightly floured
work surface and knead for about
10 minutes, or until smooth and elastic
(see Chef's techniques, page 551).

Three Return the dough to a clean,
lightly oiled bowl and turn once to coat
the surface in oil. Cover with a clean,
damp tea towel and allow to prove at
room temperature until doubled in size
(the proving time will depend on the
temperature of your kitchen).

Four Butter and flour a 1 kg (2 lb) loaf
tin, tapping out any excess flour. Turn

the dough out onto a lightly floured
work surface and knead for 1 minute.
Using your hands, pat out to a square
slightly longer than the tin and spray
with a fine mist of water. Shape the loaf
by rolling up tightly into a sausage shape
(see Chef's techniques, page 551), then
lift the bread into the prepared tin, seam
side down. Cover with a damp tea towel
and allow to rise again until nearly
doubled in size. Towards the end of this
time, preheat the oven to very hot 230°C
(450°F/Gas 8).

Five Brush the proved loaf with egg and
use a very sharp knife to make a slash
down the length of the loaf (see Chef's
techniques, page 552). Bake for about
30–35 minutes, or until the loaf is
golden brown and sounds hollow when
tapped on the base. Remove from the
tray and leave to cool completely on a
wire rack.

CHEF'S TIP *Liquid malt is available
from health food shops and has the same
consistency as honey.*

Country sourdough

Prolonged yeast fermentation gives the characteristic flavour to this sourdough loaf. The starter needs to begin fermenting about two days before the loaf is made.

Preparation time 30 minutes + proving
(2 days in advance for starter and
3 hours 30 minutes for rising)
Total cooking time 55 minutes
Makes 2 x 500 g (1 lb) loaves

STARTER
125 g (4 oz) white bread flour
1 teaspoon fresh yeast
or ½ teaspoon dried yeast
250 ml (8 fl oz) buttermilk or beer

SPONGE
1 teaspoon fresh yeast
or ½ teaspoon dried yeast
125 g (4 oz) white bread flour

2 teaspoons fresh yeast
or 1 teaspoon dried yeast
1 teaspoon salt
2 teaspoons sugar
60 g (2 oz) butter, softened
650 g (1 lb 5 oz) white bread flour
beaten egg, to glaze

One You need to make the starter two days before you want to make the bread. Sieve the flour into a large bowl and crumble the yeast over the surface. Heat the buttermilk or beer until lukewarm and mix into the flour with a wooden spoon until a smooth batter is formed. Cover and leave for about 8–12 hours at room temperature, or until the starter begins minutely bubbling.

Two Next, prepare the sponge. Add the yeast and 250 ml (8 fl oz) lukewarm water to the starter and beat with a wooden spoon until the yeast has dissolved. Stir in the flour until smooth, scrape down the sides of the bowl, then cover and leave at room temperature for 8–12 hours.

Three On the day you want to bake the bread, place the fermenting starter into a large mixing bowl or the bowl of an electric mixer fitted with a dough hook. Add the last amount of yeast, the salt, sugar, butter and a quarter of the flour, and beat until a smooth paste is formed. Add the remaining flour in three stages, beating well after each addition. You should now have a soft dough. Turn the dough out onto a lightly floured work surface and knead for about 10 minutes,

or until the dough is smooth and elastic, following the mehtod in the Chef's techniques on page 551.

Four Return the dough to a clean, lightly oiled bowl and turn once to coat the surface in oil. Cover with a clean, damp tea towel and allow to prove at room temperature until doubled in size (the proving time will depend on the temperature of your kitchen).

Five Turn the dough out onto a lightly floured work surface, divide in half and knead gently for about 5 minutes until smooth. Shape the two pieces of dough into round loaves. Dust a baking tray with flour, lift the loaves onto the tray and brush with the beaten egg. Use a very sharp knife to cut a pattern on the top of the loaves like spokes on a wheel (see Chef's techniques, page 552). Cover with a damp tea towel and allow to rise again until nearly doubled in size. Towards the end of this time, preheat the oven to moderately hot 190°C (375°F/Gas 5).

Six Bake the loaves for 45–50 minutes, or until they are deep golden with good crusts. Remove from the tray and cool on a wire rack.

about bread starters...

Sourdough bread was traditionally made using a starter fermented with wild yeasts. Today, however, as in this recipe, a little baker's yeast is used to get the starter going. The flour in the mixture gives the yeast food to live on and the buttermilk or beer helps the fermentation.

Rye bread

Rye is grown in the cool areas of northern and eastern Europe and Scandinavia, and makes a distinctively dense, slightly bitter flavoured bread.

Preparation time 30 minutes
+ proving (about 4 hours)
Total cooking time 20 minutes
Makes 2 x 410 g (13 oz) loaves

30 g (1 oz) fresh yeast
or 1 tablespoon dried yeast
1 teaspoon caster sugar
300 g (10 oz) white bread flour
250 g (8 oz) rye flour
1 teaspoon salt
15 g (1/2 oz) milk powder
15 g (1/2 oz) butter, softened

One Prepare the yeast with 300 ml (10 fl oz) water and the sugar following the method in the Chef's techniques on page 550.

Two Sieve the flours and salt into a large mixing bowl, stir in the milk powder and make a well in the centre. Add the yeast mixture and butter to the well and gradually bring the mixture together with your hands, or use an electric mixer fitted with a dough hook on slow speed, until a rough dough is formed. Turn the dough out onto a lightly floured work surface and knead for about 10 minutes, or until smooth and elastic (see Chef's techniques, page 551). Alternatively, knead in an electric mixer on medium speed for about 5 minutes.

Three Return the dough to a clean, lightly oiled bowl and turn once to coat the surface in oil. Cover with a clean, damp tea towel and allow to prove at room temperature until doubled in size (the proving time will depend on the temperature of your kitchen).

Four Turn the dough out onto a lightly floured work surface, divide in half

and knead gently for 2–3 minutes until smooth. Dust two baking trays with flour. Shape the two pieces of dough into round loaves and lift onto the trays. Use a very sharp knife to cut diagonal slashes in a crisscross pattern on top of the loaves (see Chef's techniques, page 552). Spray the loaves with a fine mist of water and lightly dust the tops with flour. Cover with a damp tea towel and allow to rise again until nearly doubled

in size. Towards the end of this time, preheat the oven to moderately hot 200°C (400°F/Gas 6) and place a tin of hot water in the bottom of the oven to produce steam that will help form a crust on the bread.

Five Bake the loaves for 20 minutes, or until browned and hollow sounding when tapped on the base. Remove from the trays and cool on a wire rack.

Pretzels

*A traditional yeasted, biscuity bread, shaped into loose knots,
sprinkled with rock salt and baked to produce a soft,
chewy texture. Serve as a snack with beer or wine.*

Preparation time 30 minutes + proving
(about 3 hours 30 minutes)
Total cooking time 25 minutes
Makes 16 pretzels

25 g (³/4 oz) fresh yeast
or 3¹/2 teaspoons dried yeast
250 ml (8 fl oz) milk
600 g (1¹/4 lb) white bread flour
2 tablespoons salt
3 eggs
30 g (1 oz) rock salt

One Prepare the yeast with the milk following the method in the Chef's techniques on page 550.

Two Sieve the flour and 1 teaspoon of the salt into a large mixing bowl and make a well in the centre. Add the yeast mixture and two of the eggs to the well and whisk with a fork for a few seconds to break up the eggs. Gradually bring the mixture together with your hands, or use an electric mixer fitted with a dough hook on slow speed, until a rough dough is formed. Turn the dough out onto a lightly floured work surface and knead for about 10 minutes, or until smooth and elastic (see Chef's techniques, page 551). Alternatively, knead in an electric mixer on medium speed for about 5 minutes.

Three Return the dough to a clean, lightly oiled bowl and turn once to coat the surface in oil. Cover with a clean, damp tea towel and allow to prove at room temperature until doubled in size (the proving time will depend on the temperature of your kitchen).

Four Turn the dough out onto a lightly floured work surface and knead gently for 2–3 minutes until smooth. Divide the dough into sixteen equal-sized pieces and roll each piece on a lightly floured work surface into 35 cm (14 inch) long sausages, covering the dough with a damp cloth while you work to prevent it from drying out. Tie each sausage into a loose knot, leaving a large hole in the centre. Butter two baking trays and cut out sixteen 15 cm (6 inch) square pieces of greaseproof paper, place one under each pretzel and lift the pretzels onto the trays, allowing plenty of space between them. Cover with a damp tea towel and leave to rise again until nearly doubled in size.

Five Preheat the oven to moderately hot 200°C (400°F/ Gas 6). Bring a large pan of water to the boil with the remaining salt (not the rock salt), then reduce the heat to simmering. Using a slotted spoon, lower the pretzels a few at a time, still on their squares of paper, into the water, being careful not to knock air out of the delicate dough. Poach for about 1 minute per batch (the paper will automatically peel off in the water, after which you can discard it). Drain on paper towels and then return to the baking trays.

Six Beat the remaining egg and brush over the surface of the pretzels. Gently press the rock salt onto the surface of the pretzels and bake for 10–15 minutes, or until pale golden. Remove from the trays and cool on a wire rack.

Pumpkin and cardamom rolls

These rolls are a golden orange in colour and their texture is crunchy with pumpkin seeds. Great with butter and honey or as an accompaniment to a bowl of winter vegetable soup.

Preparation time 25 minutes
+ proving time (about 2 hours)
Total cooking time 15 minutes
Makes 12 x 60 g (2 oz) rolls

30 g (1 oz) fresh yeast
or 1 tablespoon dried yeast
500 g (1 lb) white bread flour
15 g (½ oz) milk powder
1 teaspoon salt
2 teaspoons ground cardamom
15 g (½ oz) molasses
30 g (1 oz) butter, softened
185 g (6 oz) fresh or tinned pumpkin
purée (see Chef's tip)
60 g (2 oz) pumpkin seeds
beaten egg yolk, to glaze

One Prepare the yeast with 250 ml (8 fl oz) water following the method in the Chef's techniques on page 550.

Two Sieve the flour, milk powder, salt and ground cardamom into a large mixing bowl and make a well in the centre. Stir the molasses into the yeast mixture and add the mixture to the well along with the butter and pumpkin purée. Gradually bring the mixture together with your hands, or use an electric mixer fitted with a dough hook on slow speed, until a fairly soft dough is formed (depending on the moisture content of the pumpkin purée used, you may need to add a little additional flour). Turn the dough out onto a lightly floured work surface and knead for about 10 minutes, or until smooth and elastic (see Chef's techniques, page 551). Alternatively, knead in an electric mixer on medium speed for about 5 minutes.

Three Return the dough to a clean, lightly oiled bowl and turn once to coat the surface in oil. Cover with a clean, damp tea towel and leave to prove at room temperature until doubled in size (the proving time will depend on the temperature of your kitchen).

Four Turn the dough out onto a lightly floured work surface, add the pumpkin seeds and knead for about 3–4 minutes until the dough is smooth and the pumpkin seeds have been distributed evenly without breaking them up. Divide the dough into twelve equal-sized pieces. Using your flat palms, roll each piece on a lightly floured work surface into a 20 cm (8 inch) length and tie in a loose knot, tucking the ends underneath. Butter a baking tray and lift the rolls onto the tray. Cover with a damp tea towel and allow to rise again until nearly doubled in size. Towards the end of this time, preheat the oven to hot 220°C (425°F/Gas 7).

Five Mix the beaten egg yolk with a tablespoon of water and a pinch of sugar and salt, then gently brush over the proved rolls. Bake for 10–15 minutes, or until golden brown and hollow sounding when tapped on the base. Remove from the tray and cool on a wire rack.

CHEF'S TIP *To make the pumpkin purée yourself, steam or boil 200 g (6½ oz) peeled and cubed pumpkin until tender. Mash with a potato masher or purée the pumpkin in a food processor.*

about pumpkins...

Depending on where you are living, 'pumpkin' is a changeable term. In some countries, the name applies only to the traditional round vegetables, and in others it refers to all other kinds of squash as well. Most winter pumpkin or squash can be used for this recipe but make sure they have a hard flesh and sweet flavour.

Bagels

Whether plain or sprinkled with sesame or poppy seeds, these yeasted bread rolls, characteristic of Jewish baking, are delicious served warm with butter. The traditional shiny, hard crust is achieved by boiling the bagels before baking them.

Preparation time 50 minutes
+ 1 hour proving
Total cooking time 25 minutes
Makes 12 large or 24 small bagels

30 g (1 oz) fresh yeast
or 15 g (½ oz) dried yeast
2 tablespoons oil
2 teaspoons salt
50 g (1¾ oz) caster sugar
500 g (1 lb) strong or plain flour
1 egg, beaten, for glazing

One Dissolve the yeast in 250 ml (8 fl oz) lukewarm water, then add the oil.

Two Combine the salt, sugar and flour, then make a well in the centre. Add the yeast mixture and gradually incorporate the flour until a dough forms. Continue working the dough until the sides of the bowl come clean. Knead the dough for 10 minutes, then form it into a ball and place in the bottom of the bowl. Cover with a moist towel and set aside in a warm place to rise for about 30–45 minutes, or until doubled in size. Line two baking trays with baking paper.

Three Once the dough has doubled in size, punch it down and knead for 8–10 minutes, then divide into 12 or 24 pieces. Roll them into tight balls. Poke a finger through the centre and gently enlarge the hole until the dough resembles a doughnut. Place on a floured baking tray, cover with a moist towel and allow to rise a second time for 15 minutes. Preheat the oven to moderately hot 200°C (400°F/Gas 6).

Four In the meantime, bring a pan of water to a simmer. Cook the bagels in the water for 1 minute on each side, then remove and place on the lined baking trays. Allow to cool for 5 minutes. Brush each bagel with beaten egg and bake for 20–25 minutes, or until golden brown.

CHEF'S TIP *Once the bagels have been brushed with the egg, they can be sprinkled with poppy seeds or sesame seeds before baking.*

Fougasse

Traditionally eaten in Provence on Christmas Eve as one of thirteen desserts symbolising Christ and his disciples, each region in France now has its own version of this oldest of French breads.

Preparation time 40 minutes
+ proving (about 4 hours)
Total cooking time 10 minutes
Makes 6 x 200 g (6½ oz) rolls

15 g (½ oz) fresh yeast
or 2 teaspoons dried yeast
680 g (1 lb 6 oz) white bread flour
1½ teaspoons salt
125 g (4 oz) sugar
3 eggs, beaten
grated rind and juice of 1 large orange
2 tablespoons brandy
90 g (3 oz) butter, softened
90 g (3 oz) good-quality candied peel,
chopped
30 g (1 oz) butter, melted
2 tablespoons orange flower water

One Prepare the yeast with 90 ml (3 fl oz) water following the method in the Chef's techniques on page 550.

Two Sponge the dough by sieving the flour into a large mixing bowl, adding the salt and sugar and following the method in the Chef's techniques on page 550. In a small bowl, mix together the eggs, orange rind and juice and brandy, pour into the well after the yeast has risen and stir to form a soft dough. Add the butter, squeezing and folding it into the dough until fully incorporated. Turn the dough out onto a lightly floured work surface and knead for about 10 minutes, or until smooth and elastic (see Chef's techniques, page 551). Alternatively, knead in an electric mixer on medium speed for about 5 minutes.

Three Return the dough to a clean, lightly oiled bowl and turn once to coat the surface in oil. Cover with a clean, damp tea towel and allow to prove at room temperature until doubled in size (the proving time will depend on the temperature of your kitchen).

Four Turn the dough out onto a lightly floured work surface and gently knead in the candied peel for about 5 minutes, or until the dough is smooth and the peel is evenly distributed. Divide the dough into six equal-sized pieces and roll each one on a lightly floured work surface into a 15 x 20 cm (6 x 8 inch) oval, 1 cm (½ inch) thick. Place the fougasse on a board and use a very sharp knife to cut slashes through to the board, beginning in the centre of one side of the dough and working outwards to give shell-like grooves. Butter two baking trays and lift the fougasse onto the trays, allowing plenty of space between each one. Cover with a damp tea towel and allow to rise again until nearly doubled in size. Towards the end of this time, preheat the oven to moderately hot 200°C (400°F/Gas 6).

Five Brush the proved fougasse with half the melted butter and bake for 7–10 minutes, or until golden brown. Remove from the oven and, while the bread is still warm, brush with the remaining butter and the orange flower water. Remove from the tray and cool on a wire rack.

LE CORDON BLEU COMPLETE COOK

Challah

An impressive four-strand plaited loaf, traditionally made as a Jewish Sabbath offering, with a light, creamy inside and a rich flavour.

Preparation time *20 minutes + proving*
(about 2 hours 45 minutes)
Total cooking time *40 minutes*
Makes 1 x 1.3 kg (2 lb 10 oz) loaf

30 g (1 oz) fresh yeast
or 1 tablespoon dried yeast
1 tablespoon sugar
750 g (1½ lb) white bread flour
1 teaspoon salt
90 g (3 oz) butter, softened
3 eggs, beaten
2 beaten egg yolks, to glaze
1–2 tablespoons poppy seeds

One Prepare the yeast with 90 ml (3 fl oz) water and 1 teaspoon of the sugar following the method in the Chef's techniques on page 550.

Two Sieve the flour and salt into a large mixing bowl and make a well in the centre. Add the yeast mixture, the remaining sugar, butter, eggs and about 250 ml (8 fl oz) lukewarm water to the well. Using your hand with fingers slightly apart, gradually draw the flour into the liquid. Continue until all the flour has been incorporated and the dough comes together to form a soft ball. The dough should be soft and hold its shape without being sticky (you may need to add a little more flour or water). Turn the dough out onto a lightly floured work surface and knead for about 10 minutes, or until smooth and elastic (see Chef's techniques, page 551). Alternatively, knead in an electric mixer on medium speed for about 5 minutes.

Three Return the dough to a clean, lightly oiled bowl and turn once to coat the surface in oil. Cover with a clean, damp tea towel and allow to prove at room temperature until doubled in size (the proving time will depend on the temperature of your kitchen).

Four Turn the dough out onto a lightly floured work surface and knead for 1 minute. Cover with a clean, damp tea towel and set aside for 5 minutes, then divide the dough into four pieces. Roll each piece on a lightly floured work surface into 50 cm (20 inch) long sausages. Pinch the four strands together firmly at one end and place on the work surface in front of you with the join at the top. Starting with the left outside strand, take it under the two middle strands and then back over the top of the nearest one. Repeat with the outside right strand. Continue this sequence until the loaf has been plaited all the way to the end, then seal the ends firmly and neatly.

Five Butter a baking tray and lift the plait onto the tray. Cover with a damp tea towel and allow to rise again until nearly doubled in size. Towards the end of this time, preheat the oven to hot 220°C (425°F/Gas 7).

Six Mix a tablespoon of water with the egg yolks and brush the proved loaf with half the mixture. Bake for 10 minutes, then brush again with the yolk and sprinkle liberally with the poppy seeds. Return to the oven and bake, covering the top with foil if the loaf starts to brown too much, for a further 25–30 minutes, or until hollow sounding when tapped on the base. Remove from the tray and cool on a wire rack.

Hot cross buns

The irresistible aroma of these spiced buns, especially once they are toasted and buttered, means that hot cross buns will be baked all year round, not just for Easter.

Preparation time 25 minutes + proving
(about 2 hours 30 minutes
or overnight)
Total cooking time 20 minutes
Makes 16

30 g (1 oz) fresh yeast
or 1 tablespoon dried yeast
180 ml (5¾ fl oz) milk
500 g (1 lb) white bread flour
2 teaspoons mixed spice
60 g (2 oz) sugar
2 teaspoons salt
2 eggs, beaten
120 g (4 oz) butter, softened
120 g (4 oz) sultanas

TOPPING AND GLAZE
4 tablespoons plain flour
6 tablespoons sugar
4 tablespoons milk
½ teaspoon mixed spice

One Prepare the yeast with the milk following the method in the Chef's techniques on page 550.

Two Sieve the flour, mixed spice, sugar and salt into a large mixing bowl and make a well in the centre. Add the yeast mixture and egg to the well and gradually bring the mixture together with your hands, or use an electric mixer fitted with a dough hook on slow speed, until a soft dough is formed. Turn the dough out onto a lightly floured work surface and knead for about 10 minutes, or until smooth and elastic (see Chef's techniques, page 551). Knead the softened butter into the dough until it is fully incorporated and the dough is silky and soft.

Three Return the dough to a clean, lightly oiled bowl and turn once to coat the surface in oil. Cover with a clean, damp tea towel and allow to prove at room temperature until doubled in size (the proving time will depend on the temperature of your kitchen) or leave overnight in the refrigerator.

Four Turn the dough out onto a lightly floured work surface and knead in the sultanas until they are just evenly distributed. Divide into sixteen equal-sized pieces and roll each piece on a lightly floured work surface in the hollow of your hand until it forms a round and smooth ball. Butter a baking tray and place the buns slightly apart on the tray. Cover with a damp tea towel and allow to rise again until nearly doubled in size (the buns will be touching when they are ready). Towards the end of this time, preheat the oven to moderately hot 200°C (400°F/Gas 6).

Five To make the topping and glaze, mix together the flour, 4 tablespoons of the sugar and 2–3 tablespoons of water to form a smooth, thick paste. Place in a piping bag fitted with a small plain nozzle and pipe the paste across the proved buns in continuous straight lines so that each bun has a cross on top.

Six Bake the buns for 10–15 minutes, or until golden and hollow sounding when tapped on the base. Meanwhile, heat the milk, remaining sugar and mixed spice in a small pan until the sugar has dissolved. Brush this glaze over the buns as they come out of the oven. Remove from the tray and cool on a wire rack, then brush again with glaze. Serve plain or split and toasted with some butter.

LE CORDON BLEU COMPLETE COOK

Stollen

This sweet German Christmas bread is usually baked several weeks in advance to allow the flavour of the spices to mature. When cooked, it is liberally brushed with butter for a delicious crust.

Preparation time 1 hour + 4 hours proving + overnight marinating
Total cooking time 45 minutes
Makes 2 stollen (each cuts into 16 slices)

1 teaspoon ground mixed spice
155 g (5 oz) chopped mixed peel
45 g (1½ oz) glacé cherries, quartered
60 g (2 oz) flaked almonds
2 tablespoons rum
grated rind of 2 small lemons
155 g (5 oz) raisins
90 ml (3 fl oz) milk
30 g (1 oz) fresh yeast
or 15 g (½ oz) dried yeast
375 g (12 oz) plain flour
55 g (1¾ oz) caster sugar
185 g (6 oz) unsalted butter
1 egg, beaten
250 g (8 oz) ready-made marzipan
1 egg and 1 egg yolk, beaten,
for brushing
30 g (1 oz) unsalted butter, melted
icing sugar, to dust

One Mix the spice, peel, cherries, almonds, rum, lemon rind and raisins together. Cover and leave overnight.

Two Put the milk in a small pan and heat until tepid. Pour into a bowl and dissolve the yeast in it. Sift 125 g (4 oz) of the plain flour and 1½ teaspoons of the sugar into a bowl. Make a well in the centre and pour in the yeast mixture. Mix to a smooth paste, then cover with plastic wrap. Leave in a warm place for 40 minutes, or until doubled in size.

Three Using your fingertips, rub the butter into the remaining flour until the mixture resembles fine breadcrumbs, then stir in the remaining sugar and ½ teaspoon salt. Pour in the beaten egg and mix well.

Four Add the proved yeast mixture to the dough and mix until smooth. Add the marinated ingredients and stir in, then turn the mixture out onto a lightly floured work surface and knead to a smooth elastic dough. Place the dough in a large lightly floured bowl, cover with a damp cloth and prove in a warm place for 2–2½ hours, or until doubled in size.

Five Brush two large baking trays with melted butter. Cut the marzipan in half and roll out both halves on a surface lightly dusted with icing sugar to form two 20 x 2.5 cm (8 x 1 inch) cylinders.

Six Turn the dough out onto a lightly floured surface and knead gently for 2 minutes, or until smooth once more, then divide in half. Roll each piece into a 22 x 25 cm (9 x 10 inch) rectangle and place a cylinder of marzipan down the centre of each. Sprinkle with a few drops of water and close the dough around the marzipan, sealing the edges by pressing them together. Place on the prepared baking trays, seam side down, cover with a damp cloth and prove for 50 minutes, or until doubled in size. Preheat the oven to moderate 180°C (350°F/Gas 4). Lightly brush with the beaten egg and bake for 35–45 minutes, or until well risen and golden.

Seven Remove from the oven and, while the stollen is still warm, brush with the melted butter and dust liberally with icing sugar. Transfer to a wire rack to cool completely, then slice to serve.

CHEF'S TIPS *This recipe makes two stollen, which is perfect if you are baking for a large Christmas gathering. Otherwise, wrap one in plastic wrap, then foil, and freeze for up to 3 months.*

A stollen makes a lovely Christmas gift, wrapped in cellophane and tied with ribbon.

Panettone

*Individually made and wrapped in cellophane and ribbons, this
Milanese Christmas speciality is a wonderful gift. Good-quality crystallised
fruit will taste much better than ready-chopped candied peel.*

*Preparation time 25 minutes + proving
(about 4 hours or overnight) + 1 hour
or overnight soaking
Total cooking time 45 minutes
Makes 6 x 155 g (5 oz) loaves*

60 g (2 oz) golden raisins
60 g (2 oz) mixed candied fruits,
finely chopped
135 ml (4½ fl oz) Cointreau
1 tablespoon orange flower water
30 g (1 oz) fresh yeast
or 1 tablespoon dried yeast
90 g (3 oz) sugar
500 g (1 lb) white bread flour
1 teaspoon mixed spice
1 teaspoon salt
150 ml (5 fl oz) milk, lukewarm
120 g (4 oz) butter, softened
2 eggs, beaten
60 g (2 oz) macadamia nuts, chopped

One Prepare six tins, about 10 cm (4 inches) high and 7 cm (2¾ inches) in diameter (washed baked bean tins are ideal) by brushing with melted butter and lining the base and sides with greaseproof paper. Allow a 4 cm (1½ inch) collar to extend above the rims of the tins. Brush a second time with butter to smooth down the edges of the paper.

Two Place the raisins, candied fruits, Cointreau and orange flower water in a small bowl and leave to soak for at least one hour, or overnight if possible.

Three Prepare the yeast with 2 tablespoons warm water and a pinch of the sugar following the method in the Chef's techniques on page 550.

Four Sieve the flour, mixed spice, salt and all but 2 tablespoons of the remaining sugar into a large mixing bowl and make a well in the centre. Drain the soaked fruits, reserving the Cointreau soaking liquid, and add to the well. Add the warm milk, butter, eggs, nuts and yeast mixture. Gradually bring the mixture together with your hands, or use an electric mixer fitted with a dough hook on slow speed, until a soft dough is formed. Turn the dough out onto a lightly floured work surface and knead for about 10 minutes, or until smooth and elastic (see Chef's techniques, page 551).

Five Return the dough to a clean, lightly oiled bowl and turn once to coat the surface in oil. Cover with a clean, damp

tea towel and allow to prove at room temperature until doubled in size (the proving time will depend on the temperature of your kitchen) or leave overnight in the refrigerator.

Six Turn the dough out onto a lightly floured work surface and knead gently for 2–3 minutes. Divide the dough into six equal-sized pieces and roll each piece of dough out on a lightly floured work surface into tight balls. If any fruit or nuts break through the surface of the dough, remove these and press into the base of the balls to stop them burning. Place in the prepared tins, put on a baking tray and cover with a damp tea towel. Allow to rise again until the dough has risen nearly to the top of the tins. Towards the end of this time, preheat the oven to moderate 180°C (350°F/Gas 4).

Seven Bake the proved panettone for 30–40 minutes, or until golden brown and hollow sounding when tapped on the base, covering with a piece of foil after the first 15 minutes.

Eight Meanwhile, prepare a glaze by topping up the reserved soaking liquid from the fruit with water, if necessary, until you have 60 ml (2 fl oz) liquid. Heat in a pan with the last 2 tablespoons of sugar until the sugar has dissolved completely. Brush the baked panettone twice all over with the glaze while still warm, then remove from their tins and cool on a wire rack. The panettone can be stored in an airtight container for up to one month.

LE CORDON BLEU ✤ COMPLETE COOK

English muffins

*English muffins were originally lightly split around
the edge with a fork, then toasted on both sides,
pulled open and spread thickly with butter.*

*Preparation time 30 minutes
+ 1 hour 20 minutes proving
Total cooking time 15 minutes
Makes 12*

10 g (1/4 oz) fresh yeast
or 2 teaspoons dried yeast
400 g (12 3/4 oz) strong or plain flour
1 1/2 teaspoons salt
1 teaspoon caster sugar
1 teaspoon softened unsalted butter

One Gently heat 225 ml (7 1/4 fl oz) water
in a small pan until it feels warm, not
hot, to the touch. Remove from the heat
and stir in the yeast until it is dissolved.

Two Sift the flour, salt and sugar into a
large bowl, make a well in the centre
and pour in the yeast mixture. Melt the
butter, cool slightly and pour into the
well. Using your hand with fingers
slightly spread apart, gradually bring the
flour into the liquid and mix well. Turn
out onto a floured work surface and
knead for 2–3 minutes, or until smooth,
following the method on page 551.

Three Place the dough in a clean bowl
that has been sprinkled with a little
flour. Cover with plastic wrap and leave
in a warm place for about 1 hour, or
until doubled in size.

Four Sprinkle a baking tray with flour.
Preheat the oven to hot 210°C
(415°F/Gas 6–7). Turn the dough out
onto a lightly floured work surface and
knead until smooth. Roll the dough to
about 1 cm (1/2 inch) thick and, using a
7 cm (2 3/4 inch) plain round cutter
dipped in flour, cut out rounds and place
them on the baking tray. Re-roll any
leftover dough and repeat.

Five Cover the tray with plastic wrap
and set aside in a warm place for
15–20 minutes, or until the muffins have
risen slightly. Bake for 15 minutes,
turning halfway through the cooking
time. Remove from the tray and cool on
a wire rack.

CHEF'S TIP *These muffins can also be
cooked on top of the stove using a
griddle or dry pan over low heat. Turn
over as each side becomes lightly
browned and is cooked through.*

Crumpets

Light and airy crumpets toasted on a fork in front of an open fire have always been a tea-time delight, but they also make a special treat for breakfast and can be toasted under the grill or in a toaster.

Preparation time 10 minutes
+ 1 hour 50 minutes standing
Total cooking time 45 minutes
Makes 8 crumpets

375 ml (12 fl oz) milk
15 g (1/2 oz) fresh yeast
or 7 g (1/4 oz) dried yeast
375 g (12 oz) plain flour
1/2 teaspoon salt
1/2 teaspoon bicarbonate of soda
oil or clarified butter (see page 520),
for cooking

One Pour the milk into a saucepan and heat until warm, remove from the heat and stir in the yeast.

Two Sift the flour and the salt into a bowl and make a well in the centre. Pour in a little of the milk mixture and beat with a whisk, electric beaters or your hand to bring in a little of the flour, mixing to a smooth paste. Repeat until all the liquid has been added and all the flour drawn in, then beat until smooth. Cover with a plate or plastic wrap and leave in a warm place for approximately 1–1 1/2 hours, or until doubled in size and full of bubbles. Dissolve the bicarbonate of soda in 200 ml (6 1/2 fl oz) water. Add it to the batter and mix well. Cover and set aside for 15–20 minutes.

Three On the top of the stove, heat a griddle pan or a wide heavy-based frying pan to medium heat and brush with a little oil or clarified butter. Lightly butter or oil the inside of two or more 9–10 cm (3 1/2–4 inch) pastry cutters or crumpet rings, and put them on the pan.

Four Pour in the crumpet batter to a thickness of 1 cm (1/2 inch), lower the heat

to very low and cook for 7–8 minutes. The bubbles rise as the crumpets cook (see page 549). The crumpets are ready to turn over when the top has dried out enough to form a skin. Loosen the rings, turn the crumpets over and brown the second side for 1–2 minutes. Remove and cool on a wire rack, covered with a tea towel to prevent drying out. Repeat with the remaining batter as the rings become free. If the batter thickens on standing, thin it with a little water.

Five To serve the crumpets, preheat a grill to the highest setting and toast the crumpets well on the first cooked side, then brown more lightly on the second side. Spread the lightly grilled side generously with butter and serve the crumpets immediately.

CHEF'S TIP *If you have any fresh yeast left over, it can be stored in the refrigerator, lightly wrapped in grease-proof paper, for up to 2 weeks.*

Pikelets

These small thick pancakes are known in England as Scotch pancakes
and are served hot and buttered with a fruity
or a sweet accompaniment (pictured top right).

Preparation time 8 minutes
+ 1 hour refrigeration
Total cooking time 15 minutes
Makes 12

1 egg, beaten
50 g (1³/4 oz) caster sugar
25 g (³/4 oz) unsalted butter
280 ml (9 fl oz) milk
225 g (7¹/4 oz) plain flour
¹/2 teaspoon bicarbonate of soda
¹/2 teaspoon baking powder
¹/2 teaspoon cream of tartar

One In a small bowl, beat the egg with half the sugar. In a small pan, melt the butter with the rest of the sugar. Remove from the heat and add the milk and 1 teaspoon cold water to the pan.

Two Sift together the flour, bicarbonate of soda, baking powder, cream of tartar and a pinch of salt into a large bowl. Make a well in the centre. Pour the egg mixture and butter mixture into the well and beat with a wooden spoon or balloon whisk until the dry ingredients have disappeared and a smooth batter is formed. Cover and refrigerate for 1 hour or overnight.

Three Brush a large non-stick frying pan or griddle with melted butter and place over high heat. Using 2 tablespoons of mixture for each, drop the pikelets into the pan and cook for 1 minute, or until bubbles rise to the surface. Turn them over and cook for 1 minute, or until lightly golden. Serve immediately, or keep warm, wrapped in foil, in a low oven.

CHEF'S TIP *Serve with butter, lemon juice and sugar, maple syrup or fresh fruit conserves.*

Waffles

Waffles, made from a light sweetened batter, have a honeycombed surface
ideal for holding large quantities of sweet runny syrup or honey for those
with a particularly sweet tooth (pictured bottom right).

Preparation time 5 minutes
Total cooking time 5 minutes per waffle
Makes about 8–10 waffles

250 g (8 oz) plain flour
1 tablespoon caster sugar
1¹/2 teaspoons baking powder
¹/2 teaspoon salt
375 ml (12 fl oz) milk or buttermilk
30 g (1 oz) unsalted butter, melted
2 eggs

One Sift together the flour, sugar, baking powder and salt into a large bowl.

Two In a separate bowl, combine the milk, melted butter and eggs. Gradually add to the flour mixture and mix until well combined.

Three Preheat a waffle iron according to the manufacturer's instructions. Once hot, lightly brush with oil. Pour in the recommended amount of batter and cook until golden brown in colour and crispy. Serve with whipped butter and honey or maple syrup.

LE CORDON BLEU ✠ COMPLETE COOK

Danish pastries

Although this recipe may be time-consuming, nothing quite matches the taste of this freshly made, rich and flaky yeast dough.

Preparation time 3 hours + refrigeration
Total cooking time 30 minutes
Makes 28

1 kg (2 lb) strong or plain flour
90 g (3 oz) caster sugar
20 g (3/4 oz) salt
30 g (1 oz) fresh yeast
or 15 g (1/2 oz) dried yeast
700 ml (231/4 fl oz) warm milk
450 g (141/4 oz) unsalted butter, chilled
1 egg, beaten
50 g (13/4 oz) flaked almonds
icing sugar, to dust

PASSIONFRUIT CREAM FILLING
30 g (1 oz) caster sugar
2 large egg yolks
2 teaspoons plain flour
2 teaspoons cornflour
125 ml (4 fl oz) passionfruit juice
or pulp

OR

ORANGE CREAM FILLING
30 g (1 oz) caster sugar
2 large egg yolks
2 teaspoons plain flour
2 teaspoons cornflour
125 ml (4 fl oz) orange juice

One Butter and flour a baking tray. Sift the flour, sugar and salt into a large bowl and make a well in the centre. Cream the yeast with 50 ml (13/4 fl oz) of the milk. Stir in the remaining milk and pour into the well in the dry ingredients. Draw in the flour with your fingers until the mixture forms a soft dough. Knead the dough on a floured surface until it is smooth and elastic. Cover with plastic wrap in a bowl and chill for 10 minutes.

Two To make the passionfruit cream filling, place the sugar, egg yolks, flour and cornflour in a medium bowl and mix well. Bring the juice to the boil in a medium saucepan. Add a little to the sugar mixture, stir to blend, then add the sugar mixture to the saucepan. Bring the mixture to the boil, stirring continuously, and cook for 1 minute. Cover and leave to cool.

Three To make the orange cream filling, proceed exactly as for the passionfruit filling above, using the orange juice instead of the passionfruit juice.

Four On a floured surface, roll out the dough into a rectangle three times as long as it is wide, and 3 mm (1/8 inch) thick. Tap and roll out the butter within two long sheets of plastic wrap into a rectangle, the same width as, but two thirds the length of, the dough. Unwrap and lay the butter on the top two thirds of the dough. Fold the exposed third of the dough up over the butter and fold the top third down.

Five Turn the dough to look like a book, with the binding on the left, and roll again into a rectangle and fold into three. Repeat twice, wrapping in plastic wrap and chilling for 20 minutes between each roll.

Six On a floured surface, roll the dough into a square or rectangle 3 mm (1/8 inch) thick. Cut into 10 x 13 cm (4 x 5 inch) rectangles and place on the baking tray.

Seven To make the Danish pastries, preheat the oven to moderately hot 200°C (400°F/Gas 6). Spoon the filling into a piping bag and pipe into the centre of each pastry. Draw up the corners and press together firmly. Set aside in a warm place to prove for 30 minutes. Brush with the egg, avoiding the sides of the pastry as this will prevent the dough from rising as it cooks. Sprinkle with a few flaked almonds and bake for 15–20 minutes, or until golden. Cool on wire racks and dust with sifted icing sugar, if desired.

Orange and poppy seed muffins

Countless poppy seeds are scattered liberally throughout these muffins, filling them with a delightful flavour and delicate crunch.

Preparation time 20 minutes
Total cooking time 20 minutes
Makes 10 muffins

300 g (10 oz) self-raising flour
1/4 teaspoon baking powder
3 tablespoons caster sugar
2 tablespoons poppy seeds
1 1/2 tablespoons finely grated orange rind
100 g (3 1/4 oz) unsalted butter
105 g (3 1/2 oz) apricot jam
2 eggs
80 ml (2 3/4 fl oz) buttermilk
icing sugar, to dust

One Preheat the oven to moderately hot 200°C (400°F/Gas 6). Grease a 12-hole 125 ml (4 fl oz) muffin tin with melted butter or oil. Sift the flour, baking powder and sugar into a large bowl. Stir in the poppy seeds and grated orange rind, and make a well in the centre.

Two Melt the butter and jam in a small saucepan over low heat, stirring until smooth. Remove from the heat. Mix the eggs and buttermilk in a small jug.

Three Add the butter and egg mixtures to the well in the dry ingredients. Stir with a metal spoon until the mixture is just combined. Do not overmix—the mixture should be lumpy.

Four Spoon the mixture into 10 holes of the tin, filling each hole about three-quarters full. Bake for 12–15 minutes, or until a skewer comes out clean when inserted into the centre of a muffin. Leave the muffins in the tin for 5 minutes before carefully lifting out onto a wire rack to cool. Dust lightly with sifted icing sugar before serving.

Banana and ginger muffins

*A subtle combination of banana and ginger,
enhanced with the golden nectar of honey,
giving a lovely rich muffin.*

Preparation time 20 minutes
Total cooking time 25 minutes
Makes 12 muffins

300 g (10 oz) self-raising flour
1 teaspoon ground ginger
115 g (3¾ oz) soft brown sugar
*75 g (2½ oz) glacé ginger,
finely chopped*
60 g (2 oz) unsalted butter
2 tablespoons honey
125 ml (4 fl oz) milk
2 eggs
*240 g (7½ oz) banana, mashed
(see Chef's tip)*

TOPPING
125 g (4 oz) cream cheese, softened
2 tablespoons icing sugar
2 teaspoons finely grated lemon rind

glacé ginger, to decorate

One Preheat the oven to hot 210°C (415°F/Gas 6–7). Lightly brush a 12-hole 125 ml (4 fl oz) muffin tin with melted butter or oil. Sift the flour and ground ginger together into a large mixing bowl. Stir in the brown sugar and glacé ginger, and make a well in the centre of the mixture.

Two Place the butter and honey in a small pan and stir over low heat until melted. Remove from the heat. Whisk the milk and eggs together in a jug.

Three Add the butter mixture, egg mixture and the banana to the well in the dry ingredients. Stir with a metal spoon until just combined. Do not overmix—the mixture should be lumpy. Spoon the mixture into the muffin tin, filling each hole about three-quarters

full. Bake for 20 minutes, or until a skewer comes out clean when inserted into the centre of a muffin. Leave the muffins in the tin for 5 minutes, then lift out onto a wire rack to cool completely before spreading with the topping.

Four To make the topping, beat the cream cheese, icing sugar and grated

lemon rind together until light and creamy. Spread onto the muffins and decorate with thin slices of glacé ginger.

CHEF'S TIP *You will need about 2 bananas for this recipe. Make sure they are very ripe (even musy over-ripe bananas are fine for cooking) so give the muffins a sweet full flavour.*

Blueberry muffins

These classic muffins can be made with either fresh or frozen blueberries and are particularly good served warm for breakfast or morning tea. Try substituting raspberries or blackberries or a combination of the two, gently folding them in to keep them whole.

Preparation time 15 minutes
Total cooking time 30 minutes
Makes 6 large muffins

375 g (12 oz) self-raising flour
75 g (2¹/2 oz) plain flour
115 g (3³/4 oz) soft brown sugar
150 g (5 oz) fresh or frozen blueberries
(see Chef's tip)
2 eggs
250 ml (8 fl oz) milk
1 teaspoon vanilla extract or
essence
125 g (4 oz) unsalted butter, melted
icing sugar, to dust

One Preheat the oven to hot 210°C (415°F/Gas 6–7). Brush a 6-hole 250 ml (8 fl oz) muffin tin with melted butter or oil. Sift the flours into a large mixing bowl, stir in the sugar and blueberries and make a well in the centre.

Two Whisk the eggs, milk and vanilla together in a jug, and add to the well in the dry ingredients. Add the butter, and stir with a metal spoon until just combined. Do not overmix—the mixture should be lumpy.

Three Spoon the mixture into the muffin tin, filling each hole about three-quarters full. Bake the muffins for 30 minutes, or until a skewer comes out clean when inserted into the centre of a muffin. Leave the muffins in the tin for 5 minutes before lifting out onto a wire rack to cool. Dust generously with sifted icing sugar before serving.

CHEF'S TIP *If using frozen blueberries, use them straight from the freezer. Do not allow them to thaw, or they will discolour the muffin mixture.*

Chocolate chip cookies

These cookies, originally created at the Toll House Inn in Massachusetts in the 1920s, became so popular that small round chocolate pieces, known as 'chips', were marketed especially for them.

Preparation time 20 minutes
Total cooking time 20 minutes per tray
Makes 24

115 g (3³/4 oz) unsalted butter, softened
100 g (3¹/4 oz) soft brown sugar
100 g (3¹/4 oz) caster sugar
1 egg, lightly beaten
¹/4 teaspoon vanilla extract or essence
155 g (5 oz) plain flour
pinch of baking powder
100 g (3¹/4 oz) ground almonds
150 g (5 oz) chocolate chips

One Preheat the oven to moderate 180°C (350°F/Gas 4). Brush two baking trays with melted butter and refrigerate until set.

Two Using a wooden spoon or an electric whisk, cream the butter and sugars until light and fluffy. Gradually add the egg and vanilla, beating well after each addition.

Three Sift the flour, baking powder and ground almonds together. Fold half into the creamed mixture. When almost incorporated, add the rest of the sifted mixture, then add the chocolate chips as you fold.

Four Divide into 24 portions and roll into balls. Place the balls, spaced well apart, on the two prepared trays and flatten lightly. Bake for 15–20 minutes, or until golden brown. Remove from the tray while still hot and transfer to a cooling rack. Repeat with the remaining mixture, preparing the trays as instructed in step 1. Store in an airtight container.

Rum babas

These spongy yeast cakes soaked in a rum syrup are said to have been named by a Polish king after his storybook hero, Ali Baba. Here they are served with a vanilla-flavoured Chantilly cream and fresh fruit.

Preparation time 1 hour + 1 hour proving
Total cooking time 30 minutes
Serves 8

BABA DOUGH
250 g (8 oz) plain or bread flour
1 teaspoon salt
1 teaspoon caster sugar
15 g (½ oz) fresh yeast
or 7 g (¼ oz) dried yeast
80 ml (2¾ fl oz) milk
3 eggs, beaten
60 g (2 oz) raisins, soaked
in 1 tablespoon rum
45 g (1½ oz) melted butter, cooled

SYRUP
500 ml (16 fl oz) water
200 g (6½ oz) caster sugar
rind of 1 lemon
1 cardamom pod
2 bay leaves
½ orange, roughly chopped
2 tablespoons dark rum

CHANTILLY CREAM
315 g (10 oz) thick (double) cream
30 g (1 oz) icing sugar
½ teaspoon vanilla extract or essence

3 tablespoons apricot jam
fresh fruit, such as strawberries and raspberries, to decorate

One Brush eight individual dariole moulds or a 1 litre ring mould with melted butter, then dust with some flour and tap out the excess.

Two To make the baba dough, sieve the flour, salt and sugar into a large bowl and make a well in the centre. Place the yeast in a bowl. In a small pan, warm the milk until tepid, then add to the yeast. Stir to dissolve, then mix in 1 tablespoon flour and set aside until foamy. When foamy, add to the beaten eggs and pour into the well in the flour. Prepare the baba dough following the method in the Chef's techniques on page 549. Preheat the oven to hot 210°C (415°F/Gas 6–7).

Three Bake the rum babas for 12 minutes (or 25 minutes for a large one), or until golden. Loosen the babas and turn out of the tins onto a wire rack to cool. Prick all over with a fine skewer.

Four To make the syrup, gently heat all the ingredients except the rum together in a pan, stirring to dissolve the sugar, then bring to the boil and boil for 15 minutes to reduce the syrup and thicken slightly. Remove the pan from the stove and leave for 5 minutes to infuse the flavours. Strain, discard the flavourings, return the syrup to the pan and reheat. Remove from the stove and stir in the rum. Pour the syrup into a shallow dish and roll the cold babas in the hot syrup. Place on a wire rack over a plate to drip off excess syrup and to cool completely.

Five To make the Chantilly cream, pour the cream into a bowl and add the icing sugar and vanilla. Using a balloon whisk or electric beaters, whip the cream until it just forms soft peaks that hold as the whisk is lifted from the bowl.

Six In a small pan, heat the apricot jam with 1 tablespoon water. When the mixture has melted and begins to boil, sieve it into a small bowl and, while still hot, brush it over the babas, then leave to cool.

Seven Serve the babas with the Chantilly cream and fruit. If you have made a large baba, fill it with cream and fruit.

about rum...

Light and dark rum have different flavours when used in cooking. Dark rum still contains natural flavours from the sugarcane molasses and so has a stronger taste. Light rum has had all the pigmentation and impurities filtered out.

Shortbread

Shortbread can be made with plain flour alone, however, the texture is greatly enhanced by using a combination of flours. Adding rice flour produces a light result, while semolina gives a crunchy texture.

Preparation time 10 minutes
+ 10 minutes refrigeration
Total cooking time 25 minutes
Makes 8

120 g (4 oz) unsalted butter,
at room temperature
60 g (2 oz) caster sugar
120 g (4 oz) plain flour
60 g (2 oz) rice flour or fine semolina,
sifted twice
1½ tablespoons caster sugar,
for dusting

One Preheat the oven to moderate 180°C (350°F/Gas 4).

Two Beat the butter in a wide bowl until smooth. Gradually beat in the sugar. Add the plain flour and rice flour or semolina and stir with a knife until the mixture is well blended.

Three Press the mixture into an 18 cm (7 inch) round loose-bottomed shallow tart tin. Make sure that the mixture is level and prick the surface evenly with a fork. Place in the refrigerator to chill for 10 minutes.

Four Sprinkle the surface of the shortbread with the extra caster sugar and bake for 25 minutes, or until light golden brown.

Five While the shortbread is still hot, carefully remove the outer tin, and cut the shortbread into eight wedges with a large sharp knife. Don't separate the pieces as this will make them dry out. After 5 minutes, the shortbread will be firmer—transfer to a wire rack to cool and sprinkle the top with a little more caster sugar.

CHEF'S TIPS *The shortbread may rise or wrinkle slightly during baking—this is quite normal.*

The shortbread will keep for up to a week if stored in an airtight container or wrapped in foil.

Viennese fingers

These wonderful chocolate-dipped biscuits simply melt in the mouth.

Preparation time 25 minutes
Total cooking time 10 minutes per tray
Makes 16

120 g (4 oz) unsalted butter,
at room temperature
2–3 drops vanilla extract or essence
1 teaspoon finely grated lemon rind
50 g (1¾ oz) icing sugar
1 egg, lightly beaten
150 g (5 oz) plain flour
200 g (6½ oz) good-quality dark
chocolate, chopped

One Brush two baking trays with melted butter and refrigerate. Preheat the oven to moderately hot 200°C (400°F/Gas 6).

Two Using a wooden spoon or electric whisk, cream the butter, vanilla, lemon rind and icing sugar until light and fluffy. Gradually add the egg, a little at a time, beating well after each addition. Sift in the flour and stir to mix.

Three Spoon the mixture into a piping bag with a 1 cm (½ inch) star nozzle. Pipe enough 6–8 cm (2½–3 inch) lengths to fill the prepared baking trays, spacing them slightly apart. Bake for 7–10 minutes, or until golden brown. Cool on a wire rack. Repeat with the remaining mixture, preparing the cooled trays as instructed in step 1.

Four Half-fill a pan with water and bring to the boil. Remove from the heat, place the chocolate in a heatproof bowl and set over the steaming water. Stir until the chocolate melts. Dip one end of each biscuit in the chocolate and cool on a tray covered with baking paper.

CHEF'S TIP *For a variation, pipe the biscuits into rosettes about 4 cm (1½ inches) wide (see Chef's techniques, page 555). When cooked, divide into pairs. Spread the bottom of one with jam, then stick the two together. Dust with icing sugar and place in paper cases.*

BAKING 493

Gingernuts

*The tantalising spicy aroma of these biscuits as they come out
of the oven is bound to test your willpower. It will be difficult to wait
for them to cool and become hard and crunchy as they should be.*

*Preparation time 15 minutes
+ 1 hour 30 minutes refrigeration
Total cooking time 15 minutes per tray
Makes about 40*

*70 g (2¼ oz) unsalted butter,
at room temperature
200 g (6½ oz) sugar
1 egg
70 g (2¼ oz) treacle
2 teaspoons white wine vinegar
240 g (7½ oz) strong or plain flour
1½ teaspoons bicarbonate of soda
½ teaspoon ground ginger
pinch ground cinnamon
pinch of ground cloves
pinch of ground cardamom
sugar, to coat*

One Preheat the oven to moderately hot
190°C (375°F/Gas 5). Line two baking
trays with baking paper.

Two Using a wooden spoon or an electric
whisk, cream together the butter and
sugar until light and fluffy. Add the egg,
a little at a time, beating well after each
addition, then add the treacle and
vinegar and mix well.

Three Sift together the flour, bicarbonate
of soda, ground ginger, cinnamon, cloves
and cardamom and stir into the butter
mixture. Draw a ball of dough together
with your hands, wrap it in plastic wrap
and refrigerate for about 1½ hours, or
until firm.

Four Divide the dough into four and,
using the palms of your hands, roll each
piece into a rope. Cut each rope into 10
pieces and roll the pieces into balls.
Spread the sugar in a shallow tray. Roll
each ball through the sugar, place on
the prepared trays spaced well apart
and press down slightly to flatten.
Refrigerate the remaining dough until
needed. Bake for about 10–15 minutes,
or until golden brown. Repeat with the
remaining mixture, preparing the trays
as instructed in step 1.

CHEF'S TIPS This biscuit dough can be
prepared in advance, rolled in the sugar
and slightly flattened. Wrap in plastic
wrap and freeze as individual pieces. To
cook, place the frozen balls on a lined
baking tray and bake at moderately hot
190°C (375°F/Gas 5) for 20 minutes.

If you are cooking more than one
tray of biscuits at a time in an oven
without a fan, swap the trays around
halfway through cooking to ensure
even baking.

Chocolate brownies

The smell of brownies baking may be irresistible, but it doesn't compare with the sensation of sinking your teeth into the finished product. The thick chocolate topping makes these twice as indulgent.

Preparation time 20 minutes
+ refrigeration
Total cooking time 50 minutes
Makes about 16

200 g (6½ oz) unsalted butter,
softened
3 teaspoons vanilla extract
or essence
200 g (6½ oz) caster sugar
50 g (1¾ oz) good-quality dark
chocolate, chopped
2 eggs, lightly beaten
100 g (3¼ oz) plain flour
pinch of salt
1 teaspoon baking powder
200 g (6½ oz) walnuts,
roughly chopped

TOPPING
100 ml (3¼ fl oz) thick (double)
cream
100 g (3¼ oz) good-quality dark
chocolate, chopped
40 g (1¼ oz) unsalted butter,
softened

One Grease a shallow 20 cm (8 inch) square baking tin, and sprinkle with flour or line the base with baking paper. Cream the butter, vanilla extract or essence and sugar together in a large bowl with a wooden spoon or electric beaters, until the mixture is light and fluffy. Preheat the oven to warm 170°C (325°F/Gas 3).

Two Put the chocolate in a bowl. Half-fill a saucepan with water and bring to the boil. Remove from the heat and place the bowl over the pan, making sure it is not touching the water. Leave the chocolate to melt slowly, then remove the bowl from the pan.

Three Gradually add the eggs to the creamed butter in about six additions, beating well after each addition, then stir in the chocolate.

Four Sift together the flour, salt and baking powder and add the chopped walnuts. Add to the chocolate mixture, and stir to just combine. Pour into the tin and bake for 45 minutes, or until firm and springy to the touch of a finger. Cool in the tin.

Five To make the topping, heat the cream just to boiling point. Remove from the heat and stir in the chocolate. Whisk in the butter. Transfer to a bowl and refrigerate until cooled and slightly thickened. Spread over the brownies and chill until just set. Cut into squares.

CHEF'S TIPS *You can use pecans in place of walnuts.*

The brownies will keep in an airtight container for up to a week.

Rhubarb and almond tart

This tart has a rich, moist filling and can be enjoyed on its own, or with crème anglaise or ice cream. It keeps well and can be made a few days in advance. Fresh plums, apricots or pears can all be used instead of rhubarb.

Preparation time 1 hour
+ 40 minutes refrigeration
Total cooking time 40 minutes
Serves 6–8

PASTRY
125 g (4 oz) unsalted butter, softened
3 tablespoons caster sugar
1 egg, beaten
200 g (6½ oz) plain flour

ALMOND CREAM
100 g (3¼ oz) unsalted butter, softened
100 g (3¼ oz) caster sugar
2 teaspoons finely grated lemon rind
2 eggs
100 g (3¼ oz) ground almonds
1 tablespoon plain flour

2 tablespoons raspberry jam
1 stick rhubarb, thinly sliced
2 tablespoons flaked almonds
2 tablespoons apricot jam
icing sugar, for dusting

One To make the pastry, beat the butter and sugar in a bowl until well blended using a wooden spoon or electric beaters. Add the egg gradually, beating well after each addition. Sift in the flour and a pinch of salt and mix lightly using a flat-bladed knife until the mixture just comes together—do not overmix. Gather together to form a rough ball and place on a large piece of plastic wrap. Gently flatten to a 1 cm (½ inch) thickness, then wrap and refrigerate for 20 minutes.

Two To make the almond cream, beat the butter, sugar and lemon rind in a small bowl with a wooden spoon, whisk or electric beaters. Gradually beat in the eggs. Stir in the almonds and flour and set aside.

Three To assemble, roll out the pastry on a floured surface (or between two sheets of baking paper) 2.5 mm (⅛ inch) thick. Ease into a greased, loose-bottomed, fluted or plain flan tin, 20 cm (8 inches) across the base. Trim the edges, pierce the base lightly with a fork and spread with raspberry jam. Spread the almond cream over the top, just level with the pastry edge. Decorate with rhubarb, slightly pushing into the almond cream. Sprinkle with flaked almonds and chill for 20 minutes.

Four Preheat the oven to moderate 180°C (350°F/Gas 4). Place the tart on a baking tray and bake for 10 minutes to help set the pastry. Reduce the oven temperature to warm 160°C (315°F/Gas 2–3) and bake for 30–35 minutes, or until the almond filling is golden brown and springs back when lightly touched.

Five In a small pan, heat the apricot jam with 3 teaspoons water. When the mixture has melted and begins to boil, sieve it into a small bowl and, while still hot, brush it over the tart. Allow the jam to cool, then sift a light dusting of icing sugar across the top.

CHEF'S TIPS *Handle the pastry as little as possible: work quickly and lightly. Always rest or chill pastry before rolling to make it easier to manage. Resting just before baking helps prevent shrinkage and loss of shape.*

To make the pastry in a food processor, process the flour, butter and sugar into fine crumbs, add the egg and process in short bursts until the pastry just comes together. Tip onto a lightly floured work surface and draw the pastry together by hand.

about rhubarb...

Spring or forced rhubarb grown in hothouses has a tender stem and bright, reddish pink colour. Older field-grown rhubarb is a darker red with a tougher stem which may need to be peeled. Some rhubarb gives off more liquid than others—this may affect the appearance of the dish but it does not alter the flavour.

Madeira cake

This English favourite is a rich but simple sponge sprinkled with candied lemon rind just before baking. It is usually served with a glass of Madeira, hence the name. Some chefs also sprinkle the baked cake with Madeira before it cools.

Preparation time *30 minutes*
Total cooking time *1 hour 25 minutes*
Serves 6

1 lemon
275 g (8³/4 oz) caster sugar
225 g (7¹/4 oz) unsalted butter, at room temperature
4 eggs, beaten
250 g (8 oz) plain flour

One Preheat the oven to slow 150°C (300°F/Gas 2). Line a 1 kg (2 lb) loaf tin (see Chef's techniques, page 553). Grease the paper and dust with flour.

Two To candy the lemon rind, peel the rind from the lemon using a vegetable peeler, then with a small knife, scrape away any white pith from the inside of the strips. Place the strips flat on a chopping board and cut into fine needle-like shreds with a large sharp knife. Place the shreds in a small pan, cover well with water, and bring to the boil. Boil for 1 minute, strain and rinse with cold water, then repeat. In a separate small pan, combine 50 g (1³/4 oz) of the sugar with 35 ml (1¹/4 fl oz) water and, stirring to dissolve the sugar, bring slowly to the boil. Add the fine shreds of lemon rind and simmer for 5 minutes, or until the rind is translucent. Remove from the syrup, using a fork, and spread out on greaseproof paper to cool.

Three Following the creaming method in the Chef's techniques on page 554, cream the butter and remaining sugar and gradually beat in the eggs.

Four Sift the flour into the bowl and fold into the mixture carefully, using a large metal spoon or plastic spatula. Spoon the mixture into the prepared loaf tin and smooth the top using the back of the spoon (see Chef's techniques, page 555). Sprinkle the candied rind evenly over the top of the cake and bake for 1 hour 15 minutes, or until a skewer comes out clean when inserted into the centre (see Chef's techniques, page 556).

Five Turn the cake out to cool on a wire rack. Leave the paper on the cake until ready to serve to keep it moist.

Angel cake

Angel cake is made with egg whites and no yolks. The air beaten into the whites is what makes the cake rise. Its antithesis is the rich dense chocolate devil's cake. It is traditionally baked in an angel cake tin or ring mould but an ordinary cake tin could be used.

Preparation time 10 minutes
Total cooking time 50 minutes
Serves 6

375 g (12 oz) caster sugar
125 g (4 oz) plain flour
12 egg whites, at room temperature
1 teaspoon cream of tartar
4 drops vanilla extract or essence
2 drops almond essence
icing sugar, to dust
strawberries, halved, to garnish

One Preheat the oven to moderate 180°C (350°F/Gas 4). You will need an angel cake tin measuring 24 cm (9½ inches) across the top and 10 cm (4 inches) in depth. The tin needs no greasing or further preparation.

Two Sift 125 g (4 oz) of the caster sugar together with the flour. Repeat the sifting process six times, then set aside. Whisk the egg whites in a large bowl, using an electric whisk or beaters, until they are foamy with soft peaks. Add a pinch of salt, 1 tablespoon water, the cream of tartar, vanilla and almond essence and when bubbles form, add the remaining sugar, a few tablespoons at a time. Whisk in until all the sugar has dissolved and the meringue stands in very stiff peaks.

Three Add the sifted flour and sugar and, using a large metal spoon or plastic spatula, carefully fold in to blend thoroughly. Spoon into the tin and pull a palette knife or plastic spatula, upright in the tin and touching the base, through the mixture in a circle. This will remove pockets of air and help to blend.

Four Bake for 50 minutes, or until the cake springs back when lightly touched

(see Chef's techniques, page 556). Turn the tin upside down onto a wire rack and leave the cake to cool completely in the tin so that it will not stick when being removed. To remove, the cake may require loosening around the edge with a round-bladed knife. Transfer to a serving plate, dust with the sifted icing sugar and garnish with strawberries.

CHEF'S TIP *This cake can either be served plain with whipped cream and strawberries, or drizzled with melted chocolate. Alternatively, coat with whipped cream flavoured with coffee essence or melted chocolate.*

Black Forest gateau

This Kirsch-flavoured chocolate cake, traditionally filled with whipped cream and sour morello cherries bottled in alcohol, comes from the Black Forest region of Germany. This version uses readily available sweet black cherries.

Preparation time 1 hour + refrigeration
Total cooking time 30 minutes
Serves 8

3 egg yolks
3 eggs
130 g (4¼ oz) caster sugar
100 g (3¼ oz) plain flour
30 g (1 oz) cocoa powder
100 g (3¼ oz) good-quality dark chocolate
600–750 ml (20–24 fl oz) cream, for whipping
1–2 drops vanilla extract or essence
icing sugar, for dusting

CHERRY FILLING
2 teaspoons cornflour
425 g (13½ oz) canned pitted morello or black cherries, drained, reserving 100 ml (3¼ fl oz) of the syrup

KIRSCH SYRUP
60 g (2 oz) caster sugar
40 ml (1¼ fl oz) Kirsch

One Preheat the oven to moderate 180°C (350°F/Gas 4). Line a 20 cm (8 inch) diameter, 6.5 cm (2½ inch) deep cake tin (see Chef's techniques, page 552).

Two Bring a pan of water to the boil, then remove from the heat. Following the whisking method in the Chef's techniques on page 554, combine the yolks, eggs and caster sugar in a heatproof bowl, set over the steaming water and whisk briskly until the mixture leaves a trail on its surface when the whisk is lifted. Remove the bowl from the pan and whisk the mixture until cold. Sift the flour and cocoa powder together and, using a large metal spoon, gently fold into the cold mixture until just combined. Do not overfold. Pour into the tin and bake for about 20 minutes, or until the cake springs back when lightly touched (see Chef's techniques, page 556). Turn onto a wire rack to cool.

Three To make the cherry filling, mix the cornflour with a little syrup from the cherries to form a runny paste. Put the remaining syrup in a small pan and bring to the boil. Remove from the heat, stir in the paste, return to the heat and stir until boiling. Remove from the heat, add all but eight cherries, reserving them for decoration, and leave to cool.

Four To make the Kirsch syrup, gently warm the caster sugar with 60 ml (2 fl oz) water, in a small pan, stirring to dissolve the sugar. Increase the heat, bring just to the boil and remove from the stove. Add the Kirsch and cool.

Five Using a vegetable peeler, pare off small curls from the chocolate. In a large bowl, whisk the cream until thick and just pourable, add the vanilla and a pinch of caster sugar, then whisk until the cream forms soft peaks. Reserve one quarter of the cream for decoration.

Six To assemble the cake, use a serrated knife to cut the sponge into three layers. Spoon Kirsch syrup over each. Place the top layer on a plate or board, with the crust side down, and spread or pipe with cream. Cover with the middle sponge. Spread a thin layer of cream on top, leaving a thicker border of cream around the edge. Spread the cherry filling within the border. Cover with the last piece of sponge. Spread the top and sides of the cake thinly with cream and chill for 10 minutes. Repeat covering with the cream until it is evenly coated. Press the chocolate curls around the sides and pipe rosettes with the reserved cream on top. Decorate with the reserved cherries, sprinkle the rosettes with chocolate and dust with icing sugar.

Dundee cake

This classic Scottish fruit cake is made with raisins, candied citrus peel and almonds and flavoured with rum. With its traditional almond-covered top, Dundee cake is popular at teatime both in Scotland and throughout the rest of Britain.

Preparation time 30 minutes
+ 5 days storing
Total cooking time 2 hours
Serves 10

575 g (1 lb 2½ oz) raisins, chopped
100 g (3¼ oz) chopped mixed peel
30 ml (1 fl oz) dark rum
225 g (7¼ oz) unsalted butter,
at room temperature
225 g (7¼ oz) soft dark brown sugar
6 eggs, lightly beaten
1 tablespoon marmalade
350 g (11¼ oz) plain flour
2 teaspoons baking powder
100 g (3¼ oz) ground almonds
150 g (5 oz) blanched almonds
50 g (1¼ oz) apricot jam

One Preheat the oven to warm 160°C (315°F/Gas 2–3). Double line a 20 cm (8 inch) diameter, 8 cm (3 inch) deep cake tin (see Chef's techniques, page 553). Grease the paper and dust with flour.

Two Combine the raisins, mixed peel and rum in a glass bowl and set aside to soak. Using the creaming method in the Chef's techniques on page 554, cream the butter and sugar and gradually whisk in the beaten egg. Once all the egg has been incorporated, beat in the marmalade.

Three Sift the flour, baking powder and ½ teaspoon salt into a large bowl and stir in the ground almonds. Add the soaked fruit and rum and fold into the flour with a metal spoon or plastic spatula. Fold this into the creamed mixture in three batches, until well combined. Spoon into the tin and gently smooth the top with the back of a spoon (see Chef's techniques, page 555).

Decorate the top with the blanched almonds and bake on the middle shelf of the oven for 2 hours. Cover the cake with paper after 1 hour to prevent it browning too much. Cool on a wire rack, leaving the paper on. Store the cake in an airtight container in a cool place, so the full flavour can develop, for at least 5 days.

Four To serve, remove the paper, melt the apricot jam with 1 tablespoon water in a small saucepan and brush the top of the cake to create an attractive shine.

CHEF'S TIP *The cooking time for a fruit cake can vary considerably, depending on the temperature of your oven.*

Ginger and carrot cake

The finely chopped glacé ginger, lemon rind and combination of spices give this moist cake its delicious flavour. Enhanced by the soft creamy icing, this cake is bound to disappear quickly.

Preparation time 25 minutes
Total cooking time 45 minutes
Serves 8

6 egg yolks
200 g (6½ oz) caster sugar
250 g (8 oz) carrots, grated
125 g (4 oz) ground almonds
125 g (4 oz) ground hazelnuts
50 g (1¾ oz) cake crumbs
50 g (1¾ oz) plain flour
1 teaspoon baking powder
large pinch of ground cinnamon
large pinch of ground ginger
small pinch of ground cloves
finely grated rind of 1 lemon
6 large egg whites
4 pieces (up to 40 g/1¼ oz) glacé
ginger, finely chopped

CREAM CHEESE ICING
75 g (2½ oz) unsalted butter,
at room temperature
75 g (2½ oz) cream cheese
175 g (5¾ oz) icing sugar
½ teaspoon vanilla extract or essence

One Preheat the oven to moderately hot 190°C (375°F/Gas 5). Line a 20 cm (8 inch) diameter cake tin (see Chef's techniques, page 552). Grease the paper and dust with flour.

Two Bring a pan of water to the boil and remove from the stove. Following the whisking method in the Chef's techniques on page 554, combine the egg yolks and half the sugar in a heatproof bowl. Place the bowl over the pan of steaming water, making sure the bowl does not touch the water. Whisk until the mixture is thick and pale. Remove the bowl from the pan and stir in the carrot.

Three Sift together the almonds, hazelnuts, cake crumbs, flour, baking powder, ground cinnamon, ginger, cloves and a pinch of salt. Stir in the lemon rind.

Four In a separate bowl, whisk the egg whites until they form soft peaks. Add the remaining caster sugar and whisk until stiff shiny peaks form.

Five Using a large metal spoon or plastic spatula, fold one third of the meringue into the carrot mixture, then fold in one third of the dry ingredients. Repeat, alternating, until the mixture is almost combined. Add the glacé ginger and fold in to fully combine. This must be done gently to retain as much air in the mixture as possible. Pour into the cake tin and bake for 35–45 minutes, or until a skewer comes out clean when inserted into the centre (see Chef's techniques, page 556). Allow the cake to cool in the tin for 10 minutes before removing from the tin and transferring to a wire rack to cool completely.

Six To make the cream cheese icing, beat all the ingredients together until creamy. When the cake has cooled, spread the topping over it.

American apple pie

When pilgrims first settled in North America, they took with them apple seeds and a love of pies, sowing a national love affair with this cherished homely dessert. Cooking apples yield the best results.

Preparation time 1 hour
Total cooking time 1 hour
Serves 4–6

PASTRY
325 g (10½ oz) plain flour
180 g (5¾ oz) unsalted butter, cubed
2 tablespoons caster sugar

FILLING
800 g (1 lb 10 oz) large green apples
125 g (4 oz) sugar, plus extra for sprinkling
1 teaspoon ground cinnamon
¼ teaspoon ground nutmeg
2½ tablespoons plain flour
20 ml (¾ fl oz) lemon juice
40 g (1¼ oz) unsalted butter, cubed

One Preheat the oven to moderate 180°C (350°F/Gas 4). To make the pastry, work together the flour, butter, sugar and a pinch of salt in a food processor until the mixture resembles fine breadcrumbs. With the motor running, add 30 ml (1 fl oz) water and process until the mixture just comes together. Remove the dough, divide in half and form each portion into a thick disc. Cover with plastic wrap and chill for 15–20 minutes.

Two To make the filling, peel, quarter and core the apples, then slice thinly and place in a large bowl. Combine the sugar, cinnamon, nutmeg, flour and a good pinch of salt, and sprinkle the mixture over the apple. Add the lemon juice and toss well.

Three On a lightly floured surface, roll out a pastry portion 2.5 mm (⅛ inch) thick, and 5 cm (2 inches) wider than a greased, shallow pie tin, 23 cm (9 inches) across the base. Carefully roll the dough onto a rolling pin, or fold into quarters, then ease into the tin. With your fingertips, press the dough into the tin to remove any air bubbles. Trim the excess pastry, leaving a 2.5 cm (1 inch) border of dough overhanging the edge of the tin.

Four Add the filling, then brush the pastry edges with water. Roll the remaining dough to the same thickness as before. Dot the apple with butter, place the dough on top and cut four steam holes. Trim the excess pastry, leaving a 1 cm (½ inch) overhang, then press the edges together to seal them. Crimp the edges by pinching the pastry between thumb and forefinger into a zigzag design. Brush the top with water and sprinkle with extra sugar, then bake for 55–60 minutes. Cool the pie on a rack, and serve warm or cold.

Flourless chocolate cake

*Served with Chantilly cream and a sprinkling of flaked almonds,
this dense chocolate cake makes a lovely dessert, but is perfect
for a little chocolate indulgence on any occasion.*

Preparation time 30 minutes
Total cooking time 50 minutes
Serves 8

150 g (5 oz) soft light brown sugar
225 g (7¼ oz) unsalted butter,
softened
4 eggs, separated
200 g (6½ oz) good-quality dark
chocolate, roughly grated
230 g (7¼ oz) ground almonds
2½ tablespoons caster sugar
2 tablespoons flaked almonds

CHANTILLY CREAM
300 ml (10 fl oz) cream, for whipping
few drops of vanilla extract or essence
2 tablespoons icing sugar

One Lightly grease a 23 cm (9 inch) round cake tin and line the base with greaseproof paper. Preheat the oven to slow 150°C (300°F/Gas 2).

Two Cream the brown sugar and butter in a large bowl until light and pale. Beat in the egg yolks one at a time, beating well after each addition. Stir in the chocolate and ground almonds. In a separate bowl, whisk the egg whites until stiff, whisk in the caster sugar, then fold into the chocolate mixture in four additions. Do not overfold, or the mixture will lose its volume. When there are no more streaks of white, pour into the tin and bake for 50 minutes, or until it springs back when lightly touched in the centre. Cool completely before removing from the tin.

Three To make the Chantilly cream, whisk the cream into stiff peaks with the vanilla and sugar. Keep chilled and serve with the cake and flaked almonds.

LE CORDON BLEU COMPLETE COOK

Simnel cake

This rich fruit cake, bursting with the flavour of spices and coated with almond paste, is now associated with Easter, although it was originally made for Mothering Sunday in May.

Preparation time 50 minutes
Total cooking time 2 hours
Serves 8–12

200 g (6½ oz) unsalted butter,
at room temperature
200 g (6½ oz) caster sugar
3 eggs, lightly beaten
300 g (10 oz) plain flour
1 teaspoon baking powder
1 teaspoon ground allspice
1 teaspoon ground ginger
small pinch of ground cloves
1 teaspoon ground cinnamon
50 g (1¾ oz) ground almonds
300 g (10 oz) currants
100 g (3¼ oz) raisins
finely grated rind of 1 orange
and 1 lemon
50 ml (1¾ fl oz) Grand Marnier
600 g (1¼ lb) marzipan
80 g (2¾ oz) apricot jam
30 g (1 oz) icing sugar
few drops of lemon juice

One Preheat the oven to slow 150°C (300°F/Gas 2). Double line a 20 cm (8 inch) diameter, 10 cm (4 inch) deep, straight-sided cake tin (see Chef's techniques, page 553). Grease the paper and dust with flour.

Two Using the creaming method in the Chef's techniques on page 554, cream the butter and caster sugar together and gradually add the eggs.

Three Into a separate bowl, sift together the flour, baking powder, allspice, ginger, cloves, cinnamon, ground almonds and a large pinch of salt. Add the currants, raisins, and orange and lemon rind, and mix to combine (see Chef's techniques, page 556). Stir the dry ingredients and Grand Marnier into the butter mixture, until incorporated. Spoon half the mixture into the tin and smooth the surface using the back of a spoon.

Four Lightly sprinkle a work surface with icing sugar and place 200 g (6½ oz) of the marzipan on it. Roll out into a circle 19.5 cm (7¾ inches) in diameter. Place the marzipan onto the cake mixture in the tin and cover with the remaining cake mixture. Level the surface with the back of a wet spoon, then make a dip in the centre of the cake using the back of the spoon (see Chef's techniques, page 555). Bake for

1¾–2 hours, or until a skewer comes out clean when inserted into the centre (see Chef's techniques, page 556). Transfer to a wire rack to cool. Turn out the cake and carefully peel away the baking paper.

Five Lightly sprinkle the work surface with icing sugar again and roll out another 200 g (6½ oz) of marzipan into a circle 20 cm (8 inches) in diameter. Score the marzipan with the back of a knife in a crisscross pattern. Heat the apricot jam, with 2 teaspoons of water, in a small saucepan until melted. Lightly brush the top and sides of the cake with the warm jam and place the marzipan circle onto the cake. Divide the remaining marzipan into eleven equal-sized pieces. Using your hands, roll each piece into a ball. Place these balls around the top edge of the cake, using a little jam to make them stick, and flatten them slightly, using a palette knife.

Six Place the Simnel cake under the grill for 1–2 minutes, until the marzipan is lightly browned, then remove and set on a plate or board.

Seven Sift the icing sugar into a small bowl and mix to a stiff paste with lemon juice. Spoon into a piping bag fitted with a small writing nozzle and pipe 'Simnel' in the centre of the cake.

Iced Christmas cake

*This classic Christmas cake can be baked in November or early December
and iced closer to the day. If you are short of time, you can keep the
decorations much simpler with just holly leaves and berries.*

Preparation time 3 hours + 1 week
and 2 overnight standings
Total cooking time 3 hours
Serves 10

95 g (3¼ oz) currants
250 g (8 oz) sultanas
95 g (3¼ oz) raisins
60 g (2 oz) chopped mixed peel
60 g (2 oz) glacé cherries
160 g (5¼ oz) plain flour
120 g (4 oz) unsalted butter,
at room temperature
95 g (3¼ oz) soft dark brown sugar
3 eggs, beaten
grated rind and juice of 1 lemon
and 1 orange
½ teaspoon vanilla extract or essence
1 tablespoon black treacle
1 teaspoon ground mixed spice
200 ml (6½ fl oz) rum or brandy
100 g (3¼ oz) apricot jam
500 g (1 lb) marzipan
clear alcohol, such as gin or vodka,
for brushing
1.5 kg (3 lb) soft icing

ROYAL ICING
1 egg white
200 g (6½ oz) icing sugar, sifted
juice of ½ lemon
red, green and yellow food colouring

One Double line a 20 cm (8 inch) round cake tin following the method in the Chef's techniques on page 553. Preheat the oven to warm 160°C (315°F/Gas 2–3).

Two Place the fruit in a bowl and mix in half the flour. Beat the butter and sugar until light and creamy. Add the egg in additions, beating well between each addition. Beat in the lemon and orange rind and juice, the vanilla and treacle. Sift the remaining flour and mixed spice onto the butter mixture and beat well. Stir in the fruit.

Three Place the mixture in the prepared tin and make a dip in the centre with the back of a wet spoon. Bake for about 3 hours, or until a skewer inserted into the centre comes out clean. Cover with foil if it is browning too quickly. Cool in the tin on a wire rack, then make several holes in the cake with a skewer.

Four Without removing the paper, wrap the cake tightly in plastic wrap and store in a cool place for at least 1 week, soaking regularly with a little of the rum or brandy.

Five Level the surface of the cake with a sharp knife, then turn base-up. In a small pan, melt the jam and brush over the cake, then place on a thin 20 cm (8 inch) board. Cover the cake with marzipan and make royal icing, following the method in the Chef's techniques on page 557.

Six To decorate the cake, pull a walnut-size piece of icing from the remaining soft icing and colour it yellow. Make a small star and present shape. Divide the remaining icing into two thirds and one third. Colour the larger amount green and the smaller red. Cover and set aside the red. Roll out the green icing to a 2 mm (⅛ inch) thickness on a surface dusted with icing sugar. Cut out a 1 x 75 cm (½ x 30 inch) ribbon, cover and set aside. Cut out 8 holly leaves. Gather together the remaining icing, colour a darker green and form a Christmas tree by making a cone shape and randomly snipping the sides with scissors. Take the red icing and make a red ribbon, 12 holly berries and a small present to go under the tree.

Seven Twist the two pieces of ribbon together and wrap around the cake, fixing with some of the reserved royal icing at four intervals to give a drape effect. At each fixed point, stick on two holly leaves and three berries. Leave to dry overnight.

Eight The next day, arrange the tree and presents on top of the cake. Mix the remaining royal icing with the food colourings and pipe 'Merry Christmas' onto the centre of the cake and extra decorations on the tree and presents.

509

LE CORDON BLEU COMPLETE COOK

Mince pies

Home-made fruit mince pies are the traditional accompaniment to drinks when guests come round over Christmas. These ones are made with meltingly short pastry and a brandy-laced mincemeat.

Preparation time 1 hour
+ 40 minutes chilling
(make the mincemeat 1 week in advance)
Total cooking time 20 minutes
Makes 12

MINCEMEAT (SEE CHEF'S TIP)
250 g (8 oz) suet, shredded
250 g (8 oz) cooking apples,
peeled, cored
and roughly chopped
120 g (4 oz) chopped mixed peel
250 g (8 oz) raisins
250 g (8 oz) sultanas
250 g (8 oz) currants
25 g (3/4 oz) slivered almonds
185 g (6 oz) demerara sugar
1/2 teaspoon ground mixed spice
large pinch ground nutmeg
large pinch ground cinnamon
finely grated rind and juice
of 1/2 lemon
80 ml (23/4 fl oz) brandy

SHORTCRUST PASTRY
185 g (6 oz) plain flour
115 g (33/4 oz) unsalted butter,
cut into cubes and chilled
25 g (3/4 oz) hard white fat, such as
lard, cut into cubes and chilled
1 egg yolk
2 drops vanilla extract or essence

caster sugar, to dust

One To make the mincemeat, place the suet, apple, mixed peel and raisins in a food processor and, using the pulse button, break down roughly. Place in a large bowl, add the remaining ingredients and stir to combine well.

Two Spoon the mincemeat into four 500 ml (16 fl oz) sterilised preserving jars or jars with screw-top lids, pressing down to force out any air. Screw the lids on tightly and store in the refrigerator for at least 1 week.

Three To make the pastry, sift the flour and some salt into a large bowl and add the butter and lard. Using a fast, light, flicking action of thumb across fingertips, rub the butter and lard into the flour until the mixture resembles fine breadcrumbs. Make a well in the centre. In a bowl, mix together the egg yolk, vanilla and 1 1/2 tablespoons water and pour into the well. Mix with a round-bladed knife until large lumps form. Pull together and turn out onto a lightly floured surface. Knead very gently for no more than 20 seconds until just smooth, then wrap in plastic wrap and refrigerate for at least 20 minutes.

Four Brush a 12-hole shallow patty pan or tart tray with melted butter. Preheat the oven to moderately hot 200°C (400°F/Gas 6). On a lightly floured surface, roll out two thirds of the pastry to a 3 mm (1/8 inch) thickness. Using an 8 cm (3 inch) cutter, cut out circles and ease into the holes by pressing lightly. Chill while rolling out the remaining pastry as above. Using a 7 cm (23/4 inch) cutter, cut circles for the top of each pie. Place on a plastic-wrap-lined tray and chill for 20 minutes.

Five Fill each pastry-lined hole with 1 tablespoon of mincemeat. Take the pastry circles, brush the outer edges with water, then place, damp-side-down, on the mincemeat. Gently press the top and bottom pastry edges together to seal. Brush the tops with cold water and lightly dust with the sugar. Using the point of a sharp knife, make a small hole in the centre of each.

Six Bake the mince pies for 20 minutes, or until golden. Serve them hot with cream or brandy butter.

CHEF'S TIP *The mincemeat is best left to mature over a few weeks or months to allow the flavours to develop. Any unopened jars should be stored in cool, dark and dry conditions or in the refrigerator.*

Treacle tart

This revamped classic dessert adds a touch of glamour to an all-time favourite. The tart can be served hot or cold and is delicious accompanied by either a warm vanilla custard sauce or vanilla ice cream.

*Preparation time 40 minutes
+ 30 minutes refrigeration
Total cooking time 1 hour
Serves 8*

**1 quantity shortcrust pastry
(see page 544)
1 egg
1 egg yolk**

FILLING
*300 g (10 oz) golden syrup
150 ml (5 fl oz) thick (double) cream
1 egg
finely grated rind of 1 lemon
50 g (1³/4 oz) ground almonds
75 g (2¹/2 oz) fresh breadcrumbs*

One Brush a 20 cm (8 inch) deep loose-bottomed flan tin with melted butter.

Two Roll out two-thirds of the pastry on a floured surface into a circle about 2–3 mm (¹/8 inch) thick. Line the tin (see Chef's techniques, page 547) and refrigerate for 30 minutes. Preheat the oven to moderately hot 200°C (400°F/ Gas 6). Bake blind for 10–15 minutes, following the method in the Chef's techniques on page 547. Remove the beads and paper and cool. Reduce the oven temperature to moderate 180°C (350°F/Gas 4).

Three To prepare the lattice top, roll out the remaining pastry to 3 mm (¹/8 inch) thick. Cut strips of pastry 1.5 cm (⁵/8 inch) wide and long enough to reach across the tart. Refrigerate while preparing the filling.

Four To make the filling, place the syrup in a pan and heat gently until warm. In a bowl, mix together the cream and egg.

Add the grated lemon rind and warm syrup to the cream mixture. In a separate bowl, mix together the ground almonds and breadcrumbs, make a well in the centre and pour in the liquid. Slowly whisk in the dry ingredients until smooth and blended. Pour into the prepared flan case, filling to just below the rim.

Five Whisk the remaining egg and egg yolk together and use to brush the rim of the pastry case. Wipe off any splashes on the flan tin as they will stick and make the tart difficult to remove. Lay half the pastry strips on the surface of the tart, 1.5 cm (⁵/8 inch) apart, beginning in the centre and working outwards. Cut off by pressing down with your thumbs. Place the second layer of strips on the diagonal, again starting in the centre, to create a lattice pattern. Brush with the remaining egg wash. Bake for 25–35 minutes, or until golden brown. Allow to cool slightly before removing from the tin.

Pumpkin pie

While pumpkin pie is the traditional favourite served at America's Thanksgiving dinner, it is ideal to follow any cold-weather meal. It has a warm, spicy aroma and is delicious served with sweetened whipped cream.

Preparation time 20 minutes
+ refrigeration
Total cooking time 45 minutes
Serves 6–8

*¹/₂ quantity sweet pastry
(see page 546)*

FILLING
*200 g (6¹/₂ oz) pumpkin purée
(see Chef's tips)
2 eggs
50 g (1³/₄ oz) caster sugar
large pinch salt
small pinch of ground cloves
small pinch of ground cinnamon
small pinch of ground nutmeg
small pinch of ground ginger
30 ml (1 fl oz) double (thick) cream*

One Brush a 20 cm (8 inch) deep loose-bottomed flan tin with melted butter.

Two Roll out the pastry on a floured surface to a circle about 2 mm (¹/₈ inch) thick and line the flan tin (see Chef's techniques, page 547). Refrigerate for 30 minutes.

Three Preheat the oven to moderately hot 190°C (375°F/Gas 5). Bake blind for 10–15 minutes, following the method in the Chef's techniques on page 547. Remove the beads and paper and return the pastry shell to the oven for another 5–10 minutes, or until the centre begins to colour. Allow to cool. Reduce the oven temperature to warm 160°C (315°F/Gas 2–3).

Four To make the filling, place the pumpkin purée, eggs, caster sugar, salt, ground spices and thick cream in a bowl and whisk until smooth and blended.

Pour into the pastry case. Bake for 25–30 minutes, or until the filling is firm to the touch. Allow to cool slightly, then remove from the tin and transfer to a serving plate. Serve the pie warm, cut into wedges, or if you prefer to serve the pie cold, allow it to cool, then refrigerate for at least 30 minutes.

CHEF'S TIPS *Pumpkin purée is available tinned, but to prepare it fresh, take 300 g (10 oz) pumpkin, peel and cut into pieces, remove the seeds, and place in a pan. Just cover with cold water and add 60 g (2 oz) caster sugar. Cover and simmer until the pumpkin is tender, drain well and purée in a blender, food processor or through a sieve.*

If serving the pie cold, add shine to the surface with an apricot glaze. Melt 50 g (1³/₄ oz) apricot jam with 1 tablespoon water until liquid. Sieve, then brush the glaze evenly over the surface, avoiding going over the same area twice or you will make streaks.

Try stirring in 50 g (1³/₄ oz) chopped walnuts to the pastry dough to give added crunch.

Langues-de-chat

'Langue-de-chat', the French term for cat's tongue, is the name given to these biscuits because of their shape. Delicately flavoured, light and crisp, these biscuits can be served with a sweet soufflé or as an elegant accompaniment to coffee.

Preparation time 15 minutes
Total cooking time 10 minutes per tray
Makes about 50

100 g (3¼ oz) *icing sugar*
100 g (3¼ oz) *unsalted butter,*
at room temperature
3–4 drops *vanilla extract or essence*
3 *egg whites, lightly beaten*
100 g (3¼ oz) *plain flour*

One Preheat the oven to moderately hot 200°C (400°F/Gas 6). Brush two baking trays with melted butter and refrigerate.

Two Using a wooden spoon or electric beaters, cream the icing sugar and butter together. When the mixture is pale and light, beat in the vanilla.

Three Add the egg whites slowly, beating constantly and being careful not to allow the mixture to curdle. If it does, add a large pinch of the flour.

Four Sift the flour into the bowl, then using a large metal spoon or plastic spatula, gently fold the flour into the butter mixture, mixing lightly until combined. Spoon into a piping bag fitted with a 7 mm (⅓ inch) plain nozzle and pipe enough 8 cm (3 inch) lengths to fill

the prepared baking trays. Leave at least 5 cm (2 inches) between the biscuits as they will spread during baking. Bake for 7–10 minutes, or until the edges are golden brown, but the centres yellow.

Five Use a palette knife or fish slice to remove the biscuits from the tray while they are still warm. If they cool and become too brittle to move, return them to the oven to warm for a moment or two. Repeat with the remaining mixture, preparing the trays as instructed in step 1.

CHEF'S TIP *Langues-de-chat can be used to line moulds that are then filled with light creamy mixtures such as mousses, chilled to set and turned out. Or they can be placed around the sides of cream coated cakes. Store in an airtight container for up to 2 weeks.*

Lunettes

'Lunettes' is the French word for spectacles. Made to represent spectacles, these biscuits are elegant for teatime, but also fun for children.

Preparation time 30 minutes
+ 30 minutes refrigeration
Total cooking time 10 minutes per tray
Makes 10

45 g (1½ oz) ground almonds
110 g (3¾ oz) plain flour
45 g (1½ oz) unsalted butter, softened
1 teaspoon finely grated lemon rind
45 g (1½ oz) caster sugar
½ egg, beaten
50 g (1¾ oz) apricot jam
icing sugar, to dust
60 g (2 oz) raspberry jam

One Preheat the oven to moderate 180°C (350°F/Gas 4). Brush two baking trays with melted butter and dust lightly with flour. Sift together the almonds and flour.

Two Using a wooden spoon or electric beaters, cream together the butter, lemon rind and sugar until light and fluffy. Add the egg, a little at a time, beating well after each addition. Add the flour and almonds and stir together to form a rough dough. Draw together by hand to form a ball, wrap in plastic wrap, flatten slightly and refrigerate for about 30 minutes. Roll out the dough between two sheets of baking paper to about a 3 mm (⅛ inch) thickness.

Three Using an 8 cm (3 inch) oval cutter, cut out about 20 biscuits and transfer as many as will fit comfortably to the prepared trays. Using a 1–1.5 cm (½–⅝ inch) round cutter, or the end of a 1 cm (½ inch) piping nozzle, cut out two holes from half of the oval biscuits. These will become the tops of the lunettes. Refrigerate the rest of the dough until needed.

Four Bake for 10 minutes, or until light golden. While still warm, move the biscuits to a wire rack. Repeat with the remaining mixture.

Five Warm the jam, brush over the base of the whole biscuits and sandwich with a biscuit with holes in the top.

Six Dust with sifted icing sugar. Beat the raspberry jam in a bowl until it flows. Fill a piping bag fitted with a 4 mm (¼ inch) plain nozzle and fill in each of the holes on the sandwiched biscuits with the jam. If you don't have a piping bag, drop the jam from the tip of a teaspoon.

· LE CORDON BLEU ·

chef's techniques

Stock and sauce techniques

MAKING BROWN STOCK

Roast 1.5 kg (3 lb) beef or veal bones for 20 minutes in a very hot 230°C (450°F/Gas 8) oven. Add 1 quartered onion, 2 chopped carrots, 1 chopped leek and 1 chopped celery stick and roast for a further 20 minutes.

Transfer to a clean saucepan with 4 litres of water, 2 tablespoons tomato paste (purée), 1 bouquet garni and 6 peppercorns. Bring to the boil, reduce the heat and simmer gently for 2–3 hours, skimming the fat and scum from the surface regularly. A flat strainer is easiest to use for skimming.

Ladle the stock in batches into a fine sieve over a bowl. Press the bones and vegetables with the ladle to extract all the liquid. Refrigerate for several hours and remove the solidified fat. Makes 1.5–2 litres.

MAKING LAMB STOCK

Put 1.5 kg (3 lb) lamb bones in a large stockpot. Cover with water and bring to the boil. Drain and rinse the bones. This removes any fat.

Put the lamb bones in a clean saucepan with 3 litres of water, 1 quartered onion, 2 chopped carrots, 1 chopped leek, 1 chopped celery stick, 1 bouquet garni and 6 peppercorns.

Bring to the boil, reduce the heat and simmer gently for 2–3 hours, skimming the fat and scum from the surface regularly. A flat strainer is easiest to use for skimming.

Ladle the bones and vegetables into a fine sieve over a bowl. Press the bones and vegetables with the ladle to extract all the liquid. Refrigerate for several hours and remove the solidified fat. Makes about 1.5 litres.

Stock and sauce techniques

MAKING CHICKEN STOCK

Cut up 750 g (1½ lb) chicken bones and carcass and put in a pan with a roughly chopped onion, carrot and celery stick. Add 6 peppercorns, a bouquet garni and 4 litres water

Bring to the boil, reduce the heat and simmer gently for 2–3 hours, skimming the fat and scum from the surface regularly. A flat strainer is easiest to use for skimming. Strain the stock through a sieve into a clean bowl, then allow to cool.

Chill the stock overnight, then lift off any fat. If you can't leave overnight, skim, then drag the surface of the hot strained stock with paper towels to lift off the fat. Makes 1.5–2 litres.

MAKING FISH STOCK

Put 2 kg (4 lb) chopped fish bones and trimmings (use non-oily, white fish and remove any eyes or gills) in salted water for 10 minutes, then drain. Transfer to a clean pan with 2.5 litres water, 12 peppercorns, 2 bay leaves, 1 chopped celery stick, 1 chopped onion and the juice of 1 lemon.

Bring to the boil, then reduce the heat and simmer gently for 20 minutes, skimming the fat and scum from the surface regularly. A flat strainer is easiest to use for skimming.

Ladle the stock into a fine sieve over a bowl. Gently press the bones and vegetables with the ladle to extract all the liquid. Refrigerate until cool. Makes about 1.5 litres.

Stock and sauce techniques

TO FREEZE STOCK

To freeze, boil the stock to reduce to 500 ml (16 fl oz). Allow to cool and freeze in ice cube trays until solid. Transfer to a plastic bag and seal. To make 2 litres stock, add 1.5 litres water to 500 ml (16 fl oz) concentrated stock.

CLARIFYING BUTTER

Clarifying means removing the water and milk solids from butter, rendering the butter less likely to burn. To make 100 g (3 1/4 oz) clarified butter, cut 180 g (5 3/4 oz) butter into small cubes. Place in a small pan set into a larger pot of water over low heat. Melt the butter, without stirring.

Remove the pan from the heat and allow to cool slightly. Skim the foam from the surface, being careful not to stir the butter.

MAKING A BOUQUET GARNI

Wrap the green part of a leek loosely around a bay leaf, a sprig of thyme, some celery leaves and a few stalks of parsley, then tie with string. Leave a long tail to the string for easy removal.

Pour off the clear yellow liquid, being very careful to leave the milky sediment behind in the pan. Discard the sediment and store the clarified butter in an airtight container in the refrigerator for up to two months.

Stock and sauce techniques

MAYONNAISE

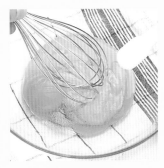

Stand a large, deep bowl on a tea towel to make it stable. Whisk the egg yolks, mustard, white pepper and salt in the bowl until evenly combined.

Whisk in the oil a drop at a time until the mixture starts to thicken, then add the oil in a thin stream. If the oil is added too quickly, the mayonnaise will separate.

After the first 100 ml (3¼ fl oz) of oil has been added, whisk in the vinegar. Add the remaining oil gradually.

HOLLANDAISE SAUCE

Whisk the egg yolks and water together in a heatproof bowl until foamy. Place the bowl over a pan half-filled with simmering water and whisk until thick. The bowl should not touch the water. Gradually whisk in the butter.

Continue adding the melted butter, over very low heat, whisking constantly. The sauce must not be allowed to get too hot, otherwise it may curdle. The sauce should leave a trail on the surface when the whisk is lifted.

Once all the butter is incorporated, strain the sauce into a clean bowl. Stir in the lemon juice and then season with salt and pepper.

Seafood techniques

SHUCKING OYSTERS

Scrub the oysters in cold water. Place an oyster, rounded side down, on a thick doubled cloth in the palm of your hand. Use a shucker with a protection shield and always protect the hand holding the oyster with a thick cloth.

Insert an oyster knife through the pointed end of the oyster at the hinge where the top and bottom shells meet. Work the knife in until at least 3 cm (1¼ inches) is inside. Twist the knife to separate the shells.

Slide the knife between the oyster and the top shell, cut through the hinge muscle and remove the top shell.

Slide the knife between the oyster and the bottom shell to release it. Remove the oyster and tip any liquid through a muslin-lined sieve into a bowl to get rid of any sand. Reserve the liquid.

PREPARING PRAWNS

Pull off the head, then peel away the shell, being careful to keep the flesh intact. Leave the tail end intact if specified in the recipe.

Make a shallow cut along the back of the prawn with a small knife to expose the dark intestinal vein.

Remove the vein with the tip of a knife and discard. Rinse the prawn and pat dry with paper towels.

Seafood techniques

PREPARING CRAB

This method can be used for most crabs. Mud crab, shown here, needs extra care as the shell is very hard. Twist the claws to remove them. Use your thumb as a lever to prise off the hard top shell. Scoop out any creamy brown meat and reserve. Wash and dry the shell well.

Discard the soft stomach sac from the main body of the crab and remove the grey spongy fingers (gills). Scrape out and reserve any creamy brown meat.

Cut the main body of the crab in half lengthways, then remove the white meat from the body with the end of a teaspoon or fork.

PREPARING MUSSELS

Clean the mussels by scrubbing the shells with a brush to remove any sand. Scrape off the barnacles with a knife.

Pull off any beards from the mussels.

Discard any mussels that are broken, or are not tightly closed and do not close when lightly tapped on a work surface.

Seafood techniques

KILLING LOBSTER

Place the lobster in the freezer for about 2 hours to desensitise it. Remove from the freezer and hold the lobster tail down under a heavy cloth. Using a large sharp knife, place the point in the centre of the head and quickly pierce right through to the board, cutting down and forward between the eyes.

REMOVING LOBSTER TAIL MEAT

Turn the lobster onto its back. Using a pair of kitchen scissors, cut lengthways down each side of the belly.

Pull the softer undershell back, exposing the meat of the lobster tail.

CLEANING SCALLOPS

Wash the scallops to remove any grit or sand, then pull away the small tough shiny white muscle and the black vein, leaving the orange roe intact.

Pull the tail meat from the shell, keeping it in a single piece.

Seafood techniques

PREPARING LOBSTER FOR BISQUE

Cut the lobster in half lengthways. Remove and discard the sac in the head and the vein down the centre of the tail.

Twist off the claws and bat them with a rolling pin or the base of a small heavy pan to crack them.

Using a large sharp knife, cut across the tail into three or four pieces.

PREPARING LOBSTER FOR AMERICAINE

Twist and remove the two main claws, if applicable, where they meet the body. Separate the head from the tail. Cook the claws and tail according to the method in the recipe.

Remove the flesh from the tail by snipping with scissors around the edge of the flat undershell and lifting it away.

Gently ease the flesh out of the tail in one piece using your fingers. Reserve the shell.

With a large sharp knife, split the head in two lengthways. Remove and reserve any coral (roe) and green-grey tomalley (liver). Discard the stomach sac found behind the mouth. Chop the head shell into large pieces.

Seafood techniques

GUTTING AND FILLETING ROUND FISH

Cut off the fins. Cut out the gills behind the head and discard.

Make a small cut at the bottom of the stomach, then cut along the underside, stopping just below the gills. Pull out the innards and discard. Rinse the inside of the fish.

Make a cut around the back of the head then, working from head to tail, cut along the backbone. Holding the knife flat, use long strokes to cut between the flesh and the bone, sliding the knife close to the bone. Pull the flesh away from the bone.

FILLETING FLAT FISH

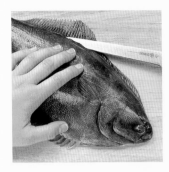

Lay the fish dark side up. Cut around the outside of the fish with a filleting knife where the flesh meets the fins.

Cut down the centre of the fish from head to tail with a sharp knife. Make sure you cut all the way through to the bone.

Working from the centre of the fillet to the edge, cut away one fillet with long broad strokes of the knife, sliding the knife close to the bone and not leaving too much flesh. Remove the other fillet in the same way, then turn the fish over and repeat.

Seafood techniques

SKINNING FISH

Lay the fillet skin side down and cut across the flesh at the tail. Dip your fingers in salt so that you can get a good grip, grasp the tail and, starting at the cut, work the knife away from you at a shallow angle using a sawing action.

PIN BONING FISH

To remove the small bones left in fish such as salmon or red mullet, run your fingers along the flesh, pressing lightly to find the bones. Remove any fine pin bones with a pair of tweezers or your fingers.

SERVING SALMON

Place the cooked salmon on a piece of greaseproof paper before you begin. Then, using a sharp knife, cut the skin just above the tail, then cut through the skin along the back and in front of the gills. Using the knife to help you, work from head to tail to peel off and discard the skin.

Place a serving plate under one side of the greaseproof paper and flip the fish over onto the plate, using the paper to help you. Remove the rest of the skin. Remove the head if preferred.

Scrape away any dark flesh with a knife. Split down the centre of the top fillet, then carefully remove and lay the two quarter fillets each side of the salmon.

Lift out the backbone by peeling it back from the head end. Snip it with scissors just before the tail. Remove any other stray bones and lift up and replace the two fillets.

Poultry techniques

JOINTING A CHICKEN

Use a pair of kitchen scissors to cut through the length of the breastbone.

Cut through the top third of the breast, leaving two even-sized portions. You can also remove the wing tips at this stage, if you wish.

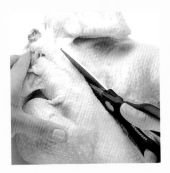

Turn the chicken over and cut down either side of the backbone to completely remove it. The backbone should come away in one piece.

Separate the leg from the thigh by cutting through the leg joint.

Following the natural contours of the thigh, cut through to separate the breast and wing piece from the thigh and leg.

You now have eight equal-sized chicken portions.

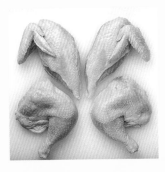

Repeat with the other half to produce four pieces.

LE CORDON BLEU ✠ COMPLETE COOK

Poultry techniques

REMOVING THE WISHBONE

The wishbone is found at the neck of the bird. Its removal makes carving the breast easier. Pull back the skin from the neck cavity. Use your fingers to feel for the wishbone just inside—you may need to slit the skin a little. Cut around the wishbone with a sharp knife, then scrape the meat away.

Cut away the wishbone at the joint and lift it out.

TRUSSING A CHICKEN

Rinse the bird inside and out, then dry with paper towels. Use ordinary household string to truss. Tie the legs together, wrapping the string under the parson's nose first.

Then take the string towards the neck of the bird, passing it down between the legs and the body.

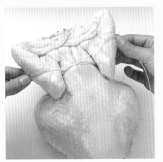

Turn the bird over and cross the string over in the centre, underneath the wings. Wrap the string around the wings to keep them flat.

Tie the string into a knot or bow to secure the chicken wings in place. Trim off the ends of the string and the chicken is ready for cooking.

Poultry techniques

SCRAPING A CHICKEN DRUMSTICK

Removing the meat from the bone can be fiddly. Pull the skin off the legs, from the fat end of the drumstick.

Hold the knuckle end of the drumstick and use a sharp knife to cut through the flesh all the way around the bone. Scrape the flesh off the bone, turning the bone as you scrape. The flesh should come off the bone in one piece.

BONING QUAIL

Pull off any feathers. Pull the skin back from the neck cavity and cut around the wishbone. Scrape away any meat and cut away at the base. Pull out the wishbone.

Place the quail breast side down and cut through the skin down the centre of the back. Using a knife, scrape the flesh away from the carcass, holding the skin as you do so.

When you reach the thigh joints, pull the thigh bones out of the joints so the legs stay attached to the skin and flesh. Continue scraping around the carcass all the way round.

Scrape carefully around the breast bone and the skin and flesh should come away in one piece as you lift out the carcass.

Carving techniques

CARVING TURKEY

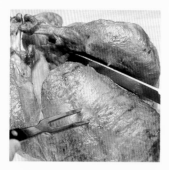

Place the turkey breast side up on a board. Cut off the wings, then the legs, cutting through the joints that connect the legs to the body.

Hold the turkey steady with a carving fork and slice down through the breast meat, holding the knife parallel to the rib cage. Carve the other side.

Cut through each thigh and drumstick joint. Hold the thigh steady with a fork and carve the thigh meat off all sides, keeping the knife parallel to the bone. Duck can be carved by the same method.

PREPARING AND CARVING HAM

With a sharp knife, make a cut in the skin at the top of the ham near the knuckle. Push your thumbs or fingers under the skin and gently pull it back from the cut and remove.

With a sharp knife, trim away the layer of fat until it is 1 cm (1/2 inch) thick. Score the fat with cuts crossways and then diagonally to form a diamond pattern. Be careful not to cut into the flesh. Cook as instructed in the recipe.

To carve the ham, cut a small wedge from the top of the ham and remove. Hold the leg steady with a carving fork and slice evenly towards the knuckle. The slices will increase in size as you carve.

Pasta techniques

MAKING AND ROLLING PASTA WITH A MACHINE

Place the flour, salt, olive oil and eggs or egg yolks in a food processor and mix in short bursts until the mixture forms large crumbs.

Gently press the mixture between your finger and thumb to check if it will come together smoothly. If not, continue to process for a few bursts.

Turn out onto a lightly floured surface and knead for 2 minutes into a smooth dough. Wrap in plastic wrap and refrigerate for 20 minutes. Secure a pasta machine to the edge of a table.

Fold the sheet into three and pass through the machine again at the thickest setting. Repeat this rolling and folding ten times, lightly flouring the pasta dough and machine to prevent it sticking.

Without folding, continue to pass the dough through progressively thinner settings, until it has passed through the finest setting. Repeat with the remaining pieces of dough.

MAKING TAGLIATELLE

Divide the dough into as many pieces as specified in the recipe. Keep covered and work with one piece at a time. Flatten into a rectangle and roll through the lightly floured pasta machine on the thickest setting.

Pass the sheet of pasta through a floured pasta machine fitted with the tagliatelle attachment. Or roll up the sheet of pasta and cut into ribbons with a knife. Cook immediately or leave to dry in a single layer. The tagliatelle may be dried on a floured tea towel hanging over the back of a chair for 1–2 hours.

Pasta techniques

MAKING AND ROLLING PASTA BY HAND

Sift the flour and salt onto a work surface. Make a large well in the centre with your hand and add the eggs or egg yolks, and olive oil.

Using your fingertips, gradually incorporate the flour into the wet ingredients.

With a pastry scraper or by hand, keep bringing the flour into the centre, forming a dough. Knead for 10 minutes, or until smooth and elastic. Divide into pieces as specified in the recipe. Cover with plastic wrap. Fresh pasta should be used on the same day it is made

To roll out pasta by hand, use a large, lightly floured work surface. Roll out the dough as thinly as possible, fold in half and roll again, bringing the furthest end over the rolling pin and gently stretching it. Roll and fold the dough ten times. Roll out to the thickness required.

MAKING RAVIOLI

Roll out a sheet of pasta and spoon the filling at regular intervals along the pasta. Lightly brush a little water or egg around each mound of filling.

Place the second sheet of pasta on top and press firmly around each mound to expel any air and to seal. Using a rolling cutter or biscuit cutter, cut out each ravioli.

Alternatively, use the ravioli cutter on a pasta machine. Place two pasta sheets in the floured machine and two mounds of filling in the grooves. Turn the handle of the machine to cut. Repeat with the remaining filling. Uncooked ravioli can be frozen in single layers between sheets of baking paper.

Vegetable techniques

PEELING TOMATOES

Using a very sharp knife, score a small cross in the base of each tomato.

Blanch the tomatoes in a large pan of boiling water for 10 seconds. Remove and plunge into a bowl of ice cold water to stop the cooking and keep the flesh firm.

Pull away the skin from the cross and discard the skin.

If a recipe calls for the removal of the tomato seeds, cut the tomato in half and use a teaspoon to gently scoop out the seeds.

PREPARING ARTICHOKE HEARTS

Break off the artichoke stalk at the bottom, pulling out the fibres that attach it to the base.

Pull off the outer leaves and place the artichoke in a pan of boiling salted water with the juice of 1 lemon. Weigh down with a plate and simmer for 20–35 minutes.

Test for doneness by pulling at one of the leaves. If it comes away easily, the artichoke is done. Cut off the top half of the artichoke and discard.

Remove the hairy choke in the middle of the artichoke heart with a spoon. The artichoke heart is now ready to use.

LE CORDON BLEU  COMPLETE COOK

Vegetable techniques

GRILLING CAPSICUMS (PEPPERS)

Grilling capsicums allows you to remove their skins and produces a delicious sweet flavour. To do this, preheat a grill. Cut the capsicums in half and remove the seeds and membrane.

Grill the capsicums, skin side up, until the skin blisters and blackens. Place in a plastic bag (the steam helps to lift the skin off the flesh) and leave to cool. When cool, peel off the skin.

COOKING ASPARAGUS

Tying a bunch of asparagus makes it easier to handle during cooking. Grasp the asparagus bunch in the centre. Holding the end of a string with thumb and finger, wrap the string around the upper part three times, cross over and wrap the lower part three times. Secure with a knot.

Cook the asparagus in boiling water until tender.

Drain, and plunge into a bowl of iced water to stop the cooking process and refresh the asparagus. This process helps retain the vibrant colour of blanched vegetables. Drain.

Vegetable techniques

PUREEING POTATOES

One way to purée potatoes is to hold a sieve securely over a bowl and force the cooked potatoes through with a wooden spoon. This gives a light, fine purée.

Another method of puréeing potatoes is to place the cooked potatoes in a mouli set over a bowl. Turn the handle to force the potato through.

Alternatively, push the cooked potatoes, a little at a time, through a ricer into a large bowl. It is important that the potatoes are evenly cooked so that they pass through the ricer evenly.

SLICING POTATOES WITH A MANDOLIN

Attach the potato to the mandolin guard. This will make it easier and safer to work with.

For thin slices, work the potato against the straight blade, set to the thickness specified in the recipe.

For long thin strips of potato, work the potato against the shredding blade.

Vegetable techniques

ROLLING UP SPRING ROLLS

Cut each spring roll wrapper in half. Divide the filling evenly among the spring roll wrappers, fold in the sides and roll up tightly. (Spring roll wrappers are very delicate and should be covered with a damp cloth while you work.) Seal the edges using cornflour mixed into a paste with a little water.

DEEP-FRYING

When deep-frying, fill the fryer only one-third full of oil: do not leave it unattended. Dry food thoroughly before deep-frying. Preheat the oil in a deep-fat fryer or deep saucepan to 180°C (350°F). Place a bread cube in the oil: if it sizzles and turns golden brown in 15 seconds, the oil is hot enough.

PREPARING MANDARIN PANCAKES

Using a fork, slowly incorporate the flour into the water until a soft dough forms. Turn out onto a floured surface and knead for 5 minutes, or until smooth. Cover and set aside for 15 minutes.

Divide the dough into six and roll into balls. Flatten one ball, brush lightly with some sesame oil and place another flattened round of dough on top. Roll out into 21 cm (8¹/₂ inch) circles, about 1 mm (¹/₁₆ inch) thick.

Heat a dry frying pan over medium-high heat. Place a pancake in the hot pan and cook for 50–60 seconds, or until blistered and coloured. Flip over and cook for another 30–40 seconds.

Transfer the pancake to a plate and while it is still hot, carefully peel it apart, being careful of any hot steam. Repeat with the remaining pancakes.

Dessert techniques

MAKING CREPES

Melt some clarified butter or oil over medium heat in a 15–17 cm (6–7 inch) heavy-based or non-stick pan. When a haze forms, pour out any excess butter.

Stir the batter well and pour into the pan from a ladle or jug, starting in the centre and swirling the pan to create a thin coating. Tip out any excess.

Cook for 1 minute until bubbles appear, the batter sets and the edges are brown. Carefully loosen and lift the edges with a palette knife. Turn and cook for 30 seconds until golden. Remove from the pan and repeat.

MAKING TARTE TATIN

Add the apples to the pan of bubbling sugar and butter and arrange upright in a circular pattern.

Make sure the apples are tightly packed as they will reduce in size as they cook. Cook and baste the apples for 45 minutes over medium heat, or until the apples are soft and the syrup has reduced and is dark brown.

Remove the apples from the heat. Working quickly, place the circle of pastry on top of the apples. Use the handle of a spoon to tuck the edges into the pan.

Dessert techniques

STEAMED PUDDINGS

Thickly brush a pudding basin with melted butter. Line the base of the pudding basin with a disc of greaseproof paper.

Lay a sheet of foil on the work surface and cover with a sheet of greaseproof paper. Make a large pleat in the middle and grease the paper with some melted butter.

Place the mixture in the basin and hollow the surface slightly with the back of a wet spoon. Place the foil, paper side down, across the top and tie string securely around the rim and over the top to make a handle.

Place a saucer or trivet in a large pan and rest the pudding basin on it. Half-fill the pan with boiling water and bring to the boil. Cover and simmer according to the recipe, topping up the pan if necessary with more boiling water.

MAKING ITALIAN MERINGUE

Boil without stirring until the syrup reaches the soft-ball stage, 116–118°C (241–244°F). If you do not have a sugar thermometer, drop ¼ teaspoon of the syrup into iced water: it should hold its shape but be soft when pressed.

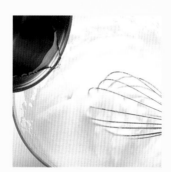

In a large heatproof bowl, beat the egg whites into soft peaks, using a balloon whisk or electric beaters. Avoiding the whisk, add the hot syrup in a thin steady stream, beating constantly until the whites are thick and glossy. Beat until cold.

HELPING A SOUFFLE TO RISE

Spoon the soufflé mixture into the dish and then run your thumb around the inside of the dish. The ridge this creates will help the soufflé rise evenly.

Dessert techniques

MAKING SUGAR SYRUP

Stir the sugar and water over low heat until the sugar dissolves completely.

Using a wet pastry brush, brush the sugar crystals from the side of the pan.

Boil, without stirring, until the syrup reaches the soft-ball stage, 116–118°C (241–244°F).

If you don't have a sugar thermometer, drop about ¹/4 teaspoon of the syrup into a bowl of iced water. The ball of syrup should hold its shape but be soft when pressed.

MAKING CARAMEL

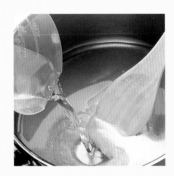

Place the caster sugar and water in a heavy-based pan. Fill a shallow pan with cold water and set it next to the stove.

Stir over low heat to dissolve the sugar. To prevent sugar crystals from forming, brush down the sides of the pan with a brush dipped in water.

Bring to the boil and simmer until the caramel takes on a deep golden colour. Swirl the pan to stop the caramel colouring unevenly.

Stop the cooking by plunging the bottom of the pan into the cold water for a few seconds.

Dessert techniques

MAKING CUSTARD

Whisk the hot infused milk or cream into the beaten eggs and sugar. Pour into a clean pan.

Stir gently over low heat with a wooden spoon for 10–15 minutes, or until the custard coats the back of the spoon and leaves a clear parting when a finger is drawn across. Do not boil, or the eggs will scramble.

Strain the warm custard through a fine sieve into a clean jug to remove any lumps.

USING GELATINE

Leaf gelatine has no flavour or colour, gives a softer set than gelatine powder, and is easier to use. Lower the leaves or sheets of gelatine into a bowl of cold water. Leave to soak for a few minutes, or until softened.

When the leaf is soft and pliable, carefully remove it and squeeze out any excess liquid. If gelatine leaves are not available and you are using powder, dissolve each teaspoon of powder in 1 tablespoon of water, following the manufacturer's instructions.

Baking techniques

PUFF PASTRY

Preparation time 1 day
Total cooking time Nil
Makes 530 g (1 lb 1 oz)

DOUGH BASE
250 g (8 oz) plain flour
1 teaspoon salt
2–3 drops of lemon juice
125 ml (4 fl oz) water
40 g (1¼ oz) unsalted butter, melted

100 g (3¼ oz) unsalted butter, chilled

One To make the dough base, sift the flour and salt onto a cool work surface and make a well in the centre. Add the lemon juice to the water, then place in the well with the butter and mix together with your fingertips. With the side of a palette knife or a pastry scraper, use a cutting action to draw in the flour and work it into the butter mixture until the dry flour disappears and the mixture resembles loose crumbs. Draw together with your hands and knead lightly, adding a few drops of water if necessary, to form a smooth soft ball of dough.

Two Cut an 'X' on top of the dough to prevent shrinkage, then wrap in lightly floured greaseproof paper or plastic wrap. Chill for 1 hour in the refrigerator—this will make the dough more pliable for rolling. Place the chilled butter between two pieces of greaseproof paper or plastic wrap. Tap it with the side of a rolling pin and shape into a 2 cm (³/4 inch) thick square. This action will make the butter pliable to roll, without melting it.

Three Unwrap the dough and place it on a lightly floured cool surface. Roll the dough from just off centre to form a cross with a mound in the centre.

Four Place the butter on the central mound and fold over the four sides of the dough to enclose it completely.

Five Roll over the top and bottom of the dough to seal the edges. On a lightly floured surface, roll the dough into a 12 x 35 cm (5 x 14 inch) rectangle.

Sift the flour and salt onto a work surface and make a well in the centre. Add the lemon juice, water and butter and blend together with your fingertips.

Cut an 'X' on top of the pastry with a sharp knife.

Unwrap the chilled dough and place it on a lightly floured surface. Roll from just off centre to form a cross with a mound in the centre.

Place the butter on the central mound and fold over the four sides of the dough to enclose it.

Six Fold in three by folding the bottom third up towards the middle and the top third down. Brush off the excess flour and ensure that the edges all meet neatly. Make an indentation with your finger to record the first roll and fold. Wrap in plastic wrap and chill for 30 minutes.

Seven Give the dough a quarter turn with the folded side on your left as if it was a book. With a rolling pin, gently press down to seal the edges.

Eight Repeat steps 5–7 three more times, remembering to record each roll with an indentation and chilling for 30 minutes after each roll. After two rolls and folds, you should have two indentations. The finished pastry should have four indentations, and will start to look smoother as you continue to roll and fold. Leave the dough to rest in the refrigerator for a final 30 minutes. The puff pastry is now ready to use. It can be frozen whole or cut into smaller portions, then used as needed.

CHEF'S TIPS *This pastry requires more effort and time than the other pastries, but the result is a lovely buttery and flaky base for any tart or pastry. If you are short of time, bought sheets or blocks of puff are a good alternative.*

When making puff pastry, work on a cool surface to prevent the butter from melting and forming a heavy dough. In hot weather, it may be necessary to refrigerate the dough for an extra 15 minutes during the final resting.

Making puff pastry is not difficult, but it is time consuming, so make two or three quantities at once and freeze the extra. Thaw the pastry by leaving it overnight in the refrigerator. Puff will keep in the refrigerator for 4 days and in the freezer for 3 months.

Seal the edges of the dough by pressing down with a rolling pin. Roll the pastry into a rectangle.

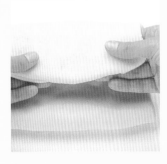

Fold the dough in three by folding the bottom third up towards the middle and the top third down.

After chilling the dough, put it on the surface in front of you as before and turn it a quarter turn so that it looks like a book with the binding on the left. Press down to seal the edges, then roll, fold and chill again.

Continue rolling, folding and chilling, trying to maintain an even finish and neat corners.

Baking techniques

SHORTCRUST PASTRY

Preparation time 10 minutes + 20 minutes chilling
Total cooking time Nil
Makes 530 g (1 lb 1 oz)

200 g (6½ oz) plain flour
large pinch of salt
100 g (3¼ oz) unsalted butter, chilled
1 egg, lightly beaten
2–3 teaspoons water

One Sift the flour and salt into a large bowl. Cut the butter into small 1 cm (½ inch) cubes and place in the flour.

Two Rub the butter into the flour with your fingertips until the mixture resembles fine breadcrumbs.

Three Make a well in the centre and pour in the combined egg and water.

Four Slowly work the mixture together with a palette knife or pastry scraper until it forms a rough ball. If it is slightly sticky, add a little more flour. Turn out onto a lightly floured cool surface and knead very gently until just smooth (no more than 20 seconds). Wrap the pastry in plastic wrap and chill for at least 20 minutes before using.

CHEF'S TIP *This quantity of pastry is sufficient to line two shallow 18–20 cm (7–8 inch) flan tins. If only making one flan or tart, divide the pastry into two and wrap separately in plastic wrap. Use one piece and freeze the other in an airtight plastic bag for another occasion.*

Put the cubes of butter in the flour and salt, and rub into the dry ingredients.

Continue rubbing the butter into the flour until the mixture resembles fine breadcrumbs.

Pour the combined egg and water into the well.

Slowly work the mixture together with a palette knife until it forms a rough ball.

Baking techniques

CHOUX PASTRY

Preparation time 5 minutes
Total cooking time 10–15 minutes
Makes 250 g (8 oz)

60 g (2 oz) plain flour
125 ml (4 fl oz) water
50 g (1¾ oz) unsalted butter, cubed
pinch of salt
pinch of sugar
2 eggs

One Sift the flour onto a sheet of greaseproof paper. Place the water, butter, salt and sugar in a pan. Heat until the butter and water come to the boil. Remove from the heat and add the flour all at once.

Two Mix well with a wooden spoon. Return to the heat and mix until a smooth ball forms and the paste leaves the sides of the pan.

Three Remove from the heat and place the paste in a bowl. Lightly beat the eggs in a small bowl. Using a wooden spoon or electric beaters, add the eggs to the paste a little at a time, beating well after each addition.

Four The mixture is ready to use when it is smooth, thick and glossy.

CHEF'S TIPS *It is essential when making choux to measure the ingredients carefully, as too much moisture can cause the choux to collapse. Traditionally, bakers weigh the eggs in order to determine the weight of the dry ingredients.*

Don't be fooled by golden coloured choux. If the cracks of the choux are still light yellow or much lighter than the rest, this indicates that the interior is not quite cooked. Reduce the oven to warm 160°C (315°F/Gas 2–3) and continue baking.

Once boiling, remove from the heat and immediately stir in the sifted flour.

Return the pan to the heat and cook until the mixture forms a smooth ball that comes away from the sides of the pan.

Remove from the heat and transfer the mixture to a bowl. Gradually beat in the eggs with a wooden spoon.

The mixture is ready to use when it is smooth, thick and glossy.

Baking techniques

SWEET PASTRY

Preparation time 10 minutes + 20 minutes chilling
Total cooking time Nil
Makes 480 g (15¼ oz)

200 g (6½ oz) plain flour
large pinch of salt
70 g (2¼ oz) unsalted butter, chilled
80 g (2¾ oz) caster sugar
1 egg, lightly beaten
1–2 drops vanilla extract or essence

One Sift the flour and salt into a large bowl. Cut the butter into small 1 cm (½ inch) cubes and place in the flour. Rub the butter into the flour with your fingertips until the mixture resembles fine breadcrumbs.

Two Stir in the sugar and make a well in the centre. Pour in the combined egg and vanilla and slowly work the mixture together with a palette knife or a pastry scraper. If the dough is too dry, sprinkle it with a little water until it just holds together.

Three Remove the dough from the bowl onto a lightly floured surface. Using the palm of your hand, smear the dough away from you until it is smooth.

Four Gather the dough into a ball and flatten it slightly. Wrap in plastic wrap and place in the refrigerator to chill for 20 minutes before using.

CHEF'S TIPS *This quantity of pastry is sufficient to line two shallow 18–20 cm (7–8 inch) flan tins. If only making one flan or tart, divide the pastry into two and wrap separately in plastic wrap. Use one piece and freeze the other in an airtight plastic bag for another occasion.*

Sift the flour and salt into a large bowl. Cut the butter into small cubes and rub into the flour.

Stir in the sugar. Make a well in the centre and add the combined egg and vanilla.

Using the palm of your hand, smear the dough away from you on a lightly floured surface until smooth.

Gather the dough into a ball and flatten slightly.

Baking techniques

LINING A FLAN TIN

Place the dough over a rolling pin and unroll loosely over the tin.

Press the pastry gently into the flutes or side of the tin with a small ball of dough.

Use a rolling pin to trim the pastry edges by gently but firmly rolling over the top of the tin. Refrigerate for 10 minutes.

Prick the pastry shell lightly with a fork to allow the steam to escape during baking. Do not make holes all the way through the pastry to the tin.

BLIND BAKING

Crush a sheet of greaseproof paper lightly into a ball. Open out the paper, then lay it inside the pastry shell.

Spread a layer of baking beads or uncooked rice or beans over the paper, then press down gently so that the beads and paper rest firmly against the side of the pastry shell.

Bake for the time specified in the recipe, or until firm. Remove the beads and paper.

If instructed in the recipe, bake again until the pastry looks dry and evenly coloured.

Baking techniques

CROISSANTS

When the dough has risen, punch it down, then roll it out to a rectangle just over twice as long as the butter and a little wider. Put the butter on the lower half of the dough and bring the dough over to enclose it.

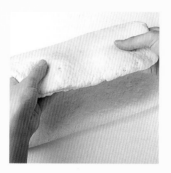

Turn the dough so the fold is on the right, then roll out into a rectangle. Fold the dough into even thirds, like a letter, with the bottom third up and the top third down. Chill, then repeat twice.

Cut the dough in half and roll out into two large rectangles. Using a triangular template, cut the rectangles into six triangles (you will be left with the two end pieces).

Roll the triangles from the wide end to form crescents.

BAGELS

Roll the dough into tight balls, then poke your finger through the centre and gently enlarge the hole until the dough resembles a doughnut.

Cook the bagels in simmering water for 1 minute each side.

Brush the bagels with beaten egg before baking them for 20–25 minutes. They can be sprinkled with poppy or sesame seeds before baking.

LE CORDON BLEU ✤ COMPLETE COOK

Baking techniques

BABA DOUGH

Using the fingers of one hand, held lightly apart, bring the ingredients together to form a soft elastic dough. Beat with the hand for about 5 minutes, or until smooth.

Add the raisins and rum and beat with your hand to combine. Scrape down the sides of the bowl and pour the warm butter over the surface of the dough.

Cover and leave to prove for about 30 minutes, or until doubled in volume. Beat the baba mixture to incorporate the butter.

Spoon the mixture into a piping bag fitted with a 2 cm (3/4 inch) plain nozzle and pipe into the tins. Cover with a damp cloth and prove until the mixture reaches the tops of the tins.

LAYERING FILO PASTRY

Place the sheets of filo pastry on a work surface and cover with a damp tea towel. Work with one sheet at a time, keeping the rest covered to stop them drying out.

Brush the first sheet with melted butter, then place another sheet on top and brush again with melted butter. Repeat until you have the number of layers specified in the recipe.

CRUMPETS

Cook the crumpets until bubbles appear on the surface. They are ready to turn over when the top has dried out enough to form a skin.

Baking techniques

USING YEAST

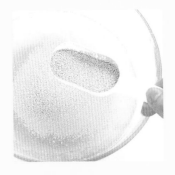

If using dried yeast, place the water in a small glass bowl and sprinkle with the yeast and sugar, if specified in the recipe. Leave to dissolve for 5 minutes, then stir with a wooden spoon.

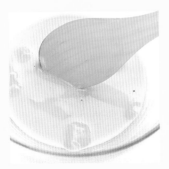

If using fresh yeast, crumble the yeast into a small glass bowl and add the water and sugar, if specified in the recipe. Cream together, then stir in a pinch of flour. Leave until bubbles form on the surface.

If using easy-blend yeast, sift the yeast into a bowl with all the dry ingredients. The yeast will be activated when the liquid is added.

SPONGING BREAD DOUGH

Sieve the flour into a large mixing bowl, add the salt and sugar, if specified in the recipe, and make a well in the centre. Add the yeast mixture.

Draw in some of the flour from the side of the bowl to form a soft paste in the well. Cover the bowl with a clean, damp tea towel and leave for about 30 minutes to expand slightly.

Add the remaining liquid ingredients, as specified in the recipe, to the well and stir in the rest of the flour to form a soft dough.

Baking techniques

KNEADING BREAD DOUGH

Place the dough on a lightly floured work surface and begin to knead it.

Flatten the dough away from you, then fold it over towards you. Continue kneading in this way.

As the dough becomes more stretchy, use the heel of your hand to push one half away from you as you pull the other half towards you. Rotate the dough as you knead.

The dough is well kneaded when it is smooth, shiny and elastic. A finger mark pressed into the dough should spring back immediately.

SHAPING A LOAF

Roll the dough out into a large rectangle, then roll it up tightly into a sausage shape and press gently to seal the seam.

Fold the dough in on itself, using your thumbs to ensure the centre is tucked in tightly (this will help give a good texture in the centre of the loaf).

Before placing in a tin or on a baking tray, simply tuck the ends under to give a neat finish to the bread.

Baking techniques

SLASHING AND SNIPPING A LOAF CRUST

Use a very sharp knife or scalpel to make slashes in the surface of the bread before or after it has proved.

Use a pair of scissors to make snips in the surface of the bread just before baking. This gives a chevron effect.

LINING A CAKE TIN

Put the tin on a sheet of baking paper and trace around the base with a pencil. Cut out the traced shape just inside the pencil marking.

Brush the inside of the tin with melted butter.

Position the piece of baking paper in the bottom of the greased tin. If stated in the recipe, line the side of the tin.

Grease the baking paper inside the tin, then sprinkle with plain flour and rotate to coat the base and side evenly. Tap out any excess flour.

Baking techniques

DOUBLE LINING A TIN

Fold a piece of baking paper in half and wrap around the tin. Mark and cut the end 2 cm (³/4 inch) longer than the circumference.

Cut two circles of baking paper to fit the base of the tin and place one on the bottom of the tin. Snip cuts along the folded edge of the baking paper.

Secure the snipped paper, cut-edge-down, inside the tin. Cover with the other circle. Grease and flour the tin if stated in the recipe.

Fold a sheet of baking paper, brown paper or newspaper in half lengthways and wrap it around the outside of the tin. Secure with string or tape.

LINING A LOAF OR SWISS ROLL TIN

Put the tin in the centre of a piece of baking paper. Make a diagonal cut from each corner of the paper to the corners of the tin.

Fold the paper between the cut edges to make it easier to put in position in the tin.

Overlap the corners of the paper and press to secure. Grease and flour the tin if stated in the recipe.

Baking techniques

CREAMING METHOD

(All the ingredients, including the eggs, should be brought to room temperature before use.) Cream the butter first, to soften, in the large bowl of an electric mixer or a large glass bowl. Beat in the sugar.

Beat the butter and sugar together until light and creamy. Use an electric mixer, electric hand beaters or a wooden spoon.

Add any flavourings and gradually beat in the eggs, one at a time, in about six additions. Beat well after each addition to prevent curdling. If the mixture does curdle, add a little flour.

WHISKING METHOD

Put the eggs and sugar together in a heatproof bowl.

Place the bowl over a pan of hot water and whisk using a balloon whisk or electric hand beaters until the mixture is thick enough to leave a trail when the whisk is lifted.

Remove the bowl from the pan and continue to whisk until cold. Gently fold in the sifted ingredients until just combined. Do not beat or overfold or you will lose the air that has been beaten into the mixture.

Baking techniques

SMOOTHING CAKE MIX

Follow the recipe instructions when preparing a cake for the oven. To prevent the cake peaking and cracking, some recipes will instruct you to make a dip in the centre of the mixture with the back of a wet spoon.

Alternatively, simply smooth the surface of the mixture with the back of a wet spoon to give the finished cake a flat top.

DROPPED BISCUITS

The dough for dropped biscuits needs to be soft enough to fall from the spoon. Scoop up balls of dough with a tablespoon and drop them onto the prepared baking tray.

PIPED BISCUITS

Piping biscuits, rather than dropping or spooning the dough, gives a more even size and neat appearance. Pipe onto the prepared baking tray with a shaped nozzle, spacing them well apart.

Baking techniques

MAKING FRUIT CAKES

Dried fruits tend to sink to the bottom of cakes. Use this method to help distribute it more evenly. Fruit for cakes should be chopped into small pieces of uniform size.

Stir the fruit through the flour mixture to help prevent it sinking during cooking.

When all the ingredients have been added, spoon the mixture into the prepared tin.

TESTING SPONGE CAKES FOR DONENESS

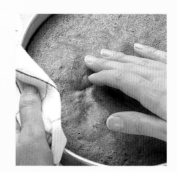

As ovens vary in their performance, cakes should be tested before removing from the tin in case they require a longer cooking time. Lightly press the centre of the cake with your fingertips—if it is done, the indentation will spring back. The edge of the cake should shrink slightly from the side of the tin.

Insert a metal skewer into the centre of the cake. It is done when the skewer comes out clean.

Baking techniques

ICING A CAKE

Decorating a cake is easy with ready-made marzipan and soft icing. To start, use small pieces of marzipan to fill in any holes in the cake.

Brush a 25 cm (10 inch) cake board with alcohol. Roll out the remaining icing and cover the board with a 5 mm (1/4 inch) layer, then trim any excess icing from around the edge. Reserve the remaining icing.

On a surface dusted with icing sugar, roll out the remaining marzipan into a circle large enough to cover the cake. Using a rolling pin, lift it over the cake.

Using two large flat implements, transfer the cake to the centre of the board.

Ease the marzipan onto the cake, smoothing out any creases. Trim the excess marzipan from around the edge of the cake, then leave to harden overnight.

To make the royal icing, beat together the egg white and half the icing sugar to form a smooth paste. Continue adding sugar until thick, then add the lemon juice to soften to a fairly stiff piping consistency.

Brush the marzipan with gin or vodka, then cover with a 4 mm (1/4 inch) layer of soft icing, using the same method as for the marzipan. Trim any excess icing from around the base of the cake.

Set aside a third of the icing, covering the surface with plastic wrap. Place the remaining icing in a piping bag with a small plain nozzle and pipe a decorative edge around the join between the cake and board.

Glossary of terms

À LA Means 'in the style of' in French.

AL', ALL', ALLA Means 'in the style of' in Italian.

AL DENTE Meaning 'to the tooth' in Italian. Pasta and risotto rice are cooked until they are al dente, meaning the outside is tender but the centre still has a little resistance or 'bite'. Pasta cooked beyond this point becomes soggy.

AMARETTI Small biscuits like macaroons, made from sweet and bitter almonds. These vary in size, but are usually 2–3 cm wide.

AMUSE GUEULE Meaning 'mouth pleaser' in French, this tiny appetiser is served before a meal, often as a complimentary taster in a restaurant.

ARTICHOKE The edible flower of a member of the thistle family. Some varieties have thorns and the types vary greatly in size. The largest artichokes are usually boiled before serving, but the smallest and most tender can be eaten raw as antipasto. Most common varieties include Romanesco (large and purple), Precoce di Chioggia (large and green), Violetto Toscano (small and tender enough to eat raw) and Spinoso di Palermo (a purple variety originating in Sicily).

BAIN-MARIE Literally a 'water bath' for gentle oven-cooking of delicate terrines and desserts. Usually the dish is placed in a roasting tin or other large ovenproof container and then boiling water is poured into the tin to come halfway up the side of the dish.

BAKE To cook in an oven in dry heat, usually until browned on the outside.

BAKE BLIND To bake a pastry case while it is unfilled to set the pastry. The pastry is usually lined with a sheet of crumpled baking paper or foil, which is then spread with a layer of baking beads or uncooked rice or beans. This stops the sides collapsing or the base from bubbling up. The pastry is sometimes baked again without the paper and beads to dry it out.

BASTE, TO To spoon melted fat or liquid over food as it cooks to stop it drying out and to add flavour.

BATON A stick of vegetable about 6 x 2 x 2 cm. Vegetables are cut into uniform batons so they cook evenly.

BATTER A mixture of flour, milk and eggs used for pancakes and to coat food before frying. Also refers to soft cake, biscuit and scone mixtures.

BEARD Also called a byssus, this is the mass of silky threads found at the opening of the shell that mussels use to attach themselves to rocks.

BEAT, TO To incorporate air into a mixture with a spoon, fork or whisk.

BLANCH, TO To cook in boiling water for a few minutes and then refresh in cold water. This keeps colour in vegetables and loosens tomato and fruit skins. Also refers to potato chips that are precooked in hot fat before being fully cooked—this improves their texture and colour.

BLANQUETTE A white stew (most usually of veal) made with white stock thickened with egg and cream.

BLEND, TO To mix together well.

BOCCONCINI Means literally 'small mouthful' and is used to describe various foods, but generally refers to small balls of mozzarella cheese, about the size of walnuts.

BONE, TO To remove the bones from a bird or piece of meat leaving the flesh in its original shape.

BOUQUET GARNI A bundle of herbs used to flavour dishes. Made by tying sprigs of parsley, thyme, celery leaves and a bay leaf in either a piece of muslin or portion of leek.

BRAISE, TO To cook slowly on a bed of chopped vegetables and with a little liquid in a covered pan.

BROWN, TO To cook food until the outer surface caramelises or a maillard reaction occurs (the reaction between a sugar and an amino acid, which causes food to brown). Browning does not mean cooking through.

BROWN STOCK Stock made from browned beef or veal bones. As beef and veal stock are usually inter-changeable, the term 'brown stock' is used. The best commercial stocks come freshly made in tubs, though stock sold in cartons and catering-quality powdered stock can also be good.

BRÛLÉ(E), BRÛLER, TO To brown or caramelise under heat. The term is usually applied to sugar, as in the dessert crème brulée. This is usually done under a very hot grill but a blowtorch can also be used.

BUTTER Butter is flavoured both by the lactic fermentation of cream and the diet of the cows from whose milk it is

made. Use either salted or unsalted for savoury dishes, but always use unsalted butter in sweet recipes.

BUTTERMILK Originally the by-product of the butter-making process—the liquid left after cream is churned into butter. Today it is made from pasteurised skim milk to which an acid-producing bacteria is added, thickening it and giving it is characteristic tang.

CALVADOS A spirit made by distilling cider, it is often used in French cooking.

CAPERS The pickled flowers of the caper bush. They are available preserved in brine, vinegar or salt and should be rinsed well and squeezed dry before use.

CARAMELISE, TO To heat food until the sugars on the surface break down and form a brown coating, which may be sweet or savoury.

CASSEROLE, TO To slowly cook a dish consisting of meat and/or vegetables on the stove or in the oven, tightly covered with a lid so that all the flavour and aroma is contained.

CEPES The French name for a porcini or boletus mushroom. Usually dried and reconstituted in boiling water, but avail-able fresh in the spring and autumn.

CHASSEUR, À LA A French term for 'hunter style', usually meaning with onions and tomatoes. Often described simply as chasseur.

CLARIFIED BUTTER Made by melting butter so that the fat separates out from the impurities and water. The fat is then either spooned off or the water tipped away and the butter reset. Clarified

butter keeps for longer than ordinary butter because all the water has been removed and can be used for cooking at higher temperatures because it has a higher burning point. It is often used in Indian cooking.

COATING CONSISTENCY A liquid that is thick enough to coat a food evenly without running off again. Test by pouring over the back of a spoon—a line drawn down the centre of the spoon should hold its shape.

CONCASSÉE Meaning finely chopped, this term is usually reserved for peeled, seeded and chopped tomatoes.

CONFIT From the French word for 'preserve', confit is usually made from goose or duck meat, cooked in its own fat and then preserved in a jar or pot. It is eaten on its own or added to dishes such as cassoulet for extra flavour.

CORAL The eggs of the female lobster, which turn red when cooked and are used for flavouring sauces. Scallop roes are also sometimes called corals

CORNICHON The French term for a small gherkin. It you can't find cornichons, you can use cocktail gherkins instead.

COULIS A thick, sieved purée, usually of tomatoes or fruit.

COURT BOUILLON A flavoured poaching liquid, most often used for cooking fish.

CRÈME DE CASSIS Originating near Dijon in France, crème de cassis is a blackcurrant liqueur used in desserts and also to flavour the drink kir.

CRÈME FRAÎCHE Lightly fermented, this is slightly tart and can often be used instead of cream in cooking.

CRIMP, TO To mark the edge of pastry or biscuits or to seal two layers of pastry together in a scalloped pattern.

CROQUETTE Mashed potato, minced meat, fish or vegetables, or any other similar mixture, made into a paste, then formed into log shapes, which are crumbed and fried.

CROÛTE, EN Enclosed in pastry before baking, for example: chicken en croûte.

CRUSTACEAN An aquatic animal, such as a crab or lobster with a hard external, segmented shell and soft body.

CUTLET A piece of meat cut through the ribcage with the vertebrae and rib bone still attached.

DARIOLE A small (individual-sized) castle-shaped mould.

DEEP-FRY To fry something in oil. The food is completely immersed in the oil.

DEGLAZE, TO To loosen meat juices and flavours that may have stuck to the bottom of the pan when frying or roasting meat. A liquid is added to the hot pan and the pan is scraped and stirred. The liquid is then added to the dish or used to make gravy.

DEGORGE, TO To salt something like eggplant (aubergine) to make it give up any bitter liquid, or to soak meat or fish in water to get rid of any impurities.

DICE Cut into small cubes. Dice are smaller than cubes.

DIJON MUSTARD A pale yellow mustard, made from verjuice or white wine and mustard seeds that have been ground to a flour. Originating in Dijon, this style of mustard is now made all over France.

DONENESS The point at which something is cooked through.

DRIZZLE, TO To sprinkle liquid in a continuous stream.

DROPPING CONSISTENCY When a mixture such as cake dough falls slowly off a spoon, that is, it won't run off or stay put.

DRY FRY, TO To cook food in a frying pan without any fat.

DUST, TO To sprinkle lightly with a powder such as icing sugar or cocoa.

DUXELLES Chopped shallots or onions and chopped mushrooms sautéed in butter.

EGG GLAZE A glaze used in baking made from eggs and water or milk.

EMULSION A stable suspension of fat in a liquid. This can be raw (as in mayonnaise) or cooked (hollandaise).

FEUILLETÉ(E) Meaning flaky and many layered. Used to describe pastries such as puff pastry.

FILLET Boneless piece of fish or meat.

FILLET, TO To take the flesh off the bones of poultry, meat or a fish.

FIVE-SPICE POWDER This Chinese spice mix is generally made with star anise, cassia, Sichuan pepper, fennel seeds and cloves, which gives a balance of sweet, hot and aromatic flavours. Five-spice may also include cardamom, coriander, dried orange peel and ginger.

FLAMBÉ (FLAMBER), TO Meaning 'to flame', this involves setting fire to alcohol in order to burn it off, leaving just the flavour behind.

FLAT-LEAF PARSLEY Also known as Italian or continental parsley. Used as an ingredient rather than a garnish, unlike curly parsley.

FLUTE Indentations made in the edges of pastry either to help seal it together or for decoration.

FOLD IN, TO To mix two things together using a gentle lifting and turning motion rather than stirring, to avoid losing trapped air bubbles. Used for cake mixtures and meringues. Usually done with a spatula.

FRENCH, TO To trim the meat away from the bones of chops or ribs leaving the bone exposed.

FROMAGE FRAIS A fresh white cheese with a smooth creamy consistency. There are a number of varieties, with their differences lying mainly in their fat content, which may affect the cooking qualities. Generally fromage frais makes a good low-fat alternative to cream.

FRY, TO To seal the surface of food quickly by cooking it in hot fat.

FUMÉ French for smoked.

GIBLETS The neck, gizzard, liver and heart of poultry. Now not often sold in a package inside the chicken, but may be bought separately.

GLAZE A coating that is applied to a surface to make it shine or to help it colour when cooked, such as an egg wash for uncooked pastry and an apricot glaze for fruit tarts.

GOOSE FAT This is a soft fat that melts at low temperature and is used a lot in the cooking of southwest France to give a rich texture to dishes. It is available in tins from butchers. Duck fat can be substituted, although it needs to be heated to a higher temperature.

GORGONZOLA A blue cheese, originally made in Gorgonzola in Italy but now produced in other regions as well. It melts well and is often used in sauces. If not available, use another strong-flavoured full-fat blue cheese, such as Stilton or Roquefort.

GOUJON A small piece of fried fish. The term is now also used for a piece of chicken breast meat.

GRUYÈRE This is a pressed hard cheese with a nutty flavour, commonly made in Switzerland and the French Alps from unpasteurised cow's milk. Although French Gruyère does have a slightly different flavour to the Swiss variety, the two are interchangeable in recipes. Gruyère is pale yellow and very firm and close-textured with a sprinkling of small holes. The best Gruyère has a slight glistening of moisture around the holes.

HAND-HOT 37°C—the temperature at which a liquid feels neither hot nor cold. Also known as blood temperature and lukewarm.

HARICOT BEANS The general French name for beans, though the term is also used to mean just a kind of small, dried bean. Dried haricot beans come in many different varieties, including cannellini (kidney-shaped beans), flageolet (white or pale green beans) and navy beans (used to make baked beans). When slow-cooked in stews such as cassoulet they become tender. They also break down very well when mashed to give a smooth purée.

HOCK The lower half of an animal's leg between the foot and lower limb.

HORS D'OEUVRES Small dishes, both hot and cold, served at the start of a meal. Soup is not an hors d'oeuvre but a separate course on its own.

HULL, TO To remove the stalks from berry fruit.

JULIENNE To cut a vegetable or citrus rind into short, thin strips (julienne strips), the size and shape of matchsticks. Vegetables used as a garnish or to be served in soups are often julienned for decorative purposes or to ensure quick even cooking.

JUNIPER BERRIES Blackish-purple berries with a resinous flavour. Used in stews and robust game dishes. Crush the berries lightly before use to release their flavour.

KNEAD, TO To mix a stiff dough by manipulating it by hand or with a mechanical dough hook in order to make it smooth. In bread-making, this also helps develop the gluten.

KNOCK BACK, TO To knead gas bubbles out of a yeast-risen dough.

KNOCK UP, TO To separate the layers of puff pastry by running the back of the knife up the sides of the cut surface.

LAMBS LETTUCE Also known as corn salad or mache. Small salad leaves which grow in rosette-like bunches.

LARDONS Short strips of pork fat or slab bacon.

LIAISON A thickening agent for a sauce, soup or stew made from eggs and cream, beurre manié or starches such as arrowroot. A liaison is added at the end of cooking.

LOIN Butchery term for the back portion of an animal comprising the last four vertebrae attached to the ribs and the ribless vertebrae along with all the attached meat. Can also be used to describe the same piece without bones.

MACERATE, TO To soak food in a liquid so it absorbs the flavour of the liquid. Often used to describe soaking fruit in alcohol and sugar syrup.

MADEIRA A type of fortified wine from the Portuguese island of Madeira. There are a number of different varieties of Madeira, from sweet (Malmsey or Malvasia and Bual), to medium (Verdelho) and dry (Sercial).

MARINADE A collection of wet ingredients in which foods are soaked so they take on flavour and, sometimes, to tenderise. Many marinades include an acid such as fruit juice (to tenderise meat) and an oil.

MARROWBONE Leg bone, usually veal or beef which contains marrow. Buy pieces already cut into sections.

MARSALA A fortified wine from Marsala in Sicily that comes in varying degrees of dryness and sweetness. Dry Marsalas are used in savoury dishes, and sweet ones in desserts such as zabaglione. Do not try to use sweet Marsala in savoury dishes.

MARYLAND An Australian term for the leg and thigh portion of chicken.

MASCARPONE A cream cheese originally from Lombardia in Italy. Made with cream rather than milk, it is very high in fat. Mascarpone is generally used in desserts such as tiramisu and is also a good substitute for cream in sauces.

MEDALLION A small round piece of lean meat.

MEUNIÈRE, À LA A lightly floured food, usually fish, cooked in butter and garnished with lemon juice and parsley.

MIREPOIX Chopped vegetables on which pieces of meat are braised. They add flavour to the finished dish.

MISE EN PLACE To collect together, weigh and prepare the ingredients of a recipe before the actual assembling or cooking takes place.

MONTER, TO To add volume to an ingredient such as cream or egg white by whipping in air, or to add butter to a sauce at the end of cooking to make it shiny.

MUSSELS Bivalve molluscs that grow in clusters around sandbanks, rocks and other objects in the sea. They hold onto rocks with a mass of long silky threads found at the opening of the shell. There are many varieties worldwide, including green-lipped mussels from New Zealand, the common mussel and the European. Smaller mussels are often more tender than large.

OLIVE The fruit of the olive tree, which was first cultivated some 3000 years ago for fruit and oil. Today, olives are grown around the Mediterranean, where they originated, but also in North and South America and Australia. Fresh green olives are available from the summer and are picked before they start to turn black, while fresh black olives are available from the autumn through to winter. Though green and black olives have a different flavour, they can be used interchangeably in recipes unless the final colour is a factor.

OLIVE OIL Extra-virgin and virgin olive oils are pressed without any heat or chemicals and are best used in simple uncooked dishes and for salads. Pure olive oil can be used for cooking or deep-frying. The colour of olive oil is goverened by the type of olive used and does not indicate quality. Olive oil is best stored in dark-coloured glass bottles or tins.

ORANGE FLOWER WATER This is produced when the flower of the bitter orange is distilled. Orange flower water is a delicate flavouring used in some dessert recipes.

OYSTERS Bivalve molluscs that grow, wild or farmed, on coastlines around the world. There are many varieties, including the European (known as 'native' in Britain), which has a round flat shell; the Portuguese, an oyster with a concave whitish-brown shell, now though to be the same as the Pacific

oyster; the greyish shelled American oyster; and the Sydney rock oyster. Oysters should be bought live, with the shells closed. If buying open oysters, prick the little hairs around the edge of the flesh—these will retract if the oyster is alive. Unopened oysters will keep in the fridge for a week. If open, store in their liquid and eat within 24 hours.

PANCETTA Cured belly of pork, somewhat like streaky bacon. Available in flat pieces or rolled up (arrotolata), and both smoked and unsmoked. Generally used, either sliced or cut into cubes, as an ingredient in dishes like spaghetti carbonara.

PAPILLOTE, EN To cook food (often fish) wrapped in a paper parcel, which puffs up. Dishes cooked like this are served at the table. Papillote also describes the white paper frill used to decorate tips of bones.

PARBOIL, TO To half-cook something in boiling water. Most commonly used for potatoes before roasting.

PARMA HAM This prosciutto comes from traditionally reared pigs fed on the whey from making Parmigiano Reggiano. It has a sweet taste and is only flavoured with salt. Parma hams can be identified by the stamp on the skin showing the five-pointed star of the Dukes of Parma. Other prosciutto can be used if Parma ham is unavailable.

PASS, TO To push food through a fine sieve.

PASSATA Meaning 'puréed', this most commonly refers to a smooth uncooked tomato pulp bought in tins or jars. The best ones have no added flavourings.

PÂTÉ A cooked paste of meat, poultry or fish, either set in a terrine or cooked in pastry 'en croute'.

PAUPIETTE A stuffed, rolled piece of meat or fish.

PECORINO One of Italy's most popular cheeses, with virtually every region producing a version. Made from sheep's milk and always by the same method, although the result varies according to the milk and ageing process used.

POACH, TO To cook gently in a barely simmering liquid.

POUSSIN A baby chicken weighing about 450–500 g (14 oz–1 lb). Poussins are often spatchcocked and grilled or stuffed. Usually one poussin is served per person, though slightly bigger ones are adequate for two people.

PROSCIUTTO Italian name for ham. Prosciutto crudo is cured ham and includes Parma ham and San Daniele. Prosciutto cotto is cooked ham.

PROVE, TO To allow a yeasted dough to rise; also to heat a frying pan or wok with oil or salt and then rub the surface, thus filling in any minute marks with the mixture and making it non-stick.

PURÉE A fine, soft, almost pourable paste of processed or pounded food.

PUY LENTILS Tiny green lentils from Puy in central France that are thought to be of a high quality. Puy lentils do not need to be presoaked and do not break down when cooked. They have a firm texture and go very well with both meat and fish. Traditionally they are served with a mustard vinaigrette.

REDUCE, TO To boil a liquid in order to evaporate off water. This thickens the liquid and intensifies the flavour.

REFRESH, TO To put just-cooked items into cold water to prevent them from cooking further.

REST/RELAX, TO To leave pastry in the fridge to allow the gluten, which will have been stretched during rolling, to contract again. Also means to leave batters until the starch cells in the flour have swelled through contact with the liquid; or to leave meat to let the juices settle back into the flesh before carving.

RISOTTO RICE Round-grained, very absorbent rice, cultivated in northern Italy. Risotto rice comes in four categories, classified not by quality but by the size of each grain. The smallest, Riso Comune (common rice) is very quick to cook (12–13 minutes) and is ideal for rice pudding. Semifino rice includes varieties like vialone nano and cooks in about 15 minutes. Fino takes a minute longer and has more bite. The largest, Superfino, includes arborio and carnaroli and takes about 20 minutes to cook until al dente.

ROAST, TO To cook in an oven at a high temperature without any covering to give a crisp, well-browned exterior and a just-cooked moist interior. Usually applied to meat or vegetables, though anything can be roasted.

ROUX A mixture of flour and fat cooked together and then used as a thickening agent, for example, in sauces and soups. A white roux is cooked until just a pale yellow, a blonde roux until it is a gold colour and a brown roux until it is a darker golden brown.

RUB IN, TO To integrate hard fat into flour by rubbing the two together with your fingertips until the mixture resembles breadcrumbs.

SAFFRON The dried dark orange stigmas of a type of crocus flower, which are used to add aroma and flavour to food. Only a few threads are needed for each recipe as they are very pungent (and expensive).

SALT COD Cod that has been gutted, salted and dried. Different from stockfish, which is just dried but not salted. Popular in northern Europe. A centre-cut fillet of salt cod tends to be meatier than the thinner tail end, and some varieties are drier than others so the soaking time does vary. Also sold as morue, bacalao, bacalhau and baccala.

SAUTER (SAUTÉ), TO To shallow-fry food in hot fat while shaking the pan and tossing the food.

SCALLOP, TO A way to decorate pastry edges by pushing in the edge with one finger while pushing the pastry on both sides of that piece in the opposite direction with the other thumb and finger.

SCORE, TO To make a shallow cut with a knife without cutting all the way through.

SEASON, TO To add flavour to something, usually with salt and pepper, or to smooth out the surface of a pan using hot oil or salt.

SEIZE When melted chocolate turns into a lumpy mass because a tiny amount of liquid, usually condensed steam, drips into it.

SHANK Part of the leg of beef, veal, lamb or pork.

SHUCK, TO To open bivalves such as oysters or to remove the husks, shells or pods from seeds.

SIMMER, TO To maintain a cooking liquid at a temperature just below boiling point.

SKIM, TO To remove fat or scum from the surface of a liquid with a large spoon, ladle or skimmer.

SPONGE A bubbly, batter-like mixture made by mixing flour, yeast and a liquid and allowing it to stand for several hours. The first step in some bread-making recipes. A type of fatless cake.

STEAM, TO To cook in the steam given off by boiling or simmering water.

STIR-FRY, TO To cook pieces of food quickly in a wok using only a little oil and moving them around constantly.

SUET Hard fat from around the kidneys which is particularly good for cooking. Buy pre-grated or grate your own from a block or piece.

TOMALLEY The green-coloured liver of a lobster.

TOULOUSE SAUSAGE A general term for meaty pork grilling sausages, often sold in a coil.

TRUFFLES Considered an expensive delicacy, truffles are the most valuable of all fungi due to their increasing rarity and the labour-intensive methods of harvest (they are sniffed out by specially trained dogs or pigs). The black truffles found in France, specifically around Périgord, are often considered the best black truffles in the world. Truffles are best eaten fresh, but can also be bought preserved in jars and only need to be used in small amounts to flavour dishes.

TRUSS, TO To hold something, usually meat or poultry, in shape with string or skewers while it cooks.

VANILLA EXTRACT Made by using alcohol to extract the vanilla flavour from pods and not to be confused with artificial vanilla essence, which is made with synthetic vanillin. The pods are picked when green, at which stage they have no flavour, and left to sweat and dry in the sun, causing them to turn deep brown. Vanilla extract is strong and should be used sparingly.

WHIP, TO To incorporate air into something by beating it (for example, cream or egg white) with a whisk or to form an emulsion by the same means (as with mayonnaise).

YEAST Available both fresh and dried. Fresh yeast is sold as a compressed solid and should be moist and creamy grey in colour and smell pleasantly yeasty. Dried yeast is sold in granules or as an easy-blend yeast (that does not need to be mixed with water first). Dried yeast has twice the potency of fresh yeast. For every 15 g of fresh yeast specified, you could use 7 g dried yeast instead.

ZEST The coloured outer layer of citrus fruit that contains the essential oils.

Index

Gorgonzola, 560
    Bruschetta with Parma ham and
Gorgonzola, 26
    Linguine with Gorgonzola sauce, 291
Gougères, 115
    Prawn gougères, 33
    Smoked haddock gougères, 167
goujon, 560
Granary bread, 463
granita, Coffee, with panna cotta, 407
Gratin dauphinois, 339
Gratin of root vegetables, 318
Gratin of summer berries, 381
gratin, Salmon, leek and potato, 179
Gravlax, 143
gravy, Thickened roast, 346
Greek salad, Rustic, 124
Green beans with bacon, 321
Green peppercorn sauce, 351
Grilled marinated vegetables, 331
Gruyère, 560
    Pasta with Parmesan and Gruyère, 305

H
ham
    Bruschetta with Parma ham and
        Gorgonzola, 26
    carving, 531
    Honey-glazed spiced ham, 272
    Parma ham and melon fingers, 40
    preparing, 531
haricot beans, 560
Herb dip for crudités, 31
herb scones
    Beef casserole with, 242
    Rabbit and marjoram cobbler with, 277
Herb tagliatelle with mushrooms and olive
    oil, 297
Hollandaise sauce, 101, 364, 521
Honey-glazed spiced ham, 272
hors d'oeuvres, 561
Hot cross buns, 474

I
ice cream, Vanilla, 409
Insalata caprese, 126
Italian meatballs, 293

J
julienne, 561
julienne strips, 561
juniper berries, 561
Jus, 346

K
Kaleidoscope salad, 121
kedgeree, Salmon, 142
kidneys, Devilled, with sage polenta
    discs, 259
kidneys, Veal, sautéed in white wine, 254
kitchen utensils, 13-15
kneading dough, 551, 561
knives, 10

L
lamb, 262
    Braised lamb with tomato sauce, 265
    Lamb cutlets with pea fritters and garlic
        cream sauce, 256
    Lamb fillets with coriander gravy, 260
    Lancashire hot pot, 264
    Navarin of lamb, 261
    Rack of lamb with a herb crust, 255
    Roasted lamb with vegetables, 262
Lamb stock, 518
lambs lettuce, 561
    Goat's cheese with watercress and lambs
        lettuce salad, 127
Lancashire hot pot, 264
Langues-de-chat, 514
lardons, 561
lasagne
    Classic lasagne, 287
    'Lasagne' of salmon with tomato and
        spinach, 171
    Vegetable lasagne, 294

leeks, 110
    Eggs en cocotte with smoked trout and
        leek, 102
    Leek and Brie flamiche, 110
    Leek tarlets, 43
    Salmon, leek and potato gratin, 179
    Smoked salmon and leek terrine with
        sauce verte, 147
lemons, 417
    Individual lemon cheesecakes, 423
    Lemon delicious, 411
    Lemon meringue pie, 417
    Lemon tart, 444
    Seafood and lemon soup, 89
    Trout flans with chive and lemon
        sauce, 158
    Veal with lemon and capers, 253
lentils
    Chicken, bacon and lentil soup, 91
    puy lentils, 562
    Warm lentil salad with mustard seed
        vinaigrette, 137
lime and yoghurt mayonnaise, Crab fritters
    with, 44
lime Chantilly cream, Smoked salmon soup
    with, 94
Lime-marinated chicken with Mediterranean
    bread, 199
Linguine vongole, 289
Linguine with Gorgonzola sauce, 291
liver
    Chicken liver pâté, 28
    Chicken liver salad with bacon and
        croutons, 136
    Chicken liver terrine, 188
    Venetian-style liver, 247
lobster, 153
    Asparagus, artichoke and lobster
        salad, 153
    Grilled lobster with buttery Pernod
        sauce, 164
    Lobster Américaine, 174
    Lobster bisque, 71
    preparing, 524-525
loin, 561
Lunettes, 515

Published by Murdoch Books®

© Design and photography Murdoch Books® 2001
© Text Le Cordon Bleu International BV 2001
All rights reserved. Published 2001
National Library of Australia Cataloguing-in-Publication Data
Le Cordon Bleu complete cook Includes index. ISBN 1 74045 094 9
1. Cookery, French. 2. Cookery. I. Cordon Bleu (School: Paris, France). 641.5944
A catalogue record of this book is available from the British Library

Editors: Kim Rowney, Jane Price
Food Editor: Lulu Grimes
Design Concept: Vivien Valk
Designer: Alex Frampton

Publisher: Kay Scarlett
Group General Manager: Mark Smith

PRINTED IN CHINA by Toppan Printing Hong Kong Ltd.
Murdoch Books® Australia
GPO Box 1203, Sydney, NSW 1045
Phone: (02) 8220 2000   Fax: (02) 8220 2558

Murdoch Books® UK
Ferry House, 51– 57 Lacy Road, London SW15 1PR
Phone: (020) 8355 1480   Fax: (020) 8355 1499

IMPORTANT: Those who might be at risk from the effects of salmonella food poisoning
(the elderly, pregnant women, young children and those suffering from immune deficiency
diseases) should consult their GP with any concerns about eating raw eggs.

ACKNOWLEDGMENTS

Murdoch Books and Le Cordon Bleu would like to express their gratitude to the Master Chefs of Le Cordon Bleu schools, whose
knowledge and expertise have made this book possible especially: Chef Terrien, Chef Boucheret, Chef Deguignet, Chef Pinaud,
Chef Bernardé, Chef Chalopin, Chef Lebouc, Chef Chantefort, Chef Thivet, Paris; Chef Lewis, Chef Males, Chef Walsh, Chef Power,
Chef Carr, Chef Paton, Chef Poole-Gleed, Chef Wavrin, Chef Barraud, Chef Bidault, London; Chef Filliodeau, Chef Guiet, Chef Beyer,
Chef Guiriec, Chef Price, Chef Baisas, Chef Pagés, Chef Lavest, Chef Irazouqui, Chef Chabert, Chef Petibon, Ottawa; Chef Summers,
Chef Beech, Chef Watkins, Chef Lowe, Adelaide; Chef Boutin, Chef Harris, Chef Rego, Chef Belcher, Chef Findlay, Chef Hood,
Chef Masse, Sydney;. Chef Benoit, Peru; Chef Yamashita, Chef Oddos, Chef Kato, Chef Poilvet, Chef Gros, Chef Hori, Chef Peguero,
Chef Honda, Chef Lederf, Chef Guilhaudin, Tokyo; Chef Martin, Chef Carmago, Brazil.

A very special acknowledgment to Denise Spencer-Walker, Kaye Baudinette, James McIntosh and Laurence Giaume who have been
responsible for the co-ordination of the Le Cordon Bleu team under the Presidency of André J.Cointreau.